THE UNFAILING LIGHT

Latest Portrait — 1943

THE UNFAILING LIGHT

Memoirs of an American Rabbi

by

Rabbi Dr. Bernard Drachman

*With an Introduction and Notes
by the Editor*

THE RABBINICAL COUNCIL OF AMERICA
NEW YORK, 1948

Copyright, 1948
by MRS. BERNARD DRACHMAN

PRINTED IN THE UNITED STATES OF AMERICA

Contents

Introduction — vii

1. Recollections of Earliest Chilhood — 1
2. Jersey City — 4
3. Jersey City—(*continued*)
   My Parents — 11
4. Jersey City—(*continued*)
   My Brothers and Sisters — 21
5. Jersey City—(*continued*)
   The Jewish Community — 27
6. The Jersey City High School — 31
7. Columbia College — 46
8. Ho, For the Old World — 58
9. Hamburg and the Trip to Nordheim — 62
10. Nordheim — 70
11. My First Day in Breslau — 88
12. First Observations of Breslau — 90
13. Activities, Contacts, and Experiences in Breslau — 97
14. Activities, Contacts, and Experiences in Breslau (*continued*) — 110
15. A Rural Wedding
    A Visit to Frankfort on the Main — 122
16. A Trip to Galicia — 128
17. Experiences in Breslau—(*continued*)
    Ph.D Degree in Heidelberg — 148
18. My Concluding Year in Breslau — 156
19. Back in America—New Problems — 164
20. American Israel at the Crossroads
    The Founding of the Jewish Theological Seminary — 176
21. Work at the Jewish Theological Seminary Begins
    Farewell to Newark
    A New Congregational Position in New York City — 183
22. I Enter the Holy Estate of Matrimony — 188

CHAPTER	PAGE
23. Startling Events in the Congregation Beth Israel Bikkur Cholim	197
24. The Congregation Zichron Ephraim is Organized	205
25. The Founding of a Hospital	217
26. Mainly About the Seminary	220
27. Jewish Activities in Various Fields The Jewish Sabbath Alliance of America	225
28. Niantic—Bay Shore—Sharon Springs A Rustic Synagogue	234
29. More About the Seminary	253
30. Working for Israel in Many Ways	262
31. New Synagogue Connections	275
32. I am Called Abroad	290
33. My Trip Through the Provinces Return to London and America Decision in the Issue of the Chief Rabbinate	306
34. Back Again to America Activities of a Strenuous Career	320
35. A Great Calamity Comes Over the World Our Attempt to Relieve It	333
36. Some Typical Incidents War Comes to America	353
37. During the War and After I Leave the Congregation Ohab Zedek	366
38. Continued Activities for Judaism A Testimonial Dinner	380
39. Tragedy Comes to Me A Glance at Canadian Jewry	390
40. A Trip to the Holy Land The Mizrachi Conference in Antwerp	396
41. My Second Romance	410
42. Houdini's Funeral A Proposed Calendar Reform	416 418
43. A Visit to California in 1928 The World Congress of Jewish Sabbath Observers in Berlin in 1930	422 425
44. Conversions to Judaism	429
45. Lighter Side of the Rabbi's Vocation	434
46. Golden Jubilee	444

List of Illustrations

Rabbi Dr. Drachman, from a Photograph taken October, 1943—Frontispiece

	FACING PAGE
Parents, from Charcoal Portraits drawn about 1887	72
Bernard Drachman, from a Photograph taken in Breslau 1883	73
The Jewish Theological Seminary of Breslau from Geschichte des Judisch—Theologischen Seminars—Dr. M. Brann 1904	104
Bernard Drachman and Sarah Weil, from Charcoal Portraits drawn about 1887	105
Facsimile of the Heidelberg University Diploma, October 31, 1884	140
Facsimile of the HATTARATH HARAAH. Granted by Rabbi Dr. Moses Gaster, Haham of Great Britain, in 1904	141
Bernard Drachman, from a Photograph taken about 1891	232
Synagogue of the Congregation Zichron Ephraim, from a Photograph taken in 1940	233
Within the Sanctuary, from a Photograph taken in 1940	264
Rabbi Dr. and Mrs. Bernard Drachman, from Photographs taken in 1930	265
Facsimile of Certificate accompanying the University Medal	392
Photograph of the University Medal	393
Columbia University Commencement, from a Photograph taken June 3, 1941. Award of Citation by Dr. Butler	424
Rabbi Dr. Drachman, from a Photograph taken in 1940	425
Home Scene—A Corner of the Study, from a Photograph taken in 1944	450

Introduction

BARELY FOUR WEEKS BEFORE THE END OF HIS LONG AND FRUITFUL life, Rabbi Dr. Bernard Drachman dictated the last sentence of his memoirs, observed, "Well, that's finished," and heaved a sigh. It was his *nunc dimittis,* his *baruch shepatrani,* the completion of his final task. For about three years he had been writing down his recollections, writing them down in long-hand, in his meticulously neat and graceful script, forming each letter with affection and care. He used an old-fashioned straight pen, which he dipped into an inkwell with determination and something of a flourish and wrote in hard-covered blank-books. Gradually he filled seventeen of them—and now, at last, that job was done.

What he wrote during that concluding period may be read in this book. He had much to remember, for his career had been an exceptionally active one, and he had a phenomenal memory which did not flag or blur for a moment until the very end. Though he never reached what might be called a dotage, he had long been living, during leisure hours at least, in a state of anecdotage—which now turns out to have been a rehearsal for the writing of these memoirs.

When he began this writing, he was over eighty years of age, but physically vigorous and mentally alert. Though he had not retired, his public activities had somewhat contracted, and in the intervals the writing of the story of his own life absorbed some of his restless energies.

It is a significant story indeed, for he was one of the key figures in the development of American Israel during the decisive period in its history, and the story is told with unusual candor. In his early years,

Bernard Drachman lived excitingly and dangerously and creatively at the very focus of activities and struggles that rocked the world of Jewry. He did this not for the love of excitement, for he was quite free from that infirmity, but solely because he felt deeply the need of helping in the effort to preserve the content of the Jewish heritage from the well-nigh overwhelming forces of disintegration with which it was surrounded. Thus his life summed up an epoch, and, though some figures of the period may seem to have been more imposing, the history of his time and the history of the man are inseparable. To understand one—fully—is to understand the other. To lack understanding of either is to misapprehend the other's significance.

The heart of the era and its attempts to find itself lay in the controversy between the Reform and the Orthodox wings of the Jewish religion. But we are beginning to understand today that it was more, far more, than a mere difference of opinion on a question of theological belief: it was the clash of two fundamental life-forces meeting for the moment at a single salient, the force of gradual assimilation into the environment and that of vigorous self-assertion for continued existence. Many events since the eighties and nineties of the past century have tended to shift the ground. The heavy immigration from Eastern Europe, the growth of Zionism and the miraculous rebirth of the Jewish national home, and, above all, the slaughter of millions of our people have all contributed to showing present-day rabbis and laymen as well that the dispute between Orthodox and Reform Judaism meant much more than a few questions of detail as to the formal routine by which congregations worship.

Bernard Drachman's part in that story was heroic, and, on careful consideration, and weighing the words with the utmost regard to their meaning, it is fitting to say that his was a heroic character. He possessed and, in his living, expressed many of the traits of true greatness. These were not always comfortable traits either for himself or for those with whom he came into contact, but they were necessary qualities in the struggle for the preservation of Jewish values, and they served to win him widespread respect and to make his life ample and significant. Therefore it may be worthwhile for the reader of these memoirs to review here a sketch of the personality of the man whose life story follows.

Introduction

First, then, there was an absolute, unquestioning and unquestionable *sincerity*. No one was ever long in doubt as to where he stood with reference to any issue that might arise. The sacrifices that he made for Judaism (many of them entirely unnecessary, according to the view of others with more adaptable consciences) should remain as proofs of this. But in his sincerity was a deeper, simpler, clearer, more inherent quality than just the negation of hypocrisy that it means to most people. His mind worked with extraordinary directness. Although he could follow, and even guide, a train of the intricate Talmudic subtleties known as *pilpul* and delighted in that kind of intellectual acrobatics, when he faced a concrete problem he tore into it with the swift, sure, intuitive accuracy of a natural force like lightning or gravitation. For him to try to deceive anyone, in even the most trivial matter, was literally inconceivable.

In this he was like one of the ancient prophets. If his concept of the truth demanded that he castigate some of our purse-proud leaders, he did not hesitate to take the risks that this course involved. If it meant that he defy the mob, he would do that too. Needless to say, he never shrank from sacrificing his own effort or his own money or convenience or health or opportunity if a good cause needed help. An awesome consciousness of duty overhung and controlled his life. He felt "called" to a mission far more exalted than any one man's interests, and, like Isaiah, he answered, *"Hineni,"* "Here I am!" He would be ready to do the Lord's work.

One must, however, avoid two misconceptions that might be read into the above: that he sought controversy, and that his life was full of gloomy broodings. Exactly the opposite is true. He was a pursuer of peace, because peace is highly esteemed in Jewish tradition. It is one of the many ironies of his life that it included many stormy incidents though there were few things that he sought more ardently than peace. Also his lofty sense of the solemnity of all existence was not of the kind to render one dismal. He was an extremely sociable man, talkative, witty, humorous, even a gay companion. He loved to laugh and to make others laugh. He enjoyed being surrounded by people and dearly relished a good joke or lively yarn. He enjoyed eating and drinking, swimming and taking long walks and horseback-riding and traveling and seeing new sights and revisiting familiar places. He was a devotee of music. He had studied art in his youth and always retained a knack of skillful drawing. For many years he practiced the hobbies of gardening and wood-chopping. He delighted in novels and plays—if only they were clean. His favorite author was Dickens, and from the master's works he would quote verbatim long passages of caricature and characterization. The versatility of his tastes was tremendous.

Nevertheless, his highest and deepest happiness was found in the practice of the Jewish religion. In this field, as in others, his youthful enthusiasm never staled. He loved the symbols and ceremonies, the rituals and gestures, the customary phrases and flavors and rhythms and melodies in which Judaism is so rich—he loved these with a touchingly beautiful affection. For his religion was no grim taskmaster imposing difficult, if necessary, burdens but a gracious hostess inviting her guests to share a hospitable feast. That this courtesy implied corresponding duties he accepted as a matter of course and all the more willingly since he was thus obliged to do what he most desired anyway. So, devoted fighter for a cause and loyal upholder of duty as he was, he found pleasure in many enjoyments, worldly as well as spiritual, and true happiness in the pursuit of the ideal.

One of his rarest traits was an everlastingly youthful freshness of approach to experiences. This is a gift characteristic of the purest and most unspoiled of geniuses, like Homer and Chaucer and the Solomon of the *Song of Songs*. Most human beings reach the limits of their capacity for appreciation early in life. After that they find repetition tiresome, and one major reason why so few people can use their abilities creatively is that nothing seems sufficiently original any longer to be worth the trouble of creation. "What's the use? Everything has been done already," is the complaint that paralyzes the imagination more and more as youth settles into maturity and thence into middle age. But in his case the world never came to appear stale, flat, and unprofitable. On the contrary, it remained year after year, decade after decade, full of the freshness which belonged to it on the morning of Creation. This was all the more notable since he never sought novelty but consistently viewed originality and innovation with a suspicious glance lest they contain some contaminating crumb of heterodoxy. Perhaps the very reason why he could cling so loyally to an unchanging creed and code was that he never grew tired of it, that it was always young and fair to him, eternally fresh and vivid and significant.

In a variety of ways he illustrated that attitude. No formulary or ritual ever received from him a casual or merely formal rendition. If there were two or three fellow-worshipers present—even if he was quite alone—he would recite and chant the service and perform the stipulated ceremonies with the same dignity and the same enthusiasm which at other times won him high acclaim from large congregations. The sight of pious men gabbling their weekday prayers as if in a race to see who could finish first and apparently with no thought of the meaning filled him with sadness and indignation. "It is on these," he would say, "that Judaism must depend, and even they fail to honor it." For himself, he invariably paid it the tribute of careful and reverent rendition. Was it an endless repetition of antique forms? He never thought so. Instead he considered it something eternal and thus forever new.

For the same reason, the struggles that it was his assignment in life to undertake were fought through valiantly and with determination. Many of these were foredoomed to defeat, and a person of less sanguine imagination might well have concluded that they would be mere repetitions of similar profitless skirmishes in the past and therefore not worth the effort of a genuine attempt. Such, for example, were the repeated campaigns to secure legislative relief from the rigors of the Sunday laws for observers of the seventh-day Sabbath. Year after year he would make his pilgrimage to Albany, accompanied by a small but faithful entourage, to appeal to committees and buttonhole politicians, few of whom considered the entire question worth a moment of their time. Every year he would feel that *this time* the Almighty would be on his side, and he would put forth gallant and hopeful exertions to deserve success.

Of course, he met with disappointments, not only in this particular enterprise but in innumerable others, and yet he never lost hope, or at any rate never remained hopeless very long. Again and again disillusionment came his way; it could never rob him of his ideals—which others often called his illusions. Institutions, movements, individuals proved recreant. He never lost faith either in human nature or in Judaism or in Providence. This particular betrayal must be borne, as part of the price of his mission, but the work must go on with absolutely undiminished devotion. Who could know? Perhaps the very next time would bring glorious fulfillment.

To carry on in that way for over six decades would have been impossible had he not been sustained by a powerful faith—faith in the essential truth and value of Judaism, faith in a just Providence who would not let wrong be forever triumphant, faith in the vitality of character, however overlaid and hidden by the corruptions of two millennia of exile and persecution, of his Jewish brethren, faith in the sense of fair play of all men, faith in the power of truth crushed to earth to rise again. It meant, too, that he had faith in himself, in the inner light that told him what to believe even when "everyone," as it seemed, was denying and ridiculing those ideals and moving in the opposite direction. And this was in no way what happens to so many old and pious men—a shutting-out of the world, to live a hermit-life of isolated religiousness; on the contrary, till the last week of his existence he was keenly aware of the currents and cross-currents of world thought, those that favored his views and those that challenged them as well. He read widely and assimilated what he read, but, to paraphrase Stevenson, he kept his soul alive by believing what his own mind approved instead of tamely following the march of the multitude.

Indeed, in this generation and even more in the generation of his youth, the normal situation was reversed. Revolt against authority was the easier, smoother, more conventional, less original, less courageous course than obedience. To uphold the banner of tradition, as he did, meant going against the force of the current, and it did not have even the romantic appeal of revolution. It was just a long, slow, hard, upstream pull, without glamor or reward, with little hope of any immediate success. Yet that was the course he laid out for himself in life, because *he was certain that it was right*. He did this unflinchingly and courageously—a simple act of duty.

Reading these recollections, you will see how very much he did in life; indeed, it may seem as though even eighty-three years could not have sufficed for so much activity and achievement. Although much of what he did showed no immediate result, it meant the building of foundations for later construction. This would have been impossible but for an exceptionally rugged constitution and great vigor both of body and of mind. He was always what is called an old-fashioned man, and the somewhat meager conditions in which his lot was cast kept him from employing modern labor-saving methods. For example, he never had a private secretary or a conveniently equipped office. A scholar's old-world study served him well enough. Every single letter of every word in all his writing, books and articles and sermons and lectures and pamphlets as well as business and personal letters and professional interchanges of ideas, was neatly and painstakingly formed by hand with a straight pen. So, too, with the other things he did—in almost every case he went to the spot in person and did the job himself. Such a career, under such conditions, demanded strength.

In one of the chapters of this book he tells how heavy a program of activities he carried and adds that he was never tired, never too tired, that is, to be restored by a night's sleep. He rarely showed fatigue. He always seemed to be alert and eager, with a thousand interests in all sorts of things. For example, he spoke at least half a dozen languages with ease and fluency and could read no fewer than fourteen. He had a remarkable capacity for remembering the most out-of-the-way facts and even statistics; he would quote, without a moment's hesitation or uncertainty, the area in square miles of Belgium or Afghanistan, would tell you what Tacitus had said about the Germans or Thucydides about the Africans, or narrate how *"der mittlere Schuster"* in his mother's Nordheim had earned the sobriquet of *"Turmhuepfer."* Everything was grist that came to his mill, and somehow, sooner or later, everything that it ground out had a Jewish flavor. But the vast quantities of it bespoke a titanic nature.

Furthermore, everything he undertook was done with a characteristic touch. Perhaps that is true of every person, once you get to know him well enough; perhaps not. At all events, it was true of him. In his case, certainly, the style was the man. It is difficult to describe that individual flavor, made up, as it was, of many different and seemingly contradictory elements all blended into a single unified quality which was readily recognized by anyone familiar with his personality.

He had his own way of speaking, of telling a story, of writing a letter, of preaching a sermon, his own way of chanting a blessing or singing a hymn—or singing a sentimental German folk ballad or an early American college song—his own typical phrases and gestures, even his own way of standing up boldly or marching through the street. It was a manner compounded of a certain stateliness and a modicum of gaiety, of rugged courage and defiance blended with the gracious courtliness of what we call the old school, implying the consciousness of standing "ever in the great Task-master's eye" and yet moving briskly through a drama with innumerable overtones of comedy, as well as high adventure.

In personal appearance he was impressive or even striking. Not above average height, he stood so erect and during most of his life had so thin a figure as to give the impression of being a tall man, a straight, upstanding tall man, black-haired and black-bearded like an ancient prophet. Yet there was nothing of the "savage Messiah" in his appearance; his black hair was always brushed with detailed exactness even including a sort of flat curl over one temple, and his black beard was trimmed neatly in the most urbane manner. His eyes were dark and restless.

He believed with considerable definiteness that a rabbi should dress appropriately. To him it seemed unfitting for a man dedicated to the work of religion to dress casually in a business suit or in lounge or sport clothes, except perhaps when on vacation. For his own use he had designed a variation of the clerical garb customarily worn by Jewish ministers in England. It consisted of a Prince Albert coat and trousers of black broadcloth and a vest of the same material with the neck-piece cut into a rectangle instead of the usual "V" shape. With this he wore a straight "stand-up" collar and a small white lawn bow tie. The cut of the vest was such that when he wore a robe the white patch of starched shirt showed through like the linen bib or "bands" that form a characteristic part of Anglo-Jewish vestments. For formal wear he used a high silk hat. At other times he would substitute a black slouch hat of almost military cut and a short black jacket instead of the coat.

His clothes were always immaculate, and this seems to have been a habit of long standing. During a visit, in 1922, to the ancestral village of Nordheim, an aged peasant woman, who had been a laundress when he stayed there some forty years previously, asked, after an exchange of warm and cordial greetings, *"Herr Doktor, Sind Sie immer noch so extra?"* ("Doctor, are you still so particular?") His students in the Seminary and the Yeshivah still recall the conspicuous tidiness of his attire. It is possible that this attention to externals was more than a mere personal habit; it may have been part of a reasoned and deliberate program to take away the ground from one of the usual criticisms of Orthodoxy—that it neglects the esthetic side and the amenities of life. Whether this is so or not, it is certain that he was always keenly aware of that criticism and strove manfully in his own congregations to remove all cause for it.

He was described more than once as a pulpit orator, and his eloquence easily merited such a description. However, his was not the rolling, orotund organ-voice that one usually associates with the term. On the contrary, he had a soft and mellow voice, more like the music of a flute than that of an organ, a tender, expressive voice that flowed without pause, a voice especially suitable for expressions of Messianic idealism, of beautiful and touching hope—a note on which his sermons often concluded. It was not ordinarily exciting or sensational, nor shocking after the manner of some orators; it was inexpressibly inspiring. His voice, though gentle and far from loud, had a clarity and crispness, a singular carrying power that made it distinctly audible to the very last rows in even a large auditorium. Indeed, it was as clear at the extreme rear as at any but the few front rows, far more easy to listen to and to hear than the shouts of many much louder speakers.

In the synagogue he wore a robe suggestive of the college gown but without its sharply angular, Gothic quality and Christian associations, over it a *talis* neatly though loosely drawn and, of course, a cap —a four-cornered velvet cap. Just as he did not thunder, he never pounded the pulpit, that "drum eccesiastick," as Hudibras calls it. His gestures were dignified and graceful. The most characteristic one was an opening out of both arms, throwing them slowly upward and outward to a sort of spread-eagle position, as if not only taking in the whole congregation but also pointing the way and leading them up to a loftier world.

It is a little unfair to mention the style of any man who speaks much in public, for he may employ many styles to suit various occasions. He had numerous styles of public speaking, of which three were most frequent and most typical. First was the sermon, already described, pronounced in a solemn though soft and appealing voice, with lofty, inspiring phrases and a nobly appealing manner. He used to prepare sermons in abstract form on a small double sheet of note paper. At the top he carefully wrote the date and the Hebrew designation of the Biblical reading for the Sabbath in question, then the Hebrew text, then "My Dear Friends," and, word for word, the introduction, which might be the statement of a religious problem or intellectual difficulty of timely or of lasting importance. The rest of the outline was briefly summarized and came in a definite order. Thus he would next present the interpretations of rabbis of Talmudic days, show their bearing upon the original text and upon the problem, then a modern solution, and the end was a clear call to hope and to strive for the realization of the glorious ideal.

Another frequent type of public address was the lecture. This would be delivered in a more objective tone, warming up to the unraveling of intellectual subtleties and often illuminated with appropriate anecdotes. In this the quotations would be more numerous than in a sermon; indeed they might come thick and fast, especially if the theme were rabbinic and the citation of specific authority played a part in its development. Third was the social address of welcome or congratulation employed at public dinners, receptions, and the like, and in these his tone was one of genial, if refined, banter. It was rich in aphorisms and epigrams and literally full of entertaining stories, yet he never opened his mouth to speak without having a tangible and fundamentally serious theme, and no amount of pleasantry could ever make him digress too far to return. He could, at a moment's notice if called upon, get up and deliver a speech of any kind, and these completely extemporaneous addresses were often brilliantly effective.

The seeming permanence of a youthful freshness and elasticity in his spirit has already been noted, and it was carried over into his appearance, manner, and voice. Of course, he did not actually look *youthful;* that would hardly be possible for any bearded man, even for one still in his twenties, but he did retain the appearance and the energy of early middle life well on into old age. When his seventieth birthday was celebrated in June, 1931, for example, he remarked (in a speech at an informal dinner) that he was not yet experiencing the "so-called infirmities of age"; and one could notice his erect and reasonably slender, almost athletic form and bearing, his dark hair and beard, his alert air, and the nimble play of his wit. It was almost six years later that he returned from a long sojourn in California with hair and beard quite white; but even then his complexion was ruddy, his eyes twinkled, and nothing bespoke the onset of age. After that he gained some weight, and then his apparently tall figure seemed to change, and with it went a not unpleasing modification of temperament; he was still alert and eager, still intrinsically earnest and still dignified, but mellower, more soothing, more ready to accept the universe and the diversity of human nature. In the last year or two he grew thin again and finally a little frail, but he still carried his aquiline head proudly and his neat white beard still jutted forward with an air of confident defiance. Through it all his voice never changed.

Such were some of the impressions he made upon one who observed him intimately over a long period of years. It would not be surprising if the reader questioned whether his character had no flaw or weakness. In full frankness, however, and without disrespect, it is possible to cite two characteristic foibles. First, despite his intense zeal, he was almost without *personal* ambition. Though intense in ideals, he gave almost no thought to his own career, and, when he did think of it, it was to spurn with contempt the kind of things that people think they must do to get on in the world. And second, he was no politician. For a publicist and communal leader, it might have been advantageous to have had some grasp of the technique of building up a clique of personal partisans to support one's efforts noisily and persistently no matter what their direction. Some clergymen have known how to advance themselves into situations of prominence, affluence, or ease —or of worthy opportunity for service—by the manipulation of groups of loyal followers. He neither knew nor cared. To him it would have seemed shameful to employ ingenious methods of winning friends by what amounts to little more than bribery or influencing people through an adroit use of flattery.

Thus in a material sense his career might well have been more successful than it was. Unlike some of the most eminent personages, whose fame rests on the positions they occupy, he was always incomparably greater than his situation. The story of his life tells of a considerable number of "opportunities" missed. In his youth, had he chosen, he could have occupied the pulpit of Temple Emanuel, the most coveted in the world of Reform Judaism, but he turned it down, with hardly a second thought, at a time when more traditional congregations worthy of his service scarcely existed in America. Later, at the peak of his activity and fame, he almost became Chief Rabbi of the British Empire, easily the most illustrious Orthodox rabbinate in the world, and this too he forfeited chiefly because of a scruple as to the propriety of the method of election. It is another of the ironies of his life that though he came so close to two positions of such eminence—and a good many more besides—those he actually filled were comparatively minor. It was the syagogue that reflected some of the luster of his name.

What, then, was his real work? It extended beyond the walls of his own houses of worship, beyond the schools and organizations for which he labored, to the community of New York, of America, of universal Israel in its difficult epoch of transition from the almost medieval European ghetto to the free democracy of modern America. In this program of bridging the gulf, his career (and this is another unique aspect of it) was the reverse of the typical one. Most contemporary Jewish leaders first entered the world and Judaism in some remote, antique environment to which no hint of alien culture or ways had penetrated, migrated to the West, experienced the shock of new ideas and customs, and finally wound up with a reconstituted, modified approach to Jewish life. Bernard Drachman, on the other hand, began his life in an America in which Jews formed only a fraction of one percent of the population, in an outlying city with only the rudiments of a Jewish community, in a home which honored Judaism but could not observe its laws fully. His growing interest in the religion of his people was cultivated first in the direction of Reform. It was only after he had studied abroad that an active devotion to the defense of tradition took hold of him. With the passage of time he moved more and more steadily to the right, specifically contrary to the seeming current of the times.

His real work was to promote in every way possible and through every conceivable instrument the vital and substantial growth of a *modern American Orthodox Judaism*. To achieve this aim he became a founder of numerous institutions and organizations and an untiring worker for many more. In reading these memoirs, one is struck by a realization of the many flourishing forces in contemporary life which received their impetus, in part at least, from his hands and his brain. He was a pioneer in the best sense of the word, one who explores new territory and clears the way for later inhabitants. He was certainly one of the first native American rabbis, possibly *the very first* in the Orthodox fold. Jews and Judaism had existed in America for two centuries before he was born, yet it is not unfair to say that the Jewish community of America had yet to be established. In that establishment it was his historic function to play a major part and especially to labor for the preservation, and against the jettisoning, of a maximum of substantial Jewish values.

So when he is described, with convenient brevity, as "an Orthodox rabbi," an inaccurate impression may be conveyed. He differed from many of his pious colleagues in that *his Orthodoxy was a conscious and voluntary choice,* a sort of revolt or counter-revolution that cost him a mighty wrench and many a tangible sacrifice, and was not a mere accident of birth. He differed, too, in another way: that he strove always to build in America a truly *American* Judaism, one that was just as true to the principles and culture of this country as to the principles and culture of his people. Others have made the same attempt, both before and since, for indeed the problem of reconciling these diverse forces is the prime challenge to the Jewish people in this era. Others, however, have often seemed to lean too far to one side or the other: either they sacrificed too much of the ancestral heritage in their eagerness to assimilate the quality of the new country, or they clung with excessive tenacity to irrelevant incidentals brought along by chance from the old one. Looked at in this way, his function was to seek a just compromise, a reasonable middle ground, to produce a harmonious blend of the two extremes, retaining, as the advertising writers say, the best features of each. From Reform Judaism he borrowed the orderly management that lends it so much impressiveness and charm, at the same time preserving all of Orthodoxy that is essential, all whose absence or modification could threaten any damage to the structure. Complete loyalty to religious law, combined with beauty of ceremonial and propriety of manner, would prove an ideal combination that should, he held, be acceptable to both parties. Thus might we do away with the disunity that is the scandal and the principal weakness of modern Jewry.

Unfortunately, the schism had already gone too far. More and more his voice fell on deaf ears in the councils of the Reform wing, which meant the small groups of influential and wealthy leaders; more and more he found that this branch would not listen to his message of peace. Inevitably he allied himself wholly with the other party. After all, in essential principles it was with these that he held, but so far as he thought legitimate he strove to adapt them to the modern culture of the American environment. He never accepted the idea that the cleavage was final and permanent but always worked, as occasion permitted, to win the wanderers back, to heal the breach. And while encouraging the more recent immigrants to adhere loyally to the duties and practices of the ancestral code, he tried to modify some of their ways to suit the new atmosphere and make the ancient faith acceptable to their own children.

Was the effort successful? If one were to judge simply by the method of *post hoc propter hoc,* the conclusion would be that it was so to a very considerable extent. In the eighties of the past century, American Judaism was almost entirely Reform. All the new developments of the period seemed to move in that direction, and Orthodoxy then was a feeble remnant constantly losing ground. Complete assimilation was taking many out of the fold. Today, the picture is quite different. Numerous and important communities now hold to the more traditional ritual and standards. Innumerable institutions, such as *yeshivoth,* or all-day schools under Jewish auspices and with rich Hebraic as well as general curricula, inconceivable a generation ago, have sprung into existence and are flourishing. The Hebrew language

Introduction

is established as part of the course of study in many public high schools and colleges. This is a far cry from the defeatist and minimalist attitude that prevailed when he began his ministrations.

It would be an exaggeration to attribute this change simply to his efforts. Many colleagues collaborated, and other factors entered, chief among them being the heavy immigration from the intensely Jewish communities of Eastern Europe. But it must have been heartening to many of those new arrivals in the land of *"apikorsim"* to find here a rabbi who, though a thorough American gentleman himself, did not tell them, like some, that in this country one gives up one's Sabbath and most of the holy days, *tephillin* and *talis*, Hebrew prayers, and dietary regulations. What influence he had in saving what has been saved it is impossible to estimate, but a good deal has been saved, and he was part of the struggle to save it.

This is not the place to discuss his other numerous achievements, his considerable contributions to scholarship, education, public welfare, Hebraic philology, and Zionism. The facts concerning these are given in the pages that follow, and the function of this preface is not to supply more facts but rather to present a personal portrait, such as an autobiographer can scarcely give of himself, and also to offer some suggestions as to the significance of his career. The publication of the story of a life calls for a justification; although any man's life story, frankly and understandingly told, may well be as interesting to read as a novel, it is only the story of a life that had some historic significance that really merits being preserved for posterity. This particular life, as has been indicated above and will be richly illustrated in the memoirs that follow, was a full life and played a meaningful part in a critical period. Further, it was a life whose value and meaning were often obscured by his own standards of self-respect or suppressed and misinterpreted by ideological opponents. Thus it is most necessary that this book reach the public and become part of posterity's record of our era. It sums up the activities of a long and fruitful life and will not let silence wash away the evidence.

Every life story is tragic, if only because it must end in death. The life story of an idealist is doubly so, because every idealist desires sincerely what no mortal has a right to expect: *that his life, his actions, his thoughts shall help to guide the course of history.* Thus every idealist, no matter how successful, must have an overflowing share of frustrations—for every victory a score of defeats. And it was perhaps the crowning irony of all in this man's life that the most frequent praise he received offered an indication that his great work was still incomplete. Time after time people would express admiration of the superb way in which he combined the attributes of ancestral piety with those of contemporary Occidental culture. Pleased as he must have been to be thus appreciated, he was wryly aware that it meant that such a combination, which he regarded as the normal and ordinary aim of every American Jew, was still far from generally achieved. The tale is instructive nevertheless, because, after all, it reports the process of the struggle for a cause.

It is for such reasons that these memoirs of an American rabbi have a legitimate place in the record of the Jewish development in America. However, as the story was actually written it is not just an account of a public career; it is also the intimate revelation of a personality. So intimate is it that the editors were faced with the problem of how much of it to give to the public, how far to alter or omit parts of the text. The writing of it had been barely completed when the end came. The author was not granted time nor opportunity to revise his first draft.

It became necessary to reduce the text by about one-third and to make other minor alterations. Here and there, where some statement has seemed a trifle ambiguous or incomplete (usually because of modest understatement) footnotes are added, each with an indication of source so that the reader may know what came from the author's hand and what from others'. The style and vocabulary have been faithfully preserved. An index has been added and so have a number of illustrations. In other respects the book is exactly as it was written.

Read it with patience and sympathy; it is the monument of a great soul.

J. M. D.

Chapter One

Recollections of Earliest Childhood

SHAKESPEARE IS OF THE OPINION OR, AT LEAST, CAUSES ONE OF HIS characters to express the opinion, that "All the world's a stage and all the men and women merely players." I do not exactly agree with this view of the Bard of Avon. The world, or let us say life, for that is what is meant by the term "world" in this connection, is not so well constructed and has not so definite a plot as a play must have to deserve the name. But it is definitely a panorama, a constant succession of ever-changing scenes, personages, and happenings.

Life has certainly been such a panorama to the writer of these pages. As I glance in mental vision retrospectively through the years that have disappeared in the abyss of the past, I behold such an infinity of varying countenances, hear such a multitude of differing voices, languages, and ideas, and see so many dissimilar places and regions that it sometimes appears, even to myself, incredible that all these kaleidoscopic changes have really belonged to my personal experience. Yet, to be sure, such varying experiences are, in greater or lesser measure, the life content of every human being. As such, they necessarily possess human interest. For, as the Roman poet says, "I am a man and nothing human do I deem alien"—and I may interpolate "uninteresting"—to me. It is my intention to narrate the experiences of my life purely for the human interest which I believe they possess.

On the twenty-seventh day of June in the year 1861 my infant eyes first opened on this troubled world. All my life I have championed the union of Judaism and Americanism. Something in the circumstances of my birth seems to have indicated this, for eight days later, when I was initiated into the Abrahamic covenant on July 4, 1861, all America celebrated a feast of great rejoicing. Sticklers for accuracy may declare that this was not on my account. They are only carping critics.

My earliest recollections are of incidents which occurred, I believe, in the fifth year of my life, in the last year of the Civil War, 1865. My parents, of blessed memory, conducted a store of so-called fancy goods in Grand Street, in the City of New York, and lived in rooms above the store. I recall that I was sitting in the store one Sunday when the store was not open for business. I was listening to a conversation between my father and a friend of his who, I can faintly remember, was named Abraham Wolf. The subject of their conversation, I faintly recall, was the relative merits of Europe and America. Mr. Wolf declared Europe superior to America, while my father defended the New World against its detractor. I was puzzled, indeed amazed, by the fact that anyone could consider any place in the world better than the place in which we were living.

Another incident which is stamped upon my memory of childhood years is that an uncle of mine, a brother of my mother, named Samuel Stein, paid us a visit. He was clad in full uniform, the blue uniform of a Union soldier. We all gazed upon him with admiration, but in my feeling there was also fascination and fear. Uncle Samuel was good nature personified, but I know that I was greatly relieved when he said, "Good-bye."

It was about this time that my father took me to see a great military parade which was taking place in New York. I remember standing on the sidewalk for a long time, holding fast to my father's hand, for fear of getting separated from him and being lost, and gazing with childish wonder at the apparently innumerable rows of brightly uniformed men marching past. There were unnumbered thousands of infantrymen tramping monotonously, with guns resting at exactly the same angle on their shoulders, many other thousands of cavalry, sitting firmly and proudly on their steeds, and hundreds of cannon drawn by stout and sturdy horses. In addition there were the drivers, with artillerymen seated on the caissons, facing the rear, their arms folded on their breasts, their eyes directed straight ahead, looking neither to the right nor to the left. I understood, of course, very little of the significance of it all, but I know that it made upon me the impression of overwhelming and invincible might.

Strange to say, my early childhood memories have little to do with things specifically Jewish. I attribute this to the fact that, because of my tender years, I was not taken to synagogue and did not yet receive Jewish instruction. There were, of course, Jewish people in the neighborhood, including several families of our relatives, with whom we associated, more or less, but my memories of our relations with them and of their characteristics are neither clear nor strong. I think I must say that my earliest experiences of life were, on the whole, very much like those of any American child in an ordinary American environment and that the Jewish influences, which were to play such a great part in my later life, had not yet begun to make themselves felt.

Chapter Two

Jersey City

IN THE YEAR 1870—I THINK IT WAS IN THE MONTH OF MAY—MY parents moved to Jersey City, in the neighboring State of New Jersey. A year previously my parents had transferred their habitation to Brooklyn, and it was from that city that they made the change to Jersey City, where they found a very fair degree of prosperity and where they were destined to abide the rest of their days in comparative peace and comfort.

I was to remain there until my twenty-first year. Jersey City was to play a great part in my spiritual and intellectual development and, while my memories of New York and Brooklyn are dim and indistinct, those of Jersey City are bright and sharply marked.

The Jersey City of those days was certainly rather primitive and provincial, very different from the great metropolis from which it was separated only by the width of the Hudson River. When we became accustomed to it, however, we found that it possessed attractive and agreeable features all of its own and we grew to love it as home. From the ferry house, at which the boats from New York landed, there extended a broad expanse of flat land leading to Bergen Heights, known in local parlance simply as "the hill." Two long straight streets, Montgomery Street and Newark Avenue, extended to "the hill." There were no apartment houses in Jersey City at that time. Most of the population lived in simple family-houses or primitive tenements, and, of course, the improvements characteristic of a later period, such as electric lights, telephones, radios, automobiles, and trolley cars, were undreamed of. The streets were lighted by dim gas-lamps, and communication was maintained by jogging horse-drawn street cars.

"The hill" itself was still quite rural in charactcer and included a fine stretch of woodland fronting on Newark Bay and known as "Curry's Woods." "Curry's Woods" was a favorite spot for excursions and picnic parties. Many were the outings which my brothers and sisters and I together with our youthful friends enjoyed in its shady recesses and verdant meadows. The outlook on the bay, picturesque and romantic, was afterwards immortalized by a pictorial representation done in watercolor by a local artist, Mr. August Will, whose beautiful and very artistic home was situated in a secluded street on "the hill" and of whom I later became a pupil and friend.

I remember an outing to Curry's Woods, taken, when I was somewhat older, with a young friend named Willie Thompson. It was a warm day, and we both became tired, hot, and thirsty, so Willie was overjoyed to spy a merry party of people of the good-natured, pleasant type characteristic of the old Germany, surrounding several kegs of beer. "I wonder," he said to me, "if they wouldn't let us have some beer, if we told them how thirsty we are. Perhaps you could ask them. You talk German." I was less pleased than he, for at that time I was a total abstainer from alcoholic drinks.

Nevertheless, I acceded at once to my friend's request and, approaching one of the men who was dispensing the Gambrinian potion, informed him, in German, that my companion was very thirsty—and would he not be kind enough to give him a glass of beer? "Indeed, I will," he replied with the utmost affability, taking me, no doubt, for a brother German, "and for you, too." Grasping two huge glasses of the type sometimes called *seidel*, he proceeded to fill them with the foaming beverage. "Thank you very much," I said, "but you needn't pour in any for me. I am only asking for my friend. I do not want any."

"And why not, pray?" the man asked in surprise, "aren't you thirsty?"

"Why, yes, I am," I answered, "but you see, I am a *Temperenzler*. I do not drink any alcoholic drinks."

The drink dispenser gazed at me for a moment uncomprehendingly; then, bursting into the exclamation, *"Gott, was gibts doch fuer Narren auf der Welt!"* (O, Lord, what fools there are in the world!) pushed away one of the glasses, filled the other and handed it to

Willie Thompson, who took it and drank its contents eagerly.

This was the first but not the last time that I have been called a fool because of loyal adherence to principle. I have been more than once honored in later years with similar expressions of opinion concerning my wisdom and have always consoled myself with the dictum of the Talmud, "It is better to be called foolish all one's life by people than to be wicked even one moment in the sight of God." Incidentally, I did not continue to adhere to the doctrine of total abstinence. It was in Germany that I changed my view on this subject so that ever since, although I have indulged very moderately in alcoholic drinks, I do not uphold the theory of Prohibition. But that is another story.

A few days after our arrival in Jersey City my father took my brothers and sisters and me to public school, to be enrolled as pupils. It was Public School No. 1, in York Street, about a block and a half from our home. The principal's name was Linsley. I do not remember with certainty his first name, but I am under the impression that it was George H. I can see him distinctly before me in my mind's eye. He was a handsome elderly man, with snow-white hair and beard, a typical American.

In those days there were no mollycoddle theories concerning the wickedness of corporal punishment. Mr. Linsley administered it vigorously to pupils whom he thought deserving thereof. His favorite implement of justice was a ruler, and it was indeed a potent means of insuring good conduct and discipline. To well behaved pupils he was kindness and friendliness personified. I certainly had no reason to complain of his treatment. Whenever we came in contact with each other, as we did occasionally on his visits to the classrooms, he was always most kindly and friendly. I looked up to him with childish reverence, and I bear him in affectionate remembrance.

My memories of Public School No. 1 are, on the whole, very pleasant. I had several teachers there during the course of my attendance, but of only one of these is my recollection clear and distinct. This was Miss Frost, a woman of middle years and of athletic build. I don't think that I ever heard her first name, but the boys, who were not over-respectful and who had nicknames for everyone connected with the teaching staff from the principal down, used to refer to her as "Jack Frost." She was a capable and conscientious teacher and a strict disciplinarian, nor did she hesitate to use her muscular ability to suppress any tendencies on the part of would-be "tough" or rowdyish pupils to disturb the order and quiet of the class. She was well liked and respected even by those pupils who had had occasion to feel her chastising hand. The boys of the school in general, and of my class in particular, were mainly friendly and well behaved but, when they could play a trick on a teacher, they enjoyed it hugely.

My association with my schoolfellows was mainly pleasant and agreeable, and I contracted some real friendships. But there was one fly in the ointment, one depressing and painful aspect of school life which, I fear, very few Jewish boys anywhere in the world are spared. That was, in a word, anti-Semitism—a term, by the way, which at that time was unknown—that unreasoning prejudice against (and antipathy to) the Jew which impels some Gentiles to heap upon the Jews with whom they come into contact all the humiliation and injury which they possibly can. Most of the boys were free from this spiritual malady, but a certain proportion were undeniable Jew-haters. I had not been many weeks a scholar of Public School No. 1, when I noticed—and, indeed, could not fail to notice—that I was the object of special dislike and antipathy on the part of certain individuals or groups of the scholars. When walking on the sidewalk approaching the school or going through the halls of the school, through groups of scholars, I would be apt to hear cries, coming apparently from nowhere and directed at no one, *"Jew," "Sheeny," "Christ-killer."* At first I would ignore these cries, thinking that they had no reference to me and were, therefore, no concern of mine. It did not take long, however, for me to recognize that I was the object of these insults. This discovery had the effect upon my emotional nature of a crushing, overwhelming shock. To be singled out as the object of special derision and contumely, to be held up to public insult and ridicule, when I was conscious of no guilt on my part and no reason why I should be treated in any way differently from the other pupils, was an outrage to my sensibilities. I was far too timid to take any action or even to protest. In school I pretended to have heard nothing, to be unaware of anything. But when I reached home, I hastened to pour out my heart to my parents. Just as words cannot describe the depth of my spiritual agony at my awful discovery, so words cannot do justice to the tender understanding and loving sympathy with which my dear father and mother sought to comfort and console me.

"Do not mind what the bad boys say," said my father soothingly. "They are rough and vulgar and you shouldn't pay attention to them. Most of the boys are nice and friendly to you, aren't they?"

"Yes, Papa, they are," I sobbed. "But what hurts me about these bad boys is that they call me names and insult me just because I am a Jew. Is there anything about being a Jew which gives them a right to be so mean to me? Are Jews worse than other people? Do they deserve to be so hated?"

"No, my son," answered my father, while my dear mother looked on, oh so kindly and pityingly. "We Jews are not worse than other people, and we do not deserve to be hated. We come from a great nation which gave to the world, thousands of years ago, a wonderful religion which teaches people to do what is right and good. Many great men, who have helped the world in many ways, are of our people. But we have had a very sad history. Our nation was overthrown a long time ago, our holy temple in Jerusalem was destroyed by the cruel Romans, and now we are in *Golus,* that is, we are scattered all over the world, and in many countries are terribly persecuted by wicked governments and people. Why God permits His holy people to be so mistreated we do not know. Perhaps it is so that we should be tried and tested to see whether we are true and faithful to our religion despite our sufferings. But God has promised, through His holy prophets, that one day He will send His *Moshiach* (Messiah) who will redeem our people and restore them to their ancient land. That is our great hope and comfort. We Jews in America have every reason to be happy and thankful to God. This is a good, noble country which gives all its inhabitants equal rights. So we must not care if a few of the people hate and insult us. They have not the power, thank God, to harm us or deprive us of our rights as citizens. Just try to be a good scholar, do your duty thoroughly and learn your lessons as well as you can, and be respectful and obedient to your teachers. Then you will have the friendship and liking of your teachers and those of your fellow-scholars whose good opinion and friendship are worth while, and you needn't care what the prejudiced and narrow-minded boys say or do."

With this explanation and these admonitions, to which my dear mother added a few words of the same general purport, uttered with infinite compassion and tenderness, I had to be content. They did comfort me somewhat and gave me an insight into the status of the Jew in the world so that I began to realize that Jewish sufferings were not merely stupid and shameful but had about them something of the glory of martyrdom and of the reverence due to those who endure tribulations for a noble cause. But they did not comfort me completely nor remove entirely my inner sentiment of rebellion against the injustice of hatred and antagonism to people who were personally without fault or wrong-doing. When I said my night prayer, before going to bed, I added a supplication of my own that God might send His *Moshiach* very soon to redeem His people and re-establish the Jewish nation as of old, so that no Jew should be persecuted or insulted any more just because he was a Jew.

I obeyed, of course, the injunction of my father and ignored any anti-Semitic cries or remarks directed at me, which were, after all, not very frequent. But as time passed I grew stronger and bolder and no longer bore my contumely in complete silence but would reply to insulting remarks with a vigorous retort. The crisis came when I was almost eleven years of age.

School had just been dismissed one day, and the boys were pouring out of the building on to the street. As it chanced, one of the Jew-haters and I came out of school and reached the sidewalk together. This fellow gave vent to one of the stereotyped anti-Semitic gibes. This time I did not remain silent or merely retort with words. Infuriated, I raised my right hand and planted a vigorous slap upon his cheek. To say that the fellow was surprised is an understatement. He was stunned and stupefied with amazement, but only for a moment. Quickly recovering, he rushed at me determined to inflict condign punishment for my audacity.

The cry "A fight! A fight!" quickly rose from youthful throats, and a crowd of the boys gathered around us to witness the battle. It was not a very long battle, but it was intense enough while it lasted. My opponent was a strong, burly boy, two or three years older than I, but wrath and indignation had given me preternatural strength. Now that I was in for it, I was determined to do the best in my power.

In five or six minutes he had had enough and had slunk off like a beaten cur. No sooner had he gone than another fellow, who could not endure the thought that the Jew should be victorious, took his place and challenged me to battle. I was still in the full heat of my rage and joy of combat. I responded with the same sort of blow I had inflicted on his predecessor, and the tussle was on. It was short and furious and ended as the first fight had. Hardly had the second fellow departed than a third anti-Semite presented himself for battle. But now I was weary and exhausted and my first rage had left me. I could no longer put up a good fight. After a few minutes of struggle, I was forced to admit defeat and went home with a bloody nose and a black eye.

Though technically defeated, the results of my battle were most advantageous to me. Americans love courage and a clean fight. It was the general consensus of opinion among the boys that little Barney—or Bernie—Drachman had shown real spunk, as they called it, and had defended his honor and the honor of his people valiantly. I suffered no more from anti-Semitism and heard no more anti-Semitic cries as long as I remained in Public School No. 1.

Chapter Three

Jersey City—(*continued*)

My Parents

LIFE IN JERSEY CITY MEANT FOR ME IMPRESSIONS CONSTANTLY growing stronger, insight into my environment steadily becoming clearer, and adaptation thereto more definite and realization of world conditions and my relation to them rising on an ever-ascending scale of understanding and adjustment. Young as I was, my contacts and relationships were, at least, threefold or fourfold. I was a Jew and an American—or perhaps I should say, an American and a Jew—I hardly know which I should mention first, so closely and harmoniously were these two aspects of my personality joined and interlocked. I was a member of a loving and tenderly attached family, and a student, with a keen desire for knowledge, of both Hebrew and secular lore. Nearest and closest to me, as it naturally is to every human being, was the family environment in which I lived and moved and had my being. It was a good, sound, normal Jewish family, with the simple, wholesome, human traits which have been characteristic of typical Jewish families since time immemorial. Rabbinical interpretation of the Bible tells us that it was the contemplation of such families that caused the poetically eloquent heathen prophet Balaam to burst forth into the exclamation, "How goodly are thy tents, O Jacob, thy dwellings, O Israel."

My parents, of blessed memory, were sincerely attached to each other in unostentatious love and devotion and to their children with solicitous tenderness and affection. There were six of us children, three sons and three daughters. I was the third of the children. My father was a native of Galicia, formerly a province of Poland but, at the time of his birth and at that period of history, a part of the

Austro-Hungarian Empire; my mother was born in Bavaria, at that time an independent German kingdom. Such difference of national origin has been known to be productive of great dissension even among persons united by the tie of Judaism, but in the case of my dear parents it certainly had no such effect. One of the reasons for this rather unusual condition was undoubtedly the fact that Father, although born and reared in a Yiddish-speaking environment, did not himself use the Yiddish but spoke and read and wrote a correct and grammatical German. This ability was so marked that it procured him recognition among the Jersey City non-Jewish citizens of German origin as one of their own, and, when a political organization of German-Americans was formed, he was invited to join. He consented to do so but only on condition that the constitution should contain no provision restricting membership to persons of German birth or descent but that membership should be open to all German-speaking citizens (*Deutschredende Amerikanische Buerger*). Father became one of the most popular members of the organization, and his voice was always lifted in behalf of Americanism and true American patriotism on the part of citizens of foreign birth. Father's culture was by no means limited to a knowledge of the German language. He was also very well acquainted with French and English, both of which languages he spoke and read and wrote fluently and correctly, without foreign accent. His knowledge of French he had acquired during a sojourn of several years in France and of English in America after his arrival in this latter country in the year 1854 at the age of twenty-six.

As a native of an originally Polish province he was, of course thoroughly acquainted with the Polish tongue. Nor was his culture merely linguistic. His mind was keen and inquiring, and he was an insatiable reader of works of science and philosophy and in most of the domains of human knowledge. This broad intellectual interest did not, however, deprive him of love for Judaism and Jewish lore. Although, as he told me, his Hebrew studies had ceased with the death of his father, which almost exactly coincided with his *Bar Mitzvah,* at the age of thirteen, he had managed in that comparatively short time to acquire an excellent knowledge of Hebrew and of a considerable portion of the Talmud and of the laws and customs of the Jewish faith. But of all the knowledge he had acquired he was most attached to Judaism and Jewish culture. While not exactly what could be called a strictly orthodox Jew, his soul was filled with a deep love for the Jewish heritage and for things Jewish. He was very anxious that his children should not grow up ignorant of Judaism and, as there was no Hebrew teacher in Jersey City when we first took up our abode there, he became the first instructor in Judaica for his offspring. I remember yet with pleasure the instruction which I received from him. He used the English language as the vehicle of instruction, and his diction, in translating the Hebrew texts or in telling of the doctrines of Judaism or the history of Israel, was so clear and simple and his manner so pleasant, that I found the lessons very enjoyable. Whenever the weather was warm or mild, which it was during a great part of the year, the instruction was given in the open air, in our back yard, which was large and breezy. I can still see myself seated with Father on the back porch of our house, listening to his kindly voice explaining the mysteries of the *Siddur** or the *Chomesh*** or telling some of the interesting and, alas, often sad and tragic events in Jewish history.

One feature of his instruction made a particularly deep impression on my youthful mind and undoubtedly had much to do with forming my later ideology. I would tell him some of the things I had heard in the public school, particularly about the great leaders and heroes of America—Washington, Lincoln, and others. He would listen with a friendly smile and, when I had concluded, he would say, "Yes, my boy, our country America has had many great men and we must respect and honor their memories, but do not forget that the Jewish people has also had not only great and holy prophets and teachers but also brave warriors and heroic champions, such as King David and Judah Maccabee and Bar Kochba."

Later, when Jersey City had developed so far as to boast of a Jewish congregation—albeit a small one—I continued my Hebrew studies with the rabbi or Hebrew teacher of the congregation, but I did not appreciate this instruction as much nor did it influence me as greatly

---

* Prayer book.
** Pentateuch

as did that which I had received from my revered father. I may add that my father was a logical and rather eloquent speaker in both English and German and was listened to with pleasure on the rare occasions when he made formal addresses. With his store of learning and ability he might very well have taken up some sort of professional or technical career. He even had several inventions to his credit which, so far as I can judge, were perfectly practical and useful. Somehow or other he did not utilize his technical and inventive ability. He had learned in his youth the trade or art of an optician and practiced it for a few years. Shortly after his marriage, he and his young wife opened a small fancy goods and notions store, and a storekeeper or merchant he remained until the end of his days. As a merchant he showed skill and energy and attended to his duties as such with the same devotion and dependability which he displayed in all his other undertakings.

Father's first name was Benjamin. His family name, which he wrote in the German fashion with two *n's,* was Drachmann, which his children subsequently Americanized slightly by dropping the final *n.* The origin of this name is veiled in obscurity. It occurs in Denmark, where it is born by a prominent Danish family of scholars and *literati,* one of them being the Danish national poet, Holger Drachmann. This family is not, as far as is known, of Jewish origin or in any way connected with Jews or Judaism. Nevertheless the identity of their name with that of the Jewish family Drachmann of Galicia has been productive of somewhat amusing—or perhaps embarrassing —misunderstandings for both families. I have been several times taken by Danes for their compatriot and asked whether I was a relative of their famous poet Drachmann. On the other hand, the editors of the *Jewish Encyclopedia,* apparently for no other reason than that of the identity of the name borne by the Danish family with that of the American Rabbi Drachman, seem to have taken it for granted that the Danish Drachmanns were Jews and have asked some of their chief members for their biographies for inclusion in the Encyclopedia. I have seen a letter written by Professor A. B. Drachmann of the University of Copenhagen in which he courteously declines to have his biography published in the *Jewish Encyclopedia* on the ground that he "did not have the honor to be a Jew and did not deserve to be included among the eminent men of that faith." My own personal opinion is that the name is of Greek origin and was originally *Drachma,* the name of a Greek coin, and was introduced into Galicia by a Hellenic Jew who bore that appellation and who settled and established a family in that country, whose members subsequently Germanized their name into Drachmann. I am under the impression that my father once made a statement to that effect.

If my memories of my father are loving and tender and tinged with reverence, those of my mother are also such, perhaps in an even higher degree. Otherwise her personality was of quite a different type. Although a woman of good understanding, tact, and prudence, with a good knowledge of German and German literature, also of English and *Juedisch-Deutsch,* and with refined and courteous manners, she made no pretense to lofty intellectuality or high cultural attainments. She considered it her chief task in life to be a loyal helpmeet to her husband, alike by presiding over the home and making it a place of comfort and happiness and by assisting in the management of the business. She possessed the abilities, rarely found in harmonious combination, of a model housewife and an efficient business woman. Her culinary achievements, conducted strictly within the limits of the Jewish dietary law, made it a gastronomical delight to eat at her table and, as for dealing with a difficult or reluctant customer, there was none of her saleswomen in the store that could compare with her. But she shone with especial radiance as a mother. Her loving kindness and tenderness were so great and her sense of duty so keen that they qualified her in ideal measure for the responsible and exacting office of a mother of children. Her conscientious care and solicitude extended to every matter which concerned the physical, intellectual, and spiritual welfare of her children. She encouraged every cultural tendency manifested by any of her children. My own cultural tastes were at first rather indefinite and excessively variegated. Dear Mother never sought to restrain or discourage me in any way. On the contrary, she permitted and even assisted me to follow my own inclination, merely remarking with a smile, "After a while, you will find out what you like best and what you want to do always." I developed a taste for music. Mother, with the approval of Father although he personally cared little for music, engaged an excellent piano teacher named, I believe, McCabe. I thought that I might like to be an artist. Mother permitted me to attend an art school conducted by a German artist named August Will, whose home was in Jersey City but whose school was on lower Broadway, New York. At this school I learned drawing and painting in watercolor. My experiences in Mr. Will's school, and with Mr. Will and his cultured family, were of the most interesting kind.

When I finally recognized that I preferred Hebrew studies to all others, dear Mother, blessed be her memory, was highly delighted and herself suggested that I should prepare myself for the vocation of rabbi. I am, therefore, directly indebted to her for the choice which I made of my vocation in life and, consequently, for whatever useful service I may have been able to render.

Mother, whose maiden name was Mathilde Stein, was reared in a manner quite different from that of the great majority of Jewish girls, especially in her time, although not infrequent in the section of South Germany where her cradle had stood. She was the daughter of a learned and strictly pious Talmudist, Rabbi Shemayah Stein, but, nevertheless, her upbringing resembled to a great extent that of a German peasant or village maiden. That unusual fact was due to a peculiar concatenation of circumstances. Her father, as already stated, was a Hebrew scholar of distinction, fully qualified, by learning and piety, to officiate as a rabbi in Israel, but his very love of his people led him, as will be told later, to abandon that calling and set up as a farmer. His farm was in the vicinity of the village of Nordheim, in the Bavarian district of Vor-der-Rhoen. All of Rabbi Shemayah's children were born in Nordheim, and thus it came to pass that my mother was reared in a thoroughly rural atmosphere and acquired many of the characteristics of a Bavarian peasant maiden. The purchase of the farm had absorbed most of Reb Shemayah's capital. He could not well afford to hire outside laborers, and thus most of the work of the farm had perforce to be done by his children. My mother, while yet a young girl, became especially proficient in this kind of work and speedily became renowned among both Jews and Gentile peasants as the Jewish girl who was a wonderful farm worker. There was nothing in the way of farm labor, plowing, planting, weeding, reaping, or other species of work, which she did not perform with zeal and efficiency. When I visited Nordheim, many years after she had left, I still found aged peasants, male and female, who remembered well her energy and activity. They all recounted, with admiration which the passing of years had not dimmed, one particular feat which Mathilde Stein, or *"die Stein's Madele,"** as they called her in their peasant dialect, had accomplished. There was a high and rugged mountain in the vicinity of Nordheim, called Gangolfsberg or, in the peasant dialect, Gangelsberg. To ascend or descend the steep primitive roads of this rough elevation, especially with a loaded vehicle, was considered a very risky undertaking. But, in the absence of anyone else to perform the task, Mathilde once drove all alone a pair of oxen, drawing a rude farm wagon, to the top of the mountain, loaded the wagon, still alone and unaided, with logs which belonged to her father, and then drove the wagon all the way down to her home in the village and placed the logs in the barn. This feat, which would have been amply difficult for a strong male laborer, perpetuated the memory of Mathilde Stein among all that generation of Nordheimers.

With Mother's arrival in America, where she came into an urban and commercial environment, these rustic accomplishments fell into desuetude. They became mere matters of memory, together with the other incidents and conditions of her youthful life. But they were very precious memories to her, and to the end of her days she was never completely reconciled to being a city dweller but always had a great love in her heart for the country and a special delight in rural sights and sounds, which she was privileged to observe only on the occasions, none too frequent, when she took a vacation from the duties of household and business. She was a living demonstration of the fact that there is room in the human heart for more than one loyalty. She was passionately attached, as I have said, to the memory of her German birthplace and its sentiments and folkways, but her heart was also full of deep and warm affection for her adopted fatherland, America, and its noble and exalted principles of liberty and democracy. In those happy pre-Hitler days, when the atmosphere of

---

* *"Madele* is Bavarian for *Mathilde*—not to be confused with *Maedel*, a young girl.—Ed.

liberty pervaded the entire civilized world, when all indications pointed to a constant increase in the power and prevalence of liberal and democratic institutions and when in Germany, too, despite its strict, monarchical form of government, liberal and progressive thought was widespread and ancient prejudices and bigotries, such as hatred of the Jew, appeared to be dying and life was kindly and courteous and filled with innocent enjoyment to a degree unequaled in other lands, such an antagonism was unthinkable.

Her third loyalty, her Jewish loyalty, meant to her a faithful adherence to the religious heritage which she had received from God-fearing, devoutly Jewish parents and ancestors. She was not, perhaps, as strict as some in fulfilling the *minutiae* of Jewish observance, but I have never known any Jewish woman in whom the consciousness of her Jewishness was keener or the reverence for the Jewish heritage profounder than in the heart of my mother. It was only natural that the gentle and persuasive influence of such parents, free from harshness and stern exercise of parental authority, inspired their children with reverence for the things that were sacred to them. It was certainly one of the causes which determined my course in life.

My mother's love for Judaism showed itself in her willing participation in all the Jewish movements that were known at the time. She was an active worker in the sisterhood or women's society of the congregation—known at that time as the Ladies Auxiliary Society—where she was highly respected and her counsel sought, and a cheerful giver to charitable causes. On the High Holy Days our store was closed and no business transacted; and on Passover, Mother saw to it that the dietary arrangements were in strict accordance with the ritual prohibition of leavened food. While I cannot claim that our home conformed in every way to the precepts of Orthodox Judaism, I know that it did so in large measure and that the spirit of reverence for Judaism pervaded it. Certainly the utter irreligion and worldliness characteristic of many so-called Jewish homes in the irreligious present were not characteristic of our home.

In other ways than that of ceremonial observance Mother showed her loyalty to Jewish tradition. One of these ways was that of hospitality and kindness, especially to the poor and needy. Mother's heart was tender and sympathetic to the *nth* degree. She could not listen to a tale of woe without trying to help, and it made no difference to her whether the one who made the plea was Jew or Gentile. Naturally, in accordance with our connections and the great number of Jewish victims of the persecutions which even at that time raged in Eastern Europe, the majority of the applicants for and recipients of help were Jewish. Our home—in this case, usually, the store—was wide open to whosoever had any legitimate reason for desiring to enter, and there was rarely a day when one or more of those who "will not cease from the midst of the land" did not present themselves, soliciting aid in their distress. None was ever turned away without help, although on some days there were, as the Jewish saying puts it, "more slaughterers than chickens," that is to say, more *schnorrers** than customers in the store.

In all these works of charity and mercy my dear father cooperated earnestly and energetically. Indeed, he sometimes performed certain kinds of charitable work in which Mother, as a busy housewife and business woman, could not very well participate. Thus I remember that in the year of the great persecutions and pogroms in Russia—I think it was in the year 1881 or a year or two before or after—when hundreds of thousands of the victims poured into America—and found here, by the way, a most cordial and sympathetic welcome, very different from the reception meted out to the victims of similar or even worse persecutions today in the calendar year 1941—Father strove strenuously to aid the new arrivals to adjust themselves to the unwonted conditions and find their places in the life of America. He took me once with him to Castle Garden, the reception station where immigrants landed on their arrival in the United States. It was a pitiable sight, the hundreds of Jewish men, women, and children, standing or sitting on benches or the floor, all with expressions of helplessness and bewilderment on their faces. Father spoke a few friendly words to a number of them in the Yiddish dialect, and it was delightful to behold the expression of pleasure and joy which lit up their countenances on hearing the words of the language they understood. Father sent out for a liberal quantity of lemonade, which he paid for out of his own pocket and which was most refreshing to the immi-

---

* Poor people, beggars.

grants, as it was midsummer and the day was very hot. He also selected a few of the refugees who were artisans and brought them, together with their families, to Jersey City, where he found homes and employment for them. One of these men I remember very well. He was a tall, slim, muscular individual, of typical Russian appearance, with a sallow complexion, pale blue eyes and blond hair and beard, and by trade a carpenter. He did not at all resemble the Jews with whom I was familiar, and, if I had met him under other circumstances, I would never have suspected that he was Jewish. But he was thoroughly so and spoke only Yiddish. When asked his name, he gave it in Yiddish as Avrohom Schlomoh. (It was afterwards Americanized into Albert Solomon.) He had a very decent and presentable family, consisting of a wife and two or three children. Avrohom Schlomoh, or Albert Solomon, supported himself and his family in Jersey City by working at his trade, largely on jobs found for him by Father, and in the course of a few years became quite Americanized and a fairly fluent speaker of English. With his children the Americanization process proceeded with such rapidity that in a year or two they hardly knew that they had ever been in Russia. Such is the miracle of America.

It was no wonder that the influence of such parents upon their children was very great. It manifested itself in all aspects of human character but was probably most marked in the domain of religious sentiment.

Chapter Four

Jersey City—(*continued*)

My Brothers and Sisters

I DO NOT KNOW WHETHER IT IS PROPERLY WITHIN THE PROVINCE OF an autobiography to devote much space or description to personages other than the one whose life history is being told. Nevertheless, I have felt justified, indeed, have thought it indispensable to devote considerable space to the description of my dear parents because of the enormous influence which they exercised upon my spiritual, intellectual, and ethical development. For the same reason I shall devote some space to the description of my brothers and sisters, for they too were influential in shaping my character and my course in life, although, of course, not to the extent nor with the force that my dear parents were. Here the influence was mutual. They influenced me, but I also influenced them, and can truthfully say that I was largely instrumental in causing them to become the men and women which they did. Speaking broadly, I may say that their influence over me prevented me from going to extremes in my Jewish religious tendencies and kept me in touch with my American and secular environment, while my influence over them prevented them from yielding excessively to that environment and kept them from drifting away from their Jewish moorings. Through this inter-relation of influences we were able to adjust ourselves harmoniously to both great aspects of our lives and of the lives of all Jews in America, Americanism and Judaism; we became real American Jews or, if you prefer the term, Jewish Americans.

Our family, as already stated, consisted of six children, three boys and three girls. A younger brother, the youngest in the family, had died in his infancy. The oldest child was my brother Louis, whose

English name corresponded to his Hebrew appellation Levi, in accordance with the Jewish custom of bearing two names, one a Hebrew name such as was borne by their ancestors in ancient times, and the other a name taken from the nomenclature of the people of the land. The Hebrew name is called *Shem Ha-kodesh,* or "holy name," and is conferred upon the child in order to preserve the continuity of the tradition of Israel; the other name is called *Shem Ha-Chol,* or "secular name," and is given to maintain the unity and sympathetic relation of the Jews with the people among whom they dwell. Louis, as the first of the children, was almost entirely a product of his American environment. As a child, he was lively and mischievous and not inclined to take anything very seriously. His school life was full of misadventures and escapades. He read books about the Wild West and once even ran away from home. After a long and varied stage of uncertainty, he joined the Democratic Club and became hail-fellow-well-met with most of the local politicians, high and low, and was not at all backward, on account of being a Jew, in his relations with them or in expressing his opinions. Thus, when he became weary of waiting for an appointment, he dramatized his indignation by bursting into the headquarters with the announcement, *"I'm going to Rome!"* It had just happened, probably for the first and perhaps for the only time in history, that a Jew named Ernesto Nathan, reputedly of English origin, had become mayor of Rome. Displaying a newspaper announcing this occurrence, he added, "That's one place in the world where a Jew can get a square deal." To the Democratic politicians, most of whom were of Irish descent and Catholic faith, these words were indeed startling. At any rate, he was given an appointment in the courthouse on the hill and held the position, rendering creditable and efficient service, until his death in 1930 at the age of seventy-six.

The second child in our family was my older sister Bessie. Her Hebrew name was Elisheba, the correct equivalent of which in English is, of course, Elizabeth. She was a gay and pretty girl, who married young and unhappily. Her husband, a handsome but incompetent fellow, turned out to be a gambler. The marriage ended in divorce, and Bessie died at thirty-two, leaving five small children, who were reared in my parents' home, educated, and prepared to find their way in life. They were not permitted to suffer in any way through the unhappy experience of their mother, and they have shown their grateful appreciation through loyal adherence to her family.

The third child of my parents was myself, of whom, for reasons which are obvious, I shall say nothing at this place, except that my name, Bernard, is a modification of the German *Baer,* a translation of my Hebrew name, *Dov.* In my childhood and boyhood this was colloquially altered into Bernie and Barney, and the true form was hardly used.

The fourth child was my brother Gustave or Gus. His Hebrew name was Jacob, or Koppel, after a remote ancestor in Germany. From the moment that we became conscious of each other's existence, Gustave and I loved each other. He was my junior by slightly less than two years, his birthday having been April 29, 1863, while mine was June 27, 1861. As children and young boys we were the most loving and devoted of comrades and playmates. I am afraid the relation was not quite equal. He was so gentle and submissive that he just naturally assumed a subordinate position while I was undeniably more self-assertive and forceful in putting through my ideas. Looking back through the vista of years, I can understand now something which puzzled me at the time. That was the fact that Gus was unquestionably Mother's favorite child and that she had an especially warm spot in her heart for him. Today I think she loved him so intensely not only because of his pure soul and amiable disposition but because there was in him that little touch of helplessness, that need of comforting and upholding, which appeals so strongly to a mother's heart. But, whatever may have been our relative rank in our relation to each other, the relation itself was most delightful. Our play together was more pleasing to us than when we played with other boys. I remember that once we played soldiers in our back yard. We had improvised uniforms after a fashion and also a wooden sword and gun. I was the general and Gus was the army, and I drilled the army in strict accordance with Upton's *Tactics,* which I had found somewhere in the house. How it came there I do not know, but I suspect that Father's cousin, the veteran, may have left it. The army was well disciplined and only failed on one occasion to comply with my orders. That was when I ordered it to *form a hollow square,* which, for some reason, it refused to do.

As Gustave grew to maturity, he entered the Law School of Columbia College and was graduated in 1885 as an LL.B. and was shortly after admitted to the bar. He did not attain to a high degree of financial success in the practice of the law, but of my own personal knowledge I can testify that any case entrusted to him was handled with skill and scrupulous care and almost invariably with success. As General Counsel of the Jewish Sabbath Alliance of America, to which position he was called on the organization of the Alliance in 1905, he defended with profound knowledge of the statutes and with rare devotion the cases of the conscientious observers of the seventh-day Sabbath, mainly Jews but also some Christians, held on charges of desecration of the Sunday by labor or business, and was usually successful in obtaining their release. This work was particularly sympathetic to him because of his own sincere and earnest Jewish religious feelings. It afforded him more pleasure to secure the release of a conscientious Jewish Sabbath observer from unjust punishment than to win a case involving many thousands of dollars but of purely mercenary and monetary concern.

Gustave married Julia Raunheim, daughter of a prominent and cultured Jewish family originating from Frankfort-on-the-Main, and lived with her many years of happy wedlock. This union was blessed with three good and worthy children. Gustave passed away in 1934 and was followed by his wife after a few brief years.

The fifth child in the Drachman family was my sister Emily, born December 31, 1865. Her Hebrew name was *Malkah,* the English translation of which is Queen. On account of the fact that her birth occurred on the last day of the year we would sometimes jestingly congratulate her on her good fortune in having managed to get born then because, we would say, if not then she could never have been born at all. . . . Which is, perhaps, not a very bright or humorous remark but, at least, served to preserve the date of her birth from being forgotten.

Emily's personality was exceptionally beautiful and noble. Even as a young girl, dignity, seriousness of demeanor, a high sense of honor, and profound ethical and religious sentiment were her leading characteristics. I cannot recall ever having observed in her any of the thoughtless merrymaking and eager pursuit of social pleasures which are supposed to be typical of females in the "flapper" stage of their existence. I was more than four years older than she, but I did not hesitate, even when I had attained to full maturity, to come to her for counsel in my difficulties, and her counsel was always one of prudence and discretion.

When Emily married, as she did in due course of time, despite her reserve and modesty, or perhaps on that very account, the opportunity came to her to establish a truly Jewish home, and she made full use of it. Her husband, Nathan Loewy, was a man of great intelligence and considerable culture, both Jewish and secular. He was an expert designer of women's dresses, and through his skill and industry accumulated quite a fortune. He was the son of strictly religious parents in Galicia and had preserved much of the religious sentiment which he had imbibed in his youth. Emily came at once, therefore, into a well provided and comfortable home and was able, with the full approval of her husband, to give that home a truly religious Jewish character. She did so with earnestness and sincerity. When children came, four splendid boys and one daughter, she saw to their religious training and sought, with much success, to imbue them with the same reverence which filled her heart for God and His holy Torah. Alas, she did not attain to real old age. She passed away at the age of sixty, greatly mourned and lamented, not only by her own family and relatives but also by a numerous group of friends who had sincerely loved and respected her.

The sixth and youngest child in our family was my sister Fannie. The name Fannie was given to her as the English equivalent of the German *Voegele,* which again corresponds to the Hebrew appellation *Zipporah.* Thanks to the mercy of a beneficent Creator, Fannie is still with her dear ones on earth, the beloved wife and mother in her family, my greatly cherished sister and friend (may the Lord preserve her for many years to come!). I am thereby inhibited from describing in full her qualities and characteristics, in accordance with the injunction of our Talmudic sages, "In the presence of thy friend, i.e., with his knowledge, thou mayest only say part of his praise, but in his absence, without his knowledge, thou mayest say all." Suffice it to say that dear Fannie is a most worthy member of our family and upholds its traditions in loyalty and sincerity. She is blessed with a noble husband, an intelligent and honorable man and loyal Jew, Aaron Wolf* by name, and with five exemplary sons, completely devoted to her and to their father. Since my other dear brothers and sisters have passed to the realm beyond mortal ken, she is the only link which binds me to my childhood days, a sweet and cherished link. May it long remain unbroken and unsevered!

I have now described for my readers the family in which I was born and reared. That description is an important and significant part of my life record. The influences in our family life were mutual and reciprocal. I was deeply influenced by my association with beloved parents, brothers and sisters and I humbly believe that from me, too, emanated an influence which tended to shape and direct their lives. The memory of their affection, of their tender devotion and cordial intimacy has been a treasured possession throughout my later years and will never forsake me as long as the breath of life stirs within me.

---

* Died February 16, 1945.—Ed.

Chapter Five

Jersey City—(*continued*)

The Jewish Community

WHEN WE TOOK UP OUR ABODE IN JERSEY CITY IN THE YEAR 1870, the Jews residing there were very few. I do not know the exact number, but I believe it was between twenty and thirty families. I refer to those residing in lower Jersey City, where we had our home. Some Jews resided on the hill and in Bergen, but they, too, were few in number and had little or no contact with their co-religionists of the lower city. Few as these latter were, they already had a rather well developed religious and social life. There was a regularly organized congregation, which bore the name of *Kehillah Kedoshah Isaac Ephraim*, that is, The Holy Congregation of Isaac Ephraim, after the father of one of the women of the group, who had contributed rather liberally to the expense of its establishment. It was a tiny affair and had no regular synagogue building but met in a hired room on the third or fourth floor above a store in Montgomery Street, about a block from our home. But small and unpretentious as it was, in it all the services ordained by the Jewish faith were conducted and a *Talmud Torah* (or Hebrew and religious school) was maintained for the instruction of the small group of children belonging to the congregation in the Holy Tongue and the tenets of the Jewish religion. I was one of the pupils of the Talmud Torah but, as already stated, I profited more by the instruction given me by my father than by that of the regular teacher. The Hebrew School was also known as *Cheder,* a term brought from Eastern Europe and originally signifying merely "room" and which, in all probability, received the meaning of "school" because the Jews in the Slavonic lands had few regular school buildings and were accustomed to send their children for instruction to the home of the teacher.

As I remember the instruction given in the Hebrew School of Jersey City in those early days, its chief characteristic was its irregularity and instability. No teacher seemed to remain very long, and the teachers were of such different types and styles that the effect on the children could not fail to be confusing. Some spoke a more or less correct English, some spoke German which could be described in the same manner, and some spoke the pure and undisguised Yiddish of Poland or Russia. The same diversity prevailed among the *Chazonim* or cantors who conducted the service. They had all possible varieties of voices and pronunciations of the Hebrew; some read the prayers in a simple, devout chant, and others essayed fanciful vocal renditions with more or less success, usually less. The congregation could not maintain a regular rabbi or preacher, but occasionally a wandering Jewish cleric visited Jersey City and would preach in our synagogue. No two of these itinerant gentlemen were exactly alike in language or method. One of them once announced that he would deliver a sermon *in English*. This announcement brought a fair-sized congregration to synagogue, and the preacher kept his promise. That is to say, his sermon, or adddress or whatever it was, was composed of English words, but these were so ponderous and unfamiliar and were strung together in such an obscure and unintelligible fashion that no one, not excluding myself, had the remotest idea what the reverend gentleman was "driving at."

But, all in all, there was surprisingly little dissatisfaction or criticism. Most of the people may have considered these conditions the normal and proper thing among Jews or may have been of a forgiving and charitable disposition or, what is most probable, may have thought that in a congregation so weak and poor as ours was at the time no higher grade of accomplishment could be expected. Evidence of the correctness of this last view may be found in the effect produced by a visit of Reverend Doctor Adolph Huebsch of the congregation *Ahavath Chesed* of New York City to Jersey City. Dr. Huebsch came to perform a marriage ceremony. He officiated, clad in his rabbinical robe, conducted a most impressive ceremony and delivered a touching and eloquent address, concluding with a solemn

Jersey City—Continued

benediction over bride and groom. The effect was immense. The entire assemblage, which included practically all the Jews of the town and a considerable number of Gentiles, was thrilled and awed, and the Finkelstein—name fictitious—marriage was the subject of admiring comment for many months.

These unfavorable conditions prevailed only in the early period of the history of the congregation. The Jewish population of Jersey City grew by leaps and bounds and increased in a few brief years to impressive proportions. At present it is a well organized community, boasting several houses of worship and necessary charitable institutions, and possessing, I doubt not, competent and well qualified synagogue and other officials as well as all other requisites of Jewish communal life.

The persons composing the community were mainly a good-natured, well intentioned, middle class group, few of whom possessed higher culture. They were, however, friendly and pleasant, with a full realization of their common faith and desirous of upholding the Jewish heritage which bound them together. They were basically loyal to their ancestral traditions, though not, perhaps, observant in the strictest sense.

As regards their countries of origin, nearly all the members were natives of Central or Eastern European lands: Germany, Austria, Hungary, Poland, Lithuania, and Russia. There was one lonely Englishman who, I think, was a *Sephardi,* that is to say, of remote Spanish origin. There was no native American among them—for that the Jersey City community was still too young. These differences of national origin had no harmful effect on their social relations. All met and associated together on the basis of their common Judaism, although there was occasionally some good-natured poking of fun of the different elements at each other, of Germans at Polish, of Galicians at Lithuanians and *vice versa.* The English language, which all spoke more or less fluently, was a unifying influence. Some of these good people possessed considerable oratorical ability, which they loved to display at meetings of the congregation and the B'nai Brith* lodge. There was Joseph Meyer, a man of considerable wealth who,

---

* "Sons of the Covenant" name of a Jewish fraternal and benevolent order.—B.D.

with his numerous relatives, formed the chief representation of the South German element in Jersey City; there were Charles Marks and Herman Koenigsberg and Joseph Levy and Benjamin Drachman, all of whom were excellent speakers and leaders of the community. There was David Cohen, a simple, unpretentious little man but with a golden heart and much respected. The other members were practically all pleasant, worthy people. As for the adolescent boys and girls, they were a lovely group, especially the girls. Most of the girls were genuinely pretty, too, and mainly of the true Hebrew type, with dark, flashing eyes, flowing black hair, alabaster skin, pearly teeth, and ravishing smiles. My admiration of them all was purely platonic. I was a retiring sort of boy, scrupulously well behaved, and permitted myself no undue familiarities with any female. Occasionally a group of boys and girls would go on outings together to Curry's Woods or some other rustic or partly rustic region not far from Jersey City. We always enjoyed these excursions immensely and really felt a strong sentiment of friendship and intimacy. I believe that there may be applied without exaggeration to the social relations existing in those early days in the Jewish community of Jersey City, among both elders and juniors, the words of the Psalmist: "Behold, how good and how pleasant it is when brethren dwell together in peace!" It is true that there were some Jews residing in Jersey City who kept themselves aloof from the community. We answered their indifference with indifference. As they deemed us strangers to them, we deemed them strangers to us. But, as for the rest of us, we certainly dwelt together not only in peace but in genuine harmony and amity. And it was not only in fair weather, when the sun of prosperity and health shone brightly on all of us, that we were friends. If misfortune came to some of us, if illness or financial reverses were uninvited and unwelcome guests in some home, the hearts of all who had been spared the affliction pulsated with intense sympathy and they made every effort to comfort the sick and to assist the needy. I remember with great joy those kindly and truly brotherly and sisterly relations. They undoubtedly had their share in filling my heart with love for my people and for the simple but sublime faith which held them together and had instilled into their being these lovable principles of conduct.

Chapter Six

The Jersey City High School

IN THE YEAR 1874, WHEN I WAS THIRTEEN YEARS OF AGE, I ENTERED the High School of Jersey City. This meant a great change in my life. I entered, as it were, into a new world. The high school building situated at that time on Bay Street, was, I believe, quite new. It certainly was a fine structure and very clean and presentable in appearance. It compared most favorably with Public School No. 1, in which I had spent the past four years of my educational career, and which was rather dingy and shabby and apparently quite old. Not only the external aspect of the high school was pleasing and impressive; its teaching staff and the educational work done by them were both of a very high type. They radiated culture, dignity, and refinement. The pupils also were of a high type. They were older in years than the pupils of Public School No. 1. That fact probably was of some influence in refining and improving their deportment and demeanor. The main reason undoubtedly was because they were almost exclusively sons and daughters of the most substantial citizens of Jersey City, children of the so-called "better classes." It may be undemocratic in America, where all citizens are presumed to be equal before the law, to speak of "better classes," but, if we wish to be realistic, we must admit that superior economic conditions entailing, as they do, not only better physical nurture but also a finer environment and a finer intellectual and social atmosphere, show their effect in the finer personal appearance, language, demeanor, and intellectual level of those fortunate enough to be reared in them. At least such was the case at that time, which belongs to the period of world history known as "mid-Victorian" and which was emphatically mid-Victorian with all that the term implies. My classmates were mainly sons and daughters of the best old families of New Jersey, partly of the original Dutch stock which had colonized this region, partly of English and partly of German origin. Their names revealed this diversity of descent. The names Van Ripen, and Wortendyke, Bierstadt and Klein, Sheldon, Carrick and Cudlipp, showed that their bearers were respectively of Dutch, German, and English ancestry. But there was no difference of external appearance or manners and no sentiment of antagonism on account of this diversity of ethnic origin. They were all splendid, clean-cut young Americans, and idiomatic American English was their common idiom.

I was, I believe, the only Jew among them, and, with one exception, their conduct toward me was as friendly and cordial as could be desired. The exception, too, did not usually show his anti-Semitic sentiments but revealed them on one important occasion, of which more anon. I enjoyed my studies immensely and profited tremendously by their instruction, so that my outlook on life became greatly broadened by my years in high school. The members of the teaching staff—I do not recall whether they bore the title of professor or not—were not young people. They were all middle-aged or elderly, a fact which did not detract from the value of their instruction. On the contrary it gave to it a special quality of maturity and authoritativeness. My respect for them was so great that I considered them—in their own domains—as practically infallible.

The principal of the high school was George H. Barton and the vice principal Edward S. Peck. They were both typical American gentlemen of great dignity and impressive appearance. The instructor whose educational work made the deepest impression upon me was Mr. W. R. Martin. He taught the classical languages, Greek and Latin, and was a master of both of these tongues and their literatures. I enjoyed especially the instruction in Latin and must have made fair progress therein, for in the examination of June, 1875, I won a prize for proficiency in that language. It was a copy of J. I. Green's "History of the English People." It was conferred upon me by Mr. Martin personally and bears an inscription in his own—incidentally very neat and legible—handwriting. I have it yet, and I treasure it as a cherished link to a happy and interesting period of my youth.

Mr. Martin was a most interesting personality. He was of striking appearance, revealing and radiating the scholar. He was tall and thin; his eyes were blue, his hair and beard auburn, his brow high and broad, and his countenance pale, "all sicklied o'er with the pale cast of thought" telling of unnumbered hours spent in study. His reality corresponded to his appearance, for he was not only a master of his own particular subject but also broadly cultured and the possessor of a keen and sound judgment in world affairs. He was not, however, at all self-assertive. On the contrary, he was of a retiring disposition and rarely spoke unless some particular reason existed for a statement on his part. He was in the habit of accompanying his instruction with running comments on many and varied topics, which happened to be suggested by the text and which were invariably both interesting and illuminating. But he was far from being a mere pedant. On the contrary, he possessed a fund of refreshing and original humor which he would sometimes use to illustrate the differences in signification of Greek and Latin words. He did this, for instance, to point out the difference between the Latin words *os*, "mouth," and *ostium*, "door" or "opening." In the German gymnasia, or high schools, he told us, it was customary to employ the Latin alike as a subject and vehicle of instruction and in conversation. It happened once that a professor and his class were sitting in the classroom during a period of instruction, when a boy, coming from outside, entered the room and left the door open behind him. It was winter and a gust of cold wind came into the room. One of the students called out to the boy, *"Claude ostium, puer"* (Close the door, boy). It was not the office of the student to give this order, and the professor rebuked him, saying, *"Claude os tuum, puer"* (Close thy mouth, boy).

Many were the humorous and yet instructive stories which Mr. Martin told and remarks which he made in order to cast light on certain points of his instruction, but I shall tell only one more. Among the students in a certain American college, he said, there was one who had considerable knowledge of Latin and was rather vain of it, so that he became somewhat careless in his homework and neglected the preparation of his Latin readings. One night he attended some sort of gay party and came to college that morning in a rather demoralized condition, with his lessons utterly unprepared. The class at that time was reading the great epic poem of Virgil, the *Aeneid*. The portion which this student was called on to translate was the speech of Aeneas in which he tells of his history and achievements and in which occurs the sentence "*Aedificavi mihi monumenta aere duriora*" (I have built for myself monuments more enduring than brass). Our student got along swimmingly until he came to this sentence. Then, momentarily confusing the verb "*aedificere*," "to build," with "*edere*," "to eat," he proudly proclaimed, "I have eaten for myself monuments more enduring than brass." "And so you see," concluded Mr. Martin, "if you don't prepare your lessons properly you may find yourselves declaring that someone had swallowed the Bunker Hill monument or run away with the Capitol in Washington or some other feat of equal plausibility."

Despite Mr. Martin's scholastic unworldliness and retiring disposition, he was a man of courage and firmness of character, who did not hesitate to defend a cause in which he believed or to insist on his rights when he thought them unjustly invaded. He demonstrated this on one occasion during the time when I was attending the high school. For some reason or other, funds were lacking at this time for the salaries of the teaching staff, and the city government sent in a request to Mr. Barton that the teachers should continue their services without pay until such time as funds would again be available. The reason for this deficit, which certainly was no credit to the Jersey City administration, I never knew. There was much angry talk among the teachers and others, attributing it to the misappropriations of corrupt city officials, but nothing definite was known, except the one fact that there was no money. Mr. Barton duly summoned a conference of the teaching staff and placed before them the request of the city government. It was received with great dissatisfaction, but none of the teachers, evidently for fear of losing their jobs, had the courage to oppose the suggestion. That is to say, none except Mr. Martin. To the surprise of all, the retiring and unassuming Mr. Martin took the floor in vigorous and emphatic opposition to the proposal, and stated that he would not serve under such conditions. And so it was. The other teachers continued their instruction without pay, but Mr. Martin stayed away until payment was resumed, which was, I believe, after a month, when he returned. No disciplinary measures were taken against him, and his fellow teachers looked upon him as very much of a hero, who had not feared to beard the lion of the city government. I had occasion to speak with Mr. Martin two or three times on Jewish topics, and I found him broadminded and with a surprisingly good understanding of the tenets of Judaism and the history of the Jewish people.*

Another teacher who impressed me greatly and for whose person and scholarship I had the greatest respect was Mr. Alfred C. Clement, the instructor in German. Mr. Clement was a typical German pedagogue, of the fine type characteristic of the Germany of that period. He was a handsome man, with a well shaped head, brown hair and beard, keen, clear brown eyes, and with a well knit, athletic figure, whose quick and graceful motions revealed the former German university student and soldier. Mr. Clement was not only profoundly learned in the German language and literature; he possessed an immense enthusiasm for them, and, best of all, he was able to communicate this enthusiasm in great measure to his pupils. Under his able guidance the German department became one of the most popular branches of instruction in the high school. I, of course, possessed a fair knowledge of German before taking it up in high school, but Mr. Clement not only gave me a more exact knowledge of its grammatical structure and rich vocabulary but also imbued me with enthusiastic admiration of the thought treasures imbedded in its great literature. When I think of the splendid intellectual and ethical heights to which the former German culture had risen and compare it with the abysmal depths of barbarism and brutality to which present-day Germany is sunk, I am not only filled with profound sorrow but also with uncomprehending amazement that such an inconceivably tragic and disastrous change should have been possible.

---

* The late Professor William Lyon Prelps, in his charming "Autobiography," devotes several pages to an account of Mr. Martin, who taught him in the Hartford High School after leaving Jersey City. He describes him as "a teacher who made a profound impression . . . six foot four, with a large red beard. . . .He was one of the most learned men I have ever known and he never published a line. . . . Later he became Professor of Ancient and Modern Languages at Trinity College, Hartford." (pp.102-3;235)
B.D., on seeing this in Phelps' book, wrote to the Yale sage, and a pleasant correspondence resulted. Mr. Martin must have been a truly remarkable teacher to have left such an indelible impression on two such men.—Ed.

The only other high school teacher of whom I have any particularly distinct recollection is Miss Annie Moore. She instructed our class in geometry, but her personal appearance and demeanor seemed oddly incongruous to her subject. There was nothing of the mathematically sharp-cut and precise about either her looks, her bearing, or her words. She was an excellent teacher and her explanations of geometrical concepts and problems were exact and lucid. She was unendingly patient too with those pupils to whom mathematical propositions present especial difficulty. I am afraid I was not one of her best pupils, for my mind is of the non-mathematical order, but I am sure I profited greatly by her instruction, and I hold her in respectful, even affectionate, remembrance.

My work at the high school did not cause me to neglect my Hebrew studies, which I continued to pursue, first under the instruction of my father, and afterwards in the Hebrew Preparatory School, which was established about this time in New York City under the auspices of Temple Emanu-El. The fact that I was studying Hebrew became known among the pupils of the high school in the following manner. Mr. Barton, the principal, had offered, as a service for the pupils, to purchase for them any books that they desired. The pupils would tell Mr. Barton the books they wished and give him the money needed, whereupon he would get in touch with the publishing houses or book dealers and obtain the books. At assemblies, when all the student body was seated in the great assembly hall, Mr. Barton would announce the books which had been bought, naming the books by their titles, and call the students who had ordered them to the platform to receive them. There was always considerable interest on the part of the assembled students in this proceeding. It was interesting, and sometimes amusing, to know the kind of subjects in which the book purchasers were interested. Taking advantage of Mr. Barton's offer, I requested him to obtain for me a copy of Deutsch's *Hebrew Grammar*, published by Henry Holt & Co. When the book arrived, Mr. Barton announced it and called me in the usual manner. There was a perceptible buzz of interest and astonishment as the title "Deutsch's *Hebrew Grammar*" was announced. I was the object of observation of all eyes as I walked to the platform and back to my seat.

About this time occurred the anti-Semitic incident to which I have previously referred and which showed how dreadful and shameful a thing is this bitter, malignant, inherited prejudice known as Jew-hatred or, in modern parlance, anti-Semitism.

There was a literary and debating society in the high school, maintained by the students under the name of the Forensic Society. It was a society of high intellectual and social type, and membership in it was greatly prized. But, while not exactly exclusive, it was rigid in its standard of eligibility. No applicant for membership was even considered unless presumably desirable and was accepted only by unanimous vote of the members. The ballot was secret, and one blackball was sufficient to reject a candidate. Several of my friends among the members suggested to me that I should apply for membership. I permitted myself to be guided by their counsel and made the application. To the surprise of all, among the ballots was one blackball. *I was rejected!* This altogether unexpected result was an indescribable shock alike for the members who had favored me and for me. The wrath and indignation of the members, especially of those who had sponsored my candidacy, knew no bounds. They were bitterly resentful of this action of an unknown enemy and greatly puzzled by it. As for me, no words can describe the intensity of the humiliation and the bitter sense of outrageous injustice which I felt. Never in my life have I been as unhappy as then.

In the meantime, my friends among the members were not inactive. They determined to get to the root of the matter, to find out who had cast the blackball and what his motives were. At first they could not attain their object. The caster of the blackball was evidently not proud of what he had done. He kept very silent about it. But at last, in an unguarded moment, he revealed the secret and avowed his motive quite frankly. He boasted that no "damn Jew" should ever be a member in a society to which he belonged. Retribution followed speedily. The members found a way to declare him unworthy of membership in the Forensic Society and expelled him. For this only a majority vote was required. I remember well the blackballer's name but shall not mention it, as he belonged to a fine well-to-do American family who may not share their scion's anti-Jewish sentiments. A delegation came to me and requested me to be a candidate for membership. At first I refused, saying that I did not care to expose myself a second time to the risk of rebuff and humiliation. But when they urged me and told me that all the members had been canvassed and that every one of them had declared that he would vote for me, I withdrew my refusal. I was duly elected and remained a member of the Forensic Society until my graduation from high school and participated with pleasure and benefit in the debates and literary meetings of the society.

Another incident which had to do with my status as a Jew occurred during my attendance at Jersey City High School and also ended favorably. Mr. Barton laid great stress upon singing by the school and there were always several songs sung at the morning assemblies. Many of these were Christian hymns with strongly Christological contents. I am not now discussing the question whether, in the public schools of a nation in which church and state are separated, the singing of specifically religious songs should be permitted. That is a question on which very much might be said, but I am now merely relating the facts as they occurred. As I could not conscientiously join in the singing of these hymns, I remained silent while they were being sung. Had I remained alone in my non-participation the matter would no doubt have passed unnoticed. But, as it chanced, quite a number of other students also abstained from singing, not because of any conscientious objections to the contents of the hymns, but simply because of disinclination to exert themselves vocally, and their non-participation became clearly noticeable. One morning, when this refusal to join in the singing was very recognizable in the diminished volume of sound, Mr. Barton became greatly enraged. He addressed the assembly very harshly, saying that refusal to join in the singing showed an insubordinate and rebellious disposition, that he would instruct the teachers to ascertain and to report to him who were the pupils guilty of such insubordination and that he would never recommend a graduate who had failed to take part in the singing, no matter how well he might have stood in his studies. This severe warning did not seem to worry the other pupils, but on me it made a deep and painful impression. I felt that I did not deserve to be condemned in this harsh fashion and that, while technically I could be included among the insubordinate ones, my reasons for refusing to participate in the singing were such as entirely to justify my conduct.

I determined to explain this to Mr. Barton. Accordingly, when the assembly was dismissed, instead of going at once to my class, I went to the platform where Mr. Barton was seated at his desk. He seemed surprised to see me but greeted me with a pleasant smile. "May I speak to you for a few moments, Mr. Barton?" I asked.

"Why, yes, Drachman," he answered. "In reference to what do you wish to see me?"

"It is in regard to not joining in the singing," I said.

"You don't mean to tell me that you were one of those disrespectful fellows who refused to sing although they know I wish it," he said. "I would never have expected it of you, Drachman. You have always been so loyal and obedient."

"I am very sorry to displease you, Mr. Barton," I said, "but I could not help myself. There is a very great reason why I cannot take part in singing most of these songs."

"And what may it be?" he asked, with just a trace of harshness in his tone.

"Well, you see," I said, "most of these songs are Christian hymns. They are full of references to Jesus and of prayer to him as the Saviour. I am a member of the Jewish faith, and so I cannot take part in worshipping one who is not recognized by my religion."

Mr. Barton looked surprised at my words, and then he asked a question and made a remark which I have been unable from that day to this to realize as possible but which he actually uttered. "Why can't you join in the singing? I understand the Jews believe in Jesus and worship also the Virgin Mary."

I was very much embarrassed by these words, but there was no evading an answer. "No, sir," I said, "we Jews believe in and worship only the One Supreme Being. We are expressly forbidden to worship any being besides Him. And so I may not take part in singing these hymns. I respect the faith of all other people, but my duty is to uphold my own. I am willing to join in the singing of all the other songs, but in the hymns I cannot."

Mr. Barton looked at me with some apparent wonderment as I spoke these words. Then he said with a pleasant smile, "Very well, Drachman. I see that your refusal to sing was not an act of insubordination. Sing whatever songs you may and, as for those which your conscience forbids, you are excused." And so this incident ended happily.

About this time—I do not remember precisely when but I believe it was while I was still attending Jersey City High School—my mother, of blessed memory, showed me one morning an article in the German language newspaper *Die Staatszeitung,* which was at that time probably the most highly esteemed and widely read newspaper of its type in America and of which Mother was an assiduous reader. The article stated that a Jewish organization of New York City had established a school for higher Hebrew education and that youths in their teens were desired as pupils. The object of the school, the article stated, was to give these youths the preliminary training required for the rabbinate. English-speaking rabbis were then very rare in America, and the members of the organization were desirous of supplying this deficiency. Knowing my interest in Hebrew studies, Mother had rightly judged that I would be interested in this announcement. I followed the suggestions in the article and applied for admission in the new school and was immediately accepted. Its official title was Hebrew Preparatory School, and it was maintained by the Emanu-El Theological Seminary Association, which was either a direct affiliate of Temple Emanu-El or mainly composed of members drawn from the congregation of that temple.

I attended the Hebrew Preparatory School for six years, and I must state that the instruction which I received there gave me a very substantial foundation of Hebrew scholarship. There were only two salaried instructors, Mr. Louis Schnabel and Mr. Arnold Bogamil Ehrlich, and they were both masters of their vocation. Three of the rabbis of the two chief reform congregations of the city, Temple Emanu-El and Temple Beth El, also took part in the instruction. They were Dr. Samuel Adler, retired Rabbi of Emanu-El, Dr. Gustav Gottheil, its officiating Rabbi, and Dr. Kaufman Kohler, Rabbi of Temple Beth El. The salaried instructors taught their classes in the building of the German-American School in East Fifty-second Street, near Second Avenue, but the rabbis gave what would be called in university phrase *seminars;* that is, they instructed selected groups of students in their homes. I participated in both forms of instruction. I took the regular courses in the East Fifty-second Street building and was also fortunate enough to be of those admitted to the seminars given by the rabbis. Both the regular instructors and the rabbis were most interesting personalities.

To begin with the elder of the regular instructors, Mr. Louis Schnabel was a striking example of the trained and systematic pedagogue. His subjects were Hebrew language, and Bible, and he taught them with rigid exactitude and accuracy, perhaps not very profoundly but with strict regard to grammatical correctness and the true, literal significance of the texts. He was, I believe, a native of what was then called Bohemia, but his pedagogical methods showed undoubted German influence. His personal appearance was striking. He was rather tall and quite thin, his face was very pale and his hair and beard snow white. His features were not characteristically Jewish but suggested emphatically the scholar. In intercourse with his pupils he was friendly and pleasant and not at all pedantic.

His associate, Mr. Arnold B. Ehrlich, was an even greater Hebrew scholar but a very different personality. He was a younger man, and his burly figure and jovial manner did not at all suggest the wealth of scholarship which he possessed. He was a native of Russia, where he had drunk deeply from the fountains of rabbinic lore, but he had also studied at German universities and imbibed much modern culture and science. His knowledge of the Hebrew language, in all its niceties and finest nuances, was extraordinary, and he used it in his interpretations of Biblical texts, which were often very far-fetched and open to great question but were certainly highly ingenious and indicative of profound scholarship. He later embodied these interpretations in two works, one in Hebrew under the title *Mikra Ki-Peshuto* (The Bible according to its literal significance) and the other a German commentary on the Psalms. He was a master of German style, which he demonstrated not only by his Psalm commentary but also by his rendition into classic German of the famous Hebrew poem *Nethanneh Tokef,* which is chanted in the synagogue on the Jewish New Year and on the Day of Atonement and which pictures in highly poetic and impressive manner the terrors of the Day of Judgment. That he had acquired in America a good knowledge of English goes without saying. His subjects included those of Mr. Schnabel and, in addition, rabbinical commentaries and Talmud. I could not always agree with his views and interpretations, but I had the greatest possible respect for his enormous erudition.

The three rabbis, while all men of outstanding ability and importance, were very different in their individual characteristics. Dr. Samuel Adler, while a leader of the reform wing of Judaism, was, in his external appearance and mannerisms, a typical representative of the old-fashioned South German rabbinate. He was a thorough Talmudist and, despite his secular and university training, thoroughly permeated with the Talmudic spirit. He taught Talmud to a small group of the students, and his method of instruction was very similar to that which I subsequently encountered in Germany.

Dr. Gustave Gottheil, Dr. Adler's successor in the spiritual leadership of Temple Emanu-El, was more the pastor or minister than the rabbi. He, too, had received a thorough rabbinical and Hebrew training in his North German home, but, before coming to America, had held for a number of years a ministerial post in England and had there acquired a splendid control of the English language and the clerical bearing and technique for which the English clergy are famous. His prominent Hebraic features and his dignified bearing made him everywhere conspicuous as a person of unusual importance. He read medieval Jewish philosophy with a group of us students, and his instruction was lucid and keenly analytical. I remember reading under his guidance the philosophic treatise *Cusari* of the great Hebrew philosopher and poet Judah Ha-Levi, and, under his illuminating interpretation, the difficult and at times obscure Hebrew text became a vivid presentation of spiritual doctrine and profound reasoning. He not only interpreted the text but described to us the inspiring personality of Judah Ha-Levi and the historical conditions under which the *Cusari* was written. In this way we derived from his words a new and very enlightening concept of medieval Jewish life. Dr. Gottheil was accustomed to accompany his instruction with observations suggested by the text and strikingly applicable to modern men and conditions. He had also a fine sense of humor and would occasionally tell a humorous tale or parable drawn from Jewish sources and with a modern application. Speaking of anti-Jewish prejudice and persecution, of which we, indeed, knew little in those happier days, he said, "Much *rishus* (anti-Jewish prejudice) is very bad, but a little *rishus* is a good thing." His idea was, of course, that it was desirable that the path of the Jew in the world should not be altogether smooth, lest he forget his Jewishness and seek to merge completely with his environment. At another time, speaking of the doctrine of the return of Israel to Palestine and the re-establishment of the Jewish nation in the Holy Land, he uttered the following words, which, coming from one who was the spiritual leader of the greatest Reform congregation in America, show an extraordinary broadmindedness and a sympathetic attitude toward the historic tenets of Judaism.

"I am sometimes asked by Gentiles, clergymen and others, what is my attitude on the question of the return of the Jews to Palestine. In such cases I examine the personality of the questioner. If I think he is a *rosho* (a Jew-hater) and his secret motive a desire to see Jews expelled from Western lands, I say, 'We Reform Jews have given up that doctrine. What we believe in and want is equal rights of citizenship in all lands in which we dwell.' But if I think he is a sincere seeker after knowledge, who desires merely to know what Jews believe and feel, then I say, 'This is a very precious doctrine and very dear to millions of Jews. Pehaps God, in His mercy, will re-establish our ancient state and restore our ancient glory. Should that happen, all Jews would rejoice.' "

The third of the rabbis who instructed in the Hebrew Preparatory School was Dr. Kaufman Kohler. He was also a distinguished scholar but a quite different personality from the other two. He was the typical German scholar of the intellectual, pre-Hitlerian type, widely read, thorough and accurate in all his knowledge, and a profound thinker. His exegetical views were very radical, and he expressed them in his interpretation of the Biblical books which he read with us. Somehow or other these interpretations did not rouse a sympathetic echo in my heart. But I had the utmost respect for his scholarship and his sincerity.

Of all the pupils of the Hebrew Preparatory School only three stand out distinctly in my memory: Richard Gottheil, Abraham Illich, and Adam Rosenberg. They were all three unusually striking personalities. Richard Gottheil was a true heir of his father's spirit, an able and diligent student, a sincere adherent of Judaism in the concept which his father represented, a thorough gentleman, and a pleasant and friendly companion. His features were strikingly Hebraic and very similar to those of his father.

Although designed for the Reform rabbinate, for some reason which I never learned he did not take up that vocation but became instead Professor of Semitics in Columbia University and served in that capacity with distinction for many years. When the Zionist movement started, he became an ardent adherent, which was hardly consistent for a follower of Reform Judaism. I believe his Zionist sentiments had their birth in his resentment at the humiliations which Jews must endure even in liberal countries and tolerant times. His was a deeply sensitive nature, and the injustices and discriminations to which Jews are subjected for no reason other than their birth grieved him profoundly and led him to think that only through the establishment of a specifically Jewish homeland could these evils be remedied.

Abraham Illich was a slight and rather frail youth, but in his frail body dwelt a keen and powerful intellect. He was, I believe a native of Albany, in the State of New York, and had come to the city of New York to pursue his studies. He was a convinced adherent of Reform Judaism and could defend his views with much cogency and logic. He often tried to convince me and was more than a little annoyed that I did not see the force of his arguments. For, although at this time I had not definitely decided to embrace the Orthodox cause and my mind was still open to conviction, I had a general concept of religion which did not harmonize with the premises on which Reform Judaism must necessarily be based. Illich died young, or else, I am convinced, he would have attained to great distinction in the Reform pulpit.

My third fellow-student, Adam Rosenberg, was poles removed in all his characteristics from the two just mentioned. He was a native of Hamburg, member of a strictly Orthodox family and himself a conscientious and strictly observant adherent of the ancient faith. He was already a fine Hebrew and rabbinical scholar, having been taught by his father, who was a learned and scrupulously pious rabbi, and why he ever entered the Hebrew Preparatory School no one knew. He was taciturn, but when he spoke his remarks showed him to be the possessor of a keen intellect and excellent ability in presenting his thoughts. While he held himself rather aloof from the other students, with me he was friendly and unreserved. He invited me to his home. It was a sincerely religious home. Not only the mother but all the children observed the precepts of Orthodox Judaism most earnestly and loyally. I was deeply impressed with what I saw in the Rosenberg family, and it had much to do with shaping my final decision as to my course in life. Despite his early and excellent preparation, Adam Rosenberg did not become a rabbi. He studied law and practiced that vocation for some years in New York City. He then became an active worker in the *Hobebei Zion,* or Lovers of Zion Society, an organization of Orthodox Jews interested in the colonization of Palestine. In this capacity he went to the Holy Land and lived for a time in a colony in the section now known as Trans-Jordania. He later returned to America, but he then disappeared from sight, and his subsequent career is unknown to me.

All in all, my experiences and contacts in the Hebrew Preparatory School made a deep impression upon me and formed a valuable and unforgettable part of my life history.

Chapter Seven

Columbia College

AT THE CONCLUSION OF THE SPRING TERM, IN THE YEAR 1878, I WAS graduated from Jersey City High School and immediately thereafter applied for permission to take the entrance examinations for the Academic Department of Columbia College (later Columbia University). Permission having been granted, I took the examinations, passed the same successfully, and was duly admitted to the fall term as a freshman in the class of 1882.

My four years in Columbia College were overflowingly rich in impressions and experiences. I became acquainted with two things of which I had previously had some idea but very little actual knowledge. They were what might be called the Anglo-American tradition, that is, the strength and the persistence in American life of the English heritage derived from colonial days, and the student spirit. The atmosphere of dignity and scholarly aloofness which encompassed alike professors and tutors, the stately academic robes which were worn, and the solemn processions and ceremonials which took place at commencements and other public occasions of importance, were all utterly new to me.

My feelings on being brought in contact with them were closely akin to awe. I speedily came to understand that all this represented the transplanting of English traditions and customs to the New World. It was evident that American universities and colleges are not only sisters but cultural children of the great academies of England, perpetuating on this continent the scholastic heritage of Oxford and Cambridge. This led me to the realization that American civilization is not merely of European but specifically of English origin and that, just as the language, so also the culture and even the political concepts of English-speaking America are deeply rooted in the soil of the

English past. As already stated, the professors and tutors fitted well into this general framework of dignity, scholarliness, and English tradition. The professors were nearly all aged men with snow-white hair and beards, and their demeanor was solemn and serious, as suited to their years and their exalted vocation. The tutors were naturally younger and also less austere, but they were looked upon as mere beginners in their vocation and relatively unimportant.

Dr. Barnard was president of the college at the time of my entrance. He was reputed a man of great scientific attainments, but as president of the college he did not personally impart instruction. He did, however, preside with immense dignity on all public occasions. Among the professors whose instruction I enjoyed or whose lectures I heard were Professors Drisler, Van Amringe, Schmidt, Short, Nairne, Root, Chandler, Alexander, and Smith. All of these, with the exception of two, were exceedingly grave and solemn gentlemen, who never unbent or surrendered aught of their professorial dignity, at least not during the hours of instruction.

The two exceptions were Professor Short, who taught Latin language and literature, and Professor Chandler, who lectured on chemistry. These two had a strong vein of humor and loved to adorn their instruction with witty comments and merry anecdotes. The students were quick to respond to this spirit and enjoyed being themselves a little humorous or jocose at the expense of the jocose professors. Two instances of this are particularly clear in my memory. It was customary, of course, for the students to take notes of the instruction and explanations given by the professors, and some of the students wrote down all the jokes and humorous remarks quite as carefully and exactly as the actual instruction. The jesting remarks of Professor Short were printed and published in book form under the title *"Short Comments on the Latin Language and Literature"* and circulated among the students. As these comments had very little to do with the actual Latin language and literature and no one had expected that they would be preserved for posterity in this manner, the publication created quite a sensation and much amusement.

One of Professor Chandler's students of the class of 1881 who had taken his course, which, I think, was on sanitation, the previous year, had made a full and faithful copy of his lectures, including all the professor's favorite jests and humorous tales. He had made a great number of copies of his notes and had sold them to the members of our class. This enabled a group of mischief-loving students to arrange a little joke on the professor, which was carried out with great hilarious success.

It was engineered as follows. The class was assembled in the lecture hall, seated in successive rows upon a great slanting gallery, as Professor Chandler began his lecture, which, I need hardly state, was profoundly scientific and very interesting, for Professor Chandler was indeed a great chemist and had a knack of presenting his thoughts in a fascinating way. Then came the first joke, a minor one. All faces remained grave and serious; no one laughed or even smiled. Professor Chandler was evidently surprised at this unusual reception of his witticism but ignored it and continued with his subject matter. A few moments later came another joke, a more important one, and the professor brought it out clearly and emphatically. Stony gravity on every side, not a trace, apparently, of comprehension of the really amusing point just made! Wonderingly and somewhat confusedly the professor tried to make the point still clearer. Then, from the extreme left-hand upper corner issued a voice, in solumn tones: *"Ha, ha, ha!"* Responding, a voice from the extreme right-hand lower corner proclaimed, *"Te he, te he!"* Then in stentorian tones from the exact center of the gallery came the words, *"Damn good joke, that!"* And immediately thereupon the entire class broke out in uproarious laughter. Professor Chandler at once saw the point.

A wondrous, delightful, and thrilling thing was the student spirit, as I saw it manifested in Columbia College. There was in it, of course, the freshness of joy and animation which are natural to those who have come to the brightest and happiest period in life, to the stage of physical vigor and energy and an eager, sanguine outlook upon the future soon to begin and to whom it seems inevitable that that future will bring fame and fortune and the glorious realization of all their hopes and ambitions. That inner sense of developing strength and ripening abilities must express itself; it bursts forth in rollicking joviality, in jest and frolic, in good-natured athletic contests and above all in the singing of the merry college songs. Along with this exaltation of the spirit, which is, no doubt, characteristic of youth the world over, there went a sort of simplicity and lack of sophistication which was peculiarly delightful and in which, I believe, the academic youth of America contrasts most favorably wiith that of the Old World.

Another American student custom marked by the same characteristics of mock hostility and real jocosity is the burning of Calculus, which occurs, I believe, in the junior year. This abstruse and difficult part of mathematics presents indeed a severe test to student mentality. When the term in which calculus is studied is concluded and the students are relieved of the necessity of further cudgeling their brains, their relief and rejoicing find vent in their triumphant burning of the loathed and detested book. A solemn funeral procession takes place, the hated work is solemnly laid upon the funeral pyre, and the fire kindled with equal solemnity. As the flames rise high, the students dance around and give vent to their feelings of triumph in fierce yells and howls of exultation. It is a weird, exciting, and yet amusing scene. The whole proceeding may seem childish, but to contrast it with the burning of books in Germany after the incoming of the Nazi regime in 1933, when the choicest products of the finest human intellects were consigned to the flames in a deliberate attempt to destroy all that is best in civilizaion, is to understand the difference between the spirit of America and that of Germany, at least in the period of Hitlerian reaction.

When I first entered Columbia, the college did not yet occupy the magnificent buildings at Amsterdam Avenue and 116th Street extending northward to 120th Street and westward to Broadway—its present home. At that time it was housed in an old rambling structure at Madison Avenue and Forty-ninth Street, which dated back apparently to Revolutionary times. The hallways were narrow and dark and gloomy and, as the students marched through them from class to class, they raised an infernal din with catcalls and the vociferous singing of college songs. The professors and college authorities must have been resigned thereto, for no objection, so far as I know, was ever raised to the practice.

These ebullitions of the student spirit were purely secondary to the serious study which went on. The atmosphere of Columbia College was one of high scholarship on the part of the professors and of assiduous intellectual labor on the part of most of the students. Some of the latter—not very many, I must confess—were typical *recluses* of the closet, burners of midnight oil, thin, frail and nervous, with countenances, to speak in Shakespearean phrase, "all sicklied o'er with the pale cast of thought." Strange to say, these diligent delvers into the wells of knowledge did not, as far as I know their subsequent careers, attain any unusual degree of success, which would go to show that success in life, even in the scholarly vocations, does not depend on book learning alone.

As for myself, I can conscientiously say that I did my best to take advantage of the splendid opportunities offered me in the college. While not as unremitting in my studies as the bookworms I have just mentioned, I sought as full and thorough a mastery as possible of all the subjects given in my courses. I must have had a fair degree of success, for I not only succeeded in passing all examinations but was also the object of favorable comment on the part of college authorities on at least two occasions. One was when I wrote an essay on a philosophic theme. The theme was "Is Materialism a Satisfactory Explanation of the Human Mind?" It was assigned by Professor Alexander, under whom I took instruction in philosophy.

This professor, apart from his standing in his subject, which was of the highest, and whose lectures were illuminating, was a most interesting personality. He was a very young man at the time, one of the youngest if not the very youngest member of the faculty, and his appearance was quite the reverse of professorial or pedantic. His face was smooth-shaven, his features were rather those of a member of "high society" than of a university faculty, and his attire was always neat and natty—indeed, he was groomed to perfection. His wife was a Miss Stevens, member of the enormously wealthy Stevens family of Hoboken, New Jersey, who had presented to the United States Government during the Civil War a great war vessel known as the Stevens Battery. No mercenary motive or need to earn a living, evidently, had induced Professor Alexander to embrace his career, but only pure devotion to the cause of abstract learning. He declared that my essay was a perfect treatise on the theme assigned and marked it 400 out of a possible 400.

The other occasion was in my senior year, shortly before graduation. Each member of the graduating class was required a write a thesis on a subject chosen by himself, the purpose of which was to show the intellectual capacity which he had attained during his college years. I chose my subject from my Hebrew studies, which I had pursued assiduously side by side with my college studies. My thesis was on the subject *Poets and Poetry of the Karaites*.* Officially no comment was made upon any of the theses, but indirectly I heard that the examiners had stated that my thesis showed a very unusual degree of learning.

But while I stood very well in most of the subjects, especially in languages, history, and abstract reasoning, the same was not the case in mathematics. There my record was but mediocre. My mind was definitely not of the mathematical order. I did not stand alone in this regard. Many of my classmates shared this disability and, in general, the record of the class in mathematics was poorer than in any other subject.

Despite my lack of mathematical ability my record in college was good. I stood among the first fourth in the graduating class. That would have entitled me to membership in the *Phi Beta Kappa*, the most highly esteemed of the Greek-letter societies which are such an important feature of the student life of American universities. But I did not apply for membership. A classmate, who was a true and undoubted friend, desiring to spare me the humiliation of a rejection, had informed me that it was the policy of *Phi Beta Kappa* not to accept Jews as members. I had no desire to repeat my experience with the Forensic Society of Jersey City High School, and, therefore, made no attempt to take advantage of my theoretical right to membership in the high and august fraternity. However, I had grown more mature and come to look upon this whole question of anti-Semitism with philosophic calm. Apart from this incident, I did not become aware of any anti-Jewish prejudice during my entire four years in Columbia. My relations with my classmates were of the friendliest and pleasantest.

---

* The Karaites are the sect of Jews originating in the 9th century C.E. adhering only to the Bible, in contradistinction to the *Rabbanites* who follow also the teachings of the Talmud. The Karaites developed quite an extensive literature in Hebrew, including many poetic writings.—B.D.

Although I was not privileged to join the *Phi Beta Kappa,* I did become a member in a most interesting society, where I probably found more mental exhilaration and real pleasure than I would have found in the great Greek-letter organization. It was called The Melancholy Club. The name was an intentional misnomer or rather a case of *lucus a non lucendo,* that is, where the name is the direct opposite of the character of the object which it is supposed to describe. There was nothing melancholy about The Melancholy Club. On the contrary, its spirit was that of pleasant social intercourse and informal *joie de vivre.* This joyous quality must not be confused with vulgar hilarity or inane carousal. The Melancholy Club had a high intellectual character. Membership was based on intellectual qualifications. No one was accepted as member unless he was possessed of some special ability in some branch of the higher human activities. But the guiding spirits of the club did not believe that intellectual power is synonymous with stiff pedantry and gloomy formalism. Their concept, and hence the concept of the club, was that higher intellectual capacity should go hand in hand with man's natural desire for happiness and should be used to make life brighter and more joyful. Hence at the meetings there were lectures and debabtes on learned topics as well as music and poetry, eating and drinking and merry-making. I was accepted as a member on the ground of my Hebrew scholarship and literary ability. Most of the members were college men but membership was not limited to them. The member whom I recall best, Leonard Wheeler, was not a college man but was an exquisite poet. His poem *Erothanatos* is one of the most beautiful and touching poetic compositions I have ever read. I joined The Melancholy Club in my sophomore year and remained a member until I left for Europe after graduation from Columbia.

With four of my classmates, Nicholas Murray Butler, William Ogden Wiley, Deas Murphy, and James Buchanan Nies, my relations were more than merely friendly and pleasant. We had a deep sympathy and respect for each other and became truly intimate, and these sentiments continued in great measure to pervade our later lives. They were all excellent scholars and most agreeable companions. Of these, Nicholas Murray Butler attained the most distinguished position in life. Beginning his career as an instructor in the college, he rose step by step until he became the President of the University and renowned throughout the civilized world for his eminently successful administration of that great institution and for his great public activity. Even as a student there was something about him which showed that he was destined to do great things. While sociable and democratic in his ways and filled with the real student spirit, his keenness of intellect and abundant energy stamped him the born leader. He and I remained on terms of cordial friendship throughout our later years.

William Ogden Wiley was the son of the head of the great publishing house of John Wiley and Sons in New York. He was a fellow of gentle and lovable nature, a handsome youth, and we early developed a great liking for each other. We were not in a position to continue our intimate relations to any great extent in later years, but I was once the recipient, through the instrumentality of Wiley, of an invitation to deliver a lecture on a Biblical historical theme before a church society in East Orange, New Jersey, the town of his residence. I had a royal reception. My lecture seemed to make a deep impression on the audience of splendid American ladies and gentlemen. Indeed, I remember the incident with great pleasure.

Deas Murphy was another classmate with whom I stood in relations of true friendship. He became a physician, of considerable eminence, I believe, in New York. I was invited to his wedding. Too, I was a guest many years later in his beautiful summer home in New Canaan, Connecticut. I happened in that year to have taken a cottage in Noroton, not far from New Canaan. Murphy learned accidentally of this and communicated with me, insisting upon my visiting him in his home. I accepted the invitation and was received most cordially by my classmate and his family.

The classmate with whom my friendship was deepest and strongest was James Buchanan Nies. Early in our college years we became strongly attached to each other, and I can say truthfully that I have never been more closely and sincerely befriended with anyone than with "Jimmy" Nies, as the classmates affectionately called him. "Jimmy" was a most interesting and lovable character. As his family name shows, he was of German descent but his given names were patriotically American. It was he who had called to my attention the anti-

Semitic tendencies of the Greek-letter fraternity, and I knew that his only motive was to save me from the distress of rejection. I considered it an act of true friendship on his part and I was truly grateful to him. Nies became an Episcopalian clergyman, but that fact had no influence on our relations, which remained as cordial and friendly as ever, so that the somewhat unusual condition resulted of a Christian clergyman and a Jewish rabbi united by ties of close and intimate friendship. During my student years in Germany Nies came out for a trip and we passed a few most pleasant days together. Of that more anon. Nies married the daughter of Alexander Orr, well known through his connection with the establishment of rapid transit in New York City. I was invited to the wedding and was treated with the utmost courtesy. We remained on most cordial and intimate terms in later years and saw each other on frequent occasions until his greatly lamented death put an end to a rare and beautiful friendship.

These student friendships are an emphatic demonstration of the falsity of the anti-Semitic postulate—now alas greatly intensified in this age of Nazism—that there is a fundamental and inevitable antagonism between Gentile and Jew, which precludes genuine friendship between them. If there was anything clearly and distinctly known in the class and the college generally, it was that Drachman of '82 was a Jew, and not only a Jew but an outspoken champion of Judaism. But that fact not only did not prevent my pleasant and friendly relations with my classmates in general but was perfectly compatible with the development of as fine and true a friendship as has perhaps ever existed between two human beings. I have known many fine and noble Jews in my time and have been closely befriended and intimate with a goodly number of them, but I must say that my friendship with "Jimmy" Nies was as warm and sincere as with the best of my Jewish brethren. I certainly did not entertain the same cordial sentiments for my Jewish classmates. Religiously we were as far apart as the poles. In our senior year there was a statistical inquiry made into the characteristics of the members of the class, their tastes, habits, desires, and views on all sorts of subjects. One of the questions concerned religion. I put myself down as Jewish. My two "Jewish" classmates evaded the question. One did not answer it; the other wrote that he was Unitarian. So that while they were nice enough young men in a superficial way, and I was not at all on unfriendly terms with them, I felt very little spiritual kinship with my two supposed co-religionists.

My dear father, of blessed memory, was accustomed to quote with approval a homely Yiddish proverb which he had heard in his youth in Galicia, *"Wie es sich Yuedelt so Christelt es sich."* The significance of this adage, which it is impossible to translate literally into English, is that despite their great differences there are also great similarities between Judaism and Christianity, that similar conditions produce similar results in both religions. I had occasion to recognize the truth of this during my course at Columbia. When I first entered the college, chapel services were held regularly, and attendance at a certain number of them was obligatory on all students. I, too, was obliged to attend the services the prescribed number of times. I understood the reason for this and did not resent it. The motives of the college authorities was to show respect for religion and to promote the spirit of religion among the students. As a private institution affiliated with the Episcopalian Church, it was only natural that the religious services were in accordance with the faith and worship of that church. As there was not the slightest attempt at proselytizing, none of the students belonging to other denominations could feel themselves aggrieved.

I made an observation at these services which was very comforting to me in regard to a matter which had often troubled me in connection with our own Jewish prayers. Jewish prayers, as is well known, are ritualistic, that is, are conducted in accordance with a certain fixed ritual or form of worship, and the offering of voluntary prayer is infrequent and a subordinate part of the service. I had often heard sharp condemnation of this from Jewish critics of Judaism, who asserted that this led to a mere mechanical repetition of words without feeling or devotion.

Of course, there are special reasons why Jewish prayer must be based on a fixed ritual, but our carping Jewish critics made no allowance for that. Probably the most important reason for the establishment of the Jewish ritual was to assure that the thoughts and sentiments expressed in the worship were genuinely Jewish and that the dispersion of Israel throughout the world should not bring about the infiltration of a host of alien views and doctrines into the faith. The use of the Hebrew language as the vehicle of worship, although it had long ceased to be the spoken language of the Jewish people, is, of course, due to the desire to preserve the unity and historic continuity of Israel and to make it possible for a Jew to feel himself at home in a synagogue anywhere on earth. But our critics contemptuously spurn these reasons and, indeed, attribute to the use of the Hebrew in the service a special share of the responsibility for the alleged lack of devotion in Jewish worship, inasmuch as many or most of the congregation do not understand it. That there is much about the synagogue service which is dearly beloved by the worshippers, even though they are not erudite Hebrew scholars, and that the beautiful Hebrew chants in themselves arouse religious emotions, these facts are calmly ignored.

I, however, had occasion to observe in the Columbia chapel that one can use a modern, perfectly understood vernacular as the medium of prayer and be perfectly independent of any printed ritual and the service be nevertheless a mechanical recitation, devoid of any soul-stirring quality. The chaplain in charge was the Reverend Cornelius Duffy, no doubt a most worthy and pious cleric. Every morning he recited, in English, of course, exactly the same prayer, in exactly the same words and with exactly the same rising and falling of the tones of his voice, and on his dignified, placid countenance not a trace of emotion of any kind was perceptible. I am not accusing the reverend gentleman of any lack of sincerity or devoutness in his prayer. I am merely pointing out that the things which are declared to be heinous offenses when committed by Jews may very well occur when there is no fixed ritual and when the medium of worship is a modern and generally understood idiom. I presume that the truth is that any observances which we constantly repeat lose a certain amount of their spontaneity and freshness, but that does not detract from the sincerity and devotion with which we perform them and that in this regard there is no difference between different faiths.

As my course at Columbia University approached its end, the board of directors of the Emanuel Theological Seminary informed me that they had settled a stipend upon me for which I was to complete my rabbinical studies at a German theological institution. I was greatly gratified by this sign of appreciation and trust and accepted it with sincere gratitude.

Although the authorities of the Emanuel Theological Seminary were themselves adherents of the ultra-Reform wing of Judaism, they did not dictate to me which one of the German rabbinical seminaries I should attend but, in true liberality of sentiment, left me perfect freedom of choice. There were at that time three institutions for the training of rabbis in Germany, the *Hochschule fuer die Wissenschaft des Judentums* in Berlin, the Hildesheimer *Rabbiner Seminar,* also in Berlin, and the *Juedisch-Theologisches Seminar* in Breslau. The first-named institution represented the Radical Reform concept of Judaism, the other two were Orthodox Jewish institutions but of somewhat different types, the Hildesheimer Seminary being reputed extremely strict in its views and the Breslau Seminary more moderate. I decided to attend the Breslau institution.

In the month of June, 1882, I was graduated from Columbia College with the degree of Bachelor of Arts. Shortly thereafter I departed for Europe to complete my preparations for the vocation to which I had finally resolved to dedicate my life, that of spiritual leader in Israel, or more modestly speaking, that of a humble worker in the vineyard of the Lord of Hosts.

Chapter Eight

Ho, For the Old World

ON THE TENTH DAY OF THE MONTH OF AB IN THE HEBREW YEAR 5642, corresponding to the 25th day of the month of July of the secular year 1882, I boarded the good ship *Suevia* of the Hamburg-American Steamship Company, on which I had engaged passage for the city of Hamburg in Germany and which was then lying at its pier in Hoboken, New Jersey. I had observed the previous day as a strict fast in commemoration of the destruction of the ancient Temple of Israel in Jerusalem. I had tasted neither food nor drink during the entire twenty-four hours beginning at sundown on the previous day. As I had also observed the eight days preceding the fast, with the exception of the Sabbath, by abstaining from all flesh food and, as it required at least fifteen or sixteen days before I could again partake, since the *Suevia* took at least that long to cross the Atlantic, and the meat on the *Suevia* was *terefa*, unclean and forbidden to the observant Jew, that meant that I would be deprived for almost a month of all indulgence in the eating of meat. But on this morning the pleasures of the palate were remote from my thoughts.

My mind was full of the pleasurable excitement incident to the venture into a new and wonderful domain. It was full of eager anticipation, too, of novel experiences and sights never before seen. The prospect of making a voyage of thousands of miles to the great continent of Europe, so famous in history and so important in the civilization of the world, entranced my youthful imagination. In addition thereto, my dear mother, of blessed memory, had given me fascinating descriptions of the land and the village in which her childhood and early youth had been spent. I was all eagerness to be in that land, to behold its beauty, to meet those exceptional people and to live with them, at least for a time, their life of peaceful contentment and spiritual fervor.

We were all up bright and early on that morning and, although the ship was not scheduled to depart until midday, we were on board shortly after nine. My parents and all my brothers and sisters were there to see "Bernie" off, and also quite a number of relatives and friends, and there was much merry conversation and wishes of *"Bon Voyage!"* and *"Gluechliche Reise!"* Conspicuous among the non-relatives were the Rosenbergs, the family of my classmate in the Hebrew Preparatory School, Adam Rosenberg, and the Reverend M. Schlesinger, cantor of our synagogue in Jersey City. The latter, by the way, had given me a letter of introduction to his sister, Frau Marcus in Breslau, at whose home I was to stay during my course at the Jewish Thelogical Seminary of that city. Finally the cry resounded, "All ashore that's going ashore." Then there were kisses and embraces. Father and Mother *benched* me, that is, they laid their hands on my bowed head and pronounced over me the Hebrew priestly benediction. Then hasty leavetakings, and suddenly I was alone among a group of strangers on the deck.

This sudden loneliness was for me, who had never been away from home, except on brief vacations in nearby country places and then only in the company of one or more members of the family, considerable of an emotional shock. But the sensation speedily wore away. It was an ideal day. The midsummer sun shone bright and warm, a mild and gentle breeze blew refreshingly on my cheeks, and the sights, as the good ship sped down New York's magnificent harbor and on to old ocean's vast expanse, were most interesting and permitted no melancholy reflections to arise. To my surprise the ocean was smooth and calm. I remained on deck for quite a time before retiring to my cabin. I did not know anyone as yet and did not speak to anyone and was not spoken to by anyone. But I felt no need of company or conversation, so fascinated was I by the weird, mystic aspect of the nightly ocean and so absorbed in my own thoughts and reflections. I rested splendidly in my berth. The gentle motion of the ship was like the rocking of a cradle, most soothing and comforting. I slept soundly and dreamlessly until morning.

The passengers on board were not very numerous. I became acquainted with quite a number of them, of whom I found several very interesting in various ways. There was an American professor and his young wife. He was a member of the faculty of a college in Maine, and they were celebrating their honeymoon by a trip to Europe. They were charming people, refined and cultured and very amiable.

There were also among my fellow-travelers a father and daughter returning to Germany after a visit to America, most charming and lovable people. Their name was Krolik. Their home was in a small town in the neighborhood of Breslau, and they had been visiting relatives in Detroit. They were co-religionists, and they possessed the qualities which I had been taught to consider the distinguishing characteristics of Israel, courtesy, gentleness, kindheartedness, and sincere religious sentiment. The father was a *Baal Ha-Bayith,* a substantial Jewish householder of the good, old-fashioned German-Jewish type, and the daughter a modest, demure maiden, a typical German-Jewish fraulein. When they heard that I was going to Germany to prepare myself for the rabbinical vocation and that I purposed to attend the Jewish Theological Seminary and the University of Breslau, they were greatly interested. They gave me much interesting and useful information concerning these two institutions and the conditions, general and Jewish, which I would encounter in the city. Fraulein Krolik was a bride, engaged to marry a distant relative who was a merchant in some Central American city, in Costa Rica or Guatemala. The marriage was to take place in Breslau after the Jewish holidays of the coming fall. They were kind enough to say that I must be their guest at the wedding, and they were as good as their word, as will be told later. I considered myself very fortunate to have made the acquaintance of the Kroliks. It took away all sense of loneliness which might otherwise have come over me, an inexperienced youth traveling alone.

The rest of the voyage passed uneventfully though pleasantly. The weather remained fair, and it was a real delight to promenade the deck and to watch the various sights which old ocean affords, a school of porpoise gamboling around, now above and now below the waves, a whale "blowing" in the distance, occasionally, though very rarely, a ship, the sight of which always created considerable excitement. Then, as we neared the other side of the Atlantic, there were also great flocks or coveys of sea gulls which hovered about our vessel, evidently on the outlook for edibles. To me these sights were all absolutely new, and I reveled in them.

In those days ocean liners did not have the speed which they now possess, and it took the *Suevia* more than fifteen days to reach its destination. On the morning of the sixteenth day we reached Cuxhaven, some miles from Hamburg, where all oceans steamers must stop, as they are not able to make the trip on the Elbe River into the port of Hamburg itself.

There we and our baggage were transferred into a smaller vessel. There had been plenty of excitement getting ready for the transfer but, once on the smaller boat, the concluding trip was very pleasant and the passengers were in quite a merry frame of mind. What struck me most was that here we were in completely German surroundings, much more so than on the ocean steamer, though there too, of course, the atmosphere had been thoroughly German. There was a band of music on the boat, very much like "the little German bands" that used to play in those days on the streets of American cities. It played characteristic lively German airs. Aproned waiters, carrying huge beakers of foaming beer, ran around and served, for pay, of course, all who were thirsty for the Gambrinian beverage, and more substantial refreshment was also obtainable.

A number of boats, loaded to the gunwales with soldiers, passed us on the river and, as they came near us, there were cheers and guttural cries of welcome on both sides. It was a combination of music and eating and drinking and militarism only possible in the Germany of that time. To me it was a thrilling spectacle, though there was a basic quality about it that grated upon me, I knew not why. As we drew nearer to Hamburg, the river became more crowded with boats of various kinds, and closely constructed rows of grimy buildings, reminiscent of days gone by, appeared on both sides of the stream. The passengers on our boat became quieter and more thoughtful, evidently in mental preparation for disembarkation. In about half an hour our boat drew up alongside a great pier, and we landed in Germany and Hamburg.

Chapter Nine

Hamburg and the Trip to Nordheim

THE FIRST THING I DID AFTER LEAVING THE SHIP WAS TO ENGAGE A droshky and direct the driver to take me and my baggage to the Hotel Hirschel, which had been recommended to me in America as a well conducted and comfortable Jewish hostelry. On my way thither I naturally gazed with close attention at the sights which presented themselves to my eyes. In appearance Hamburg was certainly very different from an American city. The streets, at least those through which we drove, were narrow and irregular and the houses mainly narrow and old-looking, and the streets were filled with a decidedly foreign appearing, typically German throng. But the streets were spotlessly clean and the people neat and decorous, so that the whole appearance was that of a "homey" comfortable town.

The hotel was a delightful haven of rest and repose after the long and tiresome sea voyage. It was not large nor elaborate, but the rooms were of goodly size and the furniture, especially the broad, old-fashioned German beds, most inviting to ease and relaxation. Everything was scrupulously clean and neat. Most attractive of all to me at that moment was the *Speisesaal,* the dining room, not because of its great proportions and luxurious furnishings—for, in truth, it was modest in size and unpretentiously equipped—but because of the entrancing prospect it offered of a genuine kosher meat meal, of which I had been deprived for almost a month. I cannot hope to convey to the mind of the reader how much I enjoyed that meal. It was a simple meal, a good plate of soup, a few slices of pot roast beef, mashed potatoes and spinach, a glass of foam-topped beer and a *demi-tasse* of black coffee. I would not have exchanged it then for ambrosia and nectar and all the delights of what Scripture calls "the corn of heaven," no, not even for the Leviathan and the fatted ox with which, the Midrash tells us, the righteous will be regaled when the great Redemption comes.

Almost as interesting to me as the meal were the people in the dining room. They were of all ages and both sexes and unmistakably Jewish. These Jews were a different type from those I had known in America. They were neatly clothed, mainly in apparel of dark colors, and they were quiet and undemonstrative in their demeanor. They were evidently very orthodox, for most of the men wore skull caps, and many of the women, especially the older women, wore *Sheitels*. The older men were an especially interesting type. I noticed a number of them washing their hands and pronouncing a blessing over pieces of bread before sitting down to their meals. Some groups of at least three persons had already finished eating and were *benshing*, that is, were chanting grace in audible voices. It was a demonstration of genuine, living Judaism such as I had not witnessed in America, and the sight impressed me greatly.

That night I retired early, for I was very tired, not so much from physical exertion as from the excitement of landing and entering a hitherto unknown place. The bed, too, was of a kind I had never seen before. It was immensely large, covered with a huge feather bed. But it was very soft and comfortable and no sooner had my head touched the pillow than I fell into a deep, dreamless sleep from which I did not awake until the morning sun, shining brightly through the great, door-like windows, called me back to consciousness. After my morning devotions and a light breakfast, consisting of only coffee, rolls and jam, the latter, incidentally, being dignified by the fancy French name *confiture*, I proceeded to attend to various matters necessitated by my impending trip to the home of my German relatives, the village of Nordheim before-the Rhoen in Bavaria. These consisted mainly of the purchase of various small articles as presents for my uncle and aunt and cousins and obtaining of my railroad ticket. The purchases were easily consummated, since there was no lack of shops where articles suitable for presents were to be had, but when it came to the railroad ticket, unexpected difficulties arose. I learned hereby that the vaunted "German efficiency" is not always what it is reputed to be. I went up to the window of the ticket seller in the railroad station and stated that I desired to buy a ticket for Nordheim before-the-Rhoen. The official behind the window gazed at me at first with an expression of mild contempt as though I were utterly unworthy of notice but that in the goodness of his heart he would condescend to consider my request. When he heard what I wished, his expression of mere disdain changed to one of furious indignation.

"What are you asking for?" he roared, while his fat, pudgy countenance grew red as a lobster. "I cannot sell you any ticket for that *nest*"—*nest* in German signifies an utterly unimportant, insignificant place, something like what we call in America a "one-horse town" but of even lower degree—"There is no railroad station by that name. Don't you know any place in the neighborhood where there is a station?"

I hastened to say that there was a town not far from Nordheim where I was sure there was a station of the railroad and that its name was Mellrichstadt.

"I never heard of that place, either," roared the ticket seller. "Don't you know of any place in the neighborhood where civilized human beings go? Isn't your place somewhere near Wuerzburg? That's a Bavarian town."

By this time I was utterly bewildered and ready to agree to anything. Besides, I had heard my mother speak of the Rabbi of Wuerzburg, so I knew it must be somewhere in the vicinity of her native place. I agreed, therefore, to purchase a ticket for Wuerzburg. After receiving my ticket, I departed humbly to find my train while the ticket seller cast after me a look of withering scorn. Whether there was anti-Semitism in that glance I do not know, but I am inclined to think there was not. As a rule, Germans only recognize the Jews of Germany and the adjacent countries, particularly the Slavonic countries, as such but not the Jewish natives of other foreign lands.

In the train I settled down to a night-and-day trip, for, as I had been informed, the railroad journey from Hamburg to Nordheim required about twenty hours. I do not recall exactly how I passed the night, whether I had a berth in a sleeping car or remained seated upon the bench of a second class compartment. All I remember is that I was exquisitely uncomfortable and found myself wondering more than once if the night would ever end. At that I was traveling in

Hamburg and the Trip to Nordheim

greater luxury than the vast majority of Germans, for the seats in the second class compartments or coupés, which most Germans do not patronize, are nicely upholstered and quite comfortable for a not-too-long journey.

There are, or were at that time, four classes of compartments in the cars of German railways. Of these the first class was fitted up with every conceivable comfort and luxury. But the price was prohibitive except for the wealthiest travelers. As the German saying puts it, "First class coupés are used only by members of the nobility, millionaires, lunatics, and Americans." I was not one of the Americans who travel first class. Second class was abundantly good enough for me and my purse. The seats in the third class were of hard, unupholstered wood, and the other provisions for comfort were very inadequate. As for the fourth class, it was devoid of the most elementary requirements for human comfort. There were not even any seats. Passengers must provide their own seats or stand. Of course, the price was extremely low, a mere fraction of the charge in the higher classes. This cheapness was naturally attractive to the very poor and to some, not so poor, of, let us say euphemistically, highly economical dispositions. Thus I was speaking once about railway accommodations to a Nordheim merchant who was not of the poorest class but was certainly very economical in his tastes, and I took occasion to condemn the arrangements in the fourth class as unworthy of human beings. He agreed with me completely. "The fourth class is certainly very bad," he said. "I only use it because there is no fifth."

If the night traveling was uncomfortable, the daytime trip certainly compensated largely for it. Hardly had the rising sun made things visible than an entrancing sight fell upon my eyes. The countryside was bedecked with luscious green, varied by occasional patches of vegetation of other colors and stretches of woodland. Everything was so neat and well cared for that to my American eyes, accustomed to the somewhat wild exuberance of American landscapes, it seemed as though we were rushing through a vast park. We passed many towns and villages, and they were all scrupulously clean and well kept, apparently without slums. The architecture, so quaint and different from that of American towns, was very picturesque and interesting. We did not make many stops—the train was evidently an express—but, when we did, the scenes at the stations were strongly reminiscent of a stage panorama. This was due not to the bustle and the excitement—they seemed quite natural and inevitable in a center of traffic—but to the diversified character of the people. Three social strata were distinctly recognizable among the passengers. There were an upper circle of gentlemen and ladies, a lower element of peasants and laborers, and, very conspicuous and dominating the scene, a strong contingent of military. The upper classes were dressed in formal traveling attire, the laborers and peasants wore simple work-a-day clothes, some of the latter, especially the peasant women, wore their traditional peasant costumes. The military, particularly the officers, were resplendent in gorgeous uniforms. The three elements did not mingle, but all were very decorous and well behaved. The familiar cry "ten minutes for refreshments" which one hears when a train stops at a wayside station in America was not heard. In its stead what may be called ambulant restaurateurs bearing trays or other receptacles filled with various edibles and the German national drink, beer, forced their way through the crowds and approached the train and sold their wares to the passengers. As I had brought some food with me from the hotel, I restricted my patronage to the purchase of a bottle of beer, which I found very palatable and refreshing. I could easily have joined in the conversation round about me, had I been so inclined, but the whole surroundings were so strange to me and I felt so shy that I made no attempt in that direction.

About two o'clock in the afternoon, however, I participated in a conversation which turned out to be of great importance to me. It was begun by a gentleman sitting opposite me in the coupé. He was a handsome man, apparently in the early fifties and dressed in perfect taste. He had been contemplating me for some time with evident interest. I had noticed this, and it embarrassed me, but I pretended to be unaware that I was the object of his observation. Finally he began to speak. He began by asking me, very courteously and excusing himself for the liberty he was taking, whether I was not an *Auslaender*, a foreigner. I answered that I was an American. "From North or South America, if I might ask?" he continued. That question seemed very queer to me, but for a German in Germany it was a perfectly natural question. To the average German, as indeed to all

Europeans in that period, America seemed as far away as the moon or the lands of which the Talmud tells "behind the mountains of darkness." I did not, however, go into any discussion of these matters but simply said that I was from the United States of North America. At this my interrogator showed greatly increased interest.

"Oh, indeed, I have heard a great deal about the United States," he said. "Many of my friends have gone to the United States. I have a brother in Chicago, who is doing very well there. Might I ask your purpose in coming to Germany?" I answered that I intended to study at a German university. He asked me which university I purposed to attend. I answered, "The University of Breslau."

He seemed surprised. "That is an unusual choice for an American. They do not go so far east. They study at Heidelberg or Jena or Berlin. Might I ask why you prefer Breslau?"

I was beginning to get annoyed at his searching inquiries into my private affairs. But I reflected that he might be connected in some way with the government and that the government in Germany desired to know exactly the reasons which impelled any alien to enter its domain. I decided, therefore, to give him full and accurate information on all subjects of his inquiries. I answered him that my primary purpose was to prepare myself for the vocation of rabbi at the Jewish Theological Seminary of Breslau, and that I would at the same time attend the university of that city with the object of obtaining a Ph.D. degree. I was surprised at the change in the expression of his face. Until then his attitude toward me had been one of courtesy and mild interest; now it became one of friendship, almost of intimacy.

"Oh, indeed," he said, while a smile of pleasure lighted up his countenance. "So you are a co-religionist. I would never have imagined it. But as soon as you mentioned Breslau, I began to suspect it. Well, I am glad to hear that our religion is developing so nicely in America that our people are beginning to train their own rabbis. You are certainly going to the right place. The Breslau seminary is a wonderful institution. Its faculty is composed of distinguished Jewish scholars. Its first director or leader was Dr. Zacharias Frankel, a very great scholar, and his successor is Dr. Israel Lewi, who is said to be the greatest Talmudist in Germany. Then there is Professor Graetz, the renowned historian, and Professor Freudenthal, Doctor Rosin, and Doctor Zuckermann, all of them distinguished authorities in their respective subjects. And Breslau is a beautiful city.

"You are not going now to Breslau, are you?" he asked. "This train is not bound in that direction at all."

I informed him that it was my intention to visit my relatives in Bavaria first and to remain with them till after the fall holidays. I informed him that their home was in a small village named Nordheim and that the nearest railroad station was a town of the name of Mellrichstadt. This information produced upon him an altogether unexpected effect. "That doesn't seem at all right (*Das stimmt aber gar nicht*)," he said. "This train doesn't go to Mellrichstadt at all. It is bound for Wuerzburg, which lies in quite a different direction. Would you mind showing me your ticket?"

In some confusion I complied with his request. He glanced at the ticket and said, "It is as you say. You have a ticket for Wuerzburg, and you are going entirely out of your way. As you are a Jew and a prospective rabbi, I presume you want to reach your destination before the Sabbath. If you go on to Wuerzbug you cannot do that. You would have to stay until the Sabbath is over, and you could not get to Mellrichstadt or Nordheim until late at night or the next day."

These words filled me with consternation. I narrated to him my experience in Hamburg with the ticket seller. He told me that he was not surprised. Some of the officials in the railway and postal service were very stupid, he said. My quandary was truly embarrassing. I knew no one in Wuerzburg, and I did not relish the prospect of being obliged to remain twenty-four hours or more in a place where I was an entire stranger. "What can I do?" I said helplessly to my newfound friend.

"The only thing you can do," he said, "is to leave this train at the next station, Erfurt. There you will find a train which goes to Mellrichstadt, and I presume someone will be waiting there to meet you. But you will have to act quickly. This train reaches Erfurt in a few minutes, and the train for Mellrichstadt leaves shortly after that. So you will have only a very little time to buy your ticket and attend to your baggage."

These words agitated me considerably, but I was grateful to my new acquaintance for having saved me from what might have been a very disagreeable situation. As soon as the train reached Erfurt, I left the train after a hasty farewell from my kind guide and counselor, and rushed into the station amidst a great throng of other passengers and went at once to the window of the ticket seller, where I was fortunately able to purchase a ticket for Mellrichstadt immediately, and then to the baggage section where I arranged for instantaneous transfer of my trunk to the other train. I boarded the Mellrichstadt train just about a minute before its departure. During my trip on the side line to Mellrichstadt—the *Werra Bahn* I believe it was called—I was too excited to pay much attention to the scenery. But I could not help noticing that it was a beautiful and truly rustic region and that we passed many picturesque villages.

At about four o'clock the train reached Mellrichstadt. On the platform were very few persons, but there was one who at once attracted my attention. He was a handsome, dark-complexioned youth whom I had never seen before but whom I at once recognized, since his photograph was in our family album in Jersey City, as my cousin Solomon. He recognized me at once too and for the same reason. We fell instantly upon each other's neck and embraced, with joyous cries of "Solomon!" and "Bernard!" A moment later we were chatting as familiarly as though we had known each other all our lives, as, indeed, we had, though not by personal contact and direct association. Solomon explained to me that the whole family would have come to meet me at the station but that, on account of the nearness of the Sabbath, they had been unable to do so. They had deputed to him the honor of receiving and welcoming their American relative. Solomon had a fine horse and carriage at the station with which to convey me to Nordheim. We rode through four miles of beautiful country and arrived at the village just in time to greet and be greeted by the family and to attend, in the little village synagogue, the evening services of the Holy Sabbath.

Chapter Ten

Nordheim*

IT WAS A FORTUNATE COINCIDENCE THAT I ARRIVED IN NORDHEIM just before the Sabbath, for I was thereby given an opportunity at once to observe the part the Sabbath played in the life of a typical rural Jewish community of Central Europe. It was a beautiful and impressive sight, the like of which I had not witnessed in America. In Jersey City the Jewish stores, with the exception of two or three, were open on the Sabbath, and only a small number of the Jewish inhabitants attended the services in the synagogue. The Jewish community of Nordheim numbered only eighteen families at that time, but they all, without exception, observed the Holy Sabbath, and all, men, women, and all but the youngest children, assembled in the House of God for worship on the Day of Rest.

It was a simple little synagogue in which the services took place, just about large enough to accommodate the fifty or sixty souls who made up the village congregation. The service was conducted in a very simple manner by the humble individual who combined the offices of reader, teacher, and *shochet* (or ritual slaughterer) in Nordheim. He made no attempt at elaborate chanting or musical effect, but to me it was, nevertheless, deeply impressive. The reason for this great impressiveness was that I recognized—and no one could fail to recognize—the utter sincerity of these simple souls, that to them their Judaism was a compellingly real and vital faith, an indissoluble part of their thought world, in fact, their very lives. Nothing there of the split and divided souls, in which contradictory and antag-

---

* I have given a full description of Nordheim in my book "From the Heart of Israel" under the title "The Village Kehillah." I am, therefore, here merely recording my general impression of the village and the life of its Jewish community.—B.D.

onistic ideologies were struggling for the mastery; nothing of the mechanical acceptance of a superficial tradition and the grudging tribute paid to it on two or three days in the year; nothing of the revolt against the time-honored religious practices of Israel shown by the cutting loose from the ancient moorings and the substitution of utterly unauthorized innovations and alterations, which I had observed in the great metropolis of America and which I knew to exist not only everywhere in that vast continent but in the great cities of the Old World as well. The Judaism of Nordheim was simple, clear, and unquestioningly loyal. In the little synagogue on that first Friday evening and during the rest of the Sabbath observance on the morrow I felt this genuineness and axiomatic loyalty and the perception and appreciation thereof penetrated to the very depth of my heart. I began to understand what real Sabbath observance is and what a hallowing and uplifting influence upon one's entire personality and life outlook it possesses.

The services concluded, the worshippers took leave of each other with friendly "Good Sabbath!" wishes and wended their way homeward. I went to the home of my relatives in the company of the rest of the family. Cousin Solomon was my especial companion. As we walked we indulged in pleasant conversation. Now I had an excellent opportunity to test my conversational ability in the German language. I was a little diffident about it because I had never been accustomed to protracted conversations in German, but Solomon—and the others afterward—was kind enough to say that I did very well.

The "good room" in the home of my relatives was refulgent in a blaze of glory in honor of the Sabbath, and in the midst of the brilliant illumination burned the Sabbath light, with a more modest glow but in a special place of honor. A tablecloth of snow-white linen covered the dining table, and on it stood the finest porcelain plates and dishes and the finest cut glass goblets and sparkling silver knives and forks and spoons that the family possessed, all in honor of the Sabbath, for it was Jewish tradition that the best of everything must be reserved for the Sabbath. The members of the family, too, were clothed in their finest raiment, for that was also a part of the Sabbath precept. There was a delightful combination of spiritual and physical joy. Uncle Koppel, his wife and children all strove to fulfill the injunction of the prophet Isaiah, "Thou shalt call the Sabbath a delight and the holy day of the Lord glorious."

On that first Sabbath evening in that little German village I first understood what the rabbis of the Talmud mean when they speak of the *Neshamah Yetherah,* "the exalted soul," as characteristic of true Sabbath observance.

It is a spiritual condition in which the finest elements of our supermundane nature are united, fervent faith in the Heavenly Father, unquestioning submission to His will, eager readiness to obey His commandments, and joyous recognition that these ennobling aspirations are all symbolized and beautifully manifested in the sacred day of rest and worship. In this spirit my relatives in Nordheim observed the Sabbath. I could see it in their earnest and solemn, yet happy and carefree faces, in the naturalness and utter genuineness of their religious emotions. I knew that these were indeed worthy kinsmen whom I would love and cherish all my days on earth.

Much of my respect and reverence went to the memory of one who no longer walked among the living but whose spirit hovered unseen over Nordheim and whose influence, even after his departure from earth, was undoubtedly responsible for the profoundly religious sentiment not only of his own descendants but of the entire Jewish community of Nordheim and the surrounding country. It was my grandfather, the father of my mother and of the Uncle Koppel in whose home I was now sojourning, Rabbi Shemayah Stein, affectionately known as Reb Shemayah. He had been educated for the rabbinate, but he had never taken it up as a vocation. Just when Reb Shemayah had received his *semichah,* or rabbinical ordination, and was also about to become the husband of the Fulda rabbi's daughter, a political event occurred, of the highest importance to the Jews of Bavaria. This event, though good in itself, destroyed Reb Shemayah's romance and completely changed the course of his life.

The medieval laws, which had hitherto prevailed in Bavaria, forbade the ownership of land by persons of the Jewish faith. Thus no Jew could be a tiller of the soil. But the breath of liberalism had begun to stir in Europe and it reached even the corner of Germany in which Reb Shemayah dwelt. The Bavarian Government repealed the prohibitory law and announced that henceforth Jews would be permitted

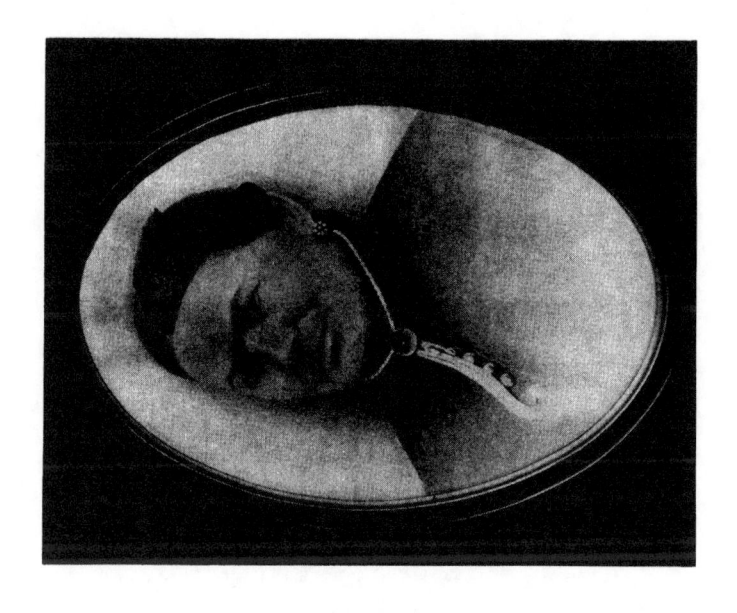

Benjamin Drachman   *Parents*   Mathilde Stein Drachman

From charcoal portraits, drawn about 1887.

Bernard Drachman — 1883
Student in Breslau

to own and till land, the same as all other citizens. It was a truly liberal legislative act, actuated by an undeniable humane purpose. Jews, however, were loath to take advantage of it. They had been unfamiliar with agriculture for centuries. They therefore hesitated to exchange the commercial pursuits which most of them followed for the calling of peasant, which stood in some disrepute, and was deemed lower than that of the merchant or the scholar. Not so Reb Shemayah. He considered the tilling of the soil the noblest occupation of man, the one most suitable to Jews, inasmuch as it had been the chief vocation of ancient Israel as long as they dwelt in the Holy Land. When he saw his Jewish brethren hesitating and undecided, he resolved to encourage them by himself setting the good example. Accordingly he took the inheritance which he had received from his parents and invested it in the purchase of a *Bauerngut,* a peasant estate or farm, in the vicinity of Nordheim, and undertook to cultivate it. The result of this action on his part was a double one: he was obliged to renounce the rabbinical vocation and also his sweet bride, for the old Rabbi of Fulda was conservative and set in his views and averred that no peasant should have his daughter. The second renunciation was especially grievous, but Reb Shemayah would not surrender his ideals for any earthly consideration and submitted in silence.

The example of Reb Shemayah worked encouragingly upon his co-religionists. Quite a number of them purchased land and tilled it, so that, in a few years, a Jewish farmer was no longer a rarity. It cannot be said that Reb Shemayah was particularly successful as an agriculturist. This was because, although he held no formal rabbinical post, he remained in spirit a religious leader and conceived his life activity as fundamentally and mainly a religious one. In the spiritual domain his success was boundless. Not only did he imbue his own progeny with profound love for the faith of Israel and unswerving loyalty to its precepts but he communicated much of his enthusiasm to the Jews of the region in general. Under the influence of his inspiring leadership Nordheim, in particular, became known as a place where piety and the fear of God were especially true and firm.

The sight of my grandfather's portrait (identical with one I had seen at home) and the living testimony to his influence which I now experienced filled me with a sort of reverential ecstasy. And this continued, though with renewed emphasis all through that first Sabbath. The *Kiddush* (or sanctification) pronounced by Uncle Koppel over a goblet of wine and two Sabbath loaves, the festal meal, of which cold fish formed the *pièce de resistance,* the chanted grace that followed, and the social hour until the approaching extinction of the lights warned us to retire—all these formed, to me, a mounting series of happy details in a process of solemn joy.

In the morning, the entire humble but obviously sincere community again packed the tiny house of worship, and again I was moved with a profounder religious emotion than I had ever felt in the most gorgeous temples in America. After the Sabbath dinner, the whole village slept—the Gentile farmers were all away in distant fields, unheard and unseen—and even the animals were silent, the cattle in the stalls, the dogs in kennels and cats beside the kitchen stove.

After the "third meal" late in the afternoon, there was another service in the synagogue. Then came the twilight interval, during which some men studied from a devotional Hebrew book, while others strolled in the fields. When it was quite dark, the *shammas* (or synagogue attendant) lit the lights, and the evening prayer, the first of the work-a-day services, was recited.

However, even after the departure of the Sabbath the people of Nordheim did not at once give up its spirit. Saturday evening was a time of social relaxation. Thus every aspect of Jewish religious life received from these good folk both scrupulous observance and loving appreciation of its inner character. I came to understand the essence and quality of a truly devout Jewish life as I had not previously understood it.

Some aspects of this profound loyalty were not devoid of their amusing quality but even they served to demonstrate the genuineness and reality of it. Thus the Jewish fathers and mothers in Nordheim were accustomed to send their offspring on fast days to the orchards and gardens to gather fruits and berries. The children of Nordheim, like children the world over, were extremely fond of sweet berries and fruits. Had they been sent to gather them on any ordinary day, it was more than probable that a considerable portion of their sweet gatherings would have disappeared down their throats. But the wise parents knew that no Jewish child in Nordheim would think of desecrating the holiness of the fast by partaking of food or drink and that, therefore, they, the parents, would obtain all that their children had gathered undiminished in quantity.

Another striking example occurred during my stay in Nordheim. It was in the synagogue a day or two before one of the minor fasts. To the understanding of this incident it is necessary to state that abstinence from food and drink is not absolutely required on the minor fast days but may be dispensed with for good and valid reasons, such as indisposition or urgent business, in which case the person breaking the fast is expected to make amends for his violation by giving charity. In order to conduct the services of the fast day, however, ten male persons, over the age of thirteen who are fasting, must be present. On the day to which I refer the *Parnass,* or president of the congregation, announced that the fast would occur on a certain date. Then he read the names of ten members who would be in duty bound to fast. One of these members, however, objected. "Excuse me, Herr Parnass," he said, "I cannot fast. I must leave town early and stay away all day. I cannot do without eating and drinking."

"I am sorry," answered the Parnass, "but I cannot excuse you. We need you for the *Minyan* (required number) and you must attend and must fast." The objecting member subsided and said no more. I was lost in amazement to think that a *Parnass* could possess such authority!

At this point let me pause in my description of general Jewish conditions in Nordheim and tell something of my relatives in the village. My Uncle Koppel and his wife Caroline and their children, three daughters and two sons, were a lovely, an ideal family. My uncle had not inherited the scholarly attainments of his learned father, Reb Shemayah. The education of the former both in Hebrew and secular subjects was moderate, but he had inherited his father's spiritual outlook and was a sincerely devout and observant Jew. By dint of natural intelligence and untiring industry he had succeeded very well economically and was reputed the wealthiest Jewish burgher of Nordheim. In the government records his name was inscribed in a threefold capacity as gentleman farmer, merchant, and financier (*Gutbe-*

sitzer, Kaufmann, und Kapitalist). And, although these pompous designations convey an exaggerated idea of his financial status, he was without doubt a man of considerable means. He used his wealth wisely and generously. He not only provided for his family most liberally in a material way but also saw to it that his children received the educational advantages which he had been unable to enjoy in his youth. He contributed generously to all benevolent purposes. He observed the Biblical law of *Maaser,* or tithes, by putting one tenth of all profits on his transactions into a special receptacle. The sums thus accumulated were used exclusively for charitable purposes.

My cousins, the children of Uncle Koppel and Aunt Caroline, were a most interesting and lovable group. Their devotion to their parents and to each other was extraordinary. The oldest, Jeannette, was a true Oriental beauty of the finest type, her features regular and delicately formed, her hair and eyes jet black, these latter brilliant, flashing and expressive, and her skin, in vivid contrast thereto, of purest alabaster whiteness. Her voice was softly melodious, like the gentle rippling of a fountain. She spoke the High German with just a touch of the Bavarian accent which made it particularly charming.

Incidentally, three forms of the German language were spoken in the village: the High or classic German, which was the language taught in the school and used at all public functions; the Bavarian peasant dialect, which was so different from the classic German as to seem almost a different language; and the Jewish-German or Yiddish which was not like either of the other two. The Yiddish, although basically nearer to the High German, was so filled with terms and expressions drawn from the Hebrew and other tongues as to be almost unintelligible to those not specifically acquainted with it. The Jewish young people of Nordheim spoke all three dialects with equal fluency but preferred the High German. It was amazing to hear Jeannette speak the Jewish-German to her parents or Jewish friends, the peasant dialect to the Gentile servants or laborers, and the High German to her Gentile acquaintances of higher rank. All three sounded pleasant and acceptable when they flowed from her lips. I will not deny that I quite lost my heart to Jeannette. But she was not destined to be mine, for in the following year, when I came for my second visit to Nordheim, I had the unwelcome privilege of being a guest at her marriage. It was a wise choice. Jeannette's husband was a good man in every way, and they were happy in their marriage.

Jeannette's two sisters, Clara and Bettie, were both unswervingly loyal to the religious and ethical traditions of their family. Clara did not survive to mature age, but Bettie, the youngest of the children, thanks to a merciful Providence, was preserved to become a wife and mother in Israel. At the time of this writing, she is still living with two of her sons in the city of Munich, amidst the tribulations and sufferings in the Germany of the Nazis.*

The two sons of Uncle Koppel and Aunt Caroline, Adolf and Solomon, were splendid youths and became, in later years, men of outstanding importance. Jewishly and ethically they were very similar, but otherwise their paths in life lay far apart. Adolf early resolved to follow the example of his practical and economically successful father rather than that of his grandfather. He took up a commercial career, in which he was successful far beyond that of his father. Adolf's outstanding achievement was the establishing of a great enterprise for the manufacture of artificial stone. He came upon the idea due to the material suited to this purpose which was found in quantities in the vicinity of Nordheim.

When I again visited Germany in the year 1922, I found Adolf at the head of this great enterprise, organized in the form of a mighty corporation under the title of *Leimbacher Kunststein Werke* (Leimbach Artificial Stone Works). He had ten plants, eight in Germany, one in Italy, and one in Switzerland. At each of these plants, I was informed, the method was the same. There were quarries in mountains from which the material was excavated. This material was then conveyed by means of an aerial railway to a factory in an adjacent town, where it was crushed and reworked into various kinds of finished products, mainly paving and building blocks and sewer conduits.

There was one such plant in Nordheim and its vicinity which I myself saw. I saw the aerial railway with its suspended cars conveying the raw material to the factory, I saw the factory with its throng

---

* The three were last heard from in 1941, the final message being that they were about to be deported to Poland.—Ed.

of busy laborers, I heard the roar and rumble of the machinery, and I beheld the heaps of finished product waiting to be taken to its ultimate destination. I must confess that the impression produced upon me by this industrial achievement was no by means all pleasant, for the romance had departed from Nordheim. It was no longer a simple peasant village, a picturesque rustic retreat. It had become a grim and grimy factory town, with different people, of an unfamiliar and less pleasing type. There was a railway station, and screeching locomotives which emitted huge trails of smoke while they dragged long trains of cars over the fields that had erstwhile been given over to smiling crops of golden grain and green vegetables and flocks and herds of peacefully grazing sheep and cattle. However, the industrial success which Adolf had attained and the economic benefit which he had brought to Nordheim and to Germany in general were undeniable. Adolf had become one of the great industrial personalities of Germany. He was reputed to be a multimillionaire. There were several thousand persons in his employ, all of whom, with the exception of a few dozen, were German Gentiles. He dwelt with his family in a mansion in Schweinfurt, not far from Nordheim, where also were located the offices of the great corporation of which he was the head. His product was mostly sold in foreign countries, so that the benefit which came to Germany from him was direct, enormous, and indisputable. All this did not, however, prevent the ruthless confiscation of his estate by the Nazis when they came to power. Adolf had, fortunately, passed away shortly before that ill-fated event. He was, therefore, spared the sight of the ruin and devastation which the totalitarian barbarians had brought upon the Jewish people in Germany. At the time of my first visit to Nordheim these tremendous changes were, of course, undreamed of, hidden in the womb of the distant future. Nordheim was still the primitive, unspoiled rustic village, and Adolf was a handsome, dark-complexioned youth, whose course in life had not yet begun to unfold. He and I were the best of friends, and he asked me many questions about America and listened with deepest interest to what I had to say about conditions in that far distant, mysterious continent.

Solomon, at that time some seventeen years of age, was about two years the junior of his brother. In personal appearance he was of the brunette type characteristic of his family, with black hair and eyes, but there was something about the expression of his countenance which was quite individual. That expression and the light which shone from his eyes indicated kindness, gentleness, and intelligence. From the first moment that we met on the platform of the railway station at Mellrichstadt, we took a great liking to each other. During my entire stay in Nordheim he and I were inseparable. We went on many long strolls together in the beautiful country surrounding Nordheim, we undertook several railroad trips together which took us away from the village for two or three days at a time, and when we were at home we were most of the time in each other's company. Incidentally, all the expenses of these excursions were defrayed by Uncle Koppel, who would not permit me to spend a cent of my own money. I found Solomon invariably kind and attentive.

We were once walking on a country road when there came along a peasant who knew Solomon and whom Solomon knew. Without any preliminary ceremony the peasant asked Solomon who the young man with him was. Solomon answered that it was his American cousin. Whereupon the peasant, with an air of superior wisdom, assured Solomon that he could not tell him any such thing as that, that he, the peasant, knew that Americans had red skins and did not wear hats upon their heads but feathers in their hair and that no one could make him believe that a young man with a white skin and wearing a hat was an American!

At another time I unintentionally shocked the whole village and terrified my relatives by eating a tomato, which, under the name of *Liebesapfel*, had the reputation of being deadly poison!

I can take to myself the credit of having influenced Solomon in the choice of his life vocation. I did not do this deliberately or intentionally. I made no attempt whatever to determine his choice. Nevertheless it was through influence emanating directly from me that Solomon's choice was made. That happened in this wise. Unlike his brother Adolf, Solomon had no taste for business or the so-called practical vocations. He was fond of reading and study, and his gentle and somewhat timid nature shrank from confronting the strenuous battle of mercantile and industrial competition. When the time came for deciding what his life's pursuit should be, as it did about that time, he found the decision very difficult. He wanted to take up some sort of learned or literary career, perhaps to seek a professorship in a university, but had reached no definite conclusion as to what he should strive to attain. Strange to say, although belonging to a family with a long tradition of Jewish piety and learning and himself sincerely religious and already equipped with a very fair knowledge of Hebrew and Biblical and Talmudic teachings, it had not occurred to him to become a rabbi. It may have been because the great majority of those who chose the rabbinate as their vocation were from poor families and he was the son of well-to-do parents that that vocation was unconsciously excluded from his thoughts.* However that may have been, my arrival in Nordheim with the avowed intention of studying for the rabbinate brought about a quick solution of the problem that had been puzzling him. Only a few days after my arrival, when we were all seated around the table, Solomon suddenly announced his decision. "I have made up my mind what I intend to be," he said to his parents and to all of us. "I am going to study as rabbi." There was some surprise, though no displeasure or objection, because of the unexpectedness of this momentous decision, and Uncle Koppel, after congratulating Solomon on having decided to walk in the footsteps of his sainted grandfather, Reb Shemayah, asked him what was his reason for making this choice.

"A very simple one," said Solomon. "I thought that if Cousin Bernard from America can be a rabbi, there is no reason why I should not be."

I can, therefore, claim to have been instrumental in giving to German Judaism one of its best spiritual leaders during the nineteenth and early twentieth centuries. For that is really what Solomon became. As Rabbi Dr. Solomon Stein, he occupied a highly honored position in the German Jewry of his time and brought to it invaluable services. He was ideally fitted for the rabbinical office. Not only did he possess the great Hebraic scholarship required for the authori-

---

* It seems that the same condition prevailed in ancient Israel as well. That is certainly the inference which may be drawn from the Talmudic dictum "Be careful in thy treatment of the sons of the poor, for from them the Torah proceeds" (*Nedarim* 81 a). The arduous preparation required for the rabbinate and its comparatively slight rewards were apparently never very attractive to wealthy youths.—B.D.

tative interpretation of Jewish law and doctrine but also the sincerity of faith and the ethical exaltation which render the occupant of the sacred office the object of profound respect and veneration. His personal amiability, his kind and gentle manner, and his charitable generosity were such as to make him equally beloved by rich and poor and equally popular with all classes of the community.

Solomon attended the *Rabbiner-seminar* of Rabbi Dr. Hildesheimer in Berlin, which was considered stricter in its Orthodoxy than the Jewish Theological Seminary of Breslau. Shortly after his ordination as rabbi, the District Rabbinate of Schweinfurt, to which Nordheim belonged, became vacant through the death of Rabbi Dr. Lebrecht, its incumbent for many years. Solomon was the logical candidate for the post mainly for three reasons: because he was a "native son" of the district and personally very popular, because he belonged to the Stein family which was highly honored and respected in the district, and, finally, because he was a descendant of Reb Shemayah, whose memory was held in deepest reverence throughout that entire section of country.

But an unexpected opposition developed. There was one other candidate for the post, a certain Dr. Koref, who was reputed to be a very eloquent preacher. Some of the leading members of the district, who desired to reorganize the Jewish community on more modern lines, preferred his candidacy to that of Solomon. It became a conflict between town and country. Most of the Jewish inhabitants of Schweinfurt, which contained the largest congregation of the district, were pro-Koref, while the Jews of the villages, almost to a man, were pro-Stein.

The day of the election was a most exciting one and attracted the attention also of the non-Jewish citizens. The poll was set up in the synagogue in Schweinfurt and was open for balloting from nine in the morning till five in the afternoon. All day long, in all kinds of conveyances and on foot, the Jews of the villages poured into Schweinfurt to cast their votes for the beloved grandson of Reb Shemayah. When the poll closed that afternoon, and the votes were counted, Dr. Solomon Stein was declared elected by an overwhelming majority Rabbi of the district of Schweinfurt. Solomon remained in this position until his retirement a few years before his death in 1939 at the age of seventy-four. He never accepted any other post although called several times to communities much larger and more important than Schweinfurt. But he felt that here, in his native region and among the people with whom he had grown up, he could do the best work for the spiritual and cultural heritage of Israel. In this sense his rabbinate was very successful and he made of the Jewish community of the district of Schweinfurt an ideal one, permeated with the Jewish spirit and unswervingly loyal to traditional Judaism. He was universally beloved and on my visits to Germany in later years, as we walked the streets of Schweinfurt together, I could see how deeply respected and honored he was by all, Jews and Gentiles alike.*

My sojourn in Nordheim, in the first year of my arrival and also in subsequent years, was rich in many more varied and interesting observations and experiences than can be narrated here. I gained an insight into German life, Jewish and Gentile both, which was very instructive and advantageous to me. On the whole the impression produced was very favorable. One observation which I made and which both pleased and surprised me—for I had expected something different—was that there seemed to be no anti-Semitism. The relations between the Jewish and Gentile inhabitants of the village and of the whole region seemed to be most cordial. I myself was the recipient of many visits from the older non-Jewish villagers, particularly the older women who, as girls, had known and associated with my mother. The interest which they took in hearing of her welfare in far distant America was unquestionably genuine and sincere. I afterwards learned that conditions were not quite as good as they seemed, that there was an element of bitter anti-Semites in the village, of venomous Jew-haters, who would not have shrunk from any deed of cruelty or savagery against their Jewish neighbors, but they were a despised minority and no one took them seriously. The air of liberty and liberalism was in the land and certainly no one dreamed that in a comparatively few years the horrors of the Middle Ages would return to Germany in increased and intensified degree.

---

* Shortly after the accession of Hitler, Dr. Stein was thrown into prison *on a charge of communism!* The evidence was that his name had appeared on a Passover relief appeal for Russian Jews. A short imprisonment so broke his health that he died a few years later.—Ed.

My observations of the religious life of the Jewish villagers were particularly enlightening. They showed me the spiritual wealth innate in Judaism when carried out normally and fully by those who profess it. Under American conditions, I had not been able to make such an observation. There may, of course, have been, among the Jewish inhabitants of Nordheim and the vicinity, a certain proportion who, in their innermost thoughts, were indifferent or even antagonistic to their ancestral faith. The overwhelming majority, however, loved their religious heritage with all their heart and soul. They carried the consciousness of it, and of their obligation to it, with them wherever they went. The following incident thoroughly confirms the statement which I have just made. Shortly after my arrival in Nordheim I heard that a cattle fair was to take place in a town called Neustadt an der Saale, that Uncle Koppel would have cattle there and would himself attend it. I was very anxious to see it. I had never attended any such fair; all I had known of them was derived from hearsay and the celebrated painting "The Horse Fair" by Rosa Bonheur. Although agricultural fairs are not unknown in America, I was very desirous of taking advantage of the opportunity to see something which I was sure would be both picturesque and highly interesting. On learning of my wish Uncle Koppel at once agreed to take me, although he warned me that the traveling there would not be very pleasant. Adolf and Solomon, who would otherwise not have gone, immediately said that they would accompany me.

On the evening before the fair I was told to go to bed unusually early as I would have to rise before daybreak. About two o'clock the next morning I was roused out of a deep sleep by a voice calling my name. It was Solomon, who was summoning me to make ready to go to the fair. It is not very pleasant to be wakened in this manner, but I arose with alacrity and hastily dressed myself. Early as was the hour, the whole household was already up. Uncle Koppel was ready for immediate departure and so were Adolf and Solomon. Aunt Caroline and the girls were awake and ready to render any needed service and so, of course, were the servants, both male and female. Within the house the lights shone brilliantly but outside pitch darkness, "the darkness of Egypt," reigned, relieved only by the occasional glimmer of a lantern borne by some worker across the spacious courtyard or the dark street. It was a rather weird and eerie scene but certainly thrilling. In about fifteen or twenty minutes we were ready to depart. In the village street in front of the house we then mounted a crude country wagon to which were harnessed two horses. Uncle Koppel and the driver sat on a bench in front, the two boys and I behind them, and the drive to the fair began. The men who were to take Uncle Koppel's cattle to the fair had already left. They were going on foot, driving the cattle before them. I will never forget that exciting ride. For me it had much of the nature of an adventure. Absolute darkness prevailed, what would today be called "a complete blackout." I could not see my hand before my face, but my fellow travelers must have possessed the owl's power of vision in the darkness, for the driver drove ahead at a good rate of speed and no one seemed to think that at all abnormal or risky. From time to time we drove through herds of cattle which were being driven to the fair. I could make out only the faintest outlines of the animals or the men. My companions, however, or at least the driver, had no apparent difficulty in that regard, for our vehicle went straight ahead without slackening its speed. There were even occasional exchanges of greetings between Uncle Koppel or our driver and men on the road. All this took place not only in intense darkness but also severe cold. Although it was still summer, the nocturnal temperature was very low. But we did not suffer from the cold. We had been warned, and were warmly clad. I certainly never had such a ride before and have never had any such since.

Neustadt an der Saale, where the fair was to take place, must have been at least twenty-five or thirty miles distant from Nordheim. It took us fully three hours to reach it. It was about half past five, the gray light of dawn was just appearing, when we rolled into the town, a typical German medieval town. We did not go at once to the fair grounds, but wended our way to a Jewish hotel or inn kept by one Moses Weglein. And here it was that I beheld the proof of Jewish loyalty to which I have referred.

The driver attended to the horses and the wagon, and the rest of our party entered the hotel. We came at once into a large room which was brightly lighted and appeared to be heated, for its temperature, compared with that of the outer air, was comfortably warm. This was evidently a combined assembly and dining room, for in it, seated or standing, a large group of Jewish men, a hundred or more, were gathered. The room was well supplied with tables covered with tablecloths and set in readiness for a meal. The men were cattle dealers who had come to Neustadt to take part in the fair. They were evidently waiting for Uncle Koppel, for as soon as we entered, one of the men came up to Uncle Koppel and said to him, "*Sholom Aleichem,** Herr Stein; now that you're here, we can begin to *or.*"** At once all the men, without exception, put on their *Tephillin* (phylacteries or prayer ornaments). A considerable number also donned their *Tallithoth* (prayer robes or shawls). One of them stood before the eastern wall of the room and began to officiate as *Chazan* (cantor or prayer leader), and all recited with him the week-day morning services. We also had brought with us our Tephillin, Tallithoth, and prayer books, and joined in the service. It was a thrilling sight. That all these men, come to this place for an ordinary commercial purpose, should first join in worship of the Most High, in accordance with the traditional ritual and usages of their faith, was an emphatic demonstration of the strength of Orthodox Judaism in these parts.

After the conclusion of the service all present washed their hands in accordance with the ritual of the Jewish faith at an antique laver which stood in a corner of the room and then, seating themselves at the table, broke bread and pronounced the prescribed benediction, also in accordance with the Jewish ritual. The meal was good and hearty. Besides the bread, it consisted of soup, substantial pieces of meat, and large cups of black coffee, all served piping hot. When the repast was finished, one of the men led in the chanting of grace and the others all joined in. Such loyalty to Jewish precepts, so natural and self-understood, was a deeply impressive revelation to me.

A few moments later all the guests—all cattle dealers—had left and gone to the fair to attend to their business. It may be mentioned here incidentally that a large proportion of the Jews residing in that section of Germany at that time were dealers in cattle and horses, so that the horse and cattle trade could not unfittingly have been called

---
* "Peace be upon you." A Hebrew salutation.—B.D.
** A German Jewish term, signifying to recite prayers, supposed to be derived from the Latin "*orare.*"—B.D.

a Jewish trade. The historic reasons for this need not be considered here, but I was interested to observe that these Jewish cattle dealers had evolved a complete Hebrew terminology with which to describe the characteristics of their animals and the various incidents of their vocation.* At the fair I saw many things that were interesting, but,

---

* e.g. "*rotzeach*" (literally "murderer") for a vicious horse, and "*chassid*" ("saint") for a gentle one.—Ed.

as the saying goes, that is another story, unrelated to the purposes of this chronicle.

All things that have a beginning have also an end, and so my idyllic visit to Nordheim reached its termination. I remained in the village, enjoying the hospitality and kind attentions of my dear relatives until after the High Holy Days, which took up the greater part of the month of September. At that time I was obliged to leave for Breslau, to take up my studies at the university and the Jewish Theological Seminary of that city. The manner of observing the High Holy Days did not differ essentially from that to which I had been accustomed, except in two particulars. On *Yom Kippur*, the Day of Atonement, every adult person in the synagogue was dressed in white. The men wore their white linen shrouds; the women, white dresses. It was an inspiring sight, the entire congregration clothed in robes of pure white, the symbol of purity and sinlessness. Also on *Succoth*, the Feast of Tabernacles, every family in Nordheim had its own *Succah*—tabernacle or ceremonial booth. The booths, built in the open air, had roofs of branches and boughs, and were ornamented in the interior according to the means and taste of the owners. Uncle Koppel had a very fine *Succah*, and the girls had joined efforts in decorating it. We spent a great deal of our time in the booth, and I found the usages connected with it most interesting. In Jersey City very few people wore white on the Day of Atonement, and as for the Succah, the number of those could easily be counted on the fingers of one hand.

At last the day of my departure arrived. My belongings were all packed. Before the house stood the wagon that was to take me to the railroad station at Mellrichstadt. To my surprise, I suddenly noticed that the day of my departure was an occasion of public observance in Nordheim. The "good room" of the Stein residence was crowded with Jewish neighbors come to bid me good-bye, and the street was filled with a throng of Gentile villagers assembled to witness the leavetaking of the "American young gentleman."

As for the Steins, to my surprise and consternation, they were all weeping—Uncle Koppel and Aunt Caroline, Adolf and Solomon, Jeannette, Clara, and Bettie. It seemed to me that the beautiful black eyes of Jeannette were especially suffused with tears, that on her lovely countenance there was an expression of great sadness. I saw no reason why anyone should weep or feel sad because I was going to study in Breslau and I tried to dispel their apparent grief, but emotions, whether joyous or sad, are contagious, and the first thing I knew I was also weeping. However, emotions cannot be permitted to interfere with necessary actions, and so we all ascended the wagon, for the entire family was determined to see me off in the train.

As the vehicle started a great shout arose, and cries of *"Lebewohl!"* and *"Glueckliche Reise!"* filled the air. At the station the scenes of leavetaking and heartfelt farewells were repeated with utmost sincerity and depth of emotion. I too was profoundly stirred by the warm affection shown by my dear relatives, far beyond anything that I felt I deserved. As the train moved away and I beheld those kind, sad faces gazing after me, I took with me indelible impressions of a peaceful, friendly village, of a true, genuinely pious and reverent Jewish life, and of the pure hearts and noble, loving souls of my dear kinsfolk.

Chapter Eleven

My First Day in Breslau

THE TRIP TO BRESLAU WAS DULL AND TEDIOUS, AND A SENSE OF loneliness pervaded me—caused perhaps by the sudden parting from the Nordheim relatives. Further, upon arriving at the home of Mrs. Marcus (the sister of the Rev. M. Schlesinger of Jersey City), where I was to board, I found everything in confusion. The family was in the throes of moving to a new apartment, which would not be ready for a few days.

Reaching the street, I debated with myself as to what I should now do and decided that the best and most advisable course was to visit the professors of the Seminary, introduce myself to them, and perhaps secure valuable suggestions as to the studies I should pursue. Accordingly, I hailed a *droschke* and had myself driven to the Jewish Theological Seminary, which was located in a street called *Wallstrasse*. Arrived at the Seminary, a fair-sized but unpretentious-looking structure, another disappointment awaited me. The Seminary appeared to be empty, except for a few persons, apparently caretakers. I was informed by them that the Seminary was not yet open for the winter semester, that the members of the faculty, who had official residences in the Seminary building, had not yet returned from their summer vacations. Noticing my consternation, the caretakers informed me that the vacation would end within a few days, that at the beginning of the following week I would find everything in full operation and that I would be able then to see everyone I wished.

With this information I had to be content, so I left with, I must admit, a heavy heart. In addition I began now to feel the pangs of hunger. I had with me the address of a kosher restaurant, which had been given me in Nordheim. It was an attractive place, kept, if I recall correctly, by a man named Sachs, and I had an excellent meal, consisting of soup, a Wiener schnitzel, i.e., a veal cutlet prepared in the Vienna manner, a *mehlspeise* (pastry) and black coffee, all very well prepared and tasty. There is something about good food that is very pleasing and satisfying alike to the physical and the spiritual parts of our nature. After my meal I began to recover from the effects of the disappointments I had suffered and to look upon the world with a more contented eye.

Night comes early in the fall of the year in those northern regions. Before it grew completely dark and the street lights began to shine, I returned to the apartment where I had rented a room. My landlady greeted me with a friendly smile and accompanied me to my room to see that everything was in order. She lit the lamp, uncovered the bed, wished me "good night and pleasant rest" (*Gute Nacht. Angenehme Ruhe*), and left. Then there came over me the most dreadful feeling of desolation and wretchedness that I had ever experienced in all my life. I sat down on the one chair in the room. The whole world seemed to collapse and crash in ruin at my feet. I felt utterly forsaken and forlorn, exhausted and miserable. It was undoubtedly homesickness, nostalgia, but let no one say that homesickness is no sickness. It may not be in the technical medical sense, but it is certainly productive of the keenest pain, akin to agony. Overcome by the weight of my desolation, I sank upon the bed and there came to me deep sleep, the deep and dreamless sleep of utter exhaustion.

Chapter Twelve

First Observations of Breslau

I AWOKE BETIMES THE NEXT MORNING. SLEEP HAD RESTED AND REfreshed me, and my frame of mind had changed. I still felt some traces of yesterday's depression, but I was resolved to overcome it and to take up the tasks of my new environment with courage and energy.

It was a fine day. The sun was already shining brightly and the air that came in through the open window was cool and invigorating. After my usual ablutions and devotions, I decided to visit the Marcuses to see what progress if any they had made in their new apartment.

I found Frau Marcus and the older daughter at home. Herr Marcus had already gone to his business, and the son and younger daughter had also left, to attend school doubtless. Frau Marcus informed me that she was practically finished with all necessary preparations to receive me, that I could take my meals there that very day, that I could occupy my room on the coming night. I took advantage of her communication by accepting her invitation to breakfast. It was, according to my American ideas, rather too simple a breakfast, a *semmel* (a kind of roll) and a half, and a cup of coffee. The whole *semmel* was buttered and the half-*semmel* was not buttered. But I afterwards learned that this was only the first breakfast, *Erstes Fruehstueck*. It was customary to eat also a second breakfast, *Zweites Fruehstueck,* about eleven o'clock, and that the second breakfast was much more substantial than the first.

Let me at this point digress a little to say something about the dietary habits of the Germans. These habits, as I became acquainted with them partly in Nordheim and more fully in Breslau, were certainly astounding to an American. The Breslau citizen could regale his inner man no fewer than seven times daily without exceeding the normal program. About seven A.M. he could visit the cow stables and drink a glass of hot milk drawn fresh from the cow. About eight he could have his first breakfast, consisting usually of rolls, coffee and *confiture* or jam. About eleven came the second breakfast, generally a chop (*schnitzel*), bread and a generous mug of foamy beer. At one P. M. was the time for dinner (*Mittagessen*), an elaborate meal limited only by his appetite and his purse. At four P. M. was *Nachmittags kaffee,* coffee and cake. About six P.M. *Abendbrot* or supper, after which the families customarily went to the *Cafe* or the *Kneipe* (liquor saloon), where *Cafe melange,* coffee with whipped cream and cakes, or huge mugfuls of beer, were consumed. How the German stomachs could endure it I cannot imagine. It must be noted, however, that this lavish indulgence was only for the well-to-do; the poor had perforce to be content with a much more restricted diet. Their food was neither abundant nor of good quality; indeed, adulteration of food products was rampant, and products were used as food which would not come upon even the poorest American table.

At breakfast, Frau Marcus conversed with me about her family. Her husband, Abraham, was classed as a *Handelsmann,* that is to say, a merchant in a small way, as contrasted with a *Kaufmann,* a merchant on a larger or very large scale. He worked very hard to support his family of three children, but times were hard and no very great success crowned his efforts. Frau Marcus asked me a number of questions about America. She was very much interested in what I told her of Jewish conditions in the New World.

Since I had no pressing engagements for the next few days, I decided to devote them to a sightseeing tour about the city. I discovered that Breslau was really a very beautiful city. There were two different sections, readily distinguishable in appearance, the old and the new. The old section, dating back to the Middle Ages, medieval in appearance, had narrow streets and antique-looking buildings. The new section, which was the greater part of the city, was thoroughly modern in its architectural layout, with broad, well paved streets and avenues and many fine buildings. Even the older section was kept scrupulously clean, nor was there any evidence, as far as I could see, of slums such as are found in the large cities of Western Europe and even in America. Neither was there a specifically Jewish section, although the Jewish population numbered upward of twenty thousand souls. A fine stream of water, crossed by bridges at intersecting streets, encompassed the city. In medieval times, this had been the moat, and was still known as the *Stadtgraben*, or city moat. The wall which had formerly stood behind the moat along its entire extent, as a part of the protective system of the city, had in modern times been removed, and in its place there had been arranged a beautiful promenade with rows of fine trees and shrubs on both sides throughout its entire length of several miles. This promenade was a favorite resort of the Breslauers and on Sundays and holidays was usually crowded with saunterers. On Sabbaths and Jewish holy days, members of the Jewish community contributed a large contingent to the throngs that strolled along its leafy walks. The promenade was at its best in the month of May when the lilacs, called in German *der Flieder*, were in full bloom. Then the sight was entrancing and the odor delicious.

The apartment houses, in which the great majority of the inhabitants of the modern city dwelt, were massive, imposing structures, but more like fortresses, or prisons, than like the homes of peaceful, every-day human beings. The entrances, immensely high, and the massive doors which closed them, created a distinctly fortress-like effect. The interior of these homes, however, was built for comfort. The rooms were large and high, and the conveniences known at that time, gas illumination and flowing water, were provided. Electric light was beginning to be known, but it was hardly in use. Elevators and telephones, to say nothing of radios, were, of course, undreamed of. The lack of elevators made it impossible to build the structures very high. They did not usually exceed five or six stories. A pleasant feature of apartment-house living in Breslau was that they usually had gardens or garden courts, planted with trees and shrubs, and each resident family had a summer house or booth of its own.

A rather quaint official, smacking of the Middle Ages, who exercised his functions in connection with the apartment houses, was the *Nachtwaechter*, or night watchman. Every block of apartment houses had such a night watchman attached to its service. These night watchmen were a sort of auxiliary police, presumably for the greater protection of the residents of the section. Their chief function, however, seemed to be to come to the aid of unfortunates who had forgotten their keys and were unable to enter their homes at dead of night. In case of such an unpleasant happening, the person affected would simply cry out, *"Waechter, waechter!"* and out of the surrounding darkness would come a speedy reply in hearty, guttural German accents: *"Ja, mein Herr, ich komm"* (Yes, sir, I am coming). The night watchman would produce the required key, open the great door of the apartment house, receive his tip, and the little incident would be finished to the satisfaction of both parties concerned. The night watchman carried a lantern which gave him a mysterious, seriocomic appearance. I had one such experience during my stay in Breslau, when everything took place in regulation manner as above described. Although I was thereby relieved from an embarrassing situation, the whole procedure struck me as irresistibly comical, suggestive of a comic opera. Even in Germany the night watchman was looked upon as a sort of comical figure, and many were the jokes made at his expense. The watchmen were supposed to have a rhyming cry of warning in rather antique German, which they called out during the night at every turn of the hour to impress upon the citizens the need of being on their guard against the danger of fire. It ran as follows:

> *Hoert, Ihr Herren, und lasst euch sagen,*
> *Die Uhr hat grade zehn geschlagen.*
> *Bewahret Feuer und Licht*
> *Dass kein Schad in der Stadt geschieht.*

Which may be freely translated as follows:

> *Listen, gentlemen, unto my word.*
> *The clock struck ten, as you've just heard.*
> *Take care of fire and light,*
> *Lest evil befall the town by night.*

But I must say that I never heard any night watchman utter this cry. No matter what may have been the case in the Middle Ages, I strongly doubt that it actually was used in modern times.

Even at that time, Germany was strongly militaristic. My casual strolls through the streets in the first few days after my arrival gave ample evidence of that fact. An infinite variety of uniforms was visible in the streets, in the *cafés,* and in other public places at most hours of the day and night. Infantry, cavalry, artillery, hussars, cuirassiers, and other branches of service were all represented, privates and officers of all ranks, from the highest to the lowest, all with special uniforms and insignia. There were other evidences of the great part which the military played in the life of Breslau. Not far from the Marcus residence was the armory of the Silesian Cuirassiers (*Schlesische Kuerassiere*)—a huge edifice, covering what in America would be called a whole square block. It needed that great space, for the regiment consisted of twenty-four hundred men and horses. Once I witnessed a full dress parade of the cuirassiers, and it was indeed a thrilling sight. The men wore uniforms of white. The upper parts of their bodies, front and back, were encased in steel cuirasses. On their feet and lower limbs they wore great leather boots with spurs attached, and on their heads steel helmets with waving plumes. The cuirasses and helmets, brilliantly polished, flashed in the sunlight, and the boots were stained a deep glistening black. The men were all sturdy, muscular-looking fellows, and the horses were fine, blooded steeds apparently of Arabian stock. The impression of overwhelming power which emanated from this tremendous aggregation of armed and armored men and horses was terrific. Mornings and evenings I could hear the bugle calls resounding from the armory. The effect was indescribably warlike. Often, too, in the mornings when returning from synagogue or when out for an early stroll, I saw detachments of infantry or artillery on their way to the drill grounds for military training. To an American, just come from a land where standing armies were an abomination and a soldier a *rara avis,* and where military displays were limited to an occasional parade by the militia, this predominance of the military element was startling. At first there was the interest of novelty, in seeing the billiant uniforms of the officers and the skillful evolutions of the rank and file, but this feeling soon gave way to one of deep disgust and something akin to horror. I realized that this militarism was not confined to Germany but was universally prevalent on the European continent, that a few miles from each other, on opposite sides of imaginary border lines, millions of men, armed to the teeth, were facing each other, ready, at a moment's notice, to spring at each other's throats. It was a most repellent thought, and I could not comprehend how cultured and civilized nations, the most advanced of the human race, living in the supposedly most advanced and progressive portion of the globe, could be guilty of something so contrary to true civilization and the ethical teachings of the religions in which the European nations were supposed to believe. I consoled myself with the thought that the danger was more apparent than real, that war was merely an ugly survival of ancient and medieval barbarism, and that the modern trend was all the other way. I hoped that the time was not far distant when the vision of the prophets of Israel, that men would beat their swords into ploughshares and no longer learn war, would become a reality and universal peace and brotherhood would prevail among men. Alas, that later years should prove that my dream was utterly unfounded!

There was, of course, in the life of Breslau, both in the general and Jewish community, much more than I was able to observe in the first few days of my arrival. But I was able to recognize that life flowed in deep and full channels and was rich in the cultural and social characteristics which go to make up a complete and highly developed human existence. The general community possessed all requisite educational institutions, from primary schools to a great university, and a multitude of establishments for the promotion of both physical and esthetic well-being and enjoyment. Breslau was in all respects a highly cultured and advanced city, a splendid example of modern Occidental life. The Jewish community was also well provided with the religious and cultural institutions required for the proper maintenance of Judaism. There were two main synagogues, the *Neue Synagoge* and the *Storch Synagoge,* presided over by distinguished and highly respected rabbis, Dr. Manuel Joel and Rabbi Gedaliah Tiktin. There were also a number of minor houses of worship and schools. The *Neue Synagoge* (New Synagogue) was an imposing structure, situated in a spacious courtyard and in a splendid location, opposite that part of the city moat known as the *Schweidnitzer Stadtgraben.* Alongside of the synagogue stood the communal building, in which the rabbi, Dr. Joel, and the other officials of the synagogue had their homes. The open and conspicuous location of the New Synagogue and the Jewish communal building was symbolic of the spirit of the new time in Germany, in which the Jews had received the full rights of citizenship and had nothing to fear and did not need to hide either themselves or their synagogues from public view.

The *Storch Synagoge,* on the other hand, still showed the influence of medieval conditions. It, too, was a large, fine structure, but was situated in an interior courtyard, with inhabited buildings in front, and was invisible from the public street. Rabbi Gedaliah Tiktin, its spiritual leader, was a descendant of an old rabbinical family of Silesia and a representative of strict and uncompromising Orthodox Judaism. There were religious differences between the two congregations but, as far as I could judge, they were not very deep-seated, nor did there appear to be any acrimonious antagonism between them. The differences were certainly not nearly as far-reaching as between American Radical Reform and Orthodoxy, and Dr Joel, though not as strict as Rabbi Tiktin, was fundamentally observant of Jewish traditional law.

The outstanding Jewish institution in Breslau was the Seminary, of which more anon. Even my first few days in Breslau were sufficient to show me that I had come to a place which was destined to exercise a profound influence upon my intellectual and spiritual make-up and upon the whole course of my future life.

Chapter Thirteen

Activities, Contacts, and Experiences in Breslau

PROMPTLY ON THE FOLLOWING MONDAY I WENT TO THE SEMINARY to make arrangements for my entrance as a student. It presented a very different appearance from that of my previous visit. Then the building was dull and almost empty; now it was a place of bustling activity. A throng of youths and young men filled the hallways, among them a few dignified elderly gentlemen. These latter were members of the faculty, whom I did not yet know. The proceedings concerning my reception were few and simple. The official in charge told me of the subjects which would be treated by the various professors and left it to me to choose whichever I wished. Instruction was to begin on the following day. I was somewhat surprised at the informality of the proceedings, but, since I had nothing further to do at the Seminary, I decided to go to the University and make application for entrance there.

The proceedings at the University were hardly more formal than at the Seminary. I was required to show my certificate of graduation from Columbia College, but that was all. No examination was required nor was I assigned to any class. Indeed, there was no class, in the American sense, in the University. Instruction was entirely by voluntary groups. This method, entirely new to me, I immediately recognized as an ideal one, perfectly adapted to the needs and desires of students and instructors alike, and suitable to the character and standing of an institution of higher learning.

There were three types of instructors: *Ordentlicher Professor*, Professor of the Order, or Full Professor; *Ausserordentlicher Professor*, or Professor Out of the Order, that is, not having full rank and recognition; and *Privatdocent,* or private instructor. The third class of instructors was a most extraordinary one, the like of which does not exist in any English-speaking country. The *Privatdocent* was an individual not appointed by the University but given, at his request, the right to instruct and lecture in the University building. Any holder of an academic degree, who felt himself qualified for a university career and desired to take it up, could apply to the University for permission to instruct, or lecture, in the University, and would at once receive such permission and have assigned to him a room and hours for his instruction or lectures. The extraordinary liberality and beneficial results of this system are self-evident. Any ambitious young man possessed of academic training could thus secure an opportunity to demonstrate his ability, and the universities could thus ascertain in an easy and natural way who were the coming men, who gave promise of rendering great service to science and scholarship in the future. Many of the greatest professors in Germany had begun their careers in this manner. Such an opportunity does not exist in America. Here, if a young man does not, by sheer good luck or by dint of influence, secure an appointment to the faculty of a university, he is barred by cruel circumstance from his desired career. Thus learning and ability are too frequently lost to the cause of scholarship. Personal reasons or unworthy prejudices may prevent his appointment. As I saw this system in Germany, it was absolutely uninfluenced by personal considerations or prejudices. There were quite a number of Jewish *Privatdocenten* and of Jewish professors who, but for this system, would in all probability never have attained their professorial eminence. The *Privatdocenten* did not receive any salaries from the university but they were at liberty to charge fees for attendance at their classes or lectures and, if they were popular and attracted many listeners, they might earn a very fair income.

The students, on taking up their studies at the university, were, as already stated, not assigned to any classes. Instead, they received a sort of notebook, called *Anmeldebuch,* literally Book of Announcement, in which they kept the record of their studies. They would present this to the professors or *Privatdocenten* whose lectures they intended to hear. They in turn would record therein the subjects of the lectures and the date of the enrollment. At the end of the semester the student would again present the book for *Abmelden,* that is, the statement that he had completed the course. Only this and nothing more. No proof of attendance and no examination in the subject taken was required. The Anmeldebuch simply served as evidence to the university from which a degree was sought that the candidate had taken the studies required for admission to the examination for the said degree. Whether the degree was granted or not depended entirly on the result of the examination and on the thesis or dissertation which accompanied it. After a certain number of semesters, four or six, a student could apply for a degree. It was not necessary to seek a degree from the university at which one had studied. Thus, although I had studied at the University of Breslau, when it came to seeking a Ph.D., I took my examination at Heidelberg.

A delightful atmosphere of liberty prevailed at the universities, in contrast to the lower schools where the utmost strictness was the rule. Many of the students, mainly those coming from wealthy families, took advantage of this academic freedom to pass a few years in idleness and pleasure-seeking before taking up their studies seriously.

The arrangements at the Seminary were, in a general way, similar to those prevailing at the University, but modified to suit the conditions of a Jewish institution. The chief resemblance was that there were no definite classes. Each student took the courses which he needed or desired, and when, in the judgment of the faculty, he had progressed sufficiently to be ripe for the rabbinate, he was admitted to the examination for the *Hattarath Horaah* or rabbinical ordination.

Before describing my experiences at the Seminary, a few words concerning the Seminary itself, its history and place in the general scheme of higher Jewish education or rabbinical training in the Germany of that period are called for. There were at that time three such institutions in Germany, the Jewish Theological Seminary, whose full title was *Juedisch-Theologisches Seminar Fraenklscher-Stiftung,* the last two words meaning "Founded by Fraenkel," in reference to the brothers Jonas and Martin Fraenkel to whose generosity the seminary owed its existence,* the *Rabbiner Seminar fuer das Orthodoxe*

---

* The Jewish Encyclopedias attribute the foundation of the Breslau Seminary to Jonas Frankel alone and do not mention his brother. According to my recollection of the story, as I heard it in Breslau, both brothers participated in the foundation of the Seminary and the other charities bearing the name of Fraenkel. I am not positive that the brother's name was Martin. If I am mistaken on this point the error is due to the inaccuracy of my memory. As the Talmud says: "There is no guardian against forgetting."—B.D.

Judenthum (Rabbinical Seminary for Orthodox Judaism) established by Rabbi Israel Hildesheimer, and the *Lehranstalt fuer die Wissenschaft des Judenthums* (Educational Institution for the Science of Judaism), which owed its inception mainly to the influence of Abraham Geiger. The latter two were located in Berlin. Of these the Hildesheimer Seminary was considered the most strictly orthodox in its attitude toward Judaism, the *Lehranstalt* the most radical or heterodox, and the Breslau Seminary as occupying an intermediary position, which might be designated as moderate or Liberal Orthodox.** The existence of three such well established and important institutions, representing the three schools of Jewish thought existing in the German Jewry of the nineteenth century, reveals a sad lack of unity among the adherents of Judaism in the concept of their inherited faith. Nevertheless it is an eloquent testimony to the keenness of their interest in their religious heritage and the earnestness of their desire to uphold and perpetuate it, each group in accordance with its understanding and conviction. Disputes and disagreements are undesirable, but where they exist there is life.

The Jewish Theological Seminary of Breslau came into existence in a most extraordinary manner. It is literally true that it owed its origin to the mistake of a clerk who was hard of hearing. Shortly after my arrival in Breslau, I learned that there were a number of charities which were maintained by funds derived from the fortune which had belonged to the Fraenkel brothers. These included, besides the Seminary, a hospital, an orphanage, a synagogue, free dwellings for worthy aged couples, and a family foundation from which maidens related to the founders received dowries.

This last charity was perhaps the most interesting of all, as it had for its result that the families in any way related to the Fraenkels guarded their pedigrees most jealously so that when the daughters became betrothed they might receive their marriage portions from

---

** I must say that I do not entirely agree with this view. The Breslau Seminary insisted upon the bindingness of Jewish law, which is after all the criterion of Orthodoxy or heterodoxy in Judaism, while the Berlin *Rabbiner Seminar* advocated the harmonious union of Orthodox faith and modern culture, which is rejected by some Orthodox elements. The Breslau and Berlin Seminaries were, therefore, in fundamental harmony on the basic concepts of Traditional Judaism and its adjustment to modern conditions.—B.D.

the family fund. The Fraenkel charities were so extensive that a special building was needed for their administration. On one of the prominent streets of Breslau there stood a fine structure which bore on its front the sign *"Verwaltungshaus des Fraenkelschen Vermoegens"* (House of Administration of the Fraenkel Estate).

The Fraenkel brothers, Jonas and Martin, were dealers in tallow in the city of Breslau, in the early and middle years of the nineteenth century. They were kind-hearted and charitable men, sincerely attached to the Jewish faith—and unmarried. They were at first only moderately prosperous. One day they received an unprecedentedly large order. As I heard the story, it was for six thousand barrels of tallow. They called in their chief clerk, informed him of the order, and told him to make every effort to obtain the needed quantity. The chief clerk happened to be hard of hearing. He misunderstood what was said to him and thought that the order was for *six hundred thousand* barrels. With the unquestioning obedience of German officials, he proceeded at once to carry out their instructions. Realizing that the obtaining of such a huge quantity of tallow was a matter of the greatest difficulty, he called together the subordinate clerks and ordered them to write to all possible sources of supply to send their entire available stocks to the firm of Fraenkel Brothers in Breslau. The clerks wrote as directed to all known dealers in tallow in all the countries of Europe.

The credit of the firm being excellent, their orders were complied with at once. Within a few days, long freight trains laden with tallow began rolling into Breslau, their cargoes consigned to the firm of Fraenkel Brothers, from all points of the compass, particularly from the countries of Central and Eastern Europe. At first the brothers were frightened and thought of taking steps to prevent the further inflow, but they speedily realized that they had involuntarily acquired possession of the entire supply of tallow in Europe. Without any effort or financial risk on their part, they had accomplished what is known in America as "cornering the market," usually a matter requiring strenuous effort and the investment of immense amounts of money. The natural results followed. The price of tallow rose. The Fraenkels disposed of their huge stocks at a handsome profit and became, so to speak "over night" enormously wealthy.

Just how large their fortune became I do not know. Judging by the extent of their philanthropic foundations, it must have been very great. One thing is certain, rarely or never has a great accumulation of capital in the hands of private individuals been devoted to better purposes. The names of the Fraenkel brothers will go down in history as those of wise and sympathetic benefactors of mankind, together with those of other great and benevolent philanthropists whose splendid contributions to human welfare have conferred undying glory on the Jewish people. Although, as stated, the Breslau Seminary was founded and endowed by the Fraenkel brothers, its income was not exclusively drawn from that source. It was an extremely popular institution and was the constant recipient of donations and subventions from Jewish organizations and individuals alike in Germany and the neighboring countries. It administered its funds not extravagantly but in what may be called a spirit of judicious liberality.

The members of the faculty were paid, according to the prevailing standards, handsome salaries. They occupied roomy and comfortable apartments in the Seminary building.* All students received stipends. The *Curatorium,* or board of governors, in the true spirit of Jewish ethics, insisted that all students, whether well-to-do or poor, should accept this stipendiary assistance. This was done in order not to humiliate those students who were in real need of financial aid. Instruction was, of course, entirely free. Nor were any nationalistic lines drawn. Youths from all countries, possessing the necessary qualifications for participation in the courses, were equally welcome. As a consequence, a large proportion, if not the majority, were not Germans but natives of the adjacent countries, mainly from Russia, Poland, Hungary, and the Balkan states. There was one American besides myself, Morris Jastrow,** son of Rabbi Dr. Marcus Jastrow of Philadelphia. Prizes, of substantial amounts of money, were given

---

* The Seminary building, a substantial though not pretentious structure, was situated in the Wallstrasse or Wall Street. This term afforded me some amusement at first on account of its similarity to the Wall Street of New York. Needless to say the Wall Street of Breslau bore no resemblance to its namesake in the metropolis of America.—B.D.

** Later famous as a Hebrew scholar, author of "The Gentle Cynic" and other classics of Hebraica.—Ed.

annually to students writing the best essays on themes from Biblical and rabbinical literature selected by the faculty.

Thus the spirit of the Seminary, alike from the scholastic and what may be called the administrative point of view, was most exemplary. It was also exemplary from the social point of view. The members of the faculty, and also occasionally curators and friends of the Seminary, made a point of inviting students to their homes and tables, particularly on Sabbaths and holidays. I was the guest, at one time or another, of all the members of the faculty, and was treated with the utmost courtesy and kindness by all of them.

The faculty, at the time of my entrance into the Seminary, consisted of five members, all of them among the most distinguished scholars in modern Jewish history. They were Jacob Freudenthal, Heinrich (or Hirsch) Graetz, Israel Lewy, David Rosin, and Baruch (or Benedict) Zuckermann. I have named them in alphabetical order because I do not know who was higher or lower in rank or whether there was any distinction of higher and lower. There was no head or chief of the Seminary, at least not of the teaching staff, although there may have been of the Curatorium.

When the Seminary was established, in 1854, Zachariah Frankel was appointed its head with the title of *Seminar Direktor*. Such was the respect for his profound scholarship and saintly character that when he died, in 1875, no one was deemed worthy of standing in his place and the title was abolished.

Israel Lewy was considered as actually, though not officially, his successor. His official title was *Seminar Rabbiner*, and his subject was the Talmud and everything connected therewith. To say that Lewy was a master of Talmudic lore is an understatement. It is difficult to find words with which to describe his phenomenal Talmudic erudition, his complete familiarity with the entire voluminous rabbinic literature, and the keenness and accuracy of his understanding of all its component parts, which are numerous and oftimes obscure. It was not easy to study under him. He demanded of his students a breadth of knowledge and a clarity of comprehension which, if not approximating his own, at least made their possessor worthy of his attention and instruction, and not all his students measured up to his requirements. He was quick-tempered and sharp-tongued with those inferior ones who could not readily grasp his abstruse interpretations. But his scholarly devotion was so sincere and his desire to share his intellectual wealth with his disciples so genuine that the severity of his methods was not resented.

It was undoubtedly due to his real interest in his students and his genuine desire that they should profit by his instruction. He was interested, too, in their personal welfare and showed it in various ways. I remember a striking instance of this. One Sabbath afternoon I was sitting in the Seminary synagogue. The afternoon prayer was over, and it was quite dark but still a little too early for the evening service. To fill out the interval I was reading a book, although it was decidedly too dark for easy or comfortable reading. Dr. Lewy was sitting in his place at the side of the ark, not far from where I was sitting. He noticed me reading but, because of the darkness, did not recognize me. "Who is sitting there reading in the dark and ruining his eyes?" he asked.

"It is I, Drachman, Herr Doctor," I answered.

"Drachman," he answered, "I am surprised. Be glad that you can do it, but don't do it." Dr. Lewy was short in stature, thin and pale, with an expressive countenance upon whose delicate lineaments scholarship and spirituality were inscribed. The general sentiment toward him was one of profound reverence.

Professor Dr. Heinrich (or Hirsch) Graetz presided over the department of Jewish history and also gave courses in Biblical exegesis and Talmud. His renown as a Jewish scholar, particularly as a historian, is so well established and universal, that it is unnecessary for me to enter into any description thereof. He is *"the"* Jewish historian *par excellence.* His monumental work *"Geschichte der Juden"* (History of the Jews) remains to this day the outstanding source of knowledge in that domain. It is easy to imagine, therefore, that his lectures on Jewish history were not only instructive but highly interesting. His exegetical instruction was also extremely interesting but for other reasons. In that field his Biblical interpretations and, particularly, his emendations of Biblical texts often aroused considerable opposition. His attitude toward Biblical criticism seemed to be in contradiction to his general religious views. He was a sturdy champion of Traditional Judaism and an uncompromising opponent of Reform

The Jewish Theological Seminary
No. 1b Wall Street, Breslau
(from *Geschichte des Jüdisch Theologischen
Seminars*) Dr. M. Brann, 1904

Bernard Drachman   *Bridal Couple*   Sarah Weil

(from charcoal portraits drawn about 1887)

innovations in the ritual practices of the Jewish faith but certainly no upholder of the authenticity of the Massoretic text of the Bible. How he reconciled this discrepancy in his views I do not know. Dr. Graetz was not only a member of the faculty of the Seminary. He held also the post of Professor of Biblical Exegesis in the University. Other Seminary students and I attended his University lectures also.

At the Seminary when Dr. Graetz read or quoted Biblical texts, he employed the *Ashkenazic* pronunciation of the Hebrew, the pronunciation customary among the Jews of Germany, with which he was familiar and in which he was perfectly fluent, but at the University he felt it his duty to use the *Sephardic* pronunciation, since that has been accepted as correct and is employed by the universities and other non-Jewish academies and theological schools. Since he was not accustomed to the Sephardic pronunciation, his tongue often tripped and he was guilty of queer mispronunciations and inconsistencies. However, that did not detract from the profound scholarship manifest in his interpretations, which were always thought-rousing and frequently gave occasion for animated discussions among the students.

David Rosin combined Jewish profundity of scholarship with typical German *gruendlichkeit*—thoroughness of knowledge and accuracy of method, and a sincere devotion to Judaism. He taught several subjects at the Seminary—Biblical Exegesis, Midrash, and Homiletics, and did them all very well. Despite his thorough German culture, Dr. Rosin was a great lover of the Hebrew language. He was the only one of the faculty, as far as I know, to publish a book in Hebrew. This was a commentary on the Pentateuch by Samuel ben Meir, one of the great Jewish scholars of the Middle Ages. Dr. Rosin edited it and provided it with an introduction and notes in excellent, almost classic, Hebrew. He was also the author of several valuable works in German.

Jacob Freudenthal, a distinguished philosopher and member of the Seminary faculty, also held the chair of philosophy at the University. He later resigned from the Seminary to devote himself exclusively to university work. He was the author of many important philosophical works, some on themes of Jewish, others of general philosophic importance. He was a *Cohen*, that is, of priestly descent, and I remember hearing him chant the priestly benediction on a holy day in the Seminary synagogue. His wife was a daughter of the renowned Berlin rabbi, Dr. Michael Sachs. Nevertheless my impression, perhaps a mistaken one, was that he was not greatly interested in Judaism. I read several of the medieval Hebrew philosophical works at the Seminary, among them the *Moreh Nebuchim* of Maimonides, the *Kuzari* of Judah Ha-Levi, and the *Emunoth Ve-Deoth* of Saadiah Gaon, but whether under the guidance of Professor Freudenthal or some of the other professors I do not now recall.

Baruch (or Benedict) Zuckermann was not perhaps one of the most important members of the faculty, but of his own subject he was a master. That subject was mathematics, particularly as represented in the Hebrew sources. With him I read the *Hilchoth Kiddush Ha-Chodesh,* the treatise of Maimonides on the Jewish calendar, and I was greatly impressed by his complete mastery of this very intricate subject. Although, as a native of Breslau, Zuckermann spoke and wrote a correct and excellent German, there was something about him of the old-fashioned Jew, reminiscent of the ghetto.

In religion he was strictly observant. He was the possessor of a private synagogue of his own, which was situated in a house which he had inherited from his father. Although he resided in the Seminary, in which there was a synagogue, he attended service daily, morning and evening, in his own place of worship, which his father had established. Zuckermann was also the librarian of the Seminary and was very helpful to the students in finding books needed by them in their studies. He was unmarried. The students would sometimes compare him to Ben Azai, the only unmarried rabbi mentioned in the Talmud, and who defended his celibacy by saying that he was married to the Torah. This comparison was certainly correct as applied to Zuckermann, for he was devoted to Judaism with all his heart and soul.

These were the men to whom I owed my preparation for the sacred calling of rabbi. None, I think, will dispute that my training could not have been entrusted to worthier and more competent teachers and guides. Not only did every one of them represent the best and most perfect in Jewish scholarship and intellectual ability but from practically all of them there emanated a wonderful spiritual influence, sincere love and devotion to the religious heritage of Israel. It was, for example, an experience to attend one of Dr. Lewy's Talmudic classes and, above all, a privilege and a revelation to hear one of his occasional brief discourses on themes of general Jewish import. To listen to him with open mind was to be thrilled with the grandeur and sublimity of Judaism.

Simultaneously with my studies at the Seminary I took several important courses at the University. I concentrated mainly on Semitic languages and philosophy, the two subjects most essential to the broadening and completing of my Seminary education. The Semitic tongues were important because they are sisters of the Hebrew and cast much light upon the significance of many Biblical terms. I needed to study philosophy because acquaintance with the views of the great thinkers of mankind is indispensable to the clarification and systemization of the doctrines of religion.

The Semitic studies I took under the guidance of Prof. Praetorius, an acknowledged master in that domain, particularly in the Arabic. Under his highly efficient instruction I read a considerable portion of the *Muallakat,* a famous collection of Arabic poetry, also selections from the *Koran*. I also took up the study of the Syriac and the Assyrian, these latter with a *Privatdocent* who was instructing in those subjects. These studies showed me clearly that while ancient Israel, of whom we modern Jews are the descendants, was one of the great family of Semitic nations, it was separated from them by a yawning chasm. It was "of them" but not "with them." Israel stood alone on a lofty eminence. A tremendous gulf of spiritual and ethical difference separated Israel from all the nations of antiquity, even from those to whom it was racially and linguistically akin. That lonely eminence was certainly not comfortable, but it was Israel's task and privilege to render to the world priceless services through the gift of the Bible.

I devoted even more serious effort to the study of philosophy than to that of the Semitic tongues. I was very anxious to know what solution philosophy has to offer of the eternal mysteries of the universe. Besides the ancient Greek philosophers, Plato and Aristotle, and the general history of philosophy, I read, under the guidance of the University professors and tutors, several of the outstanding works of modern philosophers, among them Spinoza and Kant. My general impression was one of disappointment. While I admired the profundity of thought and the brilliant concepts of these intellectual giants, I saw that their work was, after all, merely one of ratiocination and speculation, very much in the nature of guesswork. They had not found the solution of the eternal mysteries. The result of all this intellectual effort seemed to be expressed in the words of the Hebrew thinker Yedaiah Ha-Penini in his work *Bechinath Olam* (Contemplation of the Universe): "The highest height of knowledge to which we can attain is to know that we do not know."

The philosophic thought which appealed to me most, amidst the mass of theories and speculations, was that of Herbert Spencer, the distinction which he makes between the domains of the Knowable and the Unknowable. That impressed me immensely as a clear and accurate observation, definitely pointing out the limit of human knowledge, beyond which it cannot, of itself, go. Also it establishes the fact that beyond that limit there is a vast domain of truth and reality which, though closed to the ordinary perception of the intellect, may be revealed to it by some other source of communication and information. This established, in a logical and convincing manner, the relation between religion and science. Science has to do with the domain of the Knowable. There it reigns with sovereign authority and indisputable sway, and into that domain religion cannot enter to contradict or to antagonize. But in the domain of the Unknowable, of the supermundane and the spiritual, the authority of religion is equally supreme and incontestable. In that region, science, its gaze limited to material substances and forces, cannot set its foot.

This Spencerian doctrine came to me as a great comfort and satisfaction in the intellectual and spiritual struggles to which adolescent minds are liable and which were not spared me any more than other thinking youths. I found it an excellent basis for reconciling a frank and unhindered acceptance of scientific truth with sincere and loyal adherence to the religious heritage of Israel. This has been, broadly speaking, my concept of the relation between religion and science throughout my life.

Of course, I have merely given here a scanty outline of the general concept. My main purpose now is not to defend the correctness of my concept but to picture the kind of life I led during those precious three years in Breslau. It was a life of intellectual, spiritual, and esthetic exaltation and beauty, a life filled with the finest and noblest ideals and aspirations, a life eminently qualified to fit me to be a true and worthy representative of the sacred vocation to which I had dedicated myself.

Chapter Fourteen

Activities, Contacts, and Experiences in Breslau continued

I WAS DESIROUS OF TAKING ADVANTAGE OF MY STAY IN BRESLAU TO extend and broaden my general knowledge and culture as much as possible. I attended, therefore, many lecture courses at the University on subjects not at all related to those of my main studies, Judaica, Semitic languages, and philosophy. I took courses in the history of art and music, in literature and its great representatives in the various nations, particularly in Germany, in *Voelkerkunde,* that is, the study of racial characteristics and cultures. Then there were my studies in various branches of physical science, among them hygiene and its history. All this took a great deal of my time, so that I had very little leisure, but I felt that I was richly rewarded by the wealth of information and interesting points of view which poured into my mind. Of these courses the one which interested me most and is most vividly present in my memory was one of an apparently subordinate nature, a course of lectures on the History of Hygiene (*Geschichte der Hygiene*), by Professor Dr. Hirth. The reason for the exceptionally interesting character of these lectures was not so much the subject itself, although its intrinsic importance is, of course, unquestionable, but the personality of the lecturer.

Professor Dr. Hirth was indeed a rarely gifted and most interesting personage. To begin with his physical appearance, he was exceedingly good-looking, a characteristic not too frequent among Germans, especially among German professors. He was tall, with a spare, erect figure, an oval countenance with regular, finely molded features, wavy brown hair, and clear, expressive eyes, free from spectacles, also a rare characteristic among German professors. A pleasant, friendly smile lighted up his countenance most of the time and gave him a most engaging expression. His lectures were couched in a splendid literary German and illumined with not infrequent striking thoughts and flashes of humor, making them extremely attractive, even fascinating, also a rare characteristic of German professors.

In addition to his profound knowledge and his interesting manner of speaking, Professor Hirth had another quality which attracted great attention. He was extremely liberal in his views and utterly fearless in his expression of them. He spoke first of the contributions to hygiene of the ancient nations. In eloquent words he pictured what the Greeks and Romans had done to realize the ideal of *mens sana in corpore sano*—a sound mind in a sound body. He was especially eloquent in his praise of the ancient Hebrews. The Mosaic law, he declared, in its sanitary ordinances was equal, if not superior, to the most advanced hygienic practices of modern times. He described these ordinances in detail, ascribing to all of them high hygienic value, circumcision, the separation of the sexes during the period of menstruation, the segregation or quarantining of lepers and other persons with loathsome diseases, the dietary laws prohibiting the eating of the flesh of the swine and of certain other animals, birds, and fish, and of blood. He approved enthusiastically the institution of the Jewish Sabbath and holy days which gave men recurrent periods of rest and freedom from the pernicious effects of constant, unceasing drudgery.

When Professor Hirth spoke of the conditions prevailing after the rise of Christianity, especially during the Middle Ages, his handsome countenance assumed a somewhat quizzical expression. "If I am to speak of the hygienic conditions prevailing during this period," he said, "I hardly know what to say. Christianity ruled without limitation (*unbeschraenkt*) during this period on the entire European continent and controlled the thoughts and the lives of men. Christianity claims that it is not interested in the things of this world, that it concerns itself only with the hereafter. That must indeed be the case, for one thing is certain: during the entire Middle Ages the most elementary laws of hygiene were so frightfully transgressed that insulted nature could no longer endure it and tore human beings in millions by devastating plagues from the surface of the earth." The concluding sentences of Professor Hirth's address made such a profound impression upon me that their exact wording has remained indelibly stamped upon the tablets of my memory. That a Gentile professor, presumably a Christian, could speak in this manner of the dominant faith of the land filled me with amazement. It certainly showed that liberty of speech existed in the Germany of that time. In Nazi Germany such remarks would not be tolerated, not on account of the attack on Christianity, but because of the sympathetic and appreciative utterances concerning Judaism.

I had only been about a month in Breslau when the Kroliks, whose acquaintance I had made on the steamer crossing the Atlantic, celebrated the marriage of the daughter. They had not forgotten me. In accordance with their promise, I was invited to the wedding. I went gladly and had not only a royal but also a most instructive time. I was able to observe the manner in which such religio-social events were celebrated in the upper circles of religious German Jewry, and the sight was both pleasing and impressive. The ceremony was conducted in strict accordance with the traditional Jewish ritual and was beautifully rendered. The rabbi delivered an excellent wedding address in German and the cantor intoned the Hebrew ritual most melodiously. At the table a Lucullian feast was served. The Krolik family resided in Bernstadt, a small town not far from Breslau, but the wedding took place in Breslau as a more central spot for the gathering of relatives and friends. They observed also the traditional Jewish custom of the "Seven Days of Rejoicing" and, in accordance therewith, there was feasting and rejoicing for the entire week of the marriage.

Among the most precious memories of my life are those of the delightful hours which I was privileged to spend in the company of Breslau friends. Association with exalted personalities whose keen intellectuality and wit combined with artistic and musical talent and unfailing courtesy and good humor served to make my every moment a delight. I do not know whether it was any personal merit on my part or the fact that I was an American that secured me this social recognition and acceptance. I am inclined to think it was the latter circumstance, since the name of America stood in high honor in Germany in those days and to be an American almost constituted in itself a ticket of introduction to the best German society.* My friends were drawn mainly from the element of the Jewish community which combined high culture with devotion to Judaism, a circumstance which made their friendship doubly agreeable and beneficial to me.

First and foremost among these friends were Rabbi Dr. Manuel Joel and his family. Dr. Joel was looked upon with utmost respect and veneration by the Breslau population, Jewish and Gentile alike. He certainly deserved the high esteem in which he was held, for his was a rare personality in every regard, intellectual, spiritual, and ethical. He was the rabbi of the *Neue Synagoge,* the main synagogue of Breslau, whose beautiful structure was situated in a choice section of the city, opposite the portion of the promenade and the moat known as the *Schweidnitzer Stadtgraben.* His position as rabbi he filled with ability and distinction. His sermons were renowned not only for their eloquence but also for their profundity and originality of thought and attracted great congregations on Sabbaths and holy days.

His homiletic ability was only one side of Dr. Joel's attainments. He was one of the outstanding Jewish scholars of the nineteenth century, especially in the field of philosophy. In this domain, he was the author of many highly important works, in which he convincingly demonstrated the influence of Jewish thinkers on the thought of the world. He was a man of scholarly and venerable appearance, with gray hair and beard, although at this time not yet sixty years of age. His family consisted of his wife, a refined, quiet lady, and several sons and daughters. The most prominent of the children was *Herr Referendar* Joel, whose given name, if I recall correctly, was Moritz. *Referendar* is a legal title indicating that its bearer practices some branch of law or occupies some legal position, the exact nature of which I do not know, but which, I understand, carries no emolument.

---

* A number of circumstances showed the popularity of America and Americans in the Germany of that period. One such circumstance was the fact that American dentistry was considered far superior to the German, and American dentists, of whom a number were established in Germany, were patronized in preference to the natives in that profession. German dentists, in order to compete with Americans, were obliged to claim that they had learned their art in America. The sign "*In Amerika approbiter Zahnarzt*" (dentist licensed in America) appeared in many places on Breslau streets. The Breslauers attributed the superior skill of American dentists to the bad teeth of the American population, due to excessive eating of candy, the treatment of which gave American dentists an unrivalled opportunity to acquire skill.—B.D.

However, the subject never came up in our conversation, and young Referendar Joel was invariably in high spirits and the best of humor, so, whatever the financial arrangements may have been, they evidently did not militate against his comfort and well-being. In this lovely and unusually cultured family I was more than merely an honored guest, I was almost a member of the family circle. Referendar Joel and I were especially close. We met on many occasions and went together on strolls and longer excursions.

Dr. Benno Badt was another of my greatly esteemed friends. He was in his middle forties, a handsome and slightly corpulent gentleman with regular features and a full black beard. He had studied as rabbi at the Jewish Theological Seminary but had not taken up the vocation and was at this time a highly esteemed member of the teaching staff of one of the Breslau *Gymnasiums*. Although he had given up the rabbinate, Dr. Badt had by no means given up Judaism but was a sincere and loyal Jew. His keen intellect and bright wit made Dr. Badt a most agreeable companion.

There were two cultured and interesting young ladies whose friendship I was privileged to enjoy, Fraulein Martha Gutmann and Fraulein Mathilda Roth. Fraulein Gutmann delivered lectures on literature which were very popular. She later became the wife of Dr. Badt, and they were certainly ideally fitted for each other. Fraulein Roth married the world-renowned scholar, Dr. Solomon Schechter, afterward head of the Jewish Theological Seminary of America. Thus she became a resident of New York. She was indeed well known and highly esteemed throughout the length and breadth of the American continent.

I had other friends as well, even relatives in Breslau, so that I certainly did not suffer from lack of social intercourse. I sometimes wonder how I managed to combine this social life with the demands of my studious activity, which, as already stated, were highly strenuous, but I did so although the exertion required was far from small.

There was also a wonderful social or social-literary life among the students of the Seminary. This was carried on mainly through a students' society which bore the Latin name of *Amicitia*, or Friendship. This society was modeled on the great student organizations of the German universities but modified to suit Jewish conditions. It met on

Thursday evenings, when the proceedings, so I was informed, were an almost exact replica of those in the regular university student *verbindungen*. There was the same student lingo, the same singing of student songs, the same drinking of beer and beer duels, and the same spirit of youthful merriment and hilarity. In several ways *Amicitia* differed from the *Verbindungen*. Its members did not wear uniforms, did not promenade the streets leading—I had almost said in the company of—huge dogs, and they did not fight duels, and were consequently not distinguished by proudly borne *Schmisse,* or scarred countenances. But as regards the manner of conducting the meetings there was almost exact similarity.

I enjoyed these meetings immensely. The spirit was carefree and jovial, the singing excellent, and the entire proceedings so novel that I found them intensely interesting. But one evening I, unintentionally and unwittingly, created a scandal and an uproar which almost resulted in my expulsion. I did not feel like drinking beer that evening and ordered the waiter to bring me a cup of tea. The waiter looked at me with a puzzled expression but said nothing and in a few moments brought me the desired beverage.

Pandemonium at once broke loose. Unknowingly I had committed the greatest violation of the law of the *Verbindungen*. According to that law the foamy Gambrinian liquor is the sacred drink of the student world. Wine and brandy may be tolerated, but such utterly Philistine drinks as coffee or tea—*Philistine* is the German student term for the non-student world—*never!* Consequently I had shocked the sensibilities of my *commilitonen,* or fellow-students, in a most heinous manner, as they had never been shocked before. As soon as I realized the enormity of my offense, I apologize for my misconduct and strove to convince the members of the society that I had meant no offense and that my violation of the student code was entirely unintentional and due exclusively to my ignorance. At first my apology met with a very cold reception, but finally I received a grudging pardon, solely on the ground that, as an American, my plea of ignorance of the requirements of the student code might be accepted as an excuse for an otherwise unpardonable offense. Had the offense been committed by a German, no conceivable excuse would have availed to save him from swift and summary expulsion.

I attended many meetings of Amicitia after this, but was very careful never again to give any cause for criticism. I remember particularly one Purim celebration at which, in accordance with the nature of the festival, several exquisitely humorous compositions were read. Among these was one of good-natured persiflage, satirizing the strictly conscientious religious observance of *Seminar Rabbiner* Dr. Lewy, which threw the audience into paroxysms of laughter.

In the autumn semester of the year of my entrance into the Seminary the faculty posted a notice on the bulletin board in the hall, announcing the subject of the prize essay of that year. It was on the theme *"Die Stellung und Bedeutung des Jehuda Chajjug in der Geschichte der Hebraischen Grammatik"* (The Place and Importance of Judah Hayug in the History of Hebrew Grammar). Competition was open to all students and the prize was the amount of one hundred and fifty marks. The subject, a presentation of the contribution to grammatical science of the famed Hebrew grammarian of North Africa, the founder of modern Hebrew grammar through his discovery of the system of triliteral roots in Hebrew, interested me greatly. It was a theme requiring considerable research and close study, not only of the works of Hayug but also of the antecedent and contemporary sources from which an understanding of the state of Hebrew grammatical knowledge in that period could be gained. These sources were partly in medieval Hebrew and partly in Arabic, often very difficult.

I decided to enter the competition, not primarily for the sake of becoming the winner, which appeared to me a dubious and improbable result, but in order to try my hand at this kind of research and, too, with the idea of ultimately using the treatise as my dissertation when I should apply at some university for the degree of Ph.D.

I set to work very assiduously on the required study and research and in due course finished the essay and sent it to the secretary of the faculty. A few weeks later I was most agreeably surprised to be officially informed that my essay had been adjudged the best of those submitted to the faculty and had been awarded the prize. A check for one hundred fifty marks accompanied the communication. No statement was made of the number of essays that had been submitted nor of the names of their writers.

My success was greeted with general applause, and I was the

recipient of many congratulations and congratulatory messages from fellow-students, members of the faculty, and other friends. But there was one discordant note and that, strange to say, came from my fellow-American, Morris Jastrow of Philadelphia. Jastrow had also submitted an essay—a fact, by the way, which would never have become known had he not announced it. He seemed to resent my success. He made statements condemning me for undue haste in entering upon such a competition and asserting that I should have waited a year or two before doing so. Of course, I ignored his statements and they were without influence, as far as I know, on the sentiment toward me. I celebrated my success by a pleasant little dinner to seven or eight of my closest associates at Sachs', a well known and much esteemed kosher restaurant in Breslau, and by making all the members of Amicitia my guests at one of their regular Thursday evening meetings.

In the early summer of the second year of my stay in Germany I received a letter from my classmate at Columbia University, James Buchanan Nies. He informed me that he was on a tour of Europe and was, at that time, in Berlin and would very much like to meet me but that he was unable to travel further east and would appreciate it if I would meet him in Berlin to spend a few days together. I complied with alacrity.

"Jimmie" Nies was my best and most intimate friend among all my classmates at Columbia. I was delighted at the prospect of again being in his company. The semester at the Seminary was not yet concluded, but I had no difficulty in securing the necessary leave of absence. Next day I departed for Berlin, which is only a few hours distant by rail from Breslau.

Our meeting was truly cordial. We were genuinely glad to see each other, not only because of our personal friendship but because, as I have frequently noticed, there is something in Americanism which draws citizens of the great republic of the West, when they chance to meet in foreign countries, together in friendly recognition and association. Such was certainly the case with Nies and me. We felt emphatically that we were Americans, despite the fact that we were both connected with Germany by ancestry and descent and had living relatives in that land. That circumstance did not lessen our Americanism one whit. We were decidedly not "German-Americans" and were as much opposed to the concept of "hyphenated Americanism" as Theodore Roosevelt later was, although the term, naturally, did not exist. Neither did our Americanism lessen in the slightest our love and affection for our kin who still owed allegiance to foreign governments. This latter fact may seem to some illogical and self-contradictory, but it is true.

Nies was staying with relatives of his in Berlin. He had given me their address, and immediately upon my arrival in the city I repaired thither, after having taken quarters in a hotel. I found the family all at home, assembled in the *"gute Stube"* ("good room" or parlor) with Nies in their midst. The reception accorded to me, not only by Nies but by his relatives also, was most cordial. I passed a few pleasant hours in the company of my old chum and his kindly relatives and then left with the understanding that Nies and I would meet on the following morning for a sight-seeing tour of the city. Promptly after breakfast of the next day we met and started on our tour. I acted as guide for, although it was my first visit to the capital of the German empire, I was tolerably familiar, through reading and description, with the important buildings, parks and other sights of Berlin, while to Nies it was all quite new and strange. We devoted two days to our sight-seeing expedition, during which time we visited or saw most of the world-renowned edifices and places of the German capital. They were the royal palace, the great park of the *Tiergarten,* and the magnificent arch which stands at its entrance, the beautiful avenue and promenade of the *Unter den Linden Strasse,* the *Siegesallee* with its wonderful historical statues, the luxurious Hotel Adlon and many other noteworthy sights, including the splendid synagogue of the *Israelitische Kultus Gemeinde.* These are, of course, the well known sights of Berlin, seen by all or most tourists who visit the city, and need not be described here in detail.

But two incidents of our tour were of an unusual nature. They stand out vividly in my memory and merit being narrated. Among the places we visited during the first morning of our sight-seeing was Kastan's *Panoptikon.* This was a sort of museum, something like the Eden Musee in New York, which the older generation of Gothamites will remember and in which a great number of objects and persons, that were deemed curious and interesting, were exhibited. One of these particularly riveted our attention. On a platform in the center of the hall stood a large group, twenty or more, I should judge, of South Sea Islanders. They were the most extraordinary human beings I have ever seen. Their skin color was intensely black. Coal black or jet black seem hardly adequate terms with which to describe it. They had huge bushy masses of hair on their heads, massive earrings hung from their ears, and nose bars penetrated the cartilage of their nostrils, and they were almost entirely nude, with only abbreviated loincloths to cover their nakedness. They were of all ages and both sexes, and the expression of their faces varied from dull stolidity and indifference to apparently fierce resentment, like the look in the eyes of a caged tiger. Truly a weird group of representatives of the noble *Genus Homo!*

Nies and I gazed at them for several minutes in awed silence. Then Nies burst forth with a comment natural to a New York youth. "Gee, but that's a tough looking bunch," he said, looking at me.

"They certainly do look pretty bad," I answered. Neither of us, of course, imagined in the slightest that any of that group of savage and primitive beings would understood what we had said. To our intense and shocked surprise a young woman of the group, just as black, just as bushy-haired, and just as lightly clad as the others, but on whose dusky features and in whose shining eyes there hovered an expression of intelligence and good humor, who was standing at the front edge of the platform, spoke out. "You must excuse us, gentlemen," she said, in perfect and melodious English. "We don't always look as bad as this. We're doing this for business." We could hardly believe our ears, hearing such a rebuke proceeding from such a quarter. I stammered an apology, which the dark young lady received with a smile, exposing a flawless set of dazzlingly white teeth, and a regal bow of her bushy head, and we departed in considerable confusion and embarrassment.

That was one of the most thorough and lasting lessons I have ever received. It was a radical cure for any racial prejudice I may have entertained and removed completely the conceited belief, which I had shared with others whose skin happens to be white, in the inborn superiority of the Caucasian race to all other varieties of humanity.

I realized that under the skin we are all alike, that the variations of complexion and physical characteristics of human beings are only external but that intellectually and emotionally they are fundamenttally identical, and that differences of culture and ability in the arts of civilization are the result of differing environment and education, not of essential racial differences. Since then I have had abundant opportunities to recognize that the view impressed upon me by this little incident in Berlin is irrefutably true. Among the American Negroes, descendants of the primitive Africans dragged from their native lands to be slaves in America, men and women have arisen as highly gifted as any born of the most cultured Caucasian peoples, eloquent orators, golden-throated singers, able physicians and scientists, and many skilled in all the arts and trades of civilization. The same observation applies to all the other colored races, Chinese, Japanese, Hindus, and others. Formerly regarded with tolerant condescension as at best "semi-civilized," the world has now come to realize that they are in no essential respect inferior to Caucasians and that it is not at all impossible that the hegemony of the world may yet rest in their hands. The theory of the *"Herrenvolk,"* the "master race empowered and authorized by nature or nature's God to dominate over the rest of mankind, which the Nazis, accursed brood of misleaders and corrupters of German national ideals, undertook to establish and maintain impregnably and invincibly, is completely bankrupt. The very war, with which the Nazis hoped to rivet it irremovably upon the neck of mankind, has proved its undoing. The moment they, the Nazis, were obliged to seek the aid of Japan, a race as different from the German Nordics as any race can conceivably be, the Nazi theory of racial superiority suffered irretrievable shipwreck.*

For lunch, or rather noon dinner, we went to a kosher restaurant. Nies hesitated, but upon my insistence, he soon gave in, good-humor-

---

* This criticism of the concept of a "master race" must not be taken as applying to the Biblical doctrine of Israel as the chosen people of God. Israel was chosen, not to dominate but to serve the rest of mankind, to exemplify in its life and conduct the ideals of ethical purity and spiritual exaltation which it was the Divine plan that all mankind should attain. Indeed, the scorn and contempt with which the spokesmen of Nazism refer to the Biblical precepts of mercy and compassion and love for all men as brothers as *"Judische Schwachen,"* "Jewish weaknesses," is the best proof of the irreconcilable difference between the two concepts.—B.D.

edly muttering, "What wouldn't a man do for a friend?" As it happened the *Restauration* Kassel, one of the best in Berlin, was a splendidly appointed establishment, and both the dinner and the service were excellent. He enjoyed it thoroughly, and I had the additional satisfaction of seeing that he was pleased. He, too, learned something that day about how other people live.

We spent the rest of the two days in strenuous sightseeing. Nies was a delightful companion, and I loved him more than ever. I am sure that he reciprocated the sentiment. At the end of our tour we separated, after an affectionate farewell, and I returned to Breslau.

Chapter Fifteen

A Rural Wedding

A Visit to Frankfort on the Main

SHORTLY AFTER MY RETURN TO BRESLAU THE SEMINARY CLOSED FOR the summer vacation. A few days later I went to Nordheim to pass the greater part of the vacation with my dear relatives in my mother's native village. Our pleasure at meeting was mutual. I was received with open arms by my good and loving kinsfolk. A family event of the highest importance was about to take place. Jeannette, the oldest daughter, was to be married to Herr Freudenthal of Tann-an-der-Rhoen. I came just in time to be a guest at the wedding, which was celebrated in Tann.

The entire Stein family, together with some other Nordheim relatives and friends and myself, went there in three or four carriages. We were quite a cavalcade and attracted considerable attention on the part of the peasants and their wives and children in the villages through which we passed. The bride and her family were the recipients of many cordial felicitations launched at them from the roadside. The trip over the mountains was most interesting and—so it seemed to me—even somewhat adventurous. The Rhoen mountains are not classed among the great mountain ranges of the world, but they are of considerable height, several thousand feet, at least, and much of the scenery is wild and awesome. Occasionally the road skirted precipitous declivities, the prospect of a fall down which did not arouse comfortable thoughts. The upper reaches of the mountains were quite bleak and barren, but everywhere there were, at short intervals, small peasant villages, the inhabitants of which strove, with untiring effort, to wrest a living from the unresponsive soil. To me it seemed a terrific struggle for a meager livelihood, but Cousin Solomon assured me that the peasants of the Upper *Rhoenbirge* were cheerful, good-humored people and seemed quite contented with their lot.

In Tann the whole town was agog about the wedding, Jews and Gentiles alike. The ceremony took place in the Freudenthal home, which was large and commodious and beautifully furnished. Before the ceremony I listened to a discussion led by the grandfather of the groom. He was an aged man, long since retired from active business, who devoted his remaining years to the doing of *mitzvoth*—deeds pleasing in the sight of God. His particular hobby was the taking care of *schnorrers*, the poor strangers of Jewish faith who were accustomed to come to the towns and villages of Germany seeking the aid of their co-religionists. These he would look after with the utmost zeal and devotion. There was a vigorous contest—the householders comparing the number of *schnorrers* each had cared for during the year. Uncle Koppel had, I believe, cared for twelve non-paying and uninvited guests, others had been hosts to five or six or seven, and one man stated that fifteen had sojourned under his roof. Old Herr Freudenthal then said triumphantly that the number of wandering brethren who had enjoyed his hospitality during the past twelve months was forty-eight and that his main regret was that two more had not come so as to make it a round fifty. Certainly an illuminating sort of competition—would that there were more of it!

The wedding was a fine and most enjoyable affair, conducted in accordance with traditional Jewish ritual and concluded with a splendid feast.

The rest of my summer vacation I passed mostly in the company of Solomon. We were inseparable companions. We made a trip together which took us away from the village for about two weeks, in the course of which we visited a number of interesting places, notably the two cities of Wuerzburg and Frankfort-on-the-Main. In the latter place we not only saw a beautiful city but also a most wonderful Jewish community, the like of which was even then difficult to find anywhere else in the world. In size the city was not so very impressive, numbering not more than approximately twenty-five thousand souls, but in spiritual and cultural quality and importance to Judaism it was most exceptional and noteworthy. Frankfort-on-the-Main was the city of Rabbi Samson Raphael Hirsch, inspired and inspiring leader in Israel, man of God if ever there was one. His soul glowed with profound love and loyalty to the ancient faith. From his lips poured streams of eloquence to convince the doubting, to strengthen the wavering, and to satisfy and delight the already convincedly devout. The impress of his mighty spirit was upon the whole Jewish life of the queenly city. The number of business establishments closed on Sabbaths and Jewish holy days, the large and beautiful synagogues and the throngs which entered them to worship, even on ordinary days of secular occupation, and a dozen other indications, all gave unmistakable testimony to the fact that here was a city of enthusiastically loyal Jews. The Orthodox Jews, however, were not the majority of the Jewry of Frankfort. Rabbi Hirsch's congregation did not even belong to the official Jewish community. Legally and technically it was not even a congregation but only a private society, *Israelitische Religionsgesellschaft*, "Israelitish Society for Religion," but in numbers it was not greatly inferior to the main community and in zeal and religious fervor it was so superior, that its impress upon the life of the city was far greater and more significant.

The Judaism which Rabbi Hirsch taught, and for which he had gained thousands of adherents, in Frankfort and out, while unswervingly loyal to the Law and the traditions of Israel's past, was yet something different, something new. It was the religion of the ghetto without the mannerisms or the world-estrangement of the ghetto. It was indeed a wondrously perfect synthesis of the ancient and the modern, of the Oriental-Sinaitic-Talmudic precepts of faith and the life and the speech, the culture, and the demeanor of the modern time and the Occidental world. It was fittingly designated by understanding observers as *Neo-Orthodoxy*.

Solomon and I met a number of members of the Hirsch community and they all measured up to this standard. Among them were the brothers Jacob and Julius Strauss, who were relatives of Solomon, cousins of his mother, whose maiden name was Strauss. They were wealthy people, bankers doing business in a large way under the firm name of J. and J. Strauss. They were, however, more interested in Jewish religion and culture than in their business affairs.

As their guests on Friday evening, we met in the synagogue, which was filled with devout worshippers. After service we walked together to the Strauss residence, a fine and beautifully furnished apartment in one of the best streets of Frankfort. It was a memorable evening, a remarkable combination of fervent Jewishness and aristocratic demeanor, a perfect illustration of what the rabbis of the Talmud meant when they spoke of "Torah and greatness in one place." Everything was in accordance with the rabbinical precept that the best which the Jew is and has shall be reserved for the Sabbath. Such was the Friday evening in the Strauss home. Herr Jacob Strauss chanted the Hebrew prayers with dignity and reverence, and Frau Strauss was a most gracious hostess. After the sumptuous repast was concluded, and thanks duly given to the Giver of all good, we passed an hour or so in pleasant, informal conversation. Many questions about America were asked of me, and my answers were received with great apparent interest.

In connection therewith Herr Julius Strauss made a remark which showed that he was both a confirmed old bachelor "set in his ways" and a confirmed Frankfort citizen. I had asked him whether he would not like to visit America some time, to which he answered with a curt "No." Thereupon I said to him wonderingly, "Why not?" His reply was somewhat surprising but clearly indicative of his point of view. "Why shall I seek that which is good in the distance when that which is good is so near?" (*Warum das Gute in der Ferne suchen wenn das Gute liegt so nahe.*) "I never travel. It cannot be more beautiful anywhere than it is in Frankfort. Why should I tire myself out, rattling around in trains and on steamboats, when I have all the beauty anyone could want to see right here at home." To that course of reasoning no answer was possible, so I discreetly refrained from attempting to give one. After all, love of one's native place is a good quality.

The Midrash narrates that Rabbi Judah, the Prince, noticed one day that a favorite pupil of his, usually very bright and intelligent, seemed dull and unable to follow the instruction. He asked him what was the trouble. The youth answered, "I am homesick for my native town." "Is it such a beautiful place?" asked the rabbi. "No, it is not," answered the pupil. "It is very hot and there are many dangerous insects, so that when a child is born they smear its head with pitch, lest the insects sting and slay it. But still I love it." Whereupon Rabbi Judah blessed the Lord, saying, "Blessed be He who has put the love of a place in the hearts of its inhabitants." When one is a resident of so beautiful a city as Frankfort-on-the-Main, one may be excused for loving it and being a little conceited concerning it.

Solomon and I visited other relatives of ours during the course of our stay in Frankfort—Herr and Frau Friedrich Stein, whose home was not in Frankfort itself but in Sachsenhausen, an adjacent municipality or surburb. Unfortunately Herr Stein was not at home, being away on a business trip, but Frau Stein was and she received us most affably. She justified Solomon's enthusiastic description, for she was a real lady. She knew Solomon very well but, of course, did not know me. Thereupon Solomon introduced me as a cousin from America. During the course of our conversation Frau Stein kept gazing at me, courteously but wonderingly, as though there was something about me which puzzled her. Finally she asked me, "How long have you been in America?" I understood that she was not sure whether I was an American born or a German relative who had emigrated to America and was now on a visit to his native land. I answered her question, with a little waggish notion in my mind, just as she had asked it, "Twenty-one years." This answer added to her puzzlement—it was in such contradiction to my manifest youth. Suddenly the light of comprehension shone in her countenance. "Ah, then you are *born* in America!" "Yes," I said, and we all three laughed. We remained a little longer in conversation and, after the inevitable *Aufwartung*—refreshments served to guests in German homes and which it is a mortal offense to refuse—had been served, Solomon and I departed with the customary ceremonious *adieus* and *auf Wiedersehens*.

I must remark here that Frau Stein's question to me is a little puzzling to me even at this late date. As a rule I was never able to conceal my American nationality in Germany, even had I wished to, which was not the case.

Solomon and I attended a session of a study circle of some fourteen or fifteen lay members belonging to the Hirsch congregation. They were all dignified gentlemen and excellent Hebrew and Talmudic scholars, although none was a professional rabbi. I was deeply impressed and filled with admiration at the sight of a group of laymen so imbued with the love of Biblical and rabbinical lore as to devote a great part of their time to its study. I recognized that their motive was religious, rather than scholarly, and that with them, in accordance with the true Jewish concept, study of the Holy Law was really a form of worship and not merely a means of greater acquisition of knowledge. The leader, Herr Schwartzschild, was sightless but was conducting the exercises, which consisted of the translation of the *Haftarah,* or prophetic reading of the Sabbath of that week, accompanied by a running commentary. He quoted the entire Hebrew text without a single error, entirely by memory. After concluding our stay in Frankfort a few days later, Solomon and I returned to Nordheim.

Chapter Sixteen

A Trip in Galicia

NORDHEIM WAS AS PLEASANT AND RUSTICALLY ATTRACTIVE AND MY folks as friendly and hospitable as ever when Solomon and I returned from our visit to Frankfort. Nevertheless I remained there only a few days. After an affectionate farewell from my dear relatives, I left for Breslau. I had decided after a brief stay in that city to utilize the remaining weeks of my vacation to carry out a plan which I had long entertained, to visit my father's native land, Galicia, and my relatives on my father's side, who resided in the town of Brody, not far from the Russian frontier.

Accordingly, after a few days in Breslau devoted to necessary preparations for the trip, I boarded a train bound for the former Polish province of Galicia, then a province of the Austro-Hungarian Empire.

Although Galicia was directly adjacent to the German border, it was looked upon in Germany as a remote and forsaken region, not without risks and difficulties. I had been warned in Breslau that I must be prepared as well for the onslaughts of innumerable poor people who abounded there and who looked upon every visiting stranger as their legitimate prey from whom to demand charitable aid and assistance. I, therefore, made ready to meet every contingency by purchasing a return ticket to Breslau and by following Othello's advice to Iago, "Put money in thy purse, Iago, put money in thy purse." Later events showed that my precautions were indeed wise and essential.

A Trip to Galicia

All the while that the train traversed German soil the landscape presented the customary picture of neatness and order. There were the smiling, well cultivated fields, straight, smooth roads, clean, strongly constructed houses, and systematically laid-out towns and villages. It must be confessed, however, that in the section of Upper Silesia, *Oberschlesien*, the picture was far less cheerful. That was evidently a mining section, for it presented the appearance characteristic of such sections. The houses were grimier and the people shabbier and more proletarian in type than in other parts of Germany. The fundamental neatness and order of Germany still, however, prevailed.

As soon as we passed the Galician border—I think it was at the station of Oswiecim*—a great, indeed a startling change became evident. We seemed to have come to a totally different part of the world, to a country removed by hundreds of miles of distance, and hundreds of years of development from the beauty and exalted culture of the German land. The whole landscape had an aspect of wildness and primitiveness. The roads were rough and irregular as though recently hewn from the wilderness. The towns and villages were formless accumulations of frowsy and mosty small, neglected-looking buildings. On the roads and around the towns, roughly clad men on foot or driving rude vehicles, drawn by shaggy, unkempt horses, were visible. All this was startling enough to my eyes just come from the scrupulous cleanliness and faultless neatness and order of Germany, but there was also a sight which was even more startling to my vision as a Jew.

Among the people walking or riding on the roads, or standing around the towns and villages, I noticed a considerable number of persons of different appearance whom I at once recognized as coreligionists. They were Jews of a type such as I had never seen before. Men and boys, even very young boys, wore long robes reaching to their feet. On their heads they had peculiarly shaped low round hats edged with fur or high cylinders or "stovepipes." Long curls depended from their temples, in some cases reaching to their chins, or lower. The men wore full beards, the older men very long beards. Since

---

* A place later destined to immortal infamy, as the site of an "extermination camp." —Ed.

their entire costume was usually black, the result was to make them very conspicuous.

I learned afterwards that the robes were known as *jubitza* or *beckeshe* and the low hats as *streimel*. In their homes the men and boys wore small caps, known as *kapelusz* or *yarmulka*. These terms, or most of them, are, I presume, drawn from the Polish tongue but have become integral parts of the Yiddish or Jewish-German dialect spoken by the Jews of Eastern Europe. The dress of the women did not differ noticeably from that of the Polish women, but the married Jewesses wore a sort of wig or toupee, known as a *sheitel*. This was to comply with the Talmudic ordinance that married women should cover their tresses and not expose their hair to public view.

The sight of these brethren made a deep impression upon me. I saw that Judaism had survived in these regions with a strength and naturalness which it did not possess in the lands of the Western world. I had met many Orthodox Jews in Germany and some even in America, but the strictest and most observant of them were not Jewish in the sense in which these Jews of Galicia were. Everywhere in the Occident there was an effort to lessen the distinctiveness of the Jew, to minimize the external differences between Jew and Gentile, to reduce Judaism to a mere matter of religious belief, and the observance of a few ceremonies hardly perceptible in the general life of the community. As for the non-Orthodox Jews—and they were everywhere, or almost everywhere, in the Occident in the great majority—assimilation and the elimination of specific Jewish characteristics had gone so far that they were hardly more than Jews in name only.

But here was a large Jewish group, numerous enough to be considered a population, almost a million out of a total population of approximately seven million, who not only made no attempt at assimilation but even stressed and emphasized their Jewish distinctiveness to an unbelievable degree. The Jews of Galicia—and the remark applies generally to the whole of Eastern Europe—were absolutely frank and open in the complete preservation and maintenance of their Jewishness. They differed from their non-Jewish neighbors in dress, in speech, in religion, and in culture. Although religious to the fullest degree, they were not merely a sect or religious group. They were certainly entitled to be considered a national minority, for they possessed all the characteristics of nationality except the possession of a land and government of their own. All this I perceived and felt even in my first, necessarily superficial, observation.

Another thought also came to me with striking emphasis. It was that Poland was entitled to recognition as a most liberal and tolerant nation, that the Polish kings, in particular, who opened the gates of their land to the Jewish refugees fleeing from unendurable persecution in medieval Germany and Western Europe, deserved the sincere gratitude of the Jewish people for their humane and ungrudging treatment of the Jews, so different from the usual policies of the European nations in the Middle Ages. Despite occasional shadows, the picture of Jewish life in Poland had been a bright one. Israel dwelt there in security and enjoyed the full and undisturbed right to live its own life in accordance with its religious and cultural traditions. No attempt was made and no desire apparently existed, on the part of the Polish nation and government, to force assimilation or the acceptance of the Polish culture upon the Jewish population. To this extraordinary and most praiseworthy liberality alone can the development of the numerous and most genuinely Jewish community of Poland, and, secondarily, of the other countries of Eastern Europe, be attributed. It certainly was in refreshing contrast to the ruthless policy of suppressions, persecutions, expulsions, and massacres which prevaied in the other countries of medieval Europe. The Jewish gratitude for this kind and humane treatment was expressed in a rabbinical interpretation of the name of Poland. It was homiletically explained as corresponding in significance to the Hebrew words *Poh Lan,* "There it lodges," that is, there Israel shall lodge during the long, dark night of the Exile until Messiah will redeem them and bring them to the Promised Land.

The first place at which I interrupted my journey and made a sightseeing stop for a few days was Cracow. I found it a most interesting city. Both Polish and Jewish life flourished there most vigorously. The signs in the Polish language in front of business establishments and other edifices were in the majority. A goodly proportion of them was in Hebrew or written with Hebrew letters. The government of the city was in the hands of the Poles.* Of this I had convincing proof

---

* Not, as one might suppose, of the *Austrian* ruling class.—Ed.

immediately after my arrival, for on the very next morning after I had taken quarters in a Jewish hotel I was summoned to the police. The zealous guardians of the city evidently thought that anyone visiting Galicia must have some sinister purpose in mind, for they wanted to know everything about me and what my object was in coming to their province. I had considerable difficulty to convince the police officials who examined me that I was an American of Jewish faith and a student at the Jewish seminary in Breslau. My reason for visiting Galicia, I explained, was partly that of a tourist, to see the country, and partly because I had relatives in the country whom I desired to visit. They listened to me at first with apparent incredulity and suspicion but finally accepted my explanations and permitted me to depart.

The proceedings in the police office were all in the Polish language and, as far as external appearances went, it might have been the official agency of an independent Polish nation. The questions were at first put to me in Polish. I knew no Polish except a few phrases which I had picked up and I protested in them that I could not speak their language. I will put down what I said, although, from the standpoint of linguistic correctness, it must have been laughable. *"Yo no umvo Popolsky, umvo Angelsky, Nimietzky."* "I do not speak Polish; I speak English or German." When the officials saw that I could not understand their Polish, they continued their questioning, though with evident reluctance, in German. This Polish national character of the Cracow government was to me a proof of the liberal and tolerant character of the Austro-Hungarian empire. Galicia, at the time of my visit, was an Austrian province. The language of Austria was German and, if it had followed the policy of Germany in the former Polish province of Posen, Austria would have rigidly Germanized everything in Galicia. That it did not do so, but permitted the people of Galicia a degree of autonomy almost equivalent to independence, was a striking demonstration of the truly liberal and humane character of Austrian rule, a character undoubtedly derived from the example of its humane and liberal sovereign, Kaiser Franz Josef.

Another proof of the continuance and strength of the Polish national spirit was given by the Wawel, a beautiful structure dedicated to honoring the memory of the great figures in Polish history. In its magnificent hall of exhibition stood long rows of statues of the significant personages in the national annals of Poland, reigning sovereigns, members of the nobility and other distinguished individuals, all of the finest marble and carved by the most renowned sculptors of Europe. The love and patriotic devotion of living members of the Polish aristocracy—so I was informed—had furnished the means for the procurement of these splendid products of the sculptor's art. Many of the statues were ornamented with festoons of rich, broad silken bands dedicated by patriotic admirers of the personages represented by those particular statues and bearing appropriate inscriptions in golden lettering. I visited the Wawel during my tour of Cracow and was deeply impressed. The evidence of such profound and undying attachment to a cause apparently lost was truly thrilling, and I found myself involuntarily hoping that the aspiration expressed in the Polish national slogan, *"Jeszcze Polska nie zginela"* ("Poland is not yet lost"), might be realized and the Polish nation restored to a condition of true national independence. I could not help feeling, too, that the fate of Poland and that of Israel were very similar and praying inwardly that my poor, dispersed, scattered, and persecuted people might recover its ancient status of nationhood and dignity. I believe that my sympathy for the Polish nation must have been largely derived from my father, who always preserved a strong attachment to the people upon whose soil he had been born. Just as my mother was deeply attached to the memory of her native land, Germany, my father felt deep love for Poland, and these loves were never antagonistic to each other or to their Jewish loyalty. As an American, too, I felt a great sympathy for Poland, for had not Poles taken part in the battle for American independence and are not the name of Kosziusko, Pulaski, and Zabriskie written in letters of gold on the pages of American history?

Not only Polish patriotism and devotion were manifest in Cracow. Jewish sentiment and loyalty to Jewish faith were also strongly in evidence, albeit in a more modest and unpretentious way. The Jews formed a substantial part of the population of Cracow. In their disstinctive costumes they were, perhaps, even more conspicuous than their numerical proportion warranted. I witnessed the first striking demonstration of the loyalty of the Jews to their faith on a Friday afternoon. There was a great public market in Cracow, which occupied a vast square in the heart of the city. I visited this market early Friday afternoon and was much interested in the picturesque and animated scene which met my eyes. The great, far-extended space was filled with booths and stands displaying all sorts of agricultural products and merchandise. A throng of merchants and customers, of sellers and buyers, milled around them, engrossed in all-absorbing negotiations, bargaining, selling, and purchasing. The merchants were almost exclusively Jews. The purchasers in their great majority were Polish men and women. The contrast of costumes and types made a fascinating picture. I wandered around the great market-place for several hours, constantly beholding new and most interesting sights and admiring the perfect harmony and friendly relations which prevailed between the two so different ethnic elements there present.

Suddenly, at about five o'clock, a great change took place. All selling and buying ceased, the booths and stands were closed, and Jews and Poles began streaming from the market-place. The approach of the Sabbath had summoned the Jews to cease all secular activity, and all those of Jewish faith obeyed the summons. That meant the immediate closing of the market, and in less time than it takes to describe it, the great place that had just been filled with human beings and the scene of hustling, bustling activity, was empty. Silence had fallen over its vast expanse.

To me, who had never before witnessed such genuine Jewish loyalty and consistency, the sight was thrilling. I could not help contrasting it with America, where it would be hardly possible to parallel it even on the eve of Yom Kippur, Atonement Day, the most sacred day of the Jewish year.

I attended service that evening in the great synagogue of Cracow. The edifice was filled with men clad in their long silk and satin Sabbath robes. The sight of these typical Jewish figures was inspiring. Many, if not most, of the faces pale, with finely cut features and bearded, seemed intellectual, spiritual, and dignified. I do not recall seeing any women. Whether none were present, or whether they were hidden in the dark recesses of the lofty gallery, I cannot say. The service was conducted by a *Chazan* or cantor, accompanied by a choir of boys. The cantor had a high alto voice and the boys were mostly

A Trip to Galicia

sopranos. Both cantor and choir repeated large portions of the prayers many times. This was not in accordance either with my musical taste or my concept of the proper method of offering prayer, so that I cannot say that the service impressed me. But the congregation seemed to be both greatly impressed and pleased by the vocal efforts of the cantor and his *meshorerim,* or singers, so that my judgment, drawn from a different cultural environment, is perhaps not properly applicable to this case.

After the service I returned to the hotel and enjoyed a very fair meal in a genuine Sabbath atmosphere. The meal concluded, a sort of informal social gathering took place, in which a number of neighbors, who apparently were accustomed to come to the hotel for that purpose, participated. These visitors were a very interesting group. They were representative Galician *Baale Batim,* Jewish burghers of the upper class, substantial business men and cultured in their way.

They were clad in the typical Sabbath robes, made of fine material, silk, satin, and velvet, in perfect repair, and they were scrupulously clean and neat. Their language was the Yiddish but in a form closely akin to German and some of them spoke a perfectly correct German. The conversation was more than merely interesting. Much of it was highly instructive and stimulating. Several of the visitors were well versed in Talmudic lore. They interpreted obscure passages of the Talmud, and elucidated knotty points of rabbinical legislation in a manner indicative both of intellectual keenness and erudition, to their own delight and that of their listeners. Others had an excellent understanding of matters of general human interest and discussed European politics and world problems with much intelligence and accuracy of knowledge. Nor was the humorous element lacking. I heard a number of exquisite tales drawn from Jewish life, very amusing, but with the undercurrent of pathos which is seldom absent from Jewish stories and anecdotes. In all this I took no part except that of a greatly interested listener and observer. It was indeed fascinating to me to observe these men, looking in their quaint costumes and ear-locks and venerable beards as though they belonged to another age and world, and to hear from their lips veritable pearls of wisdom and utterances filled with the lightness and brightness of thought which the French call *esprit.* And over it all hovered the reverent and yet joyful spirit of the Sabbath, pervading alike the words of wisdom and the humorous tales and elevating them above the level of the merely intellectual or amusing. We remained together until a late hour and then separated for the night to meet on the morrow in the synagogue. The holy day passed in the usual manner. It was a delightful combination of spiritual exaltation and material joy.

On the following Sunday, I visited the ancient Jewish cemetery of Cracow. There lie the earthly remains of the great Rabbi Moses Isserles, usually known in rabbinic literature as *R'ma,* an abbeviated designation formed from the initial letters of his title and name, Rabbi of Cracow in the sixteenth century. My purpose was to pray at his grave and to venerate his sacred memory. He was one of the greatest of Talmudic authorities in a land rich in Talmudic authorities, profoundly revered not only for his great learning but also for his saintly character. Author of many learned works, his fame rests chiefly on the *Shulchan Aruch,* the authoritative code of rabbinical law, which, in his modesty, he called by the simple title of *Darche Mosheh,* "The Ways of Moses." Standing at the spot where rests all that was mortal of this exalted spiritual leader of Israel, I reflected on what constitutes Jewish greatness: vast learning, especially in the domain of religion but also in philosophic and secular matters, stern ethical principles, and lofty spirituality. It is a sublime combination and where it is found there is true Judaism. That glorious combination was characteristic of all the great leaders whose names adorn the pages of Jewish history and of none more than of Rabbi Moses Isserles.

The following day I left Cracow, my next objective being Lemberg, capital city of the Province of Galicia. As the train was an early morning one, I was obliged to rise with the first rays of dawn in order to attend to my ablutions, my daily devotions, my breakfast, and yet be at the railroad station in time.

Despite the early hour the station was crowded. Among the intending passengers there was a goodly proportion of my co-religionists. Conspicuous among the passengers and observed of all eyes was a group of army officers, some five or six. I do not recall whether they were Polish or German (Austrian), but they were handsome, sturdy men, with erect figures and clad in neat, well fitting uniforms. In reference to them I heard a conversation between a Jewish father and his young son which is worth narrating, because it revealed a characteristic Jewish point of view and also showed the freedom of speech prevailing in the Austro-Hungarian empire, so that people were not afraid to utter their true sentiments.

The father was a typical Galician Jew, clad in the customary long robe and with long ear-locks and beard, the son, a lad of not more than seven or eight, was, except for the beard, a miniature replica of his father. They stood directly in front of me so that I heard and, as it was in Yiddish, understood everything they said. The boy said to his father, "Look, Father, what beautiful officers!" (*Seh, tatte, wus far sheine Offiziere.*)

Whereupon the father answered, "You must never say, my son, that officers are beautiful. They may seem beautiful, but they are really ugly and hateful. Their business is to make war, and war is a terrible and wicked thing and should never be waged except to defend ourselves against those who attack us. The Torah commands 'Thou shalt not kill,' and in war they kill people by the thousands and openly break the law of God. Our prophets tell us that there will come a time when there will be no more wars and people will not even learn how to fight. When that happy time comes, Messiah will deliver us from the exile, and the world will not need either officers or soldiers or swords or guns or cannons." The boy subsided but did not seem to agree completely with the anti-militaristic views of his father.

A few minutes later the doors of the station were opened and the people entered the train. I found a seat in a section where a group of Galician co-religionists were already seated. Hardly had the train begun to move than my fellow travelers donned their *tallithoth* and *tephillin* and began to chant the morning service. I did not do so as, in accordance with my custom, I had already performed my devotions in the hotel. No one paid any attention to me. They evidently considered, since I was dressed in Occidental costume, that I was either a Gentile or a *Deitsch* (German) a recreant Jew who had adopted the customs of Germany and the Western world and was no longer to be counted among the faithful of Israel. But something occurred which called their attention to me quite strongly and sharply. It was the month of *Elul* when, in accordance with Jewish precept and in spiritual preparation for the solemn days of the New Year and Atonement Day, the Twenty-seventh Psalm is added to the daily service. Strange to say, my pious co-religionists omitted it. Noticing the omission and not averse to showing that one not of their sacred circle might also know something of Jewish things, I gave my neighbor, a fully costumed and bearded individual, a not very gentle poke in the ribs. Startled, he turned to me and demanded, *"Wus willt Ihr?"* (What do you want?)

"My friend," I answered, "you have forgotten something."

"What?"

"You have forgotten to say the Twenty-seventh Psalm. Do you not know that it is the month of *Elul*, in which we must recite the Twenty-seventh Psalm morning and evening?"

He glared at me for a moment and then said, *"Takke emess"* (That is really true). Turning to his neighbor, he communicated to him what I had said. A moment later the entire group recited the psalm in unison. I then heard him say to his friends:

"It is a shame and a disgrace that a *Deitsch* should have to remind us Galician Jews that we must say the Twenty-seventh Psalm. It is very nice of him to be so learned and pious and to remind us, but it is a disgrace for us to need to be reminded." Whereupon one of his comrades sagely remarked, "I will tell you something. A *Deitscher Deitsch* (a real German, one to the manner born) can be all right, but the Lord protect us from a Polish *Deitsch!*"

The view from the windows of the car presented a constant succession of changing pictures, possible only in Galicia or some similar portion of the world. One of these is impressed upon my memory with particular distinctness. The train stopped for a few minutes opposite some minor station. Not far from the station a house was being erected, a substantial brick structure it seemed to be, and all the workingmen connected with its erection I recognized as Jews. The hod-carriers, the bricklayers, the mixers of mortar, the truckmen, the carpenters and other workmen, all, all of them were of the posterity of Abraham, Isaac, and Jacob. While they were not garbed in the customary long robes of more formal occasions, their skull caps, beards, and ear-locks, and, in the case of some, the *Arba Kanfos* (fringed garment) on their breasts, clearly revealed their identity. That was certainly something which I had never seen before. I gazed with great interest at the unusual sight. But I soon realized that the sight was more than merely interesting; it was profoundly instructive and enlightening. It was a splendid piece of anti-anti-Semitic propaganda, better than half the learned treatises that have been written for that purpose. One of the favorite charges launched by anti-Semitic agitators against the Jews is that they perform no useful service in the community, that they are mere parasites, merchants, speculators, and adventurers, who live in comfort on the toil and sweat of the Gentiles, but who never themselves soil their hands with honest physical labor. This is, of course, a false and calumnious accusation, like all the rest of the libels hurled at the defenseless Jews by their enemies. It was most refreshing to see a living demonstration of the falsity of one favorite calumny.

The ancient Hebrews were mainly tillers of the soil and shepherds but practiced also all the arts and professions known in antiquity. Their descendants in the Middle Ages were forced into trade and money-lending because the laws prohibited them from owning land and the guilds refused to accept them as members. But whenever these restrictions were removed, the Jews took up all the vocations of civilized society.

I do not remember just how many hours the trip to Lemberg lasted, but I do remember that when I got there I was very tired. After securing quarters in a hotel and taking a light meal, I retired early.

The next morning, after the usual preliminaries, I devoted the day to sightseeing. I found Lemberg both pleasing and disappointing. It was a modern city, far more so than the other cities of Galicia. It had broad streets and avenues and many fine buildings. It was very clean, but it seemed lacking in historic atmosphere and misplaced in the Galician environment. From the historic point of view it contrasted unfavorably with Cracow, whose crooked and irregular streets and grimy buildings and whose great Wawel spoke eloquently of the Polish national past, while its Jewish section with its picturesque inhabitants and its ancient cemetery, told an equally eloquent tale of the part which the children of Israel had played in its history. It was evident also that many of the Jewish inhabitants of Lemberg had discarded the Jewish costume, for I saw many persons who I was sure were Jews but who were dressed in Occidental attire, while those garbed in Jewish fashion were not numerous. This modernity of aspect did not detract from Lemberg as a home and place of residence, for it was probably more desirable in that regard than other Galician cities, but it did deprive it of the romantic halo and charm which the undiminished preservation of historic characteristics confers. Neither did it signify that the Jewish community of Lemberg was not loyally observant, for indeed it was a venerable seat of Jewish piety and learning. Among the names on the long list of its former rabbis were several of great Talmudic authorities, though none so outstandingly important as the great Rabbi of Cracow, Rabbi Moses Isserles. It indicated that Lemberg had been more touched by the breath of Occidental culture than other Galician cities. Many of those who no longer wore the traditional Jewish attire were otherwise strictly observant. In any other country they would have been considered shining examples of Jewish Orthodoxy; here, however, they were under the shadow of non-conformity.

Incidentally the name Lemberg is not the true Polish designation of the city but was undoubtedly conferred upon it by its Austrian-German rulers. Its name in Polish is Levov or Levovo (written in Polish *Lwow*). The great penitentiary or prison of the province of Galicia was located in Lemberg and in jesting allusion to its Polish name, which happens to correspond in sound to the Hebrew term *levovo,* meaning "his heart," the Galician Jews sarcastically interpreted the second verse of the fifteenth Psalm "He speaketh the truth which is in his heart" as meaning "he that speaketh the truth will come to Levov," that is, will be put into prison.

One circumstance made my visit to Lemberg very pleasant. My classmate in the Breslau Seminary, Samuel Margulies, who, although already thoroughly conversant with the Talmud, was studying at the Seminary and the University in order to fit himself for the Western European rabbinate. He had given me a letter of introduction to the family of his wife, who were residents of Lemberg, named Menkes. They were people of wealth and high standing in the Lemberg Jewish community, and the head of the family, Reb Simchah Menkes, was a man of corresponding importance. Dignified and patriarchal in

"Doktorhut"
Heidelberg University Diploma — October 31, 1884

HATTARATH HARAAH

Certificate—one of four—of Rabbinical Ordination; this one was granted by Rabbi Dr. Moses Gaster, Haham, or Chief Rabbi of the Sephardic Congregations of Great Britain in 1904.

A Trip to Galicia

appearance in his long fine Jewish robe,* he impressed me especially. The Menkes were very proud of their son-in-law, and he indeed richly merited their high esteem. He was a man of exceptional talent and later became a distinguished figure in Italian Jewry as Chief Rabbi of Florence, head of the *Collegio Rabbinico,* the Rabbinical Seminary of Italy, and editor of *Rivista Israelitica,* the chief Italian Jewish periodical. Although, as a native of Galicia, the Yiddish was his mother tongue, he attained perfect mastery of Italian and was reputed one of the most eloquent Jewish orators in that tongue.

My next and final station in Galicia was Brody, my father's native town and the place of residence of my relatives on my father's side. Brody impressed me as very similar to Cracow, though on a smaller scale. There was much poverty in the place. I was confronted with it the moment I stepped out of the railroad station.

Opposite the station, I saw a sort of open place which was densely crowded with men and boys, so densely packed, indeed, that it seemed impossible to squeeze in another one. I wondered what that dense crowd was doing there, but I was not left long in doubt. No sooner had I appeared, together with a few other persons who had arrived on the same train, than the entire mass rushed at us simultaneously, competing with each other for the privilege of carrying our bags. They were all Jews, every last one of them. They were trying in this way to earn a few *kreuzers* to keep body and soul together. I recognized this fact at once and was filled with pity.

Just then I noticed a man and boy, evidently father and son, who were standing at the side, less obstreperous than the others. I at once entrusted my bag to the man and asked him to lead me to a hotel. As soon as I did this, the others ceased their attempts to get the bag. This must have been in accordance with an understanding among them. The man, who seemed quite a gentlemanly fellow and spoke excellent German, gave my bag to his son to carry but accompanied us to the hotel. I gave them a tip amounting, in American money, to about twenty-five cents. It must have seemed to them unusually generous, for they were both pitiably grateful.

---

* Shakespeare's reference to the "Jewish gabardine" of Shylock, is incidental evidence that the Jews of Italy in the fifteenth and sixtenth centuries wore a distinctive Jewish costume.—B.D.

My first impression of Brody was thus a decidedly unfavorable one, but it became more favorable as I became better acquainted with the town and its inhabitants. I discovered that it was not quite as poverty-stricken a place as it had seemed on first acquaintance but that there were in it a number of wealthy families and a fair proportion of moderately prosperous ones.

For instance, a rich and pious Jewish merchant named Nathansohn visited Vienna one winter, clad in traditional but elegant clothes. His luxurious and, naturally, very expensive apparel aroused the curiosity of the people in the wholesale house where he was making his purchases, and the proprietor, a German non-Jew, took the liberty of asking him some questions. "Excuse me, Herr Nathansohn," he said, "you are wearing such beautiful fur clothes, would you mind telling me what they cost?"

"Not at all," answered Herr Nathansohn. "My robe cost three thousand guldens, my cap cost one thousand, my gloves cost twelve hundred, and my fur-lined boots sixteen hundred."

"But," said the horrified wholesaler, hearing such enormous prices, "if the Jewish attire is so terribly expensive, what do the poor people in Brody wear?"

"Oh, they," said Herr Nathansohn, smiling, *"they dress in German style."*

Despite the undoubted existence of wealthy and middle class elements in the Jewry of Brody, there was an enormous amount of intense, grinding poverty everywhere in evidence. My own relatives, to whom I at once proceeded to make myself known, belonged to the middle class. They were not wealthy people, but they occupied clean and reasonably comfortable homes. What surprised me greatly was that they all bore distinctly German names—Siegel, Maiblum, Ritter, and Trachtenberg—and there was no Polish name among them. Whether this prevalence of German nomenclature was due to their descent from remote German ancestors, or whether these names were imposed upon them by the German-speaking Austrian government, I am not in a position to state. The name Drachmann was not borne by any of them. This was due to the fact that my father had been an only son. When his sisters married, they naturally received other names. There was among the relatives one name which had a Scandinavian sound, Kelsen. Of the origin of this name and why it appeared in a Slavonic-Polish environment I have not the slightest idea.

They all wore the Jewish costume except the Ritters, who appeared to be more modernized or Westernized. All the Ritters—the father, Herr Osias Ritter, and four or five quite presentable and apparently well educated sons, were clothed in Occidental raiment. Their language was, I presume, Yiddish, but I hardly know whether it should be called by that name for, with the exception of a few Hebrew and other terms and a slight difference of pronunciation, it was closely akin to the standard German. I, who had been reared in the English and German tongues, had no difficulty in understanding them and they had no difficulty in understanding my German. Under these circumstances we got on splendidly together.

My arrival in Brody was entirely unexpected by my relatives and was a great surprise to them. I had intentionally omitted notifying them of my intended visit as I did not know their circumstances and I had no desire to trouble them. My sole reason for visiting them was that I thought it only right and proper to keep up friendly relations with my kinsfolk on both sides. As for them, I am sure they no more expected a visit from an American relative than from the man in the moon. Indeed I am in doubt whether the moon did not seem nearer to them than distant America, for the moon they could see, whereas of America they could only hear, and that in dubious and uncertain tales.

However, after the first shock of surprise, they were unfeignedly glad to see me. They received me most hospitably in their various homes, which were very respectable, and did all in their power to make my stay agreeable. Of course, they were curious to know all about me, and plied me with questions about myself, about the American relatives, especially my father, about America and, most particularly, about the condition of Jews and Judaism in America. While not all my answers were pleasing to them, the general impression must have been favorable, for they finally expressed the opinion that America must be a very fine country. They also expressed the wish that they might live there and be able to meet their American relatives regularly.

I ascribe it to the effect produced by these conversations that most of my father's relatives subsequently emigrated to America, and that our family has become almost exclusively an American one. As for the German relatives, on my mother's side, they were content and happy in their native land until the accession to power of the accursed system of Nazism and its miscreant Fuehrer. They were then obliged to flee and sought refuge, most of them, in America, thus intensifying the American character of our family.

The presence of a visitor from America became known in some way or other to a goodly portion of the submerged ten thousand of Brody, and I became the object of a considerable number of requests for aid. I could not appear in the street without being implored for help from wailing men, women, or children. I refused no one as long as my money lasted, for I knew that the need was real and I obeyed the Talmudic injunction, "Whosoever openeth the hand, to him shall be given." I gave only very small amounts, but still the inevitable happened: almost before I knew it, my available cash was exhausted. With the exception of a gulden or two which I retained for unavoidable expenses during the trip, I was left penniless.

I remained only a few days in Brody. A goodly delegation of relatives accompanied me to the railroad station. We parted amid cordial farewells and mutual promises that we would correspond in the future.

I do not recall just how long the return journey from Brody to Breslau lasted, but it was a long trip, for Brody is at the extreme eastern end of Galicia, not far from the Russian frontier, while Breslau lies well to the west of the German frontier. I found it long and tiresome and I suffered from a certain depression of spirits which the sights from the car window did not dispel.

The train jogged on through a pitch-dark country until about ten o'clock, when it stopped and the *schaffner* (conductor), opening the door of the coupe, called out, *"Gleiwitz, alle aussteigen"* (Gleiwitz, everybody must leave the train). I did not like his announcement. (The term *aussteigen* simply means to leave the train but does not suggest that there is another train waiting to take passengers who are going further. Had he said *umsteigen* it would have been all right, for that term contains the desired meaning.)

Having no other choice, I descended from the train and entered

A Trip to Galicia

the station. I went up to the window of the ticket seller and asked him, *"Wenn geht der naechste Zug nach Breslau?"* (When does the next train go to Breslau?) That worthy answered me in the curt and abrupt manner characteristic of Prussian officials, *"Acht Uhr in der Frueh"* (eight o'clock in the morning). Here was a pretty kettle of fish. I was stranded in an utterly strange place, a hundred miles more or less from my destination, and without a cent in my pocket, unable to pay for a room in a hotel over night. I thought fast and furiously and decided that the only thing to do was to remain in the waiting room of the station until the train should leave in the morning. I said to the ticket seller, "I am bound for Breslau. I premuse I can wait here in the station for the train."

He answered with the same curtness as before, *"Nein, mein Herr. Der Bahnhof wird sofort geschlossen. Niemand darf sich im Bahnhof aufhalten wenn er geschlossen ist"* (No, sir. The station will be immediately closed. No one is permitted to be in the station when it is closed).

From bad to worse. To stay in the station all night was bad enough. The prospect of pacing the streets until daylight was positively dismaying. But necessity sharpens the wits and suggests expedients. I decided that I would go boldly to a hotel and state frankly the embarrassing position in which I was and ask the person in charge for permission to remain in the hotel until time for the departure of the train in the morning. If I would receive that permission, well and good. If not, I would remain in the streets for the necessary number of hours. I remembered that the Bible tells of several instances of people passing the night in the street.

I had very little hope that any hotel would permit a penniless stranger to occupy one of its rooms without paying, but things turned out better than I expected.

First it was necessary to secure the services of someone who would lead me to a hotel. I was utterly unfamiliar with Gleiwitz and could not be sure of finding my way in the black darkness in which the streets of Gleiwitz were enveloped. I saw a man standing not far from me in the waiting room who looked poor, but respectable and mild. It occurred to me that he might render me the service I required. I took the liberty of speaking to him and asked him if he could direct me to a hotel. My anticipation was correct. He at once agreed to do so and was most friendly and sympathetic.

"I heard what you were saying to the ticket seller," he said, "and I at once understood that you are in an embarrassing position (*Verlegenheit*). I will be glad to conduct you to a hotel."

"But I must tell you, my friend," I said, "that I cannot give you a tip (*trinkgeld*). I am entirely without cash and at this moment have nothing to give."

"That's no difference" (*Das macht nichts*), he said, in a most friendly tone. "Once in a while one must help a fellow-being (*Mitmenschen*) without looking for a reward."

And so this perfect stranger performed an act of true helpfulness out of pure ethical motives without any expectation of material reward. I thanked him warmly, but he put away my expressions of gratitude with a wave of his hand as though what he was doing was nothing. He led me for nine or ten minutes through a maze of streets so dark that if the term "blackout" had existed at that time that would have been the right way to describe the darkness. Then, stopping before a medium-sized, rather brightly lit building, on whose front was the sign "Hotel Hamburger," he pointed at it and said:

"There is a hotel which I think you will find suitable." Acknowledging my renewed thanks with a slight inclination of his head, he disappeared into the surrounding darkness.

Entering the hotel, I noticed at once that it was clean and neat and presumably comfortable but not large or pretentious. A number of persons were standing or sitting in the large front room. Behind the bar was an elderly, kindly-looking woman, who I at once thought was Jewish and Frau Hamburger, the proprietress or wife of the proprietor. She greeted me with a friendly smile and the inquiry, "What is your wish?" (*Was beliebt?*) I told the story of my embarrassment frankly and added that I was a student of the Breslau Seminary and that if she would accommodate me, I would send her the amount of the charge as soon as I returned to Breslau.

Her reaction was more favorable than I had dared to expect. In the friendliest and pleasantest manner and without the slightest trace of hesitation or suspicion, she agreed to my request. "Why, of course, my dear young friend," she said. "You can have the best my house affords. I could see at once that you are an honorable young man, and now that I know you are a candidate for the rabbinate, I am especially happy to be able to serve you. You shall have a good bedroom and before you leave in the morning be sure to take a good and abundant breakfast." Summoning a bellboy, she directed him to take me to room number —. Before I could recover sufficiently from my joyful astonishment to stammer forth my thanks, she said, "Good night, pleasant rest." With a smile she turned to attend to some other business.

That night I rested well in an excellent room and a soft, comfortable bed under huge German feather-filled quilts. Best of all, my faith in human beings was strengthened and intensified. I told myself that there are good, kindly and helpful people in the world, among both Jews and Gentiles. My guide had been a Gentile, and my benefactress was a daughter of Israel.

In the morning I had a very good breakfast. My kind-hearted landlady was not in evidence, but my bill was ready and it was surprisingly moderate. All's well that ends well. I got to Breslau in due course, and that very day I sent Frau Hamburger, in Gleiwitz, a letter expressing my deep gratitude for her great kindness to me and enclosing a postal money order (*Geldbrief*) for the amount of my debt to her.

Chapter Seventeen

Experiences in Breslau—(*continued*)

Ph.D. Degree in Heidelberg

I WENT TO THE SEMINARY THE NEXT MORNING AFTER MY RETURN from Galicia. There I was warmly greeted by my fellow-students. But they gave me one piece of news which had an ominous implication. A police officer had been at the Seminary on the previous day and had inquired for me. On hearing that I was not there at the time, he had left for me a *Zettel,* a slip, containing a notice from the police department summoning me to appear at police headquarters on the afternoon of the following day. The ominous implication in this was that it suggested the possibility that I might be expelled from Germany.

There was an extremely strict government in power at the time headed, I believe, by a *Reichskanzler,* or Imperial Chancellor, named Putkamer, a notorious reactionary, and it had undertaken to rid the country of all foreigners, particularly those from Russia and Poland. A number of students of the Seminary, originating from Russia or Poland, had already been affected by the decree and had been forced to give up their studies and return to their native lands.

My fellow students took it for granted that the serving of the *Zettel* had the same significance in my case as in all the others and were profuse in their expressions of sympathy. I took the matter philosophically. "If the government doesn't want me in Germany," I said, "I shall certainly not try to stay here. There is a fine rabbinical seminary in Vienna, also one in Budapest. And there is an *Ecole Rabbinique* in Paris. Of course, I should rather remain here, but if my presence is objectionable I am ready to go."

The next day, at the hour stated, I was at police headquarters. As I entered the antechamber, I saw a large number of persons, about forty or fifty, all evidently in trouble with the police for some reason or other. I went up to the clerk who was seated behind a desk opposite the door and presented my *Zettel*. The official glanced at it and said, "Ah, you are Herr Drachmann. The Herr Prefekt has left word that as soon as you arrive you are to be shown into his room."

I must admit that, on hearing these words, a violent terror seized upon me. What could be the significance of this urgent demand for my appearance? With fear and trembling I followed the clerk into the room of the *Herr Polizei Prefekt*. He was seated behind his desk, a handsome, dignified and stern-looking middle-aged man in uniform. With him was closeted a man in civil attire, with whom apparently he had been in conference. As soon as the clerk and I entered, the former showed the notice slip and uttered the words, "Herr Drachman," the Prefekt motioned to the man with whom he had been closeted, and the latter at once rose and departed, as did also the clerk.

The *Prefekt* then said to me with a friendly smile, "Please be seated" (*bitte nehmen Sie Platz*). I complied with mingled relief and apprehension. What words were to issue next from that stern and dignified mouth! He drew a sheet of paper out of a drawer and placed it before him upon the desk. It was evidently a report concerning me, for he consulted it from time to time during his conversation with me. His remarks revealed a perfect knowledge of all facts concerning my personality. The ensuing conversation was about as follows.

"Your name is Bernard Drachman?"

"Yes, Herr Prefekt."

"You come from Jersey City in America?" He pronounced it "*Yarezei Tzittee*."

"Yes, Herr Prefekt."

"You are studying as rabbi at the Jewish Theological Seminary in this city?"

"Yes, Herr Prefekt."

"You are also studying at the University in this city?"

"Yes, Herr Prefekt."

"You have relatives in South Germany and also in this city?"

"Yes, Herr Prefekt."

"Tell me, Herr Drachman, is it your intention to live here permanently and to become a German subject?"

These last words I heard with considerable amazement but I at once answered, "No, Herr Prefekt, I have no such purpose."

The *Prefekt* looked at me rather sharply and repeated, "You have no such purpose?"

I answered, "No, Herr Prefekt, I have no such purpose. I am only here for the purpose of study and as soon as I have completed my studies I intend to return to my native land."

The *Prefekt* looked at me with a glance in which there seemed to be a shade of surprise and displeasure and said, "Very well, Herr Drachman, I am glad to know your intentions. I have only called you here to let you know that, in case you should desire to become naturalized as a German citizen, there is no objection on the part of the government."

In some confusion, for I was overwhelmed with surprise by this entirely unexpected outcome of the affair, I offered my thanks to the government for the great honor which it was conferring upon me. I bowed and retired. The *Prefekt* answered my bow with a stiff and formal inclination of his head.

When I told my colleagues at the Seminary of my interview with the *Herr Prefekt,* they found it hard to believe. Nothing like that, it seems, had ever happened before. There had been innumerable instances of the expulsion of foreigners from German territory. But that the government should actually invite a foreigner, and a Jew at that, to become a German citizen—that was something unheard of. I, myself, did not feel quite as happy about the matter as my German friends thought I should. Much as I liked Germany—and Germany was indeed in those days in many ways a very likeable country and there was much about German life that was highly attractive and agreeable—I did not like it sufficiently to desire to settle there permanently. There was much in German conditions—and indeed in European conditions generally—which was repugnant to my American sentiments, to my inner consciousness of the indispensability of liberty and human rights, and I was thoroughly convinced that the only place in which an American should live his life was America.

The incident caused me to be looked upon as a prospective, or, at least, possible resident of Germany with a future career in that land. It was probably responsible for another opportunity, which came to me soon after, to make my home and take up my career in the German fatherland.

A few weeks later I was approached by the representative of the president of a congregation in a North German city with a presumably very tempting offer. He informed me that the post of rabbi in that town was vacant—a very desirable post. He added that the congregation numbered several hundred well-to-do families, and that moreover the salary was several thousand marks annually besides perquisites of an even larger amount. Also the president had a beautiful and pious daughter of marriageable age upon whom he intended to settle a very handsome dowry, that he was all-powerful in his community and could confer the position of rabbi upon anyone whom he chose and that if I consented to become his son-in-law he would have me appointed. It was a very flattering offer and almost took my breath away, but I had no difficulty in reaching a decision. Without a moment's hesitation I answered that, while I appreciated greatly the splendid proposal which was made to me, I was not yet ready to take upon myself the duties and responsibilities either of a rabbi or of a husband and that furthermore it was not my intention to remain in Germany but, after the completion of my studies, to return to America.

Meanwhile the second year of my stay in Breslau and my attendance at the Seminary was approaching its end, and I began to think of something of great importance in the scholastic equipment of a modern rabbi, the obtaining of my Ph.D. The rabbis of old did not possess nor need this degree, which is a non-Jewish one conferred by the universities and not by the *Yeshivoth* or rabbinical academies. These confer upon their graduates the title of rabbi or *Moreh Horaah* (teacher of the Law) which authorizes them to exercise rabbinical functions. That degree, which represents a vast amount of Biblical and Talmudic learning, was quite sufficient in ancient and medieval days. But with the coming of the nineteenth century and its atmosphere of emancipation and complete or partial assimilation there came an imperative demand from the Jewish communities in Western lands that their rabbis should be equipped with considerable secular knowledge. The degree of Ph.D. offers this guarantee to its holder.

In order to obtain the Ph.D. it is necessary to take an examination in at least two subjects, one major and one minor, and to submit a thesis or dissertation on some theme related to the subjects of the examination. It is customary to apply for the degree at some university other than the one at which the applicant has studied. The dissertation is first sent in to the university and, if found satisfactory, the applicant is notified to appear for examination.

I sent my treatise on Judah Chayug to the University of Heidelberg as the dissertation and stated that I desired to be examined in Semitic languages as major subject and in philosophy as minor subject. In a few weeks I was notified that my dissertation had been found adequate and I was summoned to appear in Heidelberg for examination. The receipt of this communication caused my heart to flutter. After all, the prospect of becoming a Doctor of Philosophy looms great before the imagination of a youth of twenty-three.

The journey to Heidelberg took me through pleasantly cultivated country and was marked by one instructive incident. On the train I happened to share a coupé with a group of well dressed and charmingly cultured ladies and gentlemen. We were all soon engaged in lively conversation. I bore so full a part in it that I really felt like a true member of the group.

As the train approached Heidelberg, the lady sitting next to me asked where I was to stay. In reply to my request for a suggestion, she said, "I would advise you to go to the Hotel Prinz Friedrich Karl. *All your country-people stay there.* You will find yourself in quite congenial company."

These words came to me as quite a shock. Despite my German studies and period of residence in the country, despite my earnest and confident effort to speak as well as possible, she had known I was an American the minute I opened my mouth!

This little incident taught me a valuable lesson: that one should never seek to hide one's identity. My motive had been nothing more sinister than a little linguistic vanity. Nevertheless, it was plain that one must be what one is, and it is foolish to make pretenses.

On the day following my arrival in Heidelberg I went to fulfill a duty which is incumbent upon everyone who seeks an academic degree. Academic custom in Germany requires that the candidate for the doctorate shall pay his respects to the professors who are to examine him by a formal visit to their homes. Arrayed in formal attire, in what would be called evening dress in America, a black swallow-tail coat, black vest and trousers, a stiff white linen shirt, high collar and white tie, with a high hat on my head and kid gloves on my hands, I sallied forth from the hospitable recesses of the Hotel Prinz Friedrich Karl to visit the two professors who were to decide my worthiness to become a Ph.D. They were Professor Kuno Fischer, who was to probe my philosophic attainments, and Professor Gustav Weil, who was to investigate my knowledge of the Semitic languages and literatures. Both of these gentlemen received me graciously, but there was quite a difference in the manner of their reception. Professor Fischer who, incidentally, was considered one of the greatest philosophers of Germany at that time, received me with formal courtesy and after a few minutes of perfunctory conversation, bowed me politely out of the door. Professor Weil, on the other hand, was friendliness and kindliness personified, so that I almost felt as though we had been intimately acquainted for many years. He inquired concerning conditions in America and, too, was much interested in hearing about the Breslau Seminary, as he had himself studied for the rabbinate before deciding to devote himself to Semitics. He kept me with him for about an hour, after which he accompanied me to the door, and shook hands with me when I departed.

While making these visits I did not fail to notice that Heidelberg was a beautiful town and situated in a lovely and picturesque region, on the shore of a thrillingly romantic river, the Neckar.

That night the examination took place in one of the rooms of the university. I do not deny that before the examination I felt quite nervous for, although I had prepared myself carefully and conscientiously and had stated in detail the studies which I had made, well, one never knows what may happen. The examination was close and searching but not unduly severe. It was entirely oral. Professor Fischer had me read several philosophal texts, laying especial stress on Spinoza, and asked me questions from the general domain of philosophic thought. Professor Weil caused me to read and interpret texts from the Hebrew Bible and also from various Arabic, Aramaic, and Syriac sources. He also interrogated me concerning the grammar and philology of these Semitic tongues. At the conclusion of the examination, the professors informed me that I had passed satisfactorily and that I would receive the degree of Doctor of Philosophy with the predicate *multa cum laude* (with much praise). That is next to the highest rank in the doctorate, the highest being *Maxima cum laude* (with the greatest praise). They also informed me that I would be expected to have my dissertation printed and present a certain number of copies to the university, I forget just how many. They congratulated me, bade me good night, and I departed.

As I stepped forth into the street, my spirits were in a high state of exhilaration. I was happy, deliriously happy. To have attained the rank of Doctor of Philosophy by right of a successfully passed examination and by authorization of a great and ancient German university seemed to me a distinction and a glory, compared with which the highest other earthly honors were pale and insignificant. All the circumstances of that evening seemed to confirm this feeling of exaltation and added to it an element of romance and mystic charm.

It was a little after ten when I left the university, and the nocturnal scene was one of ravishing beauty. The full moon stood high in the heavens and its bright silvery radiance lit up the streets of the town, which were already almost completely deserted and empty, and caused deep black shadows to project from the houses which intercepted its refulgence. There was a weird alternation of darkness and brightness which seemed to tell of mysteries hidden in the gloom which would be revealed and made visible in the bright light. Upon the river the moonlight shone with especial brilliance. Its long-drawn rays were stretched along the surface of the water, covering it, as it were, with a fantastic blanket of variegated illumination, while from innumerable waves and wavelets constantly changing flashes of light sparkled and scintillated. The omnipresent brightness lit up, too, the heavily forested banks on the other side of the Neckar and caused them to stand forth in somber beauty. The air was pleasantly cool, neither cold nor warm, and a balmy breeze blew on my brow and cheeks, somewhat fevered from the excitement of the examination, with delightful and refreshing coolness. On my diploma is recorded that it was conferred on me on the thirty-first day of October in the year one thousand eight hundred eighty-four, but it seems incredible that it should have been so late in the year when I recall the balmy and refreshing temperature of that glorious night, the "night of delight," in the words of Isaiah. But the record, black on white, shows that that was the date, not earlier and not later.

My heart was too full to permit me to return at once to the hotel to the prosaic act of going to bed, and so I wandered about for an hour or more, drinking in the beauty of the night and indulging my joyous and unfettered fancy. I sauntered along the bank of the Neckar, at one part of which I came upon a tavern, from whose open windows a flood of bright light poured. All the adjacent vicinity was plunged in darkness, for all the houses were closed and unlighted, so that the light from the windows of the tavern shone with uncanny brightness. A meeting of students was evidently taking place in the tavern, for the sound of lusty youthful voices, singing student songs with excellent melody and great fervor, resounded in the silent air. The contrast of the brilliant light with the surrounding darkness, and of the joyful, lusty singing with the pervading stillness, was startling. I stood fascinated for a time, gazing at the building, standing forth like a magic palace of light in the surrounding darkness and listening to the merry voices of the youthful singers. It seemed to me as though that radiance and joyous melody were related to my feelings and my experience on that auspicious night.

Sated with profound and varied emotions, I returned to the hotel and slept soundly, for I suddenly realized that I was very, very weary. On the following morning I went to the university at the hour set, received my diploma in due form and ceremony, according to academic usage, and, taking the first train, available, returned to Breslau.

Chapter Eighteen

My Concluding Year in Breslau

A Trip to England and Return to America

OF MY THIRD AND CONCLUDING YEAR IN BRESLAU AND GERMANY there is little to record. This is because, realizing that my years of study and preparation for my vocation were nearing their end and being now in possession of my Ph.D., I decided to cast aside everything not strictly related to my Hebrew and rabbinical work and to devote all, or almost all, of my time and energy to the broadening and deepening of my attainments in the domain of Biblical and Talmudic lore.

Accordingly I dropped nearly all the *allotria* to which I had given a considerable part of my time. I ceased vsiting the theater, reduced my social participation to the minimum indispensable to the maintenance of friendly relations. I even ceased my walks in the Promenade which I had enjoyed so greatly, and concentrated on my Jewish studies, Bible, Talmud, and medieval Hebrew literature, with an occasional modern Jewish work in Hebrew or German. I attended assiduously all the courses at the Seminary and I added to them by my private reading and study at home. Sometimes I did not get more than three or four hours of sleep out of the twenty-four. This exclusive devotion to intellectual activity, with practically no diversion or physical exercise and with very little fresh air was, no doubt, highly inadvisable from the hygienic point of view, but I had my good reasons for pursuing it, and I suffered no evil results therefrom. I do not recall having had even any minor indisposition, such as a headache, during this whole period, and I found the work interesting in the highest degree.

Of course, I took off enough time from my studies to attend to the printing of my dissertation, in accordance with my obligation to the University of Heidelberg. I entrusted this work to a Breslau publishing firm named Preuss. They did a very good job, printing the German, Hebrew, and Arabic text with equal clearness, distinctness, and accuracy. I was very well pleased with their performance, but their German thriftiness went a little too far, for they not only charged me for the printing and material of the book but included in their bill also the cost of the paper and ink used in corresponding with me, the time of the clerk who attended to the correspondence, and the postage. Such pettiness would be unthinkable in our happy country. I sent copies of my dissertation not only to the University of Heidelberg but also to other German universities and presented quite a number to relatives and friends.

Insensibly the closing year of my stay in Germany and my studies in Breslau slipped away. The time had come to make ready for my departure and my return to America. I notified the faculty of the Seminary of my intention and applied for rabbinical ordination. This was not a simple matter, since I had not been in attendance for the full time required. As a rule the Seminary granted ordination only to students who had attended the courses for seven years and, in a few exceptional cases, five years. The faculty was extremely well disposed toward me. They got over the difficulty by granting me a special certificate testifying to my attainments in the field of rabbinical lore, while Rabbi Dr. Joel conferred on me the specific *Semichah* or rabbinical ordination. This, being in strict accordance with traditional Jewish usage, solved the problem satisfactorily.

I was now fully prepared to return home and my ensuing actions were all performed with that purpose in view. The first steps, my leavetakings, involved more than one tug at my heart.

I had announced it as my intention to visit England on my way back to America. Some friends in Breslau, whose names I have unfortunately forgotten and who were related to Dr. Michael Friedlander, principal of Jews' College in London, gave me a letter of introduction to him. Through Professor Graetz I also received a letter of introduction to Dr. Hermann Adler, at that time Delegate Chief Rabbi* of the United Hebrew Congregations of the British

---

* Dr. Adler was then substituting for his father, the Very Reverend Dr. Nathan Marcus Adler, whom he succeeded officially in 1891.—Ed.

Empire. Before finally leaving Germany, I went to Nordheim vor der Rhoen and paid a farewell visit to my dear relatives there. I spent a few days in their very pleasant company and then, after an affectionate and tearful farewell, left for Hamburg, whence I took ship for England.

I arrived in London toward the end of the month of July in the year 1885. I naturally desired to devote a little time to seeing the sights of the vast British metropolis, but I decided to visit first the outstanding Jewish personages to whom I was fortunately in possession of introductions. My first visit was to the acting Chief Rabbi, Dr. Hermann Adler. As I approached the house, I noticed a carriage with coachman and horses standing at the curb. This caused me to fear that the rabbi was about to leave his home and would not be able to see me. Nevertheless I rang the bell and presented my card and letter of introduction to the servant who opened the door. In a minute or two I was summoned into the presence of the rabbi.

Dr. Adler received me with the utmost courtesy. He was a man of noble presence, erect and stately. His expressive countenance, encompassed by a brown full beard, revealed the inner goodness of his nature. His manner was kind and affable, utterly devoid of official stiffness and formality. I was thrilled. It almost seemed as if we were intimate friends, of many years' standing, or as if I were an eminent colleague of his. Of course, we had never met before and I was as yet only at the threshold of a rabbinical career. He explained to me that he was about to go to the funeral of Sir Moses Montefiore and that the carriage which I had seen in front of the house was to convey him to the Bevis Marks synagogue, where the funeral service was to take place. Most cordially he invited me to accompany him in the carriage. Thus it became my privilege to sit at the side of the spiritual leader of the great Jewish community of the British Empire and to be present on the historic occasion of the obsequies of the world-renowned Jewish philanthropist, the saintly Sir Moses Montefiore, whose life of piety, charity, and public beneficence had almost attained the duration of one hundred and one years. Arrived at the synagogue, Dr. Adler gave me in charge of the trustees, who assigned me to a good seat. It goes without saying that the synagogue was filled to its utmost capacity, that throngs filled the adjacent streets, and that Dr. Adler paid an eloquent and touching tribute to the great departed.

A day or two later I visited Dr. Friendlander, principal of Jews' College, and had the priivlege not only of meeting the doctor but also his good lady and his charming daughter Polly, later the wife of Dr. Moses Gaster, *Haham* (or chief rabbi) of the Sephardic community of London. Dr. Friedlander was the typical scholar, thin and pale, with a delicate countenance revealing the man whose life was all intellectual and spiritual, with next to nothing of the physical and material. His courtesy, and that of Mrs. Friedlander and Polly, to me was overwhelming, and the memory of that most impressive and enjoyable meeting will never fade from my mind while life remains.

Having made these two important and significant visits, I devoted the rest of my brief stay in London to sightseeing or rather to acquiring some knowledge of the general aspects of the life of the world metropolis. London was huge, tremendously huge, but it was a dull, monotonous, rather shabby hugeness. In the better districts unending rows of very respectable houses, almost alike, stretehed out interminably in wearisome sameness; in the slum sections, masses of wretched and repulsive structures sheltered equally wretched and repulsive throngs. The different social groups were at once recognizable by their external appearance. The prim, neat gentlemen with high silk hats, the substantial but unpretentious individuals with derbies on their heads, and the sturdy fellows with caps slanting across their brows and scarves around their necks needed no explanations to be at once identified as members respectively of the upper, middle, and lower classes. In the East End I saw numbers of forbidding-looking fellows with dogs, whom one would rather not have encountered on a dark night in a lonely street, and who might have stood—and very likely some did—as models for Dickens' character of Bill Sykes and his dog. There were many great public edifices such as Westminster Abbey or the Houses of Parliament—to mention but two—but their beauty and impressiveness were seriously marred by the grime and soot which disfigured their exteriors. After the spick-and-span elegance of Berlin, or even of Breslau, what might be called the bedraggled or "down-at-the-heels" appearance of much of London was extremely disappointing.

Another troublesome and disagreeable characteristic of London was the difference between its language and that of America. The United States of America and England are supposed to have the same national tongue, the English. That is, of course, fundamentally true, but the pronunciation and accent and the terms used to designate a multitude of articles in daily use and frequently recurring concepts and conditions differ so greatly in the two countries that an American often finds it difficult to understand an Englishman, and —I presume—the reverse is also the case. Indeed, in this regard, it may be easier and pleasanter to get along in a perfectly foreign land where an entirely different language is spoken than in a country whose speech is supposed to be the same as that of one's native land but where so many individual terms and expressions are utterly unfamiliar. In a country which is definitely foreign one learns as much as one can of the prevailing idiom and uses it as the indigenous inhabitants do; in a land possessing supposedly the same language as that of one's home country, one runs constant risk of failing to understand the local terminology or of unwittingly employing some term in an improper or even offensive way. I had a number of such unpleasant experiences. Going into a drug store—which, incidentally, is in London a "chemist's shop"—where postage stamps were sold and asking for one to take a letter to America, I was informed that it cost "tuppensapney." It was with some difficulty that I was made to understand that what was meant was "two pence half-penny." In the boarding house on one occasion I asked for a napkin. My request was received with mingled amusement and embarrassment, for which I saw no reason until I learned that in England the term "napkin" signifies the article of domestic use which in America is called a "diaper." The French term "serviette" is used in England for what Americans call a "napkin." Desiring to make a trip about London and see the sights, I asked my landlady whether there were any sight-seeing buses in London. She did not understand the term "sight-seeing buses" and asked me what they were. I explained that in America by that term was meant a kind of large vehicle with rows of seats or benches in which visitors to the city could ride around and see the important buildings and other sights. With a gleam of intelligence, she said, "Oh, *charabanks!* Certainly, we have those." I learned afterwards that the term "charabank" was an Anglicization of the French *char-a-bancs*—"a car with benches." The examples given are but an infinitesimal portion of the terms and expressions in which the speech of England differs from that of America and which, until he has learned them, makes it so difficult for an American to understand the natives. In America persons going to bed put on pajamas, in England they don pyjamas; in America persons dealing in domestic supplies are grocers, in England green grocers; those who sell vegetables from wagons in America are vegetable peddlers, in England they are costermongers; a stout wagon for the conveyance of heavy articles is in America a truck, in England a lorry; a laborer in England becomes a navvy, gasoline in England is petrol* and so on *ad infinitum*. There are also great differences in pronunciation which make it difficult for the American to understand the English of England. One such difference is the pronunciation of the syllable *ay* or *aye* as though it were *ie or eye. Day* sounds like *die or dye.*

The differences in social customs and food habits combine with the differences in language to make things embarrassing for the "green" American in England. I underwent a few of these embarrassing experiences during may stay in London. Fish is a customary breakfast food in England. My landlady served it constantly, usually in the form of fish cakes. After a few days I grew tired of the constantly recurring marine pabulum and asked my landlady whether she never served cereal for breakfast. "Cereal," she asked uncomprehendingly. "What may that be?" "Oatmeal, for instance," I answered. "And how do they prepare it in the States?" she continued. "They cook it to a mush," I answered, "and then they serve it mixed with milk and cream and sugar." My landlady's face lit up with the light of understanding. "Oh, *porridge*," she said. "Why, certainly, you can have all the porridge you want." So after that I received generous portions of porridge every morning until I tired of its superabundance.

It was rather tedious and lonesome at night-time in London. Most of the evenings I retired to my room after supper and went early to bed. One evening when I did not feel like retiring immediately I went to a music hall for diversion. I was also prompted by curiosity to see what the famous London music halls were like. I sat down at a table

---

* This, like *charabanc*, belongs to a later visit to England, of course.—Ed.

and listened to a rather poor performance. It was something like an American Negro minstrel show but decidedly inferior. Some of the actors were made up as "blackamoors" but they were the most unnatural-looking darkies I had ever seen. A waiter asked me whether I wanted any refreshment. I ordered a glass of lemonade which he brought me promptly. I did not pay at once. That was in accordance with the German custom, to which I had grown accustomed during my three years in Germany. In Germany, according to the custom prevailing at that time, the waiter who served a patron of a *café* or similar place of refreshment did not take the payment. For that purpose there was a special waiter known as the *zahlkellner* or "pay waiter." When the patron was ready to depart, he would knock on the marble table-top and call out *"zahlen"* (payment). Thereupon the *zahlkellner* would come and would ask, *"Was haben Sie gehabt, mein Herr?"* ("What did you have, sir?") The patron would state what he had consumed, pay his bill, and take his leave. In accordance with this custom I neglected to pay, subconsciously expecting that another waiter would come for the payment. But this was entirely contrary to the English custom, which is payment at once to the waiter who has served him. Since I did not do so, the waiter looked at me in surprise and withdrew a little distance away, whence he continued to eye me suspiciously. All this while I sat calmly at my place in blissful ignorance of the thoughts surging through the waiter's mind. After a few moments he must have decided that the thing had evidently gone too far. Coming up to me suddenly with a truculent air, he said:

"I sye, sir, wud you pye, sir?" I pyed.*

From London I went to Liverpool, where I was to take the steamer for America. I found Liverpool cleaner and more modern in appearance, I might say more American-looking, than London. That Sabbath I attended service in the beautiful Princes' Road synagogue. As it happened, there was a vacancy in the position of cantor in the congregation and a candidate for the office, a Rev. Mr. Rudawsky, was officiating. He was a tall, dignified-appearing man, with flowing red hair and beard and a clear, melodious voice, and he chanted the

---

* There were, nevertheless, several aspects of English culture that the author admired greatly, such as the works of Dickens, the exemplary organization of the Anglo-Jewish community, and the generally high standard of manners.—Ed.

Hebrew prayers of the ritual in a manner both pleasing and impressive. I had entered the synagogue as an entire stranger and made no attempt to make myself conspicuous. Somehow or other—I myself do not know how—attention was attracted to me. After the conclusion of the service, a number of the members gathered around me, bade me welcome to Liverpool and addressed various questions to me. Among other things they asked me my opinion of the cantor. I was glad to be able to express a very favorable opinion and I noticed that they listened very attentively to my words. The next morning before leaving the synagogue the cantor came to me, thanked me for my kind words in his behalf and said that my favorable opinion had made his election certain.

His anticipation proved to be correct. A few months later in America I chanced to see *The Jewish Chronicle,* the leading Jewish newspaper of England, and read that Rev. M. Rudawsky had been elected cantor of the Princes' Road synagogue of Liverpool. I believe that Mr. Rudawsky continued to hold that dignified and important post until his death many years later. I wonder whether he ever thought of me in later years. I never saw or heard from him again.

From Liverpool I left for America by the good ship *Aquitania* of the Cunard Line. I arrived in New York toward the end of the month of August, in the year 1885.

Chapter Nineteen

Back in America—New Problems

MY DEAR PARENTS, MY BROTHERS, MY SISTERS, RELATIVES, AND friends were at the pier to greet me when the steamer docked. Of course there was much mutual rejoicing when my dear ones and I met again after a separation of three years. After the initial greetings and embracings and exchange of questions and answers, we repaired to our home in Jersey City. There everything seemed to be absolutely unchanged, to be just the same as I had left it when I departed for Germany. The store on Newark Avenue and the apartment above the store were just about the same as I remembered them and my dear mother assigned to me the same room and bed which I had previously occupied.

But it did not take long for me to realize that a new period in my existence had begun and that I was faced by new problems of the highest importance and seriousness, which would require the utmost courage and wisdom on my part for their solution. These problems, religious in their nature, had to do with the course which I should pursue as a rabbi, as a spiritual leader in Israel. There were also grave economic questions bound up in them, and my whole economic future might depend upon the manner in which I would solve them.

I had been sent to Germany by the Emanu-El Theological Seminary, which was an affiliated institution of the Temple Emanu-El. My entire expenses in Germany had been defrayed by that institution. No influence had been exerted upon me to shape my views, no pressure of any kind had been used by the gentlemen who directed the Seminary to influence my theological opinions or rabbinical policy, but there was, no doubt, a tacit expectation that my views and actions would be in harmony with the religious standpoint of Temple Emanu-El.

My studies in Germany, however, and my contact with Jewish religious life in that country had gradually drawn me away from all sympathy with Reform Judaism as found in America and particularly as represented in the temple under whose sponsorship I had prepared myself for the rabbinate. I had become firmly convinced of the bindingness of authority and tradition upon the individual Jewish conscience and of their indispensability for the proper interpretation and fulfillment of the Jewish faith. These views were poles apart, as far, as the Hebrew phrase words it, "as the East is from the West" from the basic theories and concepts of Reform Judaism. The form of worship carried on in the Reform temples is utterly different from the traditional service of the Orthodox synagogue. Reform Jews, even rabbis of the Reform school, have not the slightest scruples at violating precepts and injunctions of the Bible and of the Talmud. How then could I, holding the convictions I did, align myself with a congregation whose views and practices I could only regard as schismatic? Still, I had been reared under the auspices of the temple, had received great benefits and kindnesses at its hands; how could I utterly fall away and show myself completely unappreciative and ungrateful?

Accordingly I visited several of the trustees, to whom I expressed my gratitude for the kindness which I had received from their congregation and its theological seminary. They were all very courteous and expressed the desire to hear me preach in the temple. Somehow I felt a restraint upon me in my conversation with them and could not tell them how different my concept of Judaism had become. Only to one of them, Mr. Rosenfeld, did I pour out my heart. He was such a perfect gentleman, refined and friendly in his manner, and showed such an unquestionably genuine desire to have me occupy the pulpit of Temple Emanu-El, that I could not withhold from him any thoughts or intentions which were in my mind but revealed to him in full how completely estranged to Reform Judaism I had become. He listened to me patiently, with a sympathetic and understanding expression on his handsome and dignified countenance, and did not in any way indicate antagonism to my views or reproach for my attitude.

When I had finished speaking, he said, in the gentlest and kindliest manner, substantially as follows: "My dear Dr. Drachman, I am pleased to see how sincere you are in your attitude to the Jewish faith. You are indeed a true rabbi, a convinced teacher of Judaism. But I am very sorry that your views seem to take you away from our temple, where you have always been greatly liked. I don't think they should. After all, we are Jews too. Our differences with our Orthodox brethren are only in the ceremonials and externals of Judaism, not in the fundamentals. I hope you will reflect again on these matters. Perhaps you will find a way to avoid estrangement and to remain in harmony with the congregation where you have been reared. At all events, if you are asked to preach in the temple, do not refuse. We certainly have a right to see what kind of man our boy has become." I was deeply moved by Mr. Rosenfeld's kindly and broadminded words. Over against such liberal and considerate reasoning, though I did not completely agree with it, I could not remain recalcitrant. I promised Mr. Rosenfeld that, if I received an invitation to preach in the temple, I would accept.

A few days later I received a formal invitation in writing to occupy the pulpit of the temple on the following Sabbath, and on that day I officiated as guest speaker in Emanu-El, the one and only occasion that I have acted in that capacity. In thus participating in the Reform service of the temple, I was confronted with a conscientious difficulty which may seem, to those unacquainted with rabbinic law, a trifling matter but which, to Orthodox Jews, is of the utmost seriousness. The services in Temple Emanu-El, as in all Reform temples of its type, are conducted with uncovered head. This is strictly prohibited by the *Shulchan Arukh,* the authorized code of rabbinic law, which ordains, in particular, that the Hebrew name of Deity shall be pronounced only by a person whose head is duly and reverently covered.

How was I to avoid violation of this precept? Had I actually conducted the service, it would have been impossible, since the Divine name occurs frequently in the ritual, but as my function was to deliver a sermon, I managed to do so by substituting the Hebrew term *Ha-Shem* ("the Name") wherever the Divine name occurred in a passage which I quoted. Actually I did not participate in the worship at all, for I had read the entire Orthodox service at home before coming to the temple, and I limited my participation in the temple service to the delivery of the sermon.

The result was as could be imagined. I will say nothing as to the quality of the sermon itself, which is not involved in this description. But my non-participation in the service and my refraining from uttering the Hebrew name of God were noticed and, quite naturally under the circumstances, aroused resentment. After the service, Mr. Rosenfeld, with regret in his voice, informed me that my principles precluded the possiblity of my becoming the rabbi of Temple Emanu-El. That was the beginning and the end of my connection with the temple.

In justice to the sense of fair play and the generosity of the people of the congregation, I must, however, state that, although they were undoubtedly disappointed in me, and displeased with my principles, I nevertheless received a few days later from the secretary of the temple an official letter of thanks and a check of one hundred dollars.

There now began for me a period of uncertainty. It almost seemed for a time that I had mistaken my vocation, that there was no room, no demand in America for an American-born, English-speaking rabbi who insisted on maintaining the laws and usages of Traditional Judaism even in the services of the synagogue. In the America of that time, Reform Judaism, mainly in the form established by Dr. Isaac M. Wise, had conquered almost the entire field of Jewish life and had been accepted by practically all the congregations of standing and importance. There were a few Orthodox congregations whose members were American-born or Americanized immigrants, and whose pulpits were occupied by English-speaking rabbis, but there were no vacancies and no immediate prospects of any. There were considerable groups of Eastern European, Polish and Russian, Jews, in the East side or Ghetto districts of the great cities, who adhered to the Orthodox traditions of their native lands, but they were Yiddish-speaking and wanted rabbis of that type. They were strange to me, and I was even stranger to them. I preached by invitation in a few of these synagogues but, while my sermons made considerable impression and there was a great deal of admiration—as well as amazement —for me as an American young man who had renounced Reform and was energetically championing the cause of the ancient traditional Jewish faith, these sentiments did not materialize in the form of a call to the rabbinate of any of these congregations.

In the meantime, time was passing and I was living at the home of my parents, dependent on their parental kindness. They were most loving and affectionate and did not in any way reproach me or even criticize or question the wisdom of the course on which I had embarked. But I could see that they were grievously disappointed and felt the gravest of forebodings concerning my future. I, too, began to think that there was really no hope, with my Orthodox views, of finding a suitable field of activity in my native land. But I was "game." I had no thought of renouncing my principles, of becoming, for material reasons, the champion or advocate of a form or system which, I was convinced, was not in accord with the true concept of Judaism. I resolved that, if I found that there was no opening for me in harmony with my religious views, I would retire from the ministry and endeavor to earn my livelihood in some other field of activity but that, under no circumstances, would I sell my soul for a mess of pottage.

I did not, however, remain passive or inactive. I spoke, as invited guest, in a number of synagogues and at meetings of Jewish organizations. Too, I contributed a number of articles to Jewish publications. In all my sermons and addresses and in all my articles in the Jewish press I spoke from the viewpoint of historic Judaism. I stressed, as fervently and eloquently as I could, the duty of modern, particularly American, Jews to remain loyal to the religious heritage which had come to them from ancient days, and I opposed with especial emphasis the idea that so-called reforms, undermining the religio-legal foundations of Judaism, were necessary in order to present our faith to the world in an esthetic and impressive manner, worthy of the culture and refinement of the modern age.

I emphasized the thought, which had been translated into reality earlier in the century in Frankfort on the Main by the God-intoxicated leader of Orthodox Judaism, Samson Raphael Hirsch, that there is nothing in the ancient faith of Israel which requires that it be carried out in the rude and uncouth manner brought about by the conditions of the Ghetto, that, on the contrary, it is worthy of being presented with all the accompaniments of beauty and splendor and impressiveness which we are capable of supplying, without, on that account, departing in the slightest from the rules and ordinances of our religious code.

Through the instrumentality of these addresses and articles, the attention of the Jewish public was attracted to me. Two or three months after my return to America, in the autumn of 1885, sitting in my parental home in Jersey City, I received an unexpected visit of a delegation of the Congregation *Oheb Sholom* of Newark, New Jersey. They came to offer me the post of rabbi in their synagogue. I had not applied for the position, had not even known of the existence of the congregation. They, however, had become aware of me through the reports of my public activities and, on the strength of these reports, were prepared to accept me as their spiritual leader without any trial sermon or other test of my ability. They assured me that, in all respects except one, their synagogue was conducted in strict accordance with the regulations of the Orthodox religious code. This exception was that at public services men and women sat together, whereas the Jewish code requires that on these occasions the sexes shall be separated. Special conditions existing in their congregation, they told me, made it impossible for them to conform to the traditional usage in this regard. Otherwise, they insisted, they were most desirous of maintaining the genuine historic tenets of Judaism in their synagogue, and especially they were anxious to have as their spiritual leader one who would strengthen them in their adherence to the true traditional faith of Israel and not one who would corrupt and weaken their loyalty and lead them astray to Reform.

Strict consistency would perhaps have required me to reject their offer, but the last-mentioned consideration decided me in their favor. I reflected that it was perhaps not wise to adopt an intransigent attitude over against all those groups who had deviated more or less but without deliberate revolutionary purpose from the time-honored paths of Judaism. I recognized the real danger in which such a group stood of falling into the hands of a mis-called rabbi who would rob them, under the guise of preaching Judaism, of all their inherited Jewish loyalty. I remembered the injunction of the Talmud: "Be gentle with Israel; it is better that they should transgress ignorantly than that they should rebel deliberately"; and I said "yes" to the committee. Thus I became the rabbi of Congregation *Oheb Sholom* of Newark, New Jersey.

I did not remain very long in that position. Owing to unexpected and unpredictable conditions, my incumbency lasted only a little over a year, but my experiences and observations in Newark were most interesting and are indelibly stamped upon my memory.

The Newark of those days, although already quite a large town of approximately a hundred thousand population, had many characteristics of a rural settlement. Many parts of the town, especially in the upper section, where the synagogue of Congregation *Oheb Sholom* was situated, were practically open country with cultivated fields and empty lots; a goodly part of the population lived in small cottages and kept cows and poultry, and social life had the friendliness and simplicity characteristic of rural districts.

The Jewish community, although working together in matters of public concern, was divided into four distinctly recognizable groups, in accordance with the countries of their origin. They were the Germans, the Bohemians or Czecho-Slovakians, the Poseners—people originating from the province of Posen in Prussia, sometimes called "*Herzogthuemers*," because Posen had formerly been a *Herzogthum* or duchy—and the Russian-Polish. Each element was represented by a main congregration or synagogue. The Germans were represented by the Radical Reform Temple, the Bohemians by the Congregation *Oheb Sholom*, the Poseners by the Congregation *B'nai Abraham*, and the Russian-Polish by the Congregation *Anshe Russia*. These divisions were not absolute, for the common Jewish heritage had caused many individual Jews to join congregrations whose main membership was not that in which they had been born.

The first thing which impressed me was the great difference between the Jewish communities of Newark and Jersey City, in which the early years of my life had been passed, despite their great topographical nearness. Only a few miles separated the two communities, but they were as different as though they were hundreds of miles removed from each other. The Jewish population of Newark was far greater than that of Jersey City. It numbered twenty thousand souls, more or less, while the Jews of Jersey City numbered not more than a few hundred families. Neither was there in Jersey City the sharp division into different elements characteristic of Newark. The Jewish life of Newark was also, I must admit, far deeper and stronger than that of the home of my youth. I noticed these things and, wonderingly, I said, "So near and yet so far apart." I could think of no reason for these differences. But so it was!

When I got to know the people of my congregation, which I did very quickly, I liked them very much. I had never before met Bohemian Jews to any extent. What I saw of their ways and characteristics was quite a revelation, and a very pleasing one. They were, on the whole, very similar to the Jews of South Germany, but there were also strong differences. Their native tongue was German, but in America they had largely adopted the English, and the speech of the younger generation was almost exclusively English. Their religious life, I observed with pleasure, was sincerely and loyally Jewish. Nearly all the homes were observant of the dietary laws, quite a number were Sabbath-keeping, and even some of the stores kept by Bohemian Jews were, a rare thing in America, closed on the Sabbath day. The services in the synagogue were, with the one exception above noted, absolutely in accordance with Orthodox usage. The strong religious feeling of the congregation was evidenced by the fact that it maintained a Talmud Torah and laid great stress on the Jewish education of the children. It was a part of my duty as rabbi to act as superintendent of the school and instruct the highest class. I accepted this task with pleasure, for I have always believed in the fundamental importance and necessity of thorough instruction in the spiritual and cultural heritage of Israel for the upbringing of a loyal and competent Jewish generation. Besides, I personally enjoy the work of teaching. To expound the beauties of the Holy Tongue and the sublime spiritual and ethical teachings and symbolic usages of Judaism has always been a delight to me. So, although in many congregations the rabbis are not required to do this work, I cheerfully agreed to undertake it and, as long as I was connected with the congregation, I devoted myself to the task of teaching as conscientiously and faithfully as to any other of my rabbinical duties.

Shortly after my election as rabbi, the congregation celebrated the event by a formal installation. There was a double celebration, a solemn religious service in the synagogue and a banquet in a hall in the lower section of Newark. The chief speaker at the synagogue service was Rabbi Dr. Alexander Kohut, who had been called shortly before from Hungary to the pulpit of Congregation *Ahawath Chesed* of New York City. Dr. Kohut was renowned as a brilliant orator and a great Hebrew scholar, undoubtedly one of the greatest Talmudists who have ever been in America. He was the author of a monumental dictionary of the Talmudic Hebrew, the *Aruch Ha-Shalem* or *Aruch Completum*. Although he had accepted a call to a Reform congregation, Dr. Kohut was strongly conservative in his views and had become involved in a sharp controversy with leaders of Reform on the question of the bindingness of tradition in Judaism, in which he defended his side of the controversy with profound erudition and consummate ability. I will not deny that this fact had much to do with the influencing of my choice of Dr. Kohut as the rabbi to officiate at my installation. Dr. Kohut also attended the banquet, which was furthermore graced by the presence of the Mayor of Newark, Hon. James J. Haynes.* The mayor was a most democratic individual and his informal ways were a source of constant wonderment to Dr. Kohut, accustomed to the hauteur and reserve of Hungarian officialdom. Thus, when a Negro waiter greeted the mayor and the latter cordially responded and shook the waiter's hand, Dr. Kohut looked on in amazement and, turning to me, said, *"Das waere in Ungarn unmoeglich. Hier sieht man die echte Demokratie."* ("This would be impossible in Hungary. In this country one sees genuine democracy.")

Among the members of Congregation *Oheb Sholom,* who were, on the whole, of a very respectable middle-class type, there were a number of interesting personages and fine, outstanding characters whom I remember with pleasure and respect. The most outstanding was undoubtedly Rev. Isaac Schwarz, with whose family I made my home on taking up my residence in Newark. Mr. Schwarz was of distinguished Jewish ancestry, being a brother of two prominent Bavarian rabbis, Israel and Joseph Schwarz. The latter was the more famous of the two, having been the author of a highly esteemed Hebrew

---

* I am not sure that I remember the first name of the Mayor correctly. His surname was, however, without doubt as given, Haynes.—B.D.

work, "*Tebuoth Haaretz*," on the geography, geology, and history of Palestine, of which land he became a resident, at a time when to reside in the Holy Land was very unusual and a sign of exceptional piety. This work was translated into both German and English, the German version, entitled *"Das Heilige Land"* ("The Holy Land") being by Israel Schwarz, and the English version entitled *"A Descriptive and Historical Sketch of Palestine"* by the well known American rabbi Isaac Leeser. Isaac Schwarz was a worthy brother of these distinguished leaders of Israel.

The Loewenstein family was related to the Schwarzes and marked by similar characteristics. Mrs. Loewenstein, in particular, was a lady of great culture and refinement as well as of sturdy Judaism. The two Kohn brothers were fine typical Jewish *baale batim,* or householders, and pillars of the congregation. Mrs. Rosa Kohn, wife of one of the brothers, in whose home I boarded during the second period of my stay in Newark, was a woman of exceptional spirituality and delicacy of sentiment, for whose nobility of character I had the greatest admiration. The Kohn family contributed a most worthy member to the Conservative rabbinate of America, Dr. Jacob Kohn, for many years in New York, at present in charge of a prominent congregation in Los Angeles. Miss Sarah Kussy, the well known Zionist worker, is also a native of Newark and related to the Kohn family. At the time of my stay in Newark she was a little girl. There were many other excellent people and loyal Jews connected with the congregation.

At the time of my election the post of *chazan,* or cantor, was vacant. The congregation left the choice of the cantor to me. That was a most unusual proceeding. My choice fell on the Rev. Solomon Rappaport, and he was elected. He was well worthy of the post, being a young man of fine Jewish background, a member of the well known Jewish family Rappaport of Galicia, of handsome and dignified appearance and the possessor of a very melodious and cultured voice. A somewhat humorous incident occurred in connection with his candidacy. On the occasion of his trial officiation, his rendition of the service aroused great enthusiasm. One of the most enthusiastic of his auditors was an elderly man named Matz, a native, I believe, of Alsatia, that border province which has been alternately French and

German for a century or more. This man, who was very fond of *Chazonuss*, the traditional Hebrew chants and melodies of the ritual, was unfortunately afflicted with a throat trouble which rendered his voice extremely hoarse and his words very difficult to understand. When the service was concluded a number of people went up to Mr. Rappaport to offer their congratulations on his beautiful officiation. Among them was Mr. Matz. Filled with a desire to express his unbounded admiration he approached the cantor, extended his hand, and said, in his Alsatian Jewish German, and in a hoarse and almost inaudible tone, *"Shkoach, Sie haben wunderbar georht, Sie bekommen meine Stimme."* ("I congratulate you. You officiated wonderfully. You will get my vote.") A burst of laughter greeted these words. Unfortunately the German word *stimme* signifies not only *vote* but also *voice,* and they took it in the latter sense. Horrified, Mr. Rappaport exclaimed, *"Gott soll hueten dass ich Ihre Stimme bekomme!"*) (The Lord forbid that I get your voice!) Matz joined in the general laughter which followed.

The social life in the congregation was very pleasant. Not only did the members and their families come together quite frequently in social gatherings but the prevailing tone was truly friendly and brotherly. The congregation was a true brother band, very much, indeed, like a big family. The religious spirit was equally true and genuine. Quite a number of the members were profoundly devout and imbued with sincere love for Judaism, its teachings and practices. This religious zeal showed itself in the many questions concerning Jewish doctrines and precepts which were addressed to me and the almost pathetic eagerness with which they listened to my answers. It was evident that they took their Judaism very seriously.

The two families in whose homes I had the privilege of living while in Newark, the Schwarzes and the Kohns, were particularly fine representatives of the religious fervor of the community. It was a spiritual privilege to dwell with them, so true and fervent was the Jewish atmosphere which prevailed in their homes.

In the midst of this community I labored with joy and contentment, feeling that I was really rendering some service to the cause of Israel. In addition to my routine duties as rabbi, preaching, teaching, officiating at ceremonies, and answering religious questions, I was quite active in public life. I participated in public movements and addressed meetings of organizations, usually in English but occasionally in German. But, as already stated, I was not destined to remain there long. An event of great significance to American Jewish life in general forced me out of my quiet and sheltered nook to take part in the broad, continent-wide activity of the American Jewish world.

Chapter Twenty

American Israel at the Cross Roads

The Founding of the Jewish Theological Seminary

DOCTOR ALEXANDER KOHUT, WHO HAD INSTALLED ME AS RABBI OF the Congregation *Oheb Sholom* of Newark, New Jersey, had come to America in 1885. He had been called from his native Hungary to the post of rabbi of the Congregation *Ahavath Chesed* of New York, N. Y., a large and important organization. There may have been something providential in our practically simultaneous arrival in America. Divine Providence may have designed that we, together with several other sincere and earnest Jewish spiritual leaders, should be the instruments for the creation of a new era in American Judaism.

Dr. Kohut was a strong believer in the authority of Jewish tradition and the bindingness of rabbinic law on the conscience of modern Israel. How he reconciled this conviction with the acceptance of a post in a Reform congregation which had departed in many ways from the precepts of rabbinic law I do not know. Shortly after his arrival in America he openly and energetically espoused this view in a series of lectures on the *Pirke Aboth*, "The Chapters of the Fathers," a Talmudic treatise containing the statements on doctrinal and ethical themes of many of the Talmudic sages.* These lectures, which were

---

* I had occasion to become personally aware of his respect for Rabbinic ordinances. Calling upon him one day shortly before the Feast of Tabernacles, I found him absorbed in the study of the *Shulchan Aruch*, the code of Rabbinic law. He had been asked by one of the members of his congregation to perform a marriage ceremony in *Chol Ha-Moed*, the intermediate period of the festival, when marriages are forbidden by Rabbinic law except in certain emergencies. He was looking to see whether a permission could be found. He asked me what I did in such cases. I answered that I declined to perform such ceremonies. He subsequently inquired of a well-known Conservative rabbi and was amazed and horrified to hear from his lips that he followed his own sweet will without regard to the precepts of the Rabbinic code. Dr. Kohut strongly condemned such an irreverent attitude over against the traditional law and usages of Israel.—B.D.

in the nature of a summons and appeal to American Jews to depart from the paths of Reform and to return to the unaltered and unadulterated Judaism of their forefathers, coming, as they did, from one who enjoyed the highest reputation for Hebrew scholarship and who stood at the head of a great and prominent Reform congregation, produced a tremendous furore in the ranks of Reform Jewry. A vigorous controversy followed. In their pulpits, the leaders of Reform attacked Dr. Kohut, who defended his views with energy and keen reasoning. His vast erudition enabled him to use both most effectively, and with brilliant eloquence.

Not content with mere pulpit fulminations, the Reform leaders summoned a congress or conference of those who agreed with their views in order to put the standpoint of Radical Reform before the American Jewish public with the utmost possible force. This conference took place at Pittsburgh, Pennsylvania, on November 16th to 18th, 1885. It became notorious for the boldest negation of fundamental doctrines of Judaism in the history of American, and, indeed, of world Jewry. It rejected the idea of Divine revelation and the entire ceremonial legislation of the Mosaic code, acknowledging as binding only the moral laws. It specifically permitted the reception of male proselytes into the Jewish fold without circumcision, a rite traditionally considered most sacred and binding upon the native-born male Israelite and convert alike. It endorsed Sunday services as a sort of substitute for, or rival of, the historical seventh-day Sabbath worship.

The conference was not numerically impressive, with only nineteen rabbis attending it, but among these were the most prominent representatives of the Reform rabbinate of the time, Doctors Kaufman Kohler of New York, Isaac M. Wise of Cincinnati, and S. H. Sonnenschein of St. Louis. This fact, coupled with the wide publicity given it, made the conference very important. The purpose of its promoters was palpably to deal a mortal blow to Orthodox Judiasm. If so, they failed completely in their attempt, for the very reverse was the effect.

All those to whom the historic concept and the traditional laws and usages of Judaism were precious were shocked and horrified. These included not only the strictly Orthodox but also many of the Conservative who, though permitting themselves certain deviations were in substantial agreement with the Orthodox. They were stirred to action. They felt that something must be done if the ancient faith of of Israel was to be preserved from utter disintegration and downfall in the New World. The rabbis of both Orthodox and Conservative congregations began to confer as to what form this so urgently needed action should take. The leading figures in this movement were the rabbis of the Sephardic congregations of the America,* Sabato Morais of the Congregation *Mikveh Israel* of Philadelphia, Henry Pereira Mendes of the Congregation *Shearith Israel* of New York, and Meldola de Sola of the Congregation *Shaar Ha-Shamaim* of Montreal, Canada. These were men of profound religious feeling and sturdy loyalty to the tenets of Traditional Judaism, ideal types of the Jewish minister.

Sabato Morais was undoubtedly the one of outstanding importance. A native of Italy, he combined remarkably the ancient faith and culture of Israel with the literary and esthetic qualities of his native land. He was a master of the Hebrew language, which he wrote with classic purity and beauty. His ethical standards were of the highest. He was an earnest and impressive preacher in lofty and well worded English, and his manner and bearing had the gravity and dignity which comported well with the noble ideals which he championed. Henry Pereira Mendes and Meldola de Sola were also splendid representatives of the Orthodox Jewish ministry. Mendes had a truly spiritual concept of the Jewish faith and was an untiring worker in every cause which promised to bring spiritual and ethical exaltation to the Jewish people. De Sola was especially known for his courageous and uncompromising defense of Orthodox Judiasm against the inroads of Reform.

Of rabbis representing the *Ashkenazic* section of the American Jewish community, Henry W. Schneeberger of the Congregation *Chizuk Emunah* of Baltimore, Maryland, Moses Maisner of the Congregation *Adath Israel* of New York, and I were the chief participants. Like myself, Schneeberger was of American birth and had

---

* The term *Sephardic* designated the Jews of Spanish or Portuguese ancestry. The Jews who originate directly or remotely from Germany are known as *Ashkenazim*. There are slight differences of ritual and Hebrew pronunciation between the two elements, but they are united in their adherence to Orthodox Judaism.—B.D.

received his rabbinical training in Germany. He was a man of sincere piety and loyal observance, and his congregation was drawn from the relatively small but earnest element of Jews of German origin who had not succumbed to the allurements of Reform but had remained faithful to the historical concept of Judaism prevelant in the land of their ancestry. Moses Maisner was a native of Hungary, trained in the *Yeshivoth*, or Talmudic academies, of his native land, learned in rabbinic lore and strictly adherent to Orthodox tradition. His congregation, too, composed of Jews of mainly German origin, was conducted along strictly traditional lines. I participated in the movement not only in accordance with my own inner convictions but at the special and urgent request of Rabbis Morais and Mendes.

Immediately after the Pittsburgh conference had taken place, I had received letters from both of these noble representatives of Orthodox Judaism, whom I did not at the time know personally. They pointed out the crisis in Jewish affairs which that sacrilegious gathering had produced. They assured me that they had taken note of my outspoken utterances in behalf of Traditional Judaism, and they asked my assistance in repelling the onslaught of Radical Reformers on the sacred traditions of the ancestral faith. I answered, assuring them of my complete agreement with their view of the situation created by the Pittsburgh conference and my sincere cooperation in any effort to strengthen the cause of Israel's ancient faith. The only rabbinical representative of Conservative Judaism whom I can recall as having taken part in the movement was Dr. Alexander Kohut, but he, with his vast erudition and fiery eloquence, was a tower of strength and an inspiring and very attractive influence to many who might otherwise have held aloof.

The Orthodox and Conservative Jewish laity of America was splendidly represented among the participants in the movement. While their number was not very great, they were without exception men who, by virtue of their fine standing as citizens and their sincere loyalty to Traditional Judaism, were eminently fitted to launch a purely religious movement of this nature. They were a truly representative cross-cut of the religious element of American Jewry, with the exception of one section thereof, the Jews of Eastern European origin. These stood mainly aloof, not because of any fundamental ideological difference (for they were, in their overwhelming majority, loyal adherents of the traditional concept of Judaism) but because they were not yet completely integrated into American life and did not feel entirely at home in the company of their brethren of other origin.

Among the laymen most conspicuously identified wiith the movement and whom I best remember were A. R. Altmayer, Louis Ash, Joseph Blumenthal, Max Cohen, Dr. S. Solis-Cohen, Newman Cowen, Dr. Aaron Friedenwald, Daniel P. Hays, Nathan Hirsch, S. W. Korn, L. Napoleon Levy, Moses Ottinger, Edgar J. Phillips, S. M. Roeder, Edward L. Rothschild, A. S. Solomons, and Jonas Weil. These, and the many other participants not mentioned here, were practically all either American-born or thoroughly Americanized gentlemen who were at the same time sincere upholders of the traditional concept of Judaism. Most were members of Orthodox congregations, both Sephardic and Ashkenazic, some of Conservative congregations, but all were strongly opposed to the destructive tendencies of Radical Reform, as had been expressed in the Pittsburgh Conference.

After a sufficient number of congregations and individuals had signified their assent to the movement, its inaugurators called a conference or convention to consider the steps to be taken. This convention took place in the early days of January 1886, in a hall on Sixth Avenue in the neighborhood of Thirty-fourth Street, New York City, which bore, if I remember rightly, the name of Liberty Hall. It was a highly successful convention, indeed, the most emphatic demonstration of the strength of the historical religious sentiment that had yet been given in the history of American Jewry. The number of congregations represented and the number of delegates in attendance, not only from New York but also from Philadelphia and Baltimore and several other cities and towns, while not very great, was amply sufficient to show that a very considerable section of the American Jewish community was still loyally attached to the traditional concept of the Jewish faith. Above all, the convention was successful through the magnificent spirit which prevailed. It was a spirit of grave earnestness and of firm determination, of full realization of the difficulties to which the maintenance of the ancient faith was exposed under

American conditions. A high resolve prevailed to do something real and substantial for the improvement of those conditions and for the bringing about of a better and happier future.

The addresses delivered by the rabbis and several of the laymen were on a high plane of eloquence and earnest thought. In these I took part, and I contributed, I trust, some useful service to the solution of the problems before the assembly. After full and earnest debate, it was resolved that the best and most advisable action for the defense of Traditional Judaism from the inroads of Radical Reform and its protection against unauthorized and improper innovations, in doctrine and practice, would be the establishment of a Jewish Theological Seminary, in which rabbis would be trained who would uphold and promulgate the authentic tenets of Judaism. Amid great enthusiasm and, as far as I can recollect, without a single dissenting voice, the gathering voted to organize the Jewish Theloogical Seminary Association of New York and to charge it with the task of establishing and maintaining the seminary. Two bodies were chosen to conduct the affairs of the seminary, the board of trustees to attend to its financial and material interests, and the faculty to arrange and supervise the course of instruction. Joseph Blumenthal was elected president of the board of trustees, and Dr. Sabato Morais president of the faculty. Dr. Morais was given full authority to select the individuals who would constitute the actual teaching staff. The convention then adjourned, with delegates and visitors alike inspired by the conviction that a most important step had been taken for the defense and permanent maintenance of Historical Judaism in America.

Although a certain proportion of the organizing delegates and participating rabbis belonged to the Conservative wing of Judaism, the principles of the seminary, as declared in its charter of incorporation, granted by the Legislature of the State of New York on the ninth of May, 1886, were those of uncompromising adherence to the tenets of Orthodox Judaism. They are there stated in the following clear and unambiguous language: "The purpose of this association is the preservation in America of the knowledge and practice of historical Judaism, as ordained in the Law of Moses and expounded by the prophets and sages of Israel in Biblical and Talmudical writings." The specific term "Orthodox" is not used, but the definition of Judaism given in this statement of principles is in exact accordance with the significance universally attached to that term.

A few days after the close of the convention, I received from Dr. Morais a letter requesting me to meet him for the purpose of discussing with him matters relating to the work of the seminary. At the meeting, which took place in the vestry of the Spanish and Portuguese Synagogue in New York, at that time situated in West Nineteenth Street, Dr. Morais informed me that he desired to appoint me a salaried member of the teaching staff of the seminary and asked me whether I would be willing to accept such appointment. I answered that I felt greatly gratified by the offer and that I should be glad to accept, as the work was exactly after my heart, but only if he was thoroughly convinced of my worthiness for the post. We then read together some Biblical and rabbinical selections—it was a sort of informal examination, though not technically so—and discussed various questions of Jewish lore, after which Dr. Morais declared that he was thoroughly satisfied with my attainments and qualifications and that he appointed me to the post in question. My precise title and the subjects I was to teach were left for later decision.

Thus began the second period of my career in America, my connection with the Jewish Theological Seminary in its work of training the leaders and teachers of Historical Judaism in the New World. It was destined to last many years, to be exact twenty-three in all, and to exercise, I may say without self-praise, an appreciable influence upon the course of Judaism in America and Europe alike.

Chapter Twenty-one

Work at the Jewish Theological Seminary Begins

Farewell to Newark

A New Congregational Position in New York City

THE PROCESS OF LAUNCHING THE SEMINARY UPON ITS APPOINTED task was carried out energetically and speedily. Dr. Morais did not permit any "grass to grow under his feet." The establishment of an institution for advanced instruction in Hebraic lore meant for him the realization of a life-long dream, and he proceeded to carry it out with the enthusiasm and thoroughness which come from the fulfillment of one's long-cherished ideals.

His first act was to organize the teaching staff. He appointed as instructor or preceptor in Talmud Dr. Gustave Liebermann, a splendid representative of the finest and highest type of Hungarian Orthodox Jewry. He had been a student at Hungarian *Yeshivoth* and had received a thorough training in Biblical and Talmudic lore purely out of love for the religious and cultural heritage of Israel. At the same time, he had been thoroughly grounded in the secular culture of the age. After failing in business, he left his native land, together with his wife and a family of five young children, two sons and three daughters. He had arrived in America two or three years before the establishment of the Seminary. In this country he did not hesitate to make use of his Hebrew attainments for the purpose of supporting himself and his family and had, in this manner, attracted the attention of Jonas Weil, a religious and philanthropic co-religionist of German origin who became his sincere admirer and devoted friend.

Dr. Liebermann was introduced to Dr. Morais, who at once recognized his outstanding abilities and appointed him to the seminary post of preceptor in Talmud.

The other members of the faculty, except myself, were all voluntary instructors. They were Dr. Morais, Dr. Kohut, Dr. Mendes, and Dr. Maisner. I do not remember just what subjects each taught, but among them they covered the various parts of Biblical and rabbinical instruction. As for me, in the course of my connection with the Seminary I have taught, at one time or another, practically all the subjects which belong to a rabbinic course: Hebrew language, Biblical exegesis, medieval Jewish philosophy, Talmud, rabbinic codes, and homiletics. I was a sort of rabbinic "general utility man" and did whatever was necessary or desirable at any particular time, without overmuch consideration of the monetary reward, which was, at least in the early days of the Seminary, very moderate.

I enjoyed the confidence and trust of Dr. Morais until his greatly lamented demise in 1897. A few years after the establishment of the Seminary I was made dean of the faculty, I think in 1889, and held that post until the reorganization of the Seminary in 1901 under the presidency of Dr. Solomon Schechter.

The opening of the Seminary attracted a splendid group of youths as students, not very numerous, but of outstanding quality. They were almost entirely of European birth and had already received substantial preparatory training in European Jewish schools. Of these I especially recall Herman Abramowitz, Bernard Ehrenreich, Michael M. Eichler, Leon M. Elmaleh, Michael Fried, Israel Goldfarb, Julius H. Greenstone, Emanuel Hertz, Joseph Herman Hertz, Hirschman Hillel Kauvar, Bernard S. Kaplan, Mordecai M. Kaplan, Morris Mandel, Elias S. Solomon, and Henry Speaker. Most of these became in later years respected and valued spiritual leaders of Jewish congregations; some attained to great distinction. The outstanding figure among them is undoubtedly Joseph Herman Hertz, who, after serving with great ability and success in important congregations in Syracuse, N. Y., in South Africa, and in New York City, was chosen in 1913 Chief Rabbi of the United Synagogue of the British Empire, the most exalted Jewish position on earth—with the possible exception of the chief rabbinate of Palestine—which pre-

eminent post he still—1943—occupies with great renown and honor.*
The fact to be stressed is that, with the establishment of the Jewish
Theological Seminary of New York and the training of a goodly
number of spiritual leaders dedicated to the Orthodox and Conservative concepts of Judaism, the flood of Radical Reform, which had
threatened to overflow all America and wash away every trace of
respect for and loyalty to the historic landmarks of the Jewish faith
and to spread its baleful influence to the ancient communities of
Israel in the lands of the Old World, had been definitely checked.
Since this saving deed the name America is no longer synonymous
with the negative and destructive tendencies in Judaism and Jewish
thought. Indeed, there has been a true revival of Historic Judaism.
In bringing about this change of sentiment and of conditions, the
Jewish Theological Seminary of America has been an important,
though by no means the only, influence.

When I accepted the appointment to a preceptorship in the Seminary, my idea was to combine it with my position of rabbi to the
Congregation *Oheb Sholom* of Newark and to perform the duties of
both places. I soon found that this was not practicable. The time
consumed in traveling between the two cities and the difficulty of
avoiding conflict in the hours of instruction rendered it impossible to
do justice to both positions. Nor was the congregation satisfied with
a rabbi of divided allegiance. They wanted a spiritual leader who was
entirely their own, a point of view which I could not but recognize as
justified. Proverbially no man can serve two masters. Thus it became
necessary for me to decide which master I should serve. After earnest
and profound reflection I decided that I could render more valuable
service to Judaism in the Seminary than in an individual congregation, especially when located in a somewhat distant city. Accordingly,
after a month or so of fruitless endeavor to accomplish loyal service
to both, I resigned my post in the Congregation *Oheb Sholom* to devote myself henceforth to the service of the Seminary. The congregation was sorry to see me go, and I have retained pleasant memories
of my connection with it and friendly relations with some of its people
up to the present day.

---

* Chief Rabbi Hertz died in Jan. 1946, at the age of 73.—Ed.

Moving to New York, I sought and found an ideal home with the Rosenberg family, residing in Fifty-second Street between First and Second Avenues. They were really a remarkable family and, in fact, were among the determinative influences of my life. Never before or since have I met people of such profound piety and fear of God, of such sincere and conscientious observance of the precepts of Judaism to the smallest detail.

There was an aged grandfather, the father of Mrs. Rosenberg, named Herzberg—Rabbi Eliezer Herzberg he was called, although he was not, to the best of my knowledge, an officiating rabbi. His mode of life can only be called saintly. He was at this time retired from all secular activity and devoted himself exclusively to the service of religion and charity. When he was not praying or studying the Holy Law, he was busily occupied in raising funds for the relief of the poor, especially those of the Holy Land, and he was very successful in this. Indeed, he was so successful that once when he planned to settle in Palestine himself, the rabbis of Jerusalem cabled him in alarm that he should by no means come, lest it would involve the cessation of the invaluable aid which he was rendering to the poor of the Holy Land.

Rabbi Eliezer's two daughters and sons-in-law and their families were passionately loyal to Jewish tradition. Never will I forget how on *Tishah B'Ab,* the ninth of Ab, the day on which the destruction of the Temple and the downfall of the Jewish nation are annually commemorated in Jewish homes with fasting and lamentation, on returning from the synagogue I found the entire Rosenberg family sitting on the floor weeping and reciting the *Lamentations* of Jeremiah. It was a thrilling and moving sight. It almost seemed as though the grief-laden elegy of the Psalmist were being enacted before my eyes: "By the rivers of Babylon, there we sat, yea, we wept when we remembered Zion."

About this time a new synagogue was opened in New York City which, it appeared to me, would be a very promising field for true Jewish spiritual activity as I conceived it, and I longed to devote my energy and whatever ability I possessed to its cultivation and development. It was erected in a splendid location in upper New York City, at the corner of Lexington Avenue and Seventy-second

Street by the Congregation *Beth Israel Bikkur Cholim,* whose former house of worship had been situated in Chrystie Street on the lower East Side. This was one of the older congregations of the city, having been founded in 1847, and its members consisted mainly of Americanized Jews of Polish origin and their American-born posterity. The downtown synagogue had always been conducted in strict accordance with Orthodox tradition. The history and composition of the congregation seemed to indicate that it would be naturally receptive to my concept of Judaism, the union of loyal adherence to the precepts of the historic faith with modern culture and demeanor. My position in the Seminary offered no obstacle for, being located in the same city, there were no difficulties caused by the necessity of traveling a long distance; and the rabbi, I understood, would have an abundant teaching staff and would not be expected himself to conduct a class in the school of the congregation.

I sent in my name as candidate and was invited to preach. My sermons and my general characteristics met with approval, and I was duly elected rabbi of the congregation in the early part of 1887. The election at first filled me with great joy. I was young, overflowing with energy and zeal, and eager to make a substantial contribution to the triumph of Historic Judaism on the glorious continent of America. I felt that this might be the beginning of the realization of my dreams and hopes. But my dreams and hopes were doomed to disappointment, and my connection with the Congregation *Beth Israel Bikkur Cholim* was destined to be of but short duration.

Chapter Twenty-two

I Enter the Holy Estate of Matrimony

ON SETTLING IN THE CITY ONE OF THE FIRST MATTERS WHICH I TOOK up was the selection of a house of worship* which I would attend. There were two synagogues adhering to the Orthodox ritual within a short distance of the home of the Rosenberg family with whom I was boarding. One was the synagogue of the Congregation *Orach Chaim*, to which the Rosenbergs belonged; the other that of the Congregation *Adath Israel*. The first-named synagogue was situated in Fiftieth Street between First Avenue and the river, and the other on Fifty-seventh Street, a few doors west of First Avenue. I attended alternately at both but more frequently at the synagogue of Congregation *Adath Israel*. At the time, the Congregation *Orach Chaim* worshipped in small rented premises and had no regular officials, whereas the *Adath Israel* had its own synagogue building, its own rabbi, Dr. Moses Maisner, and its own cantor, Rev. David Cahn. Though both were, of course, acceptable, I found more spiritual satisfaction in a well conducted service.

At the synagogue of the Congregation *Adath Israel*, I became ac-

---

* This evidently goes back to a period before his election as Rabbi of *Beth Israel Bikkur Cholim*. Even after the election, it appears that he still attended services for a time with one or another of the two small Orthodox congregations in the neighborhood, since the building erected for his new synagogue was not complete.
  It should be noted that during the period in question the Yorkville neighborhood was richly supplied with Reform temples, including: *Beth-El* at Fifth Avenue and Seventy-sixth Street, *Rodeph Sholom* at Lexington Avenue and Sixty-third Street, *B'nai Jeshurun* at Madison Avenue and Sixty-fifth Street, the Central Synagogue at Lexington Avenue and Fifty-fifth Street, and, a little further, Temple *Emanu-El* at Fifth Avenue and Forty-third Street, and the Park Avenue Synagogue, at Eighty-sixth Street near Lexington Avenue. In contrast to this array of large and pretentious Reform temples, some of which were presided over by famous rabbis, there were then only the two inconspicuous Orthodox groups, one of which had not even a building of its own.—Ed.

quainted with a number of the more prominent members, among them Mr. Jonas Weil. Mr. Weil was—or had been—president of the congregation. At all events, he was one of the pillars of that house of God. He was a splendid example of the good, old-fashioned type of German Jew. Born in a small town in the Dukedom of Baden, he had absorbed Jewish piety and the culture of both Judaism and Germandom. His memory was exceptionally powerful and retentive; he knew the entire contents of the Five Books of Moses in Hebrew by heart. The family in which he had been born was not wealthy in Germany, but in America his intelligence and untiring industry had speedily brought him a high degree of financial success. Starting at the lowest rung of the ladder, he had risen to great affluence, first as a wholesale butcher, and afterwards as an owner and operator in real estate. In both of these businesses he was associated with his cousin and brother-in-law, Bernhard Mayer.

At the time when I became acquainted with Jonas Weil he was in the real estate business as senior member of the firm of Weil and Mayer but devoted himself mainly to synagogue and philanthropic activity. I could not fail to notice that Mr. Weil took considerable interest in me. He would converse with me after service in the synagogue. He inquired concerning my history, my family, my work at the Seminary and my prospects in my vocation as rabbi, all of which questions I answered with entire frankness. After several such conversations, he invited me to visit him and his family at a family gathering on the following Sunday evening. I accepted with thanks and was indeed sincerely grateful, for I had but little opportunity for social intercourse in New York and was happy at the prospect of friendly intimacy with a Jewish family of such fine character and high standing.

The family gathering on the following Sunday evening was a very pleasant and rather elaborate affair. The Weil family occupied a high-stooped brownstone house, of the type so highly esteemed in the New York of that period, in East Fifty-first Street, between First and Second Avenues, and on that evening the great parlor was completely filled. In addition to Mr. and Mrs. Jonas Weil and their children, two sons and two daughters, the relatives on both sides, and they constituted a numerous clan, were almost all present. Socially and economically they were a very impressive group. On Mr. Weil's side there were present his brother-in-law Ferdinand Sulzberger together with his wife, Mr. Jonas Weil's sister Rosa, and his brother Samuel Weil and wife. These two men were among the greatest figures of the industrial and commercial world of New York at that time. Ferdinand Sulzberger was head of the great wholesale packing firm of Schwartzschild and Sulzberger.* On Mrs. Jonas Weil's side there were present her three sisters, Adele, Babette, and Sophie, and their husbands, Moritz Weil, Lazarus Weil, and Moritz Gruenstein, also her brother, Bernhard Mayer, and his wife. As the children of these couples and some other relatives were also present, the spacious parlor was taxed to its capacity. I was introduced to the senior members present and was cordially received by all. But there was one person present, belonging to the junior element, who stood out from all, who immediately attracted my attention. It was Sarah, the eldest daughter of my host. She was then approximately nineteen or twenty years of age, not a pretentious beauty, although her features were regular and well formed, her eyes clear and bright and her figure graceful and erect. She was not gorgeously attired but was clad in a simple though becoming gown. She was modest and reserved, even demure, in demeanor, but there rested upon her a dignity and a charm which revealed a pure and beautiful soul and a gracious and kindly personality. As I gazed at her there came to me a thought which, even as I thought it, seemed to me presumptuous and hopeless. "Perhaps," so I thought, "I have found my *Bath Zug*, my Divinely appointed life-partner; perhaps this is the woman whom the Lord has assigned to me as the companion of my joys and sorrows." "There are some," so the rabbis say, "who come to their destined mate and some to whom the mate comes." "Perhaps," I thought, "the first part of this rabbinical dictum has been fulfilled in me and I am now gazing at my appointed affinity." But even as the thought arose in my mind I dismissed it as utterly unreasonable and improbable.

Nevertheless, a few moments later something occurred which seemed to confirm or add probability to what I had thought. The young folks stormily demanded that she recite something for them.

---

* Later known as Wilson & Co.—Ed.

I Enter the Holy Estate of Matrimony

In particular they demanded that she recite a German poem called *"Mein Erwaehlter"* (My Chosen One). With evident reluctance she yielded to their urgent request. In this poem a young maiden describes the ideal man whom she would wish to wed. She pictures him as handsome, with dark eyes and hair, of medium stature, neither too tall nor too short, of pure and righteous character, refined and gentle manners, and courteous and courtly speech, and she declares that she looks not for wealth but only for a modest competency, adequate for a decent and worthy life.

As Sarah recited, she blushed and grew embarrassed but managed to finish the recitation, which was greeted with enthusiastic applause. As she recited, it seemed to me that some of the people were looking at me in a peculiar manner, but I pretended not to notice it and joined heartily in the applause and offered Sarah my personal congratulations. I remained some time longer and then took formal leave of most of the assembled company, including Sarah, and received a cordial invitation from Mr. and Mrs. Weil to call again. I promised to do so and left for home, my head in a whirl. It was a case of "love at first sight." Indeed it was more than merely love. It was a case of deep respect and admiration for a manifestly fine and noble character.

On my way home and after reaching it, my thoughts were mainly preoccupied with the new problem which had suddenly risen in my life. On the whole they were pessimistic. I could not see any justification for believing that if I were to ask the hand of Sarah Weil in marriage my suit would be successful. After all I was only a poor young rabbi, while she was the daughter of wealthy parents. At best my income must seem pitifully small to people accustomed to think in terms of hundreds of thousands or millions of dollars. However I turned the question in my mind I could only come to the conclusion that for me to seek the hand of the daughter of Jonas Weil would be presumption. Nevertheless I decided to take advantage of the very cordial invitation I had received to visit the Weil family. It would be pleasant to be on terms of social intercourse with these very worthy people, and as for other possibilities, well, one never knew what might happen.

Accordingly, a week or so later, I called on the Weil family and was received with the utmost cordiality. Sarah was present, and we had some conversation which increased my good opinion of her intelligence, fine character, and modesty. I called on several later occasions and became a sort of regular guest of the family.

My intimacy with the Weil family and my secret affection for Sarah grew and increased simultaneously. But still I did not dare make any open declaration. How long this mental state might have continued I do not know, but it found a sudden and unexpected termination.

I was teaching my class one afternoon in the Jewish Theological Seminary, at that time temporarily housed in the synagogue of the Spanish and Portuguese Congregation *Shearith Israel* in West Nineteenth Street, when we received a visit from Rev. Dr. Aaron Wise, whose son Stephen was destined to become a generation later the well known pulpit orator and Zionist leader. Dr. Aaron Wise was on a visit of inspection to the Seminary. He listened to the instruction in the classes and when these had been dismssed, he remained for a little conversation with me. He was interested in my experiences since my return from the Breslau Seminary, and I described them to him in some detail. I also told him of my friendly relations with the Weil family and of my high respect for them. Nor did I conceal my affection and admiration for the oldest daughter Sarah.

When I had finished my enthusiastic description, Dr. Wise said to me with a smile, "Since you think so well of Miss Weil, why don't you ask her to marry you?"

I was very much taken aback by this unexpected question but managed to answer that I would be glad to do so but that, in view of the disparity in our financial conditions, I did not consider myself justified in such a proposal, or that I had any prospect of success if I should seek its fulfillment.

At this, Dr. Wise smiled a little more broadly than before and said, "My dear Dr. Drachman, I don't think you need have any anxiety on that score. I was speaking recently with Mr. Weil and he told me about you, how much he and his family, including Sarah, and the whole relationship think of you. I advise you to go right ahead. Remember, '*frisch gewagt ist halb gewonnen,*" (boldly dared is half won)."

I Enter the Holy Estate of Matrimony

These words of Dr. Wise turned my thoughts into a different channel. On my next visit to the Weils, I sought and obtained the opportunity of private conversation with Sarah. I think it was at the piano in reference to some new piece of music. Once alone I told her what was in my heart and asked her if she would be my wife. Her response was exactly in accordance with her sweet and gentle nature, filial loyalty, and innate dignity. The parental consent was readily and joyfully given, and thus Sarah Weil and Bernard Drachman were betrothed.

We were very happy. I know that I was very happy indeed, so happy that sometimes it seemed to me as though I were dreaming, that the fulfillment of my ardent hopes and desires was too glorious to be real, that "it was too good to be true," but, thank, God, it was real and true and, though my experiences in life were by no means always pleasant and agreeable, no external event ever affected my happiness either in my betrothal or, later, in my marriage.

Our betrothal took place in the spring of 1887 and our marriage was planned for the autumn of that year. The family went for a summer vacation to Saratoga, where a Jewish hotel, the Oakwood House, conducted according to the dietary laws—a rare thing in those days—had just been opened, and I accompanied them. We returned to New York for the autumn Holy Days, with the intention of celebrating the marriage immediately after the close of the festival season. Unfortunately Mr. Weil's sister, Mrs. Rosa Sulzberger, died, and it was decided that the marriage should be postponed for several months. On February eighth, 1888, Sarah Weil and I became husband and wife. The nuptial ceremony was celebrated in the synagogue of Congregation *Beth Israel Bikkur Cholim* at the corner of Lexington Avenue and Seventy-second Street, of which I was the rabbi at the time. The officiating rabbis were my friends and colleagues, Rev. Drs. Henry Pereira Mendes and Moses Maisner. A great throng filled the beautiful edifice and showed the greatest interest in the ceremony. The wedding dinner took place in Vienna Hall, at Lexington Avenue and Fifty-eighth Street, at that time the chief hall of public entertainment among the Jews of New York. In addition to Drs. Mendes and Maisner, two of the most prominent Conservative rabbis of the period, Drs. Alexander Kohut and Aaron Wise, were among the throng of relatives and friends attending the wedding feast.

After the wedding we took up our residence at 329 East Fifty-first Street, which was a private house directly adjacent to the Weil residence at 327 East Fifty-first Street and which had been presented to us as our home by Mr. Weil, who had also settled a very comfortable dowry on Sarah. Here and in later homes we were destined to dwell for a goodly number of years, not altogether free from distressing and exciting happenings, but in true and ideal harmony.

Here is the right place to speak briefly of my marriage and of my dear Sarah as a wife in Israel. The old saying is, "Matches are made in heaven." If that saying is ever true, it certainly was true of my marriage to Sarah Weil. I do not claim any of the merit of this for myself. I am no different and no better, I imagine, than the average husband. But Sarah, I am convinced, was infinitely better and infinitely superior to the vast majority of American wives, Jewish or Gentile. I do not think that I exaggerate when I say that her disposition was angelic. In all the years of our marriage, and we were privileged, through the mercy of Divine Providence, to live together for thirty-seven years, there was never between us anything even approaching the semblance of a quarrel. There were occasional differences of opinion, but they were always adjusted in accordance with reason and right and without any recourse to dispute and strife.

Sarah's leading principle was loyalty to duty. She was conscientious, even scrupulous, in performing what she recognized as her duty, to her parents, to her husband, to her children, to her fellow beings, to her God. We were blessed with a large family, five sons and two daughters—our first-born, a son, had died in early infancy. As each child came, she greeted it with joy and gave it the same full measure of loving care and devotion. Although a daughter of wealthy parents, she cared little for fashion and society, for her tastes were simple and almost exclusively domestic. Her home, her husband, and her family—they were her world, from which she cared but seldom to depart. Her absorption in her domestic obligations did not permit her to participate, to any great extent, in the activities of synagogue or communal organizations.

There was in her an ever ready kindness and sympathy, a perfect willingness to share my joys and my sorrows. Thus our nuptial history was one of complete understanding and harmony, of mutual trust and confidence, and no words can adequately describe how much strength and encouragement I found on my ofttimes thorny path of rabbinical duty through her sweet and blessed companionship.

Almost exactly a month to the day after our marriage, on March 12, 1888, there took place, or rather began, for it lasted two full days, the great blizzard, famous in the history of New York.

It was certainly a stupendous event, an unparalleled manifestation of the overwhelming forces of nature. There may not improperly be applied to it the words with which Scripture describes the plague of locusts in Egypt in the days of Moses and Pharaoh: "Before it there was no such plague of locusts and after it there will not be." For sheer fury and intensity it has no associate or rival among the storms of recorded history.

We were snowed in, but I doubt whether those confined to their homes by the ordinary snow storms of winter have anything of the feeling of utter helplessness and desolation which were ours when we saw ourselves the prisoners of an irresistible monster, of an almost inconceivably wild and furious tempest. It drove before it huge masses of icy, hail-like snow with such violence and overwhelming force that we could not restrain an uneasy apprehension that perhaps even the houses might not be able to withstand the titanic onslaught.

For approximately forty-eight hours this furious raging of the tempest continued, producing confusion and disturbance in the life of the great metropolis and the surrounding area. Traffic and traveling were utterly suspended, neither street cars nor elevated trains could move, and the ferry boats were unable to push themselves through the dense masses of ice which covered the North and East Rivers. Uncounted thousands of residents of New Jersey and Long Island were thus prevented from reaching their homes. The same experience befell vast numbers of Manhattanites, whom the lack of opportunity of street travel kept away from their abodes. The jam and crush in the hotels can be easier imagined than described.

Many were the victims of the blizzard who, seeking to reach their homes on foot, succumbed to the exposure and the strain which they were forced to endure. An especially sad case of this kind, which subsequently aroused much regret and sympathy, was that of the Honorable Roscoe Conkling. Mr. Conkling was a man high in public life—United States Senator from the State of New York, if I recall correctly—and a famous orator. He was caught by the blizzard in an office in lower New York and could find no means of transportation to take him to his home in East Seventy-second Street. He undertook to make his way there on foot and managed, after several hours of struggle, to reach there utterly exhausted. The following day he developed pneumonia, to which, after several days, he succumbed.

Toward the end of the second day, the thirteenth of March, the blizzard abated and ceased. The city presented a most curious appearance after its cessation. Huge masses of snow covered the streets and all exposed surfaces. The snow masses driven by the fury of the wind, had assumed strange and fantastic shapes. In many places they were piled tremendously high. It was weeks before New York was able to dig itself out of the snow masses and resume its normal appearance.

The blizzard will never be forgotten in New York, and for decades, yes, in all probability for centuries to come, when people speak of "*the* blizzard" they will mean the blizzard of March, 1888.

Chapter Twenty-three

Startling Events in the Congregation Beth Israel Bikkur Cholim

IN THE SPRING OF THE YEAR 1887 I HAD BECOME THE RABBI OF THE Congregation *Beth Israel Bikkur Cholim,* a splendid new synagogue in the uptown district at the corner of Lexington Avenue and Seventy-second Street. During the entire period of its existence on the lower East Side, already then an almost exclusively Jewish district, and sometimes called, on that account, the Ghetto, it had adhered without question to the traditional ritual and customs of the synagogue. On this account it had seemed to me a very suitable field for my activity, where I would be able to propound the traditional concept of Judaism and gain adherents for it among the rising, American-born generation. This had, indeed, been the main reason that I accepted the call. Besides, I considered that any other attitude would be inconsistent with my holding a position on the faculty of the Jewish Theological Seminary.*

I had not held my post in the congregation very long when I discovered that my concept of it had been erroneous. A goodly proportion of the membership were loyally attached to Traditional Judaism. But I soon found that there was a considerable element desirous of Reform and that they looked to me to aid them in attaining their objective. In accordance with the usual method pursued by would-be Reformers in Jewish congregations, they only demanded the changing of an ostensibly unessential synagogue custom, the manner of seating the worshippers at service.

The orthodox custom, which the congregation had hitherto followed, was that the men were seated on the main floor and the women

---

* This incidental remark very neatly points up the original character of the Seminary as an Orthodox institution and thus helps to cast light on later developments.—Ed.

in the gallery. This, the Reform-inclined members maintained, was without significance from the religious point of view, but was out of harmony with American customs and offensive to the fair sex and should, therefore, be changed and both sexes should be seated together throughout the building. They found no aid or assistance in me for this object. I told them in clear and emphatic terms, when they suggested this to me, that I would not authorize any change. My words were at first effective, and agitation for a change in the rule ceased for a time.

Let me explain here that the insinuation or open charge that the reason for the rabbinical prohibition of the seating together of the sexes at public worship is a lack of respect for the female sex is utterly baseless. The great men whose precepts and ordinances constitute the Talmudic law had the profoundest respect for womanhood, which they expressed in numerous eloquent and instructive dicta. They were supremely anxious to preserve in Israel the womanly modesty and virtue which are the essential prerequisites of that respect and enacted many ordinances for the securing of that objective. One of these ordinances is that men and women shall not mingle in too close association, especially not in the house of worship, where such close intermingling may tend to lessen the devout sentiment which is essential to true prayer. Indeed, it is to an actual occurrence of this kind that the Talmud attributes the adoption of the rule that men and women shall be separated at prayer (*Succah,* 51, b).

To modern Orthodox Jews the point of view expressed in the Talmud is not exactly the reason that they deem this ancient rule binding upon them. As modern men they are accustomed to mingle freely with women in public gatherings of many kinds and do not find such association disturbing to their serenity of mind or destructive of their devoutness on occasions devoted to prayer or religious discourses. But Orthodox Jews believe in the bindingness of authority. Since the downfall of the Jewish state and the cessation of the *Sanhedrin,* the highest judicial and religio-political legislative body in Israel, there *has been no authority competent* to modify or discard any of the existing institutions of Judaism or to introduce new ones. There is no legal or historical basis for such a movement as Reform, that is to say, the rejection of the established ordinances of the Jewish faith, as enunciated in the Talmud and the rabbinical codes, and the introduction of unauthorized innovations.

Having taken my stand on the platform of the bindingness of Talmudic authority, there was no course open to me but to refuse to permit deviations from the established usages of the Jewish faith. That, accordingly, was the decision which I rendered, but I used my best efforts to show that my attitude was not arbitrary but based entirely upon the authentic teachings of Bible and Talmud and, indeed, the only attitude which a sincere adherent of Traditional Judaism could logically and consistently assume. As already stated, my words were at first effective. The element desirous of innovations apparently accepted my decision as authoritative and desisted for a time from any agitation for the attainment of their desires. I believe that my impending marriage had something to do with determining their course of action. Under the circumstances they apparently did not wish to cause disturbance or excitement in the congregation.

Shortly after my marriage, however, the agitation was renewed with increased force and intensity. The seekers after reforms demanded a special meeting to consider the question of the seating of the sexes in the synagogue, and it was accorded them. The meeting was attended by practically all the membership of the congregation and it was marked by stormy and excited debates. I was present and Mr. Weil, who had become a member of the congregation, was also present.

Before the vote was taken, I addressed the meeting. I spoke in a mild and conciliatory manner, pointing out that I had no desire to force these views upon them because they were my personal convictions but that I spoke as the voice of the true and authentic teaching of our holy faith. I reminded them that their congregation had always loyally upheld the true historic concept of Judaism and that there was no reason, just because their new synagogue had been built in a more fashionable section of the city, that they should change their policy in matters of religion, and I concluded with an earnest appeal to them to revere the memory of their departed parents and ancestors and to continue to conduct their house of worship in a manner which would have met with their approval.

I noticed that the reception given my words was a mixed one, that, while many of the members present were in full agreement with my sentiments, others evidently disapproved them, but it seemed to me that the majority was in my favor. The president, whose name, if I recall correctly, was Harris (or Marx) Bennett, then put to a vote the question before the house. The result of the vote was an even division! Exactly one half of the members voted in favor of retaining the separate seating of the sexes, and one half voted to introduce their joint and intermingled sitting.

The decision was therefore up to the president. He looked at me a little shamefacedly, muttered a few apologetic words, and then said, "I am sorry to displease our worthy rabbi, but I vote that we shall have pews—that is, that the ladies and gentlemen shall sit together in our synagogue."

Words cannot adequately describe the shock which this statement of the president gave me. It meant that the decision had gone against me, that the congregation had deliberately rejected my declaration of their religious duty as Jews, had flouted my rabbinical authority. The vote, it is true, was very close; the result had been brought about by the action of one man, but it was just as decisive as though the majority had been great. I was so overwhelmed that I could not speak. The president, noticing my agitation, addressed me briefly, saying that he hoped that the result of the vote would not affect my attachment to the congregation. He assured me that he and the congregation appreciated my ability and my services very much and trusted that this incident would not disturb the cordiality of our relations, inasmuch as it did not indicate any lack of esteem but only a difference of opinion. I did not, I could not, answer him. I remained seated for a moment or two and then, rising, I went to where Mr. Weil was sitting and said to him, "Father-in-law, let us go home." He arose and together we left the room.

One thought was clear in my mind. I could not remain in the congregation. The blow which had been struck at my rabbinical prestige was too great. It had completely undermined my position, had deprived me of all moral justification for continuing in a supposed spiritual leadership which had become a mockery. On our way home I communicated this thought to my father-in-law. Somewhat to my surprise, he fully agreed with my point of view. I had feared that he might advise me to compromise, that he might say that I had shown my loyalty to Orthodox Judaism with perfect clearness and that, if the congregation did not wish to abide by my interpretation of the law, it was not my fault. But he said nothing of the sort. On the contrary, in his simple but blunt and direct way, he said that I was perfectly right, and that I should by no means remain in a place where my dignity and authority were not respected. He advised me, however, not to resign silently but to deliver a farewell sermon in which I must tell the congregation in unmistakable words what I thought of their action and fling their position back in their teeth.

I had already determined to do as Mr. Weil advised, but when I heard him uphold and encourage me so emphatically in this course of action, it added greatly to the firmness and definiteness of my resolution. It convinced me that my proposed action would meet with the approval of all right-thinking Orthodox Jews, that it would be a proper and thoroughly justified deed in defense of the authority of Jewish law in Israel, in other words, what is called in Talmudic phrase a *Kiddush Ha-Shem,* or Sanctification of the Divine Name, a bold and unyielding demonstration of the truth that loyalty to God and His Holy Torah stands higher than all earthly considerations.

The meeting had taken place on a Wednesday evening, and I devoted most of the two following days to the preparation of my sermon for the ensuing Sabbath. Early on the following Sabbath morning, before I had yet left for synagogue, Mr. Weil visited me at my home for the express purpose of confirming me in my resolution. I was rather surprised at the warmth of his feelings in the matter, but it certainly showed the genuineness of his adherence to Orthodox Judaism and the courage and energy with which he upheld his convictions.

On the Friday evening preceding I had attended service in the synagogue, but I did not refer to the result of the meeting nor indicate in any way my thoughts and intentions. I noticed that some of the people appeared surprised and gratified. I attributed it to an impression on their part that I was becoming reconciled to the new conditions that were to be introduced into the congregation. On the Sabbath morning I went to synagogue, immediately after Mr. Weil's visit, and was present at the very beginning of the service. I donned my official cap and robe and took my accustomed seat on the platform. The service proceeded in the customary manner, and nothing unusual occurred until the Scroll of the Law was returned to the Ark and the time had come for the delivery of the sermon. I then ascended the pulpit for that purpose.

While walking to the pulpit, knowing the nature of the address I was about to deliver and realizing the tremendous consequences it might involve, sudden qualms came over me and I felt a momentary hesitation as to whether I should deliver the sermon which I had prepared or whether I should not rather switch to some innocuous, non-controversial topic. But these feelings were only momentary. My mind was fully made up, my purpose was inflexible, and there was no turning back.

There is no need to give a full presentation of the contents of my sermon. Suffice it to say that I made my attitude in the question which had arisen in the congregation abundantly and most emphatically clear. I spoke with a fire and force quite unusual for me, who am, as a rule, inclined to be calm and sedate in my speech and no seeker after the sensational. But my feelings on this subject were so deeply stirred that once I began to speak I put my whole soul into my words. I told my listeners that a rabbi must be a true and sincere interpreter of the word of God, that he must not misinterpret it or consent to its being disregarded lest his ministry become a mockery and a sham. I added that just as the rabbi is in duty bound to propound the true doctrines of Judaism, so the individual Israelite and the congregations of Israel are in duty bound to accept these true interpretations and to abide by them willingly and loyally. No one, I insisted, may presume to set aside a precept of the Torah on the ground that it is unimportant; for it is not for human beings to decide which of God's commandments are important or unimportant, since we know not what is important or unimportant in the sight of the Most High. These thoughts and several similar ones I illustrated with appropriate Biblical passages and Talmudic dicta. I concluded, most emphatically and energetically, with the declaration that, since they had acted in direct opposition to these principles, I no longer considered the rabbinical post in their congregation a worthy one, and that, with the conclusion of the present service, I would cease to be their spiritual leader.

Intense excitement followed this declaration. As soon as I had finished my sermon and returned to my seat, people began to speak to each other excitedly and a buzz of agitated conversation filled the synagogue. The president rose from his seat and went down to the floor of the auditorium, where he exchanged some hasty remarks with two or three of the trustees. They looked at me as though they desired to speak with me, but they did not do so. Now that I had cleared my breast I was perfectly calm and collected. I remained during the rest of the service and, when it was concluded, I went to the robing room, exchanged my clerical robe for my ordinary attire and then left the synagogue in the company of my father-in-law. Several persons tried to speak with me on the way out, but I declined to enter into conversation with anyone.

This incident created a great sensation in the city and, indeed, in Jewish circles throughout the country and, to a considerable extent, throughout the world. The press, both Jewish and general, described it and reporters interviewed me in order to obtain a full explanation of the reasons for my action. The matter was extensively reported also in the Jewish press of Europe, even in the Hebrew press of Eastern Europe. I was also the recipient of many letters, most of them from adherents of Orthodox Judaism who expressed high approval of my action, and a few from believers in Reform who denounced me as a reactionary and a fanatic. I had, of course, expected to be judged in different ways according to the viewpoint of the persons judging me, so that I was neither unduly elated nor depressed by the varying reactions to my step.

The bright glare of publicity which now shone upon me had a sobering and, at the same time, inspiring and exhilarating effect upon my mentality. I realized that I had suddenly become the cynosure of all eyes that gazed with interest at that which was done in Israel, that I had been identified, in a measure, with the cause of Orthodox Judaism, and that my actions thenceforth would redound to the credit or discredit of the ancient faith of my people. The effect of this realization was to strengthen my resolve that, come what might, I would dedicate every atom of my strength to the holy cause which I had espoused and to the endeavor to secure for it the utmost measure of recognition and support among my brethren in the New World.

The question now was, what next? The answer was natural and direct. I must obtain the position of rabbi in a congregation from the pulpit of which I could proclaim the truths of Judaism as I saw them. Mr. Weil, with whom I naturally discussed the question, was most emphatically of this opinion too. This was not conceived in any materialistic or mercenary spirit, but that I might have the power and the following which would enable me to carry out what I now recognized as my mission, to defend and to propagate Orthodox Judaism in America. To obtain such a position and opportunity, that was the next step to which I directed my attention.

Chapter Twenty-four

The Congregation Zichron Ephraim is Organized

HAD MY OBJECT BEEN MERELY TO OBTAIN A RABBINICAL POST, ITS attainment would have been attended with no difficulty. My name had become well known to the Jews of America. There was considerable respect for both my character and my scholarship, and the occurrences in the Congregation *Beth Israel Bikkur Cholim* had attracted much attention to me and been productive of considerable comment. This comment was not all favorable; for to the Reformers both my attitude toward Judaism and my activity in its behalf were extremely unwelcome, but to the Jews of orthodox inclinations they came as a sweet and comforting message and were greeted with great enthusiasm.

Hardly had the news of my resignation from the *Beth Israel Bikkur Cholim* Congregation become known than calls came to me from various Orthodox congregations to accept the post of rabbi. Several of these calls were from New York City congregations, others from congregations in out-of-town cities. While highly honorable and gratifying in themselves and greatly appreciated by me, they were, for various reasons, unacceptable or, at least, not in accordance with my true inner aspirations and ideals. Some of the out-of-town congregations were important and of high standing, but I did not want to leave New York. I felt that the great metropolis of America, the home of more than half the Jewish population of the Western Hemisphere, was the most important and promising field of Jewish activity in this part of the world, perhaps in the whole world. Since I had become its resident, I decided to devote whatever strength or ability I possessed to the upbuilding of Historic Judaism in its majestic domain. The New York City congregations, on the other hand, due to reasons connected with their location or their type of membership, did not seem to me fertile soil for the development of the harmonious combination of Orthodox Judaism and Americanism which to me was the true concept of the ancient faith of Israel on this continent. Good and worthy people as they were and sincerely Orthodox Jews, I thought it more likely, if I accepted a post in their midst, that they would draw me to their type than that I could draw them to mine.* I was torn by conflicting thoughts and found it very difficult to decide what to do. Considerable time passed in this state of indecision.

Mr. Weil took the greatest interest in these matters but did not at first attempt in any way to influence my decision. One day, however, he said to me, "Bernard, I see that it is hard for you to make up your mind. Would you like to know what I think should be done?"

"Why, of course, Father-in-law," I answered. "I would be glad to hear whatever you wish to suggest."

"I think," he said, "we should organize our own congregation. It is right that you should want to officiate in a congregation entirely in harmony with your ideas and where you feel sure you could do the best work. That is hardly possible in any of the already existing congregations. You will always find in them people who have their own ideas of how a congregation should be and how a rabbi should be and you are liable to have trouble. You don't want to have happen again what happened in the Seventy-second Street *shool*. But if you organize your own congregation things will be entirely different. The people who come in will do so because they believe in you and want to help you carry out your ideas. From the very beginning everything will be arranged in accordance with your plans, and you will have a real opportunity to show what you can do for Orthodox Judaism in America."

I heard the words of Mr. Weil with great joy. He had spoken out of my own heart. He had expressed thoughts which my observations and experiences had convinced me were correct but which I had hesitated to utter because I saw that their realization was a matter of great difficulty. To establish a congregation worthy of my ideals would

---

* A clear reference to the predominance of the East European atmosphere in most of the Orthodox groups of that period and to his sense of the urgent importance of developing an *American* Orthodox Judaism rather than a direct transplantation from older countries.—Ed.

mean not only the acquisition of a great number of adherents but also the erection of a large and dignified synagogue. The building would have to be equipped with all necessary furnishings and appurtenances of fine and impressive quality and would necessitate the raising of great funds. I expressed these thoughts to my father-in-law. He answered quietly that he realized the difficulties but had every confidence that they could be overcome, that if I were to launch such a movement, he would be willing to do his share also in a financial way. These words decided my action. I began at once to take steps toward the organization of a congregation, and Mr. Weil gave me vigorous aid.

I answered many of those who had written me letters approving my course in the matter of the Congregation *Beth Israel Bikkur Cholim* and informed them of my purpose to establish a congregation in which my concept of Historic Judaism would be carried out. I received a goodly number of answers requesting me to place the names of the writers on the roll of members of the proposed congregation. Mr. Weil, in a similar manner, obtained quite a number of accessions. I do not recall the precise number of persons who thus declared their desire to cooperate, but it was not far from two hundred. Almost all were heads of families, which, of course, meant that their families, too, would be numbered in the ranks of the congregation. What especially pleased me was the evident sincerity and earnestness with which they declared their desire to join such a movement. It gave me courage and firmness of resolution to continue the task which I had begun.

The movement for the organization began in the late autumn of 1888 and continued during the greater part of 1889. A number of meetings were held in various places of assembly, during which the plans for the work of the new congregation were discussed and funds for preliminary expenses collected. In 1889 the organization was completed by the adoption of a constitution and the election of a board of trustees. That the members thoroughly understood the purpose of the congregation and that they were in entire accord with my concept of Judaism is shown by the preamble to the constitution which they adopted. This is so important and significant that it shall be here transcribed in full. In it my spirit speaks as perhaps nowhere else.

PREAMBLE

"Whereas the history of Judaism and the experience of Jewish congregations in the United States of America have shown the great dangers to the safety of our religion which arise from unauthorized and improper changes in the historical observances and laws of our faith, we, men of Israel, impressed with the deep conviction that it is an imperative necessity to make a determined effort for the maintenance of our faith and its defense against those dangers, and deeming it necessary to establish a congregation in which the orthodox doctrines, observances, and laws of Judaism shall be firmly and unalterably maintained, do hereby organize this congregation and enact the following Constitution and By-Laws for its government, hoping that through it Almighty God may be pleased to furnish a strong bulwark against the inroads and encroachments of unbelief and innovation and for the support and perpetuation of the sacred faith of our fathers in all its historical purity and completeness."

The deep religious faith and profound earnestness of the organizers of the congregation could not be better shown than by the adoption of this constitution. Shortly before this step was taken, Mr. Weil had announced that he would supply the main amount of funds required for the erection of a suitable synagogue and that his brother Samuel would cooperate with him by giving a substantial donation. In recognition of their generosity the meeting voted that the congregation should bear the name of *Zichron Ephraim,* or Memorial of Ephraim, in memory of their father, Ephraim Weil, of Emmendingen, Baden, Germany. The first board of trustees of the congregation consisted of the following gentlemen: Jonas Weil, *President,* Lewis Myers, *Vice President,* William Prager, *Honorary Secretary,* Leo Hutter, *Treasurer,* Barnett Sturman, Abraham Rothstein, Emanuel Arnstein, Carl Heller, and Adolph Guggenheim—all substantial householders and loyal Jews.

The best Orthodox elements of the city were represented among the membership. They were not of one class or national origin, as was usually the case in the Orthodox congregations of that time, which, as a rule, were formed by immigrants from the same European country, but came from all the various elements of the Jewish community of New York. There were among them Jews of Russian, Polish, Hungarian, German, and other ancestry, a fair proportion of them being of native American birth. The congregation was, therefore, of broadly representative character and could be correctly designated as a genuine American Orthodox Jewish group. The new congregation constituted a truly creditable addition to the forces of Orthodox Jewry, from which great service to the cause of the ancient faith could be justifiably expected.

On Thanksgiving Day of the year 1889 the cornerstone of the new synagogue was laid with appropriate ceremonies. A fine piece of land, seventy by one hundred one feet in dimensions, on Sixty-seventh Street, between Third and Lexington Avenues (in the Yorkville district of New York City), had been secured, mainly through the efforts and generosity of Mr. Weil. The event aroused widespread interest in New York and was attended by a large gathering. I was, of course, the chief speaker, and among the others were Rev. Dr. H. Pereira Mendes and Hon. Joseph Blumenthal, president of the Jewish Theological Seminary Asssociation. The architects of the synagogue were Messrs. Schneider and Herter, German-born architects and masters of their profession. Under their skillful direction a beautiful edifice was destined to arise, of rarely artistic design, and considered for many years the most beautiful structure devoted to Orthodox Jewish worship in New York City.

The rest of the year 1889 and the greater part of 1890 were devoted to the completion of the synagogue and the strengthening of the membership. On August 26, 1890, I was formally elected rabbi of the congregation for life and I received a contract to that effect. An exceptionally able and gifted *Chazan* or cantor was also chosen at the same time. He was the Reverend Moses Lublinsky, who had been chief cantor of the city of Thorn in Prussia but had been expelled, because of his Polish birth, by the Prussian government, which even at that time was, in many ways, harsh and inhuman. At my suggestion the congregation also voted to appoint a paid male choir, in order to adorn the service with every feature needed to make it esthetically gratifying as well as impressive. They chose as choir leader Hyman Kantrowitz, a musician of rare ability.

A few weeks later the synagogue was solemnly dedicated to the service of God Almighty through the traditional Jewish faith. The dedication was attended by a throng which filled every available seat in the spacious edifice and overflowed into the street outside. The synagogue presented a most beautiful appearance. The architects had understood to combine the lines and proportions suggestive of a religious purpose with a touch of the Oriental so that its very external appearance told of the faith to which it was dedicated. I had had the name of the congregation, *Zichron Ephraim,* and a verse from Psalm One Hundred, "Enter into His gates with thanksgiving and into His courts with praise," in Hebrew and beautifully carved in polished granite, placed on its front, so that the holy purpose of the building and its Jewish character could not fail to be recognized even by the casual observer.

The interior of the synagogue was even more strikingly beautiful than its exterior. The chaste lines of its construction, its arches, the impressive design of the ark, the altar and the pulpit, of massive and exquisitely carved hard wood, the glorious stained-glass windows, and the rich carpets and draperies combined to make a ravishing picture of artistic beauty and spiritual appeal. There was a special choir loft over the ark—a most unusual feature in Jewish houses of worship—from which the voices of the unseen singers resounded with touching melodiousness. The basement of the synagogue contained a spacious hall of assembly, four classrooms for the *Talmud Torah* or Hebrew and religious school, and a small synagogue for week-day worship. The beauty of the synagogue and its excellent adaptation to its purpose aroused general admiration.*

---

* The synagogue is, indeed, still a unique architectural gem. Neither extraordinary in size (seating capacity about nine hundred) nor as expensively equipped as some temples, it is nevertheless large and elaborate enough to be classed with the finest. Its design combines in an absolutely individual fashion the solemnity of a shrine with a touch of a lighter sort, so that it also suggests the fairy-tale palace of a child's dream or an Arabian Night's fantasy. A young boy, visiting it for the first time, described it as "a friendly place."

In general, its style is Oriental, principally (though not exclusively) Byzantine, with a great profusion of small, bulbous cupolas, set at various levels, each surmounted by a slender rising shaft supporting a six-pointed Star of David. From the outside, the facade is not clearly visible, unless you get well across the street, for the main structure soars from behind an elaborately arched portico. At either wing rises a decorative square tower, one higher than the other but both richly carved and arched and star-crowned. The most remarkable feature is the beautiful rose-window, worthy to be recorded in a history of art.

The Congregation Zichron Ephraim is Organized

Public services were first held in the synagogue on the High Holy Days of the year 5651 (1890). They were most impressively conducted by the Reverend Moses Lublinsky, assisted by his splendid choir under the direction of Hyman Kantrowitz. I, of course, delivered the sermons. Every seat had been taken, and the synagogue was completely filled. The universal judgment was that the services could not have been better rendered, from any point of view, and that the synagogue and the services together constituted a most significant demonstration for American Orthodox Judaism.

From that day on the Congregation *Zichron Ephraim* has never ceased its activity in behalf of the ancient faith of Israel. The synagogue has been open daily, morning and evening, and at many other times, for prayer and the study of the Holy Law and the traditional Jewish literature and for public gatherings for social purposes or in behalf of worthy and deserving causes, Jewish and non-Jwish.

Immediately after the opening of the synagogue the congregation established a school* (*Talmud Torah*) for the instruction of children in the Hebrew language, Biblical history, and the principles of the Jewish faith. This became at once very popular and was attended by approximately two hundred and fifty children, boys and girls, who were taught by four teachers. I acted as superintendent. Owing to a change in the character of the district, the number of children decreased considerably in later years, but the work of the school has continued unaltered, and it is at present (1943) still composed of four classes under the tuition of two teachers.

Shortly after the opening of the synagogue a Sisterhood or Women's

---

* At first called "The Hebrew Free School of Congregation *Zichron Ephraim*." The term "*Talmud Torah*" was adopted about twenty years later.—Ed.

One appreciates that feature more fully from within, where it appears that there are two such glorious circles—one above the Ark rich pink and blue and silver, which we called the Moon, and the other, known as the Sun, in the rear wall, facing the street, all dazzlingly bright and vast.

The prevailing color scheme of the interior was originally white and light blue, lit with jets of gold, the great altar-wall, including the Ark and choir-loft gracefully and intricately carved with loops and pointed cupolas leading the imagination from enchanted stage to higher and higher stages, until one is almost ready to believe that the lofty, vaulted, spangled, and delicately buttressed roof might truly be the doorstep of Heaven itself.—Ed.

Society was organized by some zealous and devout women. This organization has always labored zealously to assist the congregation and has frequently contributed considerable sums to the congregational funds. Early in its career it took upon itself the responsibility of maintaining the Talmud Torah, thereby freeing the congregation from the entire burden of its upkeep. It has never faltered in the performance of this self-imposed task and is loyally and conscientiously continuing to perform it at the present time (1943). In addition to this specific congregational work the Sisterhood contributes from time to time to general charitable causes. A chief activity of this kind is its annual subvention of several hundred dollars to the Passover Relief Association of Yorkville, for the purpose of providing the Jewish poor of the Yorkville district with the unleavened bread and groceries required for the proper observance of the Passover festival.

The records have not been preserved and I do not recall who the ladies were who first organized the Sisterhood. I am unable, therefore, to give their due meed of praise to these noble souls. But I am able to mention some of those who have in later years devoted their time and energy to the cause of the Sisterhood, and I feel it incumbent upon me to do so. The list will necessarily be far from complete. It is headed by Mrs. George Harris, one of the original founders. Mrs. Rose Szobotka Katz, Mrs. Y. Somberg, and Mrs. Marcus Schoen have been presidents of the Sisterhood and have labored with zeal and devotion in its behalf. Mrs. Jacob Harris has been for years its faithful and most efficient secretary. Among the other loyal and zealous members may be mentioned Mrs. M. Keller, Mrs. J. Ungar, Mrs. Samuel Weiss, Mrs. M. Sobel, and Mrs. Bernard Drachman. Mrs. George Harris is greatly respected for her exceptional and profound piety. In this she follows the example of her sainted husband, an American-born, scrupulously observant Jew, as strictly exact in his fulfillment of the commandments as any inhabitant of the ancient centers of European Jewry.

It would be impossible and would probably serve no good purpose to enumerate and describe the qualities and characteristics of all the good men and loyal Jews who have, at one time or another, been members of Congregation *Zichron Ephraim* during the more than fifty years which have elapsed since its founding. But a few of the more prominent of those connected with it, especially in its earlier years, shall be mentioned, because it shows what a fine representative of Orthodox Judaism the congregation has been since its inception and is also a contribution to the general history of American Jewry.

Jonas Weil, its founder and first president, needs no description at this place. Lewis Myers, the first vice-president, was a fine example of the harmony which may exist between Americanization and ancestral piety. A native of Russia, where he had absorbed and made his own the strictest principles of Judaic piety, he had become in external appearance and demeanor a true American without sacrificing a whit of his inherited devoutness. He and his wife and large family of handsome sons and daughters occupied a fine home in which they practiced the ceremonies of Judaism in a dignified and beautiful manner. Sender Jarmulowsky, Joseph Oshinsky, Baruch David Kaplan, Fisher Lewine, Joseph Polstein, Abraham Siegel, and Meyer Vesell were, together with others unmentioned, fine representatives of American Orthodor Jews of Russian origin. They were learned, loyal, and generous. The outstanding member of this group was unquestionably Sender Jarmulowsky. He was an exceptional Hebrew scholar, might, indeed, be truthfully called a great Talmudist, far greater than many professional rabbis, but was by vocation a banker, head of an important private bank on the lower East Side.

There was a splendid group also of a different type, thoroughly Americanized Jews of German origin. These were not as deeply learned as some of the Russian-Polish group but they were fully as sincere in their devotion to Orthodox Judaism. The chief representatives of this element were the four Arnstein cousins, Emanuel, Max J., Samuel and Sigmund, members of a large and very devout family, Julius J. Dukas, Adolph Guggenheim, Paul Hirsch, Jacob Katz, and Max Landauer. These were all generous supporters of the congregation as well as sincere upholders of its principles. The most prominent of these in public matters was Julius J. Dukas. He was a man of great energy and during his lifetime was probably the most strenuous worker in the field of Jewish education and philanthropy in the City of New York. Two important institutions bear testimony to the success of his efforts in these fields, the Jacob Joseph School and the Hebrew Free Loan Association. After the death of Jonas

Weil in 1917, Dukas became his first successor in the presidency of Congregation *Zichron Ephraim,* and he held this position for two terms.

There were also a number of families of Hungarian origin connected with the congregation, all very worthy people and sincerely attached to Orthodox Judaism. Outstanding members of this class were Dr. Gustave Liebermann, Simon Stern, Max Friedman, David Weisz, Jonas Ungar, and Joseph Greenberg. With Dr. Liebermann the reader has already become acquainted as the first instructor in Talmud in the Jewish Theological Seminary of America. Simon Stern was sexton of the congregation for several years preceding the first World War and came to an untimely and tragic end in the early weeks of that titanic conflict, while he was on a vacation in Europe. His remains were brought to New York and he received the exceptional honor of a burial from our synagogue. He was a man of culture and refinement and a learned and pious Jew. Max Friedman and David Weisz were both greatly respected and were chosen presidents of the congregation for several consecutive terms.

My congregational activities have been very numerous and extremely varied. Suffice it to say that in all my activities I have been impelled mainly by two aspirations: first to serve faithfully the cause of traditional Judaism and increase its respect and prestige in the sight of the world and, secondly, to aid, to the extent of my power, in solving the spiritual problems of those to whom I have been privileged to minister, to rejoice with them in their joy and to comfort them in their sorrow.

In the pursuit of the first named objective I have given great care to the sermons which I delivered and have striven to make them express the sublime message of Judaism, as laid down in the Bible and illustrated by the wise interpretations and quaint parables of the Talmud. I have never considered my office as an impersonal one, rendered to an impersonal being called a congregation, but as a personal and individual one, of interest and importance to every individual human soul. My sermons have been mainly in English, but, since some of the members of the congregation have been of foreign origin, I have delivered a certain proportion of them in German—mainly at the Sabbath afternoon services. I have used a simple Ger-

The Congregation Zichron Ephraim is Organized

man vocabulary, avoiding the use of rare or technical terms, so that those of my hearers whose native idiom is the Yiddish should have no difficulty in understanding me. I have also, on a few occasions, employed the ancient tongue of Israel, the Hebrew, as the vehicle of expression.

In accordance with my conviction of the indispensability of a good knowledge of Judaism and Jewish culture for the making of a true Jew, I have bent every effort from the inception of the congregation toward its maintenance of an efficient *Talmud Torah* or Hebrew and religious school, for the instruction of the children alike of its members and non-members. Our school has had a very fair degree of success. Thousands of boys and girls have gone through its courses during the many years of its existence and have derived from it the understanding and love of Judaism which they have needed for spiritual stability and loyalty in their adult years. In order to intensify that understanding and to strengthen that love I have frequently visited the classes and addressed the school assemblies regularly on Sunday mornings. I have aimed to interpret for the children the Biblical portion of the week and to rouse their Jewish consciousness by commenting on world happenings from the Jewish point of view. The present (1943) teachers of the school are Mr. William Rosenberg and Miss Rose Harris, who have been in charge of their classes for many years and have performed their tasks efficiently and to the satisfaction of the parents and the Sisterhood.

I have also encouraged other forms of activity which go to strengthen interest in the congregation and Judaism in general, such as the formation of Young People's Societies and public lectures on themes of Jewish importance, sometimes given by me, sometimes by outside speakers of prominence. These activities have served to bring both young and old together as Jews, outside of the formal occasions of worship, for the rousing of interest in things Jewish and the strengthening of their attachment to our holy faith.

And thus the years have flown away and sunk into the abyss of the past. Most of those associated with the founding of Congregation *Zichron Ephraim* have passed to the Great Beyond. Men have come and gone, and tremendous, epoch-making happenings have stirred the world and have had their repercussions upon our congregation.

The congregation still stands firmly loyal to the purpose for which it was established—to be a strong bulwark and citadel for the ancient faith of Israel. Some of these happenings and how they affected the congregation as well as the humble part I had in them will be told, please God, in later chapters of this veracious chronicle.

Chapter Twenty-five

The Founding of a Hospital

MR. WEIL HAD MUCH PLEASURE IN THE SYNAGOGUE OF WHICH HE was the principal founder. Whenever he saw the beautiful building in which it was lodged and especially whenever worshipping or visiting throngs filled its spacious interior, great satisfaction and joy filled his heart.

After a time, however, he became painfully aware of an accusation that Orthodox Jews are more pious than philanthropic. This is, of course, a pure calumny, just one of the stock libels by which the opponents of Orthodox Judaism seek to discredit the ancient faith. Mr. Weil, however, felt personally insulted by the insinuation that he was a mere formalist, that he deemed words of prayer entirely adequate as service to the Most High but that his ears were deaf to the cry of the afflicted. He expressed to me his indignation at this false accusation. I told him that we Orthodox Jews were constantly the victims of such and other false charges, that we could not waste our time in perpetual controversies, and that our lives were the best refutation of the calumnies launched against us.

Mr. Weil, however, felt that in view of the damaging effect of these accusations, it was necessary to do something constructive to demonstrate convincingly their falsity. After considerable discussion we reached the conclusion that a hospital, conducted in accordance with the best and most modern scientific methods but in which the religious precepts of Othodox Judaism would be respected, would be the most suitable institution to demonstrate the union of charity and religion. As a necessary feature of this concept we agreed that, as far as the benefits of the hospital were concerned, it must be strictly nonsectarian—that is to say, its services must be rendered to all suffering human beings, without distinction of race or creed.

For the name of the proposed hospital, I suggested "Lebanon"—first, to follow the precedent of Mount Sinai Hospital (whose conduct, however, was not in accord with Jewish law) through the use of a Biblical mountain as a title, but also for another reason. The *Midrash* states that the name "Lebanon" was sometimes applied to the *Beth ha-Mikdash,* the Temple on Zion's height. *Lebanon* signifies "white"—the color of purity and spiritual exaltation, as appropriate an implication for a place devoted to works of mercy and sympathetic aid as to a place of prayer and atonement.

The next step taken was the organization of a corporation for the maintenance of the hospital. This was duly done, and Jonas Weil became its first president. The same zealous service and generous support which he gave to the synagogue he extended also to the hospital.

A more difficult problem than these preliminary matters was the provision of a suitable building. Mr. Weil and I agreed that, if feasible, a suitable building should be bought, thus saving the time required to erect a new one. Considerable time passed in this search, but there seemed to be a dearth of such properties, and we both began to get discouraged.

One day an advertisement in the *New York Times* attracted my attention. It stated that a property, consisting of a large building, suitable for institutional purposes, and approximately forty lots of land, and situated in the upper part of the city, was for sale. I immediately went to the office of the agent, Mr. Xavier Roth. I found him a very courteous gentleman with a touch of the clerical about him and, despite his German name, apparently a perfect American. He informed me that the property in question was the convent of the Ursuline Sisters and was situated on Westchester and Cauldwell Avenues in the Bronx.

We went immediately to the convent—a trip of several hours in those days—and were received by the Mother Superior. I saw at once that the property was ideal for the purposes of a hospital. The building was large, containing several large rooms, suitable for wards, and many smaller rooms adapted for the reception of private patients. It stood on the top of a hill, where the air was, naturally, pure and fresh, and in the midst of extensive park-like grounds admirably fitted for rest and recuperation of convalescent patients. The price, though many thousands of dollars, seemed to me, considering the extent of the property and its fine location, very reasonable indeed.

A day or two later Mr. Weil and I visited the property together, and Mr. Weil's enthusiasm was fully as great as mine.

The rest of the story is quickly told. Mr. Weil purchased the property and presented it to the Lebanon Hospital Association. On Washington's Birthday, February 22, 1893, Lebanon Hospital opened its portals to the ill without distinction of race or religion. From that day to this it has dedicated itself to the task of demonstrating that in Judaism the love of God and the love of man, religious observance and ethical principles, are inseparably united, that, in fact, the ethical is an essential and irremovable part of the spiritual. I accepted, when the hospital began its activity, the post of supervisor of the *Kashruth,* or ritually permissible character of the dietary, and have found great satisfaction in the consciousness that I was privileged to aid in maintaining the truly Jewish religious standards of the hospital.

This year (1943) witnesses the completion and opening for service of a new Lebanon Hospital, housed in a magnificent building, equipped with all the latest discoveries and inventions which science employs for the improvement of the medical art. It adheres nevertheless without alteration or modification to the principle of the union of religion and ethical practice. It maintains, as ever, a strictly permissible dietary system as enjoined by the precepts of Orthodox Judaism. The two sons of the founder, Mr. Victor Weil and Mr. Benjamin J. Weil, are continuing the work of their father and are serving the hospital with zeal and devotion. The former is the present president (1943) and the latter a member of the board of directors.

Chapter Twenty-six

Mainly About the Seminary

WHILE THE EVENTS NARRATED IN THE TWO PREVIOUS CHAPTERS WERE occurring, I continued my activities in other fields of Jewish endeavors with full force and intensity. In connection with my work as rabbi of the Congregation *Zichron Ephraim* I strove to carry the message of Orthodox Judaism and Jewish culture to the broad masses of our people by frequent contribution of articles and letters to the Jewish—and occasionally to the general—press and by the delivery of lectures and addresses to public gatherings outside of the synagogue. These engagements naturally kept me very busy, and I speedily found that, for the performance of marriage ceremonies and for their sad converse, funerals, the demands made upon my time were extreme. The multiplicity of my activities did not weary me. I was young, ardently devoted to my vocation, and filled with zeal to accomplish tangible results, and, however arduous the tasks which confronted me, a gracious Providence gave me the strength to cope with them. If sometimes I was very tired, it seemed to be a natural, healthy weariness which sound sleep—"tired nature's sweet restorer," as the poet calls it—quickly dispelled.

My work at the Jewish Theological Seminary constituted a very great part of my activities, perhaps the greatest part. I have already stated that I was, so to speak, a "man of all work," and this condition was not altered by the fact that in 1889, only three years after the opening of the Seminary, I had been appointed dean of the faculty. I have before me as I write a schedule of hours for the winter term of 5654 (1893-94) which shows clearly how numerous were the hours and how varied the subjects of my instruction in the Seminary. My weekly hours of instruction were fifteen and were devoted to the following subjects. On Sundays I read the Talmudic treatise *Sanhedrin* with the Senior B class and Jewish history with the Preparatory A class. On Mondays I read the prophet *Hosea* with the Junior class and *Psalms* with the Preparatory A. On Tuesdays I lectured on the history of Jewish philosophy to the Senior B class and taught Hebrew grammar and composition to the Junior and Preparatory A classes. On Wednesdays I lectured on the history of Jewish philosophy to the Senior B class and taught Hebrew grammar to Preparatory B. On Thursdays I read the *Cuzari,* the celebrated philosophical work of the renowned medieval Hebrew poet and philosopher Judah Ha-Levi, with the Senior A class, and the *Emunoth Ve-Deoth,* the great philosophic work of Saadiah Gaon, with the Senior B Class, and the book of Daniel and other Aramaic selections with the Junior class. On Friday, *Erev Shabbos,* the eve of the Sabbath, I was free from duty, but on Saturday evenings, after the going out of the Sabbath, I read the Talmudic treatise of *Rosh Ha-Shanah* with the Juniors. This is a specimen schedule of studies, as carried on during the winter term of 5654 (1893-94).

In other years I taught a variety of other subjects, including homiletics or the art of preaching. Too, I trained the students in the practical methods of preaching and I supervised their homiletic efforts in the Seminary synagogue. Then there were frequent meetings of the faculty, which I attended. Since matters affecting the conduct of the Seminary were, in the absence of Dr. Morais, referred to me as dean, it will readily be seen that my position was no sinecure.

During the greater part of the earlier period of the history of the Seminary the faculty was composed of the following members: Rev. Dr. Sabato Morais, President, Rev. Dr. Alexander Kohut, Vice Chairman, Rev. Dr. Bernard Drachman, Dean, Rev. Dr. M. Maisner, Rev. Dr H. Pereira Mendes, Dr. A. J. Joffe, and Mr. H. Speaker. Dr. Gustave Liebermann, the first instructor in Talmud, resigned his post after the establishment of the Lebanon Hospital to accept the superintendency of the latter institution He was succeeded at the Seminary by Dr. A. J. Joffe.

The Seminary led rather a wandering existence in its earlier period. The first place in which sessions were held was in the vestry rooms of the Spanish and Portuguese Synagogue in West Nineteenth Street,

New York City. After a comparatively short sojourn there, the Seminary was transferred to quarters in the Cooper Union. This was, for several reasons, an unsuitable location and was, probably from its very inception, only considered a temporary abode. From there the Seminary moved to East Twelfth Street, where the association had rented a floor in a so-called "flat" building. From here, too, it moved after a stay of short duration, this time to a building at 735 Lexington Avenue, between Fifty-eighth and Fifty-ninth Streets. This was quite a capacious structure and, as the Seminary had the use of the entire building, it was possible to provide excellent accommodations for the classes and other requirements, as well as for Sabbath services and public meetings. For the last named purpose the entire parlor floor was reserved and it was fitted up as a synagogue, with an *Aron Ha-Kodesh,* or Holy Ark, and a *Ner Tomid,* or Perpetual Light. Here the Seminary remained, and carried on its work very satisfactorily, until the year 1903 when it was transferred to a splendid new building at 531-535 West 123rd Street which had been presented to the reorganized Seminary Association by the well known banker and philanthropist Jacob H. Schiff.

In seven or eight years the labors of those who had founded the Jewish Theological Seminary of New York began to yield fruit. The first class of rabbis graduated, if I remember rightly, in 1894. It was not a numerous class, only six or seven graduates, but they were all able young men and well qualified for their chosen vocation. That the founders of the Seminary had done well in deciding upon such an institution as a desirable instrumentality for the uplifting of Orthodox Judaism was shown by the avidity with which congregations seized upon these young men to be their spiritual leaders. Hardly had they been graduated, in some cases even before their graduation, than they were called to the rabbinate of excellent congregations.

The outstanding member of the first graduating class was unquestionably Joseph Herman Hertz. With his career I was most directly connected. In the spring of the year 1894 the Congregation *Adath Jeshurun* of Syracuse, New York, applied to the Seminary for a suitable incumbent for the pulpit of their synagogue. In my capacity as dean I recommended Hertz, whereupon he was invited to deliver there a trial sermon in the synagogue on the first day of Passover. I accompanied him on the trip and was present in the synagogue when he delivered the sermon. It is no exaggeration to state that Hertz took the congregation by storm. He surprised even me. It was a masterly effort and revealed oratorical and interpretative gifts the existence of which even I, his teacher in homiletics, had not suspected, although I had heard him several times in the pulpit of the Seminary synagogue. In June 1894 Hertz was formally installed as rabbi of the Syracuse congregation. His subsequent career, a distinguished, though somewhat stormy one, led finally in 1913 to the incumbency of the highest Jewish post in the world, that of Chief Rabbi of the British Empire, with his seat in London.

For the next few years there is little of special interest to record of the Jewish Theological Seminary and of my connection with it. Everything moved along smoothly and well. The academic work continued uninterruptedly and the position of the Seminary as a great spiritual and intellectual force in American Jewry became ever clearer and stronger. The importance and value of the service to American and universal Israel rendered by the men who went forth into the Jewish world under its auspices became recognized as of great value. In making possible the training of these men I had my full share. My services, too, were fully appreciated by those in whose hands lay the destiny of the Seminary during its earlier period. Above all, it was my privilege to enjoy the complete confidence and esteem of the pure-souled and saintly Jew who, more than anyone else, was the initiator and creator of the Jewish Theological Seminary—the Reverend Doctor Sabato Morais, of blessed memory.

All too soon the fell hand of the Angel of Death began to strike gaps in the ranks of the first founders and leaders of the Seminary. On May 25, 1894, Dr. Alexander Kohut, the distinguished scholar and warm-hearted Jew, at only fifty-two years of age, passed away. Although he had occupied the pulpit of a Reform congregation, he had felt himself drawn toward those who were striving to perpetuate the ancient faith of Israel in America. Indeed, he had cooperated zealously in the establishing of the Seminary and its scholastic work.

A little over three years later, on November 11, 1897, our revered president of the faculty, Dr. Sabato Morais, was called to the realm beyond the grave. And on March 2, 1901, the president of the board of directors, Mr. Joseph Blumenthal, was taken from us. Mr. Blumenthal was unquestionably the outstanding layman in the Seminary Association, an energetic worker and a generous supporter. Though not learned in Hebraic lore, he was a devout adherent of Orthodox Judaism and a bold and outspoken champion of the principles for which the Seminary stood. He was a member of the Spanish and Portuguese congregation, and such was the esteem in which he was held by the congregation that, although he was not a *Sephardi*, they had chosen him as president for several terms.

These severe losses left the Seminary weakened both spiritually and materially. They also gave the opportunity to another group, not identical in spirit with the founders, to take over the control of the Seminary. Of this great change, of its influence upon the character of the Seminary, and my relation to it, more anon.

Chapter Twenty-seven

Jewish Activities in Various Fields

The Jewish Sabbath Alliance of America

IN THE SEMINARY I WAS A "MAN OF ALL WORK," AND IN THE GENERAL field of Jewish life I may apply the same designation to myself. Wherever I saw an opportunity to strengthen the Jewish consciousness, to make it easier for Jews to be Jews or to increase their desire to be Jews, I was glad to render whatever service was in my power.

I was especially interested in the youth, because it is an axiomatic matter, which all leaders of men recognize, that he who has the youth has the nation. Transferred to the Jewish domain, that means that only if the Jewish youth, or, at least, a goodly portion of them, feel and think, and act Jewishly, there will be a Jewish future. I recognized, too, that the Talmud Torah cannot alone solve the problem. The children who attend the Talmud Torah are in the receptive period of life. They are under the ideological domination of their elders and teachers. But in the later period of youth, when adolescent boys and girls are confronted with the ideological difficulties presented by modern science, as well as with the economic difficulties of life, there is a rude assault upon their childish faith, and too often that faith succumbs. It was clear, therefore, that an effort must be made to hold the adolescents for the concepts and usages of Traditional, or Orthodox, Judaism. With this object in mind I sought to influence the students of the Seminary and other youths and maidens in the same period of life, to organize a movement for the winning of adolescents for Traditional Judaism.

The fruit of my efforts was The Jewish Endeavor Society. The idea was enthusiastically espoused by the Seminary students. Among its organizers were many who afterwards became prominent as rabbis of great congregations or leaders of communal organizations. In a list of the officers of the Jewish Endeavor Society from the year 1900 we find the names of Herman Abramowitz, President, now (1943) and since many years rabbi of the great McGill College Avenue synagogue in Montreal, Canada, Gabriel Davidson, executive manager of the Jewish Agricultural Society, and Charles Kauvar, now rabbi of a great congregation in Denver, Colorado. Elias Solomon, now rabbi of the Congregation *Shaarey Zedek* of New York, was also a member. Israel Goldfarb, for many years rabbi of a congregation in Brooklyn and renowned as an authority in the field of Hebrew ritual music and the possessor of a fine singing voice, was one of the founders of the Jewish Endeavor Society. He was usually chosen to conduct the service at the prayer gatherings of the Endeavor Society. The society laid great stress upon these prayer gatherings or meetings, because they made it possible to bring the message of Judaism to the rising generation in strict conformity with the traditional rules and in a refined and decorous manner which appealed to their esthetic taste as young Americans who possessed American culture.

These services were very popular with the young people on the lower East side of New York City. They were usually held on Sabbath afternoons and consisted of the regular Hebrew service of the occasion and a sermon or address in English. They generally took place in synagogues, which were gladly placed at the disposal of the society by various congregations. I was the speaker at a number of these gatherings.

The Jewish Endeavor Society continued its work for Orthodox Judaism for several years with considerable success. It then began to decline and finally ceased to exist. The reason was that so many of its leading spirits and chief workers found their life work in other fields and other places and were unable any longer to devote their efforts to its service. But the work which it was created to do, the winning and holding of American-born Jews for the ancient faith, did not, on that account, fall into utter neglect and desuetude. Another organization, Young Israel, drawn from other circles and a different element of people but actuated by the same convictions and desires, has taken up the work where the Jewish Endeavor Society relinquished it and has met with a considerable measure of success. It has influenced thousands of adolescent Jews and Jewesses to remain loyal to their inherited religious principles, and it has succeeded in forming model Jewish communities, composed of young married couples, in several sections of Greater New York. In these communities the Jewish spirit and the traditions of Judaism are loyally and sincerely maintained. Like the Jewish Endeavor Society, Young Israel lays great stress upon religious services and devotional and educational addresses and lectures. My attitude over against Young Israel has always been one of warm sympathy and approval. I have addressed their public gatherings on various occasions.

In 1905, I took up a form of Jewish work which I considered—and still consider—of the highest importance to the welfare of Judaism and to which I have devoted my energies unceasingly ever since. I refer to the promotion of the observance of the Holy, or seventh-day, Sabbath. Why Sabbath observance is so important, indeed fundamental, in Judaism, is—or should be—a matter of general knowledge and should need no detailed explanation. Suffice it to say that the sanctification of the Sabbath is enjoined in the first chapter of the first book of the Bible, *Genesis,* that it is one of the Ten Commandments, and that its observance is continually impressed upon Israel as a sacred duty throughout the Scriptures and the Talmud. Until comparatively recent times the Jewish people have clung unyieldingly to the observance of this sacred precept. Even in the great Dispersion, in lands of oppression and in the midst of hostile and malevolent populations, wherever Jews dwelt, the Holy Sabbath was loyally and undeviatingly observed. Its influence for good upon the Jewish ideology was very great. It cast a glamor upon the humble dwellings of the Jewish people and filled their lives with an atmosphere of sacredness.

But for reasons which are difficult to understand, about the middle of the nineteenth century great laxity in Sabbath observance began to prevail among the Jews in Western Europe. Stranger yet, in America, where complete political and religious liberty prevailed and where no legal disability of any kind stood in the way of undiminished adherence to Judaism and fulfillment of its precepts, our people grew lax. The Jews, who came here in their multitudes in order to enjoy the freedom and economic opportunities of the land, seemed to think there was something in the American atmosphere which made the religious loyalty of their native lands, and especially the olden observance of the Sabbath, impossible. Desecration of the Sabbath, particularly through the pursuit of secular occupations and business, became very widespread indeed. It became an exception, even a rarity, for a Jewish mercantile establishment or shop to be closed on Israel's sacred day of rest. Jewish leaders early recognized and deplored these conditions but seemed unable to prevent or even to improve them.

In the nineties of the nineteenth century, there were in existence two organizations for the promotion of Sabbath observance, one in the upper part of the city, the other on the lower East Side. They were both under the leadership of good men and loyal Jews. The uptown society was led by Mr. David Piza, a Sephardic Jew of earnest character and sincere piety. The downtown oganization was conducted by Mr. Isser Reznik, a Russian Jew, possessed of great love for Judaism and things Jewish. The name of the uptown society, if I recall correctly, was Jewish Sabbath Association; the downtown organization bore the Hebrew appellation of *Agudath Am Israel,* or League of the People of Israel. I joined the uptown organization but was unable to influence it to any extent. Whatever may have been the cause, neither of these organizations, despite the undoubted sincerity and good intentions of their leaders and members, was able to carry out its purpose. The Sabbath Association soon ceased to exist, and the *Agudath Am Israel* vegetated aimlessly.

These conditions grieved and distressed me greatly. I did not entertain the Utopian idea that I might completely solve the tremendous problem of Sabbath desecration, but I resolved to use my utmost efforts to bring about a change for the better. Impelled by this thought, I sought the cooperation of those who felt as I did for the purpose of forming a society for the promotion of Sabbath observance. This society, I hoped, would differ from the previous organizations, through the adoption of more practical methods and the greater energy and intensity with which they would be carried out. I found loyal co-workers, mainly among our brethren of Russian and Polish origin but including also a number of co-religionists of other descent.

Together we formed a society to which we gave the Hebrew name of *Tomche Shabbath,* that is, Supporters or Upholders of the Sabbath. A very intelligent and energetic man, Mr. Zvi Jacob Luria, was chosen for the all-important post of executive director, to be my right hand* in the putting into action of the plans which I had formed.

These plans were on an extensive scale, corresponding to the many aspects of the difficult and complicated Sabbath problem and designed to cope with these difficulties in a practical manner.

In an effort to relieve one of the most painful and distressing situations in American Jewish religious life, there was to be an employment bureau for Sabbath observers. This problem affected practically every observant family. The extreme difficulty of obtaining employment for its sons and daughters without the need of work on the Sabbath day was crucial. For Sabbath-keeping employment-seekers to find positions where consideration would be given to their conscientious scruples was an almost impossible task. It was the proverbial "looking for a needle in a haystack" The conflicts between religious loyalty and economic compulsion, and the domestic tragedies caused by the opposing sentiments of parents and children involved in this situation were numberless. But the situation, though grave in the extreme, was not utterly hopeless. There were still establishments in existence in which the holy Sabbath was observed. If the Sabbath-keeping employer and the Sabbath-keeping employment-seeker could be brought together, the problem would be solved for many, if not for all, of those affected by it. To accomplish this result was the task contemplated for the employment bureau.

Propaganda for the Sabbath was to be another form of work to which the new organization would devote much attention. In normally constituted Jewish communities, such as had existed in the Old World since time immemorial, propaganda, that is, deliberate and systematic efforts to induce Jewish people to observe the Sabbath, or any other of the precepts of the faith, would have been utterly superfluous and unthinkable. Here, however, disregard for the Sabbath had become so general that for multitudes of Jews the day had lost all sanctity and these multitudes were utterly unconscious that any duty rested on them to abstain on that day from secular labor and business and to observe it as holy time. In those numerous cases where Sabbath-

---

* Curiously, the writer forgets to mention that he was elected president of the new association.—Ed.

violating Jews had known different conditions, having been reared in pious and God-fearing environments, it was necessary to arouse their slumbering religious emotions and to appeal to them not to forsake the sacred heritage of their ancestors but to preserve and maintain it even in the changed conditions of modern days. For those other multitudes—and they were and are, unfortunately, very numerous—who had never had the inspiring experience of life in a truly Jewish environment, who had grown up in a spiritually barren and Jewishly moribund atmosphere, it was necessary to provide instruction, to tell them of the wondrous exaltation of the Jewish life and the sacred delight of the Sabbath which they had never known. Propaganda, therefore, of this fine and appealing type was to be an important part of the work of the Supporters of the Sabbath.

Intercession with employers was to be an important part of the work of our Sabbath society. In order to understand its need we must take a glance at conditions in the great metropolis of New York. When our immigrant brethren arrived and settled in the great city, it was natural for them to set up their homes and businesses on the lower East Side. They found there a great community of their country folk and a thoroughly Jewish atmosphere. The Sabbath was universally observed, and so they continued to observe the Holy Day, as they had done in their native lands. But when, after a few years, they prospered, as many of them did, and felt the urge to transfer their business activity to the upper city, they came into contact with new elements of people and with conditions they had not previously known. Here their loyalty to the Sabbath was put to a severe test. In the new district the influence of observant Jewish neighbors was lacking, and many of the newcomers succumbed only too easily to the spirit of the new environment and opened their establishments on the Sabbath day.

This action affected not only the employers and the office personnel but also, what was, from the religious point of view, far more important, the working people employed in the shops. In hundreds of these shops many thousands of workers had enjoyed the privilege of Sabbath rest and had been thus enabled to continue their religious life as they had been accustomed to in their East European homes. But when their employers decided to open on the Sabbath, it meant, almost invariably, that the shop, too, would be opened and the workers be compelled to work as on any ordinary week-day.

The gravity of the blow thus struck at Jewish religious observance and the Jewish religious spirit. To tear these thousands of workers from the historic moorings of Judaism, to accustom them to the desecration of the Sabbath, meant giving them over to every radical and subversive influence, to making them the easy victims of anti-religious agitators.

There was but one thing that could be done to counteract this threatening danger. It was to intercede with the employers to desist from work in the shops on the Sabbath day. Intercession with the employer, therefore, became a main feature of our work for the Sabbath and with blessed and happy results.

Legislative action was also recognized as a necessary and very important part of our work. The ideal democratic way of dealing with the problem is that the state should recognize the abstention from labor or commercial activity by the seventh-day-observing citizen as identical in legal value with the same abstention on the first day by the Sunday-observing citizen and that therefore the seventh day observer should be entitled to attend to his secular occupation or vocation on the six other days of the week, including Sunday. Unfortunately very few of the states have regulated their rest-day legislation in accordance with this natural and truly democratic principle.

Of the forty-eight states of the Union twenty-four, or exactly half, prohibit all work or business on Sunday. Of the remaining twenty-four, the majority grant partial exemption from Sunday laws to the observer of the seventh-day Sabbath. Three of the far Western states, California, Oregon, and Washington, and the District of Columbia, it may be incidentally remarked, have no Sunday laws. The State of New York, in which the bulk of the Jewish population of this country dwells, has a partial and very limited exemption law. It recognizes habitual observance of another day of the week as "holy time" as a valid *defense against prosecution* for work or labor done on Sunday. It does not protect against arrest for such labor nor does it permit traffic or business on Sunday at all.

None can deny, therefore, that the way of the conscientious Sabbath observer is a hard one, even in this land of supposed religious liberty. Even where exemption from Sunday laws is granted, that does not compensate financially for the loss and injury caused by closing one's business on Saturday, the busiest and most profitable day in the week. But without such exemption and under the necessity of remaining closed one hundred and four days in the year while one's competitors close only fifty-two days, it becomes practically impossible for many merchants and manufacturers to continue the observance of the Sabbath. It was clear, therefore, that the protection of the legal rights of the Sabbath observer must be an essential part of the work of our society.

In view of the peculiar nature of the New York statute, it was clear that it would be necessary for our society to employ counsel for the defense of Sabbath-observing workingmen and others haled to court on charges of violating the Sunday law. This position was filled from early after the organization of the society until his death in 1934 by my brother, the late Gustave S. Drachman, with rare fidelity, ability, and success. He procured the acquittal of many defendants who, if undefended or incompetently defended, would have been found guilty and fined, perhaps heavily fined. The present (1943) counsel of the society is Mr. Herman Koenigsburg, who performs the duties of the office with devotion and ability.

There is another feature of the work of our Sabbath Society on which we at present lay great stress but which was not thought of when the society was first organized—the effort to secure the general adoption of the five-day working week, that is to say, that the working week shall consist of five days, from Monday to Friday inclusive, and that *both* Saturday and Sunday shall be days of rest, for all citizens, Jews and Christians alike.

The difficulties of Sabbath observance are many. There is a widespread fear of arousing anti-Semitism by observers making themselves unduly conspicuous. There was, too, the practical loss involved in refusing to do business on the week's busiest day. Man has need, besides, of two kinds of release from work—physical recreation and spiritual renewal.

These very real and weighty causes led to the proposal that the working or business week be limited to five days, with both the Saturday and Sunday observed as days of rest and abstinence from busi-

Bernard Drachman at the Beginning of his
Rabbinical Career about 1891

Synagogue of the Congregation Zichron Ephraim
163-167 East Sixty-Seventh Street, New York

ness by all merchants, Jewish and Gentile alike. That would automatically free the Jewish merchant from the fear of arousing anti-Semitism through stressing his separateness and would prevent all improper competition, since all would stand on an equal, indeed, on the same basis.

Furthermore, one rest day in the week is not adequate to serve both the religious and the social needs of the community. A weekly day of rest is required for two purposes, to enable human beings to turn their minds from earthly things and to worship their Maker and to give them a period of recuperation from the drudgery and grind of work and business. One day cannot serve both purposes. The clergy, both Christian and Jewish, naturally stress the religious purpose, indeed, are inclined to look upon any other employment of the day as a desecration. The workers and other employees of commercial and industrial establishments, especially the younger element, on the other hand, want the day of rest as a time of recreation and recuperation.

The only way in which these conflicting tendencies can be reconciled is to arrange that both Saturday and Sunday shall be observed by the entire community, Jews and Christians alike, as days of rest. Under this arrangement Christians, except the seventh-day observing sects, would devote the Sunday to religion and the Saturday to recreation, while the Jews would reverse the process. It would mean, for all concerned, an eminently satisfactory solution of a most thorny and vexing problem. As already stated, I did not take up this form of work immediately on the organization of our Sabbath society but only a number of years later.

Chapter Twenty-eight

Vacations—Niantic—Bay Shore—Sharon Springs

A Rustic Synagogue

IT MIGHT BE THOUGHT THAT VACATIONS FORM NO ESSENTIAL PART OF the life of a rabbi and that to describe them is quite superfluous. But I look upon my life as a sort of panorama and am trying to depict my experiences as they occurred. Besides, they have not infrequently been instructive and conveyed lessons of value, of general importance or of special significance, to an adherent or teacher of Judaism. For reasons of space I shall limit myself to the description of a few vacations which stand out in my memory with especial vividness because of their highly interesting quality or particular significance. .

The first such vacation was in the year 1900. My family and I had become the summer paying guests of a Jewish farmer named Isaac Wilinsky. His farm was located in the vicinity of Niantic, Connecticut, in the township of Lyme. My family consisted then of my wife and myself and our five children, herewith mentioned in the order of their ages: Beatrice Beruchah, Edgar Jacob, Julian Moses, Albert Isaiah, and Mathilde Madeline, of whom the oldest was ten years of age and the youngest two. Mr. and Mrs. Isaac Bernheim, friends of ours, accompanied us. They too boarded at the Wilinsky cottage.

The country around Niantic was the most thoroughly rural, almost primitive, of any region I have ever visited. It was surprising to me that a region of this nature could be found so near to the great metropolis. The hand of man had changed it very slightly. The roads, in those pre-automobile days, seemed hardly more than scratches on the surface of an unchanged wilderness. They were lined on both sides with an exuberant vegetation, barely kept down in the middle by the occasional passing of vehicles. The great fields through which the roads passed, with their abounding wealth of variegated plant life, seemed more to reflect the natural state of a fertile, aboriginal land than the artificial product of human skill and industry. The not infrequent stretches of forest, in whose dark recesses one could well imagine that wild creatures still lurked, strengthened these impressions. The habitations of man in this region fitted harmoniously into the picture. They were mostly low, sprawling structures, equipped with the rude comforts of a pioneering population but devoid of the refined provisions for catering to a pampered taste known as "modern improvements." The old-fashioned wells, with their primitive superstructures and moss-covered buckets, stood not far from the farm houses. These wells spoke of colonial days, when the settlers, in order to insure their supply of water, were obliged to draw it themselves from the bowels of the earth. But the aqueous fluid thus primitively obtained was wonderfully cool and fresh, superior, indeed, to that supplied by the elaborate aqueduct systems of the great cities.

The mode of life of the inhabitants and the easy manner in which they accommodated themselves to conditions which persons of more delicate sensibilities would consider unbearable hardships also amazed me. Take the case of Farmer Johnson. Talking to me one day, he told me about his life in winter. He said he lived in a remote part of the back country and was generally snowed in for two months or more. Incidentally, he was a widower without children and lived alone. I asked him how he managed to get along under such conditions.

"Oh, that's easy," he answered. "In November I buy a barrel of pork and a barrel of crackers and I have my food for the whole winter. Every day for breakfast I eat crackers and pork, for dinner I eat pork and crackers, and for supper I eat crackers and pork."

"But aren't you awfully lonely when you're snowed in?" I asked. "What do you do to pass the time?"

"I'm not a bit lonely," he answered. "Sometimes I set and think, and *sometimes I just set.*"

In this thoroughly rural region amidst a mainly Yankee population, a not inconsiderable number of our Jewish brethren had found homes. They were mostly Russian refugees who had fled from the empire of the Czars to escape the bloody pogroms and persecutions which raged against the Jews in that benighted land. They had found refuge in free and—at that time—hospitable America. Many of them had purchased abandoned farms, of which there were many in the region, and which they were inhabiting and cultivating. There were also several Jewish colonies in the neighborhood. Our landlord, Isaac Wilinsky, was a Jewish farmer of the first mentioned type.

Practically all the Jewish farmers added to their incomes by taking summer guests. These vacationists had brought about the creation of a new term in the Russian-Yiddish dialect which the farmers spoke. They called them *"pleasurenikes,"* "seekers of pleasure," a combination of the English word "pleasure" and the Russian ending *"nik,"* meaning "someone characterized by, or addicted to."

Though the furnishings were the reverse of luxurious, the food certainly compensated for this deficiency, for, though simple, it was very good indeed. The vegetables, berries, milk, cream, butter, and eggs were all supplied by the farm and they were not only of superb quality but had the indefinable charm which comes from perfect freshness and ripeness and of which city dwellers have very little idea. The other dietary components, such as meat, poultry, fish, bread, rolls, tea, coffee, and the rarer fruits, Wilinsky obtained from New London, about fifteen or sixteen miles away, where there were kosher butcher shops and well stocked grocery and provision stores. Two or three times a week he would harness up his truck and repair thither to bring the needed supplies. I accompanied him on one of these expeditions—a mad dash over pitch-dark roads.

I made a special study of the Jewish settlers in the region. I was greatly interested in them and very desirous of knowing how the sudden change from their native Russia to the great republic of the western world had affected them and influenced their outlook on life. I found them a hard-working, industrious people, happy in their new homes and very anxious to achieve prosperity for themselves and a successful future for their children. Physically they seemed more Russian than Jewish; at all events the Semitic type was not at all frequent among them. Our Mr. Wilinsky, for instance, was typically Slavonic, tall and strong, with reddish hair and sallow complexion.

His wife and children were similar in appearance. Mrs. Wilinsky was rather good-looking and the boy and girl were darling little ones, but there was nothing Semitic or Oriental about them. There was a Russian Gentile laborer on the farm and I also had occasion to meet two converts, a father and son, who had accepted the Jewish faith in Russia and had come to America together with the Jewish exiles, but I could perceive no difference in physical type between them and the other farmers.

Religiously I was surprised and grieved to find that America had influenced them unfavorably. They had all been strictly observant of Jewish precepts and traditions in their native land, but many of them seemed to think that in America that was not possible.

Even into this secluded rural region, I noticed, anti-Semitism had made its entrance. It was not of a dangerous or vicious kind—under American conditions it could hardly be—nor would I say that it was generally prevalent, but it grieved me greatly to find it at all where the bitter competition and rivalry of commercial and professional life was lacking. It saddened me to observe how this senseless psychical malady of Jew-hatred, whether instinctive or acquired, follows its unfortunate victims wherever they wander. Often it is due to mere ignorance, as will be illustrated by the following incident.

I was sitting one afternoon on the porch of the Wilinsky cottage, when a buggy containing an aged couple, typical Down East Yankees, came along on the road and stopped opposite the house. The only other person on the porch at the time was the little daughter of the Wilinskys, a pretty child of six or seven years with fair hair and complexion and blue eyes. Addressing me, the old man said, "We have heard that there is a Jewish child here. Would you mind showing it to us?" Without answering in words I pointed to the Wilinsky child. The couple looked at her and I noticed a puzzled expression on their countenances. Then, turning to his wife, the man said in a tone indicating both surprise and disappointment, "Jee whillikens, Jerushah, she looks like any other kid." It was clear that they were completely ignorant of the fact that Jews are Caucasians and expected the child to show the complexion and physical characteristics of some strange, outlandish race.

Later my father, of blessed memory, was to stay with us for a few weeks. On the day when he was to arrive I spoke to Wilinsky and asked him to take me in his buggy to the railroad station, which was about five miles away, to meet my father and bring him to the farm. Wilinsky and his men were extremely busy with farm work and could not spare the time. I then asked him to let me have the rig and I would myself drive to the station and bring my father. To this he readily agreed but warned me that the only horse available was the bronco. I heard this statement with consternation. The bronco was a fractious, ugly-tempered brute who enjoyed the reputation of being utterly uncontrollable by anybody. Several of the Jewish farmers, including Wilinsky himself, had tried to drive him but without success. The severest beatings could not make him budge. To drive such an animal to the station seemed utterly impossible. But to permit my father to arrive at the station and to find no one there to welcome him, and bring him to his destination, was out of the question.

By some sort of inspiration the thought came to me that perhaps by kindness and gentleness I might persuade the bronco to do my will. I had him harnessed and brought, together with the buggy, to the open space before the cottage. This he was willing to do, but as he stood there I thought I noticed in his eyes an ugly look, as much as to say, "Make me go any further, if you can." I went up to him, stroked him gently and softly on his forehead and neck several times and whispered into his ear, "Bronco, be a good boy. Don't let me disappoint my father. Take me to the station and back and I will be forever grateful to you. Do now, that's a good boy."

I then mounted the buggy, took the reins in my hand and said in a gentle voice, "Gee up!" To the surprise of all the onlookers, myself included, Bronco started off at a fair pace. He kept this up until we reached the station. He seemed to know the way, for he required no urging by me, and when we arrived at the station he stopped of his own accord. He waited patiently until the train bearing my father arrived, and then he brought us back with the same ready obedience and the same steady and rapid amble. I saw to it that he was rewarded with a couple of apples and an extra portion of oats. This incident filled the farmers with amazement. They said the bronco must have had a Jewish soul since he showed respect and deference to a rabbi. I thought that it was simply a demonstration of the power of gentleness, that it as potent with the lower animals as with human beings. It was an illustration of the meaning of Solomon when he said, "A soft answer turneth away wrath."

One day, in conversation with one of the guests at Wilinsky's, I learned of the existence of two towns in the neighboring State of Rhode Island, Westerly and Ashaway, whose inhabitants, Christian Sabbatarians, were strict observers of the Jewish, or seventh-day, Sabbath. This information interested me greatly. I was anxious to see a place in America where the Sabbath of Israel was observed by the general community and where its influence was recognizable in the public life of the town, even though those who observed it were not of the seed of the patriarchs. I determined to make the trip thither and see for myself. I inquired first whether there was any religious Jewish family in either of these towns, where I could obtain ritually permitted food. I was informed that there was such a family in Westerly named Soloweitzik. My informant added that they were in humble circumstances, the husband being only a customer-peddler. I answered that their financial condition made no difference to me, so long as I knew that they were conscientious in their Judaism, and that their food was ritually permissible.

I wrote accordingly to the Soloweitziks, inquiring whether they could accommodate me at their home for a few days including the Sabbath. Mr. Soloweitzik answered that he and his wife would be glad to have me as their guest. The very next day, I believe it was Thursday, I took the train for Westerly, which is about three hours by rail from Niantic, having previously sent the Soloweitziks a telegram announcing the hour of my arrival. When the train stopped at the Westerly station I saw a good-looking, neatly dressed gentleman of early middle age, who appeared to be looking for someone. Coming toward me, he inquired, "Are you the Rabbi Dr. Drachman?" I answered in the affirmative and said that he was no doubt Mr. Soloweitzik. My assumption was correct, although I was surprised to find him much better-looking and more genteel than I had been led to expect.

"I have my rig here," he said, "and I will be glad to take you to my home at once."

On the other side of the station were standing a horse and buggy.

The horse was a fine, coal-black animal. The buggy was an elegant vehicle, apparently almost new. This did not agree at all with my preconceived notions about my prospective host. I could not refrain from asking:

"Are these yours?"

"Yes," he answered. "But I only use them for visiting and riding around. For business I have a wagon and a different horse."

The streets through which we at first drove were rather poor-looking—it was evidently the poorer section of the town—but we soon entered very handsome streets and drove between rows of fine cottages. I especially admired the splendid old trees which lined both sides of the street. We came to what was evidently a great estate, an extensive tract of land enclosed with a massive fence, in the midst of which stood a large building, a real mansion. Here my host turned and began to drive through the great central entrance. I was amazed and could hardly believe my eyes. In my amazement I said to Mr. Soloweitzik, "Are you driving in here?" "Yes," he answered. "This is where I live, this is my home." He then explained to me, smiling at my manifest astonishment, that he was not the owner of this splendid property, that it belonged to an American Gentile physician and that he, Mr. Soloweitzik, was his tenant. The physician and his family, consisting, if I remember aright, of his wife and several daughters, occupied the lower part of the building and Mr. and Mrs. Soloweitzik the upper part. A considerable part of the land was covered by a vegetable garden which produced a great quantity of fine vegetables, of which the Soloweitziks were entitled to one half, as well as to an equal share of all the privileges and prerogatives connected with the estate. The physician and family, Mr. Soloweitzik informed me, were most delightful people, friendly and sociable, and his and his wife's relations with them were most agreeable. We then ascended a broad and elegant staircase to the Soloweitzik apartment. I was received most hospitably by Mrs. Soloweitzik, a youthful and very good-looking woman. The apartment consisted of ten rooms and those which I saw were handsomely furnished. I could not restrain my curiosity from inquiring what rent the Soloweitziks were paying. Lo and behold! The remuneration for all this comfort and beauty was the munificent sum of ten dollars monthly.

I spent three delightful days in Westerly, where I learned a great deal about it, both from what I observed while walking through its streets in the company of Mr. Soloweitzik and from what my companion told me. I found it a most interesting place from two points of view, the religious and economic. Religiously it was most astonishishing to me to observe how zealously and conscientiously the Sabbatarians, who constituted approximately half of the population, kept the Seventh-Day Sabbath, the Sabbath enjoined by the Holy Torah of Israel. I saw throngs of devout worshippers going to their churches on Friday evening and Saturday morning and afternoon, and there was a weird similarity to the manner in which we Jews attend our *Kabbalath Shabbath* and *Shacharith* and *Minchah* services on the Sabbath day, except that the churches were far better attended than the generality of American synagogues.

There were great mills and factories and stores belonging to Sabbatarians, all strictly closed on the Sabbath day. I was informed that the neighboring town of Ashaway was even more of a Sabbath-keeping place than Westerly for, while in the latter town only about half of the population were seventh-day observers, in the former place that was true of all the inhabitants.

The religious conditions among the Jews were not nearly as satisfactory. There were only eight Jewish heads of families in Westerly, four of whom kept the Sabbath while the others did not. The four Sabbath-keepers were all customer-peddlers. The other four were storekeepers, and all of them kept their places of business open on the Sabbath day. This condition of affairs made me very indignant. I took the liberty of rebuking one of the Sabbath desecrators, the proprietor of a large establishment.

"Aren't you ashamed," I said, "to be *mechallel Shabbos* (to break the Sabbath) in a place like this? If you were in a place where the Sunday is kept by the majority of people, you would have an excuse. You could say that you cannot afford to be an exception. But here, where the Gentiles are keeping our Sabbath, you have no such excuse. On the contrary, here, by keeping open on Sabbath you make yourself an exception and bring a bad name on the Jews." This reasoning, I believe, is logical and correct, but it had no influence on this individual. He did not attempt to refute me, but I could see by his expression of face that he was unimpressed. I could only say to myself that "habit becomes second nature," or, to put it with the Talmud, "when a person transgresses and repeats his transgression several times, it becomes to him like a thing permitted."

My hosts were sincerely religious and strict observers of the Sabbath. There was no synagogue and no public Jewish service in Westerly, but we, Mr. Soloweitzik and I, reciited all the prayers and read the Biblical portions of the day in the home. Mrs. Soloweitzik had fulfilled the other precept of the Sabbath by preparing excellent meals, so that I passed a very enjoyable Sabbath indeed.

Economic conditions in Westerly were surprisingly good. Rents were particularly noteworthy for moderation. A fairly comfortable worker's cottage could be rented, I was informed, for five dollars monthly. Food was also extremely moderate in price. On the other hand, wages were high and earnings large. This made the vocation of customer-peddler very profitable. I do not know whether these ideal economic conditions were restricted to Westerly or were prevalent throughout the entire region. Neither do I know whether the same conditions prevail there today (1943). I am inclined to think that such is not the case, that this region has been affected by the general rise in prices and the process of urbanization which have gone on all over this country.

I was really sorry to take leave of the Soloweitziks. They were such friendly and hospitable people that we became real friends. I had, of course, intended to pay them for entertaining me, but they would accept no remuneration. On the contrary, after returning to New York I was surprised one day to receive a beautiful cushion which Mrs. Soloweitzik had made and on which she had embroidered my initials "B. D." most artistically in silk lettering, as a memento of my visit with them.

In the summer of 1901 we rented a cottage at Bay Shore, Long Island. There, on the nineteenth of July, my fourth son, Myron Joshua, was born. The event was not only a joyous one for me and my family but aroused great interest among our neighbors.

Eight days later the *Brith Milah,* the formal initiation of the infant into the Covenant of Abraham, took place. It was, naturally, a joyous family event, as had been the similar events in the lives of my older sons, and was celebrated with the customary solemnity and rejoicing. The grandparents of the infant, with the exception of my mother, of blessed memory, who had passed away in 1896, and most of the members of the families on both sides had come from the various places where they were passing the summer. Mr. and Mrs. Jonas Weil, my parents-in-law, came from Sharon Springs, New York, where they had taken a cottage for the heated season.

After the ritual act of the circumcision, and the feast in connection therewith, were concluded, Mrs. Weil made a very unexpected and pleasant announcement to my wife and me. "I have seen a very nice cottage at Sharon," she said. "It has quite a number of rooms and is in very good condition. It also has a nice piece of land attached to it. I think it would be just the right thing for you and your family. I have taken an option on it, and if you both are satisfied I would like to present it to you."

And thus we became the possessors of a summer home at Sharon Springs. Of course we could not occupy it that summer, but in the following summer, of 1902, it became our home during the months of July and August and a little before and after. Although it had been in quite good condition when purchased, Mr. Weil had quite extensive external and internal repairs and improvements made, which made it an ideally comfortable summer residence. It served this purpose for fully nineteen years, during which time most of my sons and daughters grew up to manhood and womanhood.

Our summers in Sharon Springs were most pleasant and enjoyable. For the children especially they were the acme of what growing boys and girls require for health and happiness. The country around Sharon is most picturesque and truly rustic. Situated in the heart of the beautiful and romantic Mohawk Valley with its entrancing scenery and its memories of colonial and pre-colonial history, it fairly urged one to forget the great city with its congestion and its artificiality, to yield to the charm of unspoiled nature and to inhale with delight the cool ozone which exudes from forest and mountains.

I encouraged my children in their youthful love of sport and play and participated to a considerable extent in their outings and hikes through the countryside. I rode horseback and also had them taught horseback riding, at which they became quite expert. The surrounding country afforded an ideal opportunity for this form of health-bringing enjoyment.

Shortly after we had settled down in the cottage in our first season, my brother-in-law, Mr. Benjamin J. Weil, presented the children with a goat, together with a goat carriage and the necessary harness. Words cannot describe the delight with which the children received this present or the pleasure they derived from it. For years it was a source of pleasure for the children, especially the younger ones, and became well known in the vicinity.

It attracted considerable attention a few years later and, incidentally, brought some fame to my younger daughter Mathilde Madeline —we called her Mattie for short, and call her so to this day—who was at the time eight or nine years of age. There was a so-called field day in Sharon Springs that summer and one of the features of the celebration was a procession of ornamental or show vehicles. Little Mattie got the idea that she might compete in the procession through the aid of the goat and his carriage. Accordingly my wife and some of our female relatives dressed Mattie in a picturesque costume and also decked the goat and the carriage in appropriate adornment. Mattie was a most charming little figure, and the goat and carriage presented a picturesque and unusual sight. There was nothing like them in the procession and both Mattie and her equipage aroused great admiration.

The piece of land on which our cottage was situated was large enough to enable us to have a vegetable garden of our own. When I subsequently enlarged it through the purchase of an additional piece of land from a neighbor, it became more than sufficient for that purpose, and made it possible for us to keep a cow. Our garden and cow not only provided us with an unfailing supply of fresh vegetables and pure milk and cream but also with wholesome and delightful occupation. The garden was planted in the spring before our arrival by the neighbor who took care of the cottage. After our arrival, however, my boys and I took care of it for the rest of the summer. The boys even learned how to milk the cow. My third son, Albert, became particularly skillful thereat, but I never acquired that ability. As a rule the cow was milked and cared for by a neighbor, whose reward was a goodly portion of the daily yield of milk.

Our life in Sharon was, therefore, from the physical point of view, most pleasant, and from the spiritual standpoint it was equally satisfactory. I had indescribable joy in offering up my prayers to the Almighty morning and afternoon and evening while God's cool breeze fanned my cheeks and all the surroundings spoke of a Merciful and Loving Creator. I never had greater intellectual and spiritual satisfaction than when I sat in my cozy, airy room in our cottage in the quiet, shady village street and read the messages of the prophets of Israel or pored over the abstruse discussions of the rabbis of the Talmud—I had brought copies of the Hebrew Bible and one or two Talmudic treatises along for that very purpose. I continued the Hebrew and religious instruction of my children just as I had imparted it in the city.

Our Sabbaths were particularly delightful. On Friday evenings, our house was a picture of a typical Sabbath in a Jewish home. The table was set with the best of silver, glass, porcelain, and linen which our household afforded. On it stood, in its center, the Sabbath chandelier which my wife had lit with a devout blessing just before the shades of evening began to fall. All the other lights in the house were also lit. At first we had only kerosene oil lamps, but later on electric illumination took their place—so that the whole house shone with the bright radiance which, according to Jewish tradition, is symbolic of spiritual enlightment and joy. Our Sabbath meals were delightful. As I sat at the head of the table, my dear wife opposite me and our children on both sides, I was reminded of the words of the Psalmist: "Thy wife shall be like a fruitful vine within thy home, thy children like olive plants round about thy table. Behold, thus shall be blessed a man who feareth the Lord." (*Psalm CXXVIII*, v. 3 & 4). And I felt that this blessing had been fulfilled, however unworthily, in me. Our children were all thoroughly familiar with the prayers and chants of the Sabbath, and when I, or one of the boys, led in the chanting of the grace, all participated with perfect harmony and correct melody. Sometimes we had guests on Friday evening or Sabbath by day, and they were always as much impressed by our reverential and melodious services as they were pleased with the palatable meal.

When we first took up our summer residence in Sharon Springs, it was a place hardly known to the Jewish community and rarely visited by our co-religionists. My mother-in-law, Mrs. Therese Weil, had heard of the curative properties of its mineral waters and had gone there seeking healing. In the first summer of our occupation of the cottage Mrs. Amelia Rosenberg, with whom I had boarded in New York previous to my marriage, came to Sharon also in pursuit of health. We invited her frequently to our cottage in order that she might have the opportunity of eating a good kosher meal, which it was not possible to obtain otherwise in the village.

Mrs. Rosenberg was looking at that time for some source of income, and Mrs. Weil suggested to her that she should open a boarding house in Sharon Springs. With Mrs. Rosenberg's splendid reputation for strict reliability in the observance of the dietary laws, and her thorough respectability, Mrs. Weil said, there was little or no doubt that she would obtain the patronage of the best Jewish families.

Mrs. Rosenberg acted upon this suggestion, purchased a cottage which was then available, made the necessary alterations and improvements, and in the following summer opened it as a strictly kosher hotel, to which she gave the name of Hotel Rosenberg. Mrs. Weil's prediction came true. The Hotel Rosenberg became at once a decided success, patronized by a select clientele of Jewish residents of New York and Baltimore.

Our taking up of our summer residence and Mrs. Rosenberg's opening of her hotel called the attention of Jewish people generally to Sharon Springs, and it speedily became a favorite summer and health resort for our co-religionists. At the present time (1943) it may truthfully be called a Jewish resort. Almost all of the hotels, of which there is a goodly number, and the great majority of the summer residents, are Jewish.

In the first year of our residence in Sharon I made no attempt to have congregational services. I read the prayers and the Scriptural portions in our cottage. My wife and children were my congregation. But the summer wore on, and the great fast of *Tisha B'Ab*, the ninth of Ab, which commemorates by fasting and lamentation the destruction of the Temple and the downfall and dispersal of the Jewish nation, was approaching. I determined to try to bring together the required *Minyan*, or quorum of men, ten, so that we might have a congregational service at least on the evening with which, like all Jewish holy days, the *Tisha B'Ab* begins. A few days before the holy day, I began canvassing the village, to see whether I could find the requisite number and to induce them to attend the service. I worked with great energy, even entering houses where I had no reason to anticipate the presence of any Jew. On the eve of the fast I had found nine Jews who had promised to come to our cottage for the service. But the indispensable tenth one was lacking.

The time for service arrived. The nine were already assembled in our cottage. Almost in despair I went to the main street and had hardly stepped upon it when I saw approaching a man whom I knew well and who might help us out of our difficulty. This was a man of Jewish birth, but not at all observant of Jewish religious precepts. (His name, incidentally, was Ochs.) I greeted him with joy.

"Tonight is *Tisha B'Ab*," I explained. "I am trying to arrange *Minyan* and we are just one man short. Won't you come with me and help complete the *Minyan?*"

He smiled. "If you can use such a Jew as I am to *Minyan*, I don't mind going with you," he said.

We had a very reverent and impressive service. I chanted the prayers and the lamentations of Jeremiah, and Mr. Ochs joined in as devoutly as the most Orthodox Jew. After the service I thanked him for his courtesy in coming at my request. He said to me, "You know, Dr. Drachman, I think Sharon Springs is the queerest place in the world. Everywhere in the world ten Jews are needed for *Minyan*. Here, in Sharon Springs, I see you can get along with nine Jews and an ox." I softened the asperity of his self-criticism by assuring him that such an ox would be acceptable for *Minyan* everywhere in the world.

After Mrs. Rosenberg opened her hotel, I arranged, with her consent, that we should have public services in the parlor of the hotel on Friday evenings and Sabbath mornings and also occasionally on week days. It was a handsomely furnished, pleasant room, well adapted for moderately large gatherings. There was a good attendance from the start, both from the guests of the hotel and outsiders, as there was already a sufficient number of Jewish summer visitors in Sharon to insure a very fair-sized congregation. The prayers were read by the *shochet*, or ritual slaughterer, of the hotel, who was also a well qualified cantor, and I usually delivered a sermon at the Sabbath morning service.

But I soon found that services in the hotel parlor were not completely satisfactory. After all, a hotel parlor is not an ideal place for permanent religious services. Not all the hotel guests were spiritually inclined and interested in religious services. They would show their lack of interest by remaining on the porch and indulging in ordinary conversation while the services were going on. This manifest indifference and open disrespect offended many of the worshippers, among them, I must admit, myself. The services would also be disturbed in other ways, innocent, indeed, and without evil intent, but very disagreeable nevertheless.

Contemplating these conditions, I came to the decision that the only proper place for a permanent religious service is a regular synagogue, a House of God, built for and consecrated exclusively to the holy purpose of the worship of the Supreme Being. I resolved that I would endeavor to bring about the erection of such an edifice in Sharon Springs.

That very summer I began my efforts to accomplish this purpose. I announced my intention and requested and received financial aid for its accomplishment from a number of summer guests both at the Sabbath morning services in the Rosenberg Hotel and in private. I also visited the Jewish hotel keepers—there were already several Jewish hotels in Sharon—and requested their cooperation. I took the view, and expressed it to them, that Jewish hotel keepers should be especially interested in promoting the establishment of a Jewish house of worship in the town, as it would add to the attractiveness of the place in the eyes of the Jewish public and would tend to increase the number of visitors and hotel guests. I also looked about for a suitable site for the proposed synagogue and spoke to several of the town residents in reference thereto.

My efforts met with a mixed reception. All but one of the hotel men were enthusiastically in favor of the idea and assisted me with their contributions, but that one was violently opposed. He told me that he would not give one cent for the erection of a synagogue but that he would be willing to contribute several hundred dollars to prevent it. He was one of the class of Crypto-Jews who believe there is safety in concealing their identity.

Also among the non-Jewish inhabitants the proposal to erect a synagogue evoked a divergence of opinion. A meeting of residents was called—so I was informed by one who claimed to have been present—to consider the question as to the attitude which the villagers should take toward the proposal to establish a synagogue in Sharon Springs. At this meeting, my informant stated, one of those present, a Gentile hotel keeper, took a distinctly anti-Semitic attitude. He advised the people of Sharon to discourage the growth of the Jewish element in their town, using the familiar anti-Semitic calumnies to impress their undesirability upon those present. He proposed that no Gentile owner of real estate should sell his land for the erection of a synagogue.

It looked for a time, so I was told, as though this view might prevail. But the situation was saved by the action of the oldest and most respected resident and land owner of Sharon, whose name I have pleasure in mentioning, Judge Jackson. This gentleman warmly opposed the anti-Semitic views of the previous speaker. He said that the Jews, as American citizens, had a perfect right to settle in Sharon Springs either permanently or as summer visitors if they so desired, and that the people of Sharon should be glad to welcome them, as peaceful and progressive people, through whose presence the prosperity of Sharon could only be increased. He concluded by saying, with a smile, that he owned a piece of land which he thought well adapted for a synagogue and, if Rabbi Drachman desired to purchase it for that purpose, he would be very glad to sell it to him. The liberal and truly American views of Judge Jackson decided the issue. Accordingly the meeting resolved not to take any action of an anti-Jewish nature.

As it happened, I did not have to put the liberal resolutions of the meeting to the test. I chanced to become acquainted, I do not recall just how, with a co-religionist, a Mr. Bernard Bondy, who was the owner of a piece of land which was ideally suited for the purpose I had in mind. This was a lot situated in a side street of the village, a street lined with splendid shade trees and at the intersection of a picturesque country lane. There was a small cottage on the lot, but the unoccupied portion of the land was amply sufficient for the erection of another building. Mr. Bondy was also willing to grant very liberal terms, to accept the few hundred dollars which I had thus far collected as a down payment, and to wait for the payment of the rest until such time as would be convenient for me to make it. Without consultation with anyone and entirely upon my own responsibility, I purchased the property. Immediately thereupon I made the necessary arrangements for the construction of the building. I returned to New York with the assurance that the summer of the coming year would see a Jewish house of worship in Sharon Springs—the only one not only there but in the entire surrounding country for many miles. The first thing I did after our return to the city was to look up an architect to design the plan which should guide Mr. Hoffman, our builder, in the construction of the synagogue.

My next task was to raise the funds which were still needed for the completion of the edifice, not a very large sum but still several thousand dollars. I found the task easier than I had anticipated. I called personally on a number of prominent co-religionists and sent letters to others. Hardly any refused to contribute. The spirit of understanding which I encountered was most gratifying.

From beginning to end it required about seven thousand dollars to acquire the property, construct and furnish the building, excavate the soil, build the retaining wall, sod the ground, and plant bushes and trees. The result was a charming edifice, surrounded by attractive grounds. Its seating capacity was not very large, only sufficient for three hundred worshippers, but it became so popular that during the summer season it was filled to its utmost capacity on every occasion of public worship.

The formal consecration or dedication of the new synagogue took place on the afternoon of the 22nd of July, 1904. This was, of course, an event of outstanding importance in the village. It brought Jews and Judaism to the attention of the country people as they had never been brought before. The news of the forthcoming event had spread far and wide, and a great throng, not only of Jewish summer boarders but also of residents of Sharon and the surrounding country, came to participate. Every seat in the synagogue was occupied and many persons, who had not been able to secure admission, stood outside and gazed through the open windows and listened to the proceedings.

The program consisted of Psalms and Bible readings, which were impressively rendered by the cantor, musical selections by the village band, and addresses. The consecration sermon was delivered by me, and the principal other address was by the Reverend Mr. Armstrong, Episcopal clergyman of the village, whose church was very near the synagogue and whom I had invited as a sign of interdenominational comity. Mr. Armstrong's sermon was a noteworthy one, not only because it conveyed a truly spiritual message in beautiful English and with much eloquence but because of its modesty of attitude and profound appreciation of the importance of the Jewish religion in the religious history of the world. I was greatly impressed by the fair and just views of Mr. Armstrong, which are, to say the least, none too frequent among non-Jewish appraisers of Judaism, and I remember them with grateful pleasure to this day. Mr. Armstrong was, incidentally, a native of England, and, in appearance and manner, a typical English curate.

The dedication ceremonies were followed by the regular services of Friday afternoon and Sabbath evening. The twenty-second of July in that year fell on a Friday. From that time on, the Sharon Springs synagogue has remained undeviatingly devoted to Jewish worship, not only while my family and I continued to make Sharon our summer home but also after we left it in 1921, even until the present day. It was always conducted, during my connection with it, I can truthfully say, in a manner calculated to please and stir the religious emotions of its visitors.

I was, at the same time, its rabbi, financial manager, and caretaker. (For these services, I need hardly add, I received no manner of material compensation.) I preached on almost every Sabbath, and I also saw to it that its financial obligations were met and that the building and grounds were maintained in a condition of perfect cleanliness and order. The services were in accordance with Orthodox Jewish ritual and usages. Perfect order and decorum prevailed, and congregational singing, in which my children and I took a leading part, added harmony and melody. As a result, the synagogue found favor in the sight of all elements of the Jewish summer visitors. Many Reformers, who at home never attended an Orthodox service, were among its regular Sabbath attendants. Through the influence of the synagogue, and also other efforts on my part, Jewish life in Sharon took on a more religious character than in many other places of summer resort. When we left Sharon in 1921, I handed over the synagogue, free and clear of debt, to a committee of Jewish hotel keepers. It still serves its holy purpose.

Chapter Twenty-nine

More About the Seminary

THE PASSING AWAY OF THE DISTINGUISHED MEN AND NOBLE LEADERS of Judaism who had been chiefly instrumental in the founding of the Jewish Theological Seminary brought with it many changes. A new and, from a certain point of view, more brilliant period speedily began for it. It found new friends, particularly one very potent friend, Mr. Jacob H. Schiff, multimillionaire, leading banker of New York City, and outstanding Jewish philanthropist. What the motive of Mr. Schiff was which induced him just at that time to give the Seminary the generous assistance which he had not given during the lifetime of its original founders and leaders, I do not pretend to know. Certain it is, however, that he did give it, and with a degree of generosity and lavishness unparalleled in the history of Jewish philanthropy and communal beneficence in America and only surpassed in two or three instances in the Old World. He caused the Seminary to be transferred from its modest home at 736 Lexington Avenue to a palatial structure in West One Hundred and Twenty-third Street, erected at a cost of a half-million dollars or more, and he provided the funds necessary for the carrying on of the educational work of the Seminary in a manner consistent with the splendor of the building in which it was housed.*

A distinguished Anglo-Jewish scholar, Dr. Solomon Schechter, renowned through his discovery of the original Hebrew text of Ben Sira in the Cairo *Genizah,* was called to the presidency of the faculty, and several other European Jewish scholars were added to the faculty: Dr. Louis Ginzberg as Professor of Talmud, Dr. Israel Fried-

---

* This does not refer to the even more magnificent building, occupying an entire block on Broadway from One Hundred and Twenty-second to One Hundred and Twenty-third Streets in which the Seminary is now located, but to the comparatively modest annex just around the corner. *Sic transit gloria mundi!*—Ed.

lander as Professor of Biblical exegesis, and Dr. Alexander Marx as Professor of history and librarian. Rabbi Joseph Mayer Asher became professor of homiletics. The reorganized Seminary became thus quite a different institution from the modest academy of Jewish learning which I had assisted in founding.*

How did these changes affect my position? Not favorably, I am sorry to say. I had been dean of the faculty under Dr. Morais. I had taught, as we have seen, almost every subject in the Jewish curriculum. I was the logical candidate for the successorship to Dr. Morais; the least to which I was logically entitled was a professorship in some major subject. My just claims were apparently not even considered. I was offered the position of instructor in Hebrew and acting reader of rabbinical codes. It was a tremendous come-down, but, after an internal struggle, I decided to accept. I was so greatly interested in the Seminary and the cause to which it had been devoted from its inception and which it would now presumably be better able to serve than ever before, that I did not want to leave it, and I hoped—I was still young—that with unremitting devotion to the duties of my appointed task I would be able to win the approval of the new powers that be.

After I had accepted my new and humbler post in the Seminary, the atmosphere appeared cordial, and the prospects of rising in the reorganized institution to something of the dignity and influence which I had previously enjoyed seemed not unpromising. Dr. Schechter welcomed my acceptance in a letter couched in the most cordial terms.

THE JEWISH THEOLOGICAL SEMINARY OF AMERICA
Tannersville, Greene Co.,
New York, Aug 6th, 1902

Rev. Dr. Bernard Drachman
Sharon Springs, New York.
My dear Sir.

I am in receipt of yours of the third inst and beg to express to you my satisfaction at your accepting the office of Instructor in the Jewish Theological Seminary of America. I have no doubt

---

* At this time its official title was changed from the Jewish Theological Seminary of New York to the Jewish Theological Seminary of America.

that your long experience as a teacher in the Seminary for the last sixteen years, your personal acquaintance with the students and your theological attainments will be of the greatest service to our Institution in particular and to American Judaism in general. I extend to you my greeting as a "good colleague" (*Chaver tov*) in our common work of the future. P.G. The Seminary will be opened on the fifteenth of September. When will you be back in town? I should like to arrange for a meeting of the Faculty on the eighteenth of September. Will this suit you? I am going to draw up the curriculum of our work during the next academic year where your share will be assigned to you—subject, of course, to such modification as our personal meeting will suggest. I remain, dear sir

      Yours faithfully,

            S. Schechter.

The favorable augury suggested by this letter seemed at first certain of fulfillment. The first meeting of the new faculty took place as arranged by Dr. Schechter, and the prevailing spirit was one of mutual respect, sincere friendship, and a high resolve to so conduct the work of the Seminary as to render the utmost possible service to the cause of Hebrew scholarship and Traditional Judaism. The work assigned to me was that of Hebrew language, Biblical exegesis, and rabbinical codes. I took it up with the sanguine anticipation that a new period of Jewish history in America was now beginning which might rival or exceed the glories of the Golden Age of Judaism in medieval Spain, that there might be fulfilled in the new Seminary over against the old what the prophet Haggai says of the latter Temple: "Greater shall be the glory of this latter house than of the former, saith the Lord of Hosts, and in this place will I give peace" (*Haggai*, II, 9), and that my part in this new development would be one of increasing value.

In order to contribute my share to the fulfillment of this anticipation, I devoted myself to the performance of my allotted task with the utmost diligence and conscientiousness. I must have succeeded, for I never heard any word of criticism or noticed any sign of dissatisfaction with my work, either on the part of Dr. Schechter or anyone else connected with the administration of the Seminary. With my students I was immensely popular. Not only did they show the liveliest interest in my instruction but would often remain after the lesson to discuss the subjects taken. The personal relations between me and my students were of the most cordial and friendly kind.

Such was the case also with my relations with my colleagues of the faculty. Although my position on the teaching staff was now a subordinate one, I sat at the meetings of the faculty as an equal among equals, and my views on the subjects under discussion were listened to with respect and even deference. There did not appear to be any cause which might disturb these friendly and promising relations. My social relations with Dr. Schechter and his cultured and intellectual family were also of the most cordial and pleasant kind. I had known Mrs. Schechter in her maidenhood in Breslau, during my student years at the Seminary there, when she was the intimate friend and associate of my good friend, Fraulein Gutmann, afterwards Frau Professor Badt, and we had pleasure in exchanging reminiscences of those happy early days.

In the second year of my connection with the reorganized Seminary, 1904, I was officially designated for an honorable function which was an undeniable proof of trust and confidence. The Jewish Theological Seminary of Breslau was to celebrate in the autumn of that year the fiftieth anniversary of its foundation. It had been established in 1854. They invited the other Jewish seminaries of the world to be officially represented at its celebration. The board of directors of the Jewish Theological Seminary of America, with the approval, and probably at the suggestion, of Dr. Schechter and the faculty, appointed me as their representative. The circumstance that I alone, of all the teaching staff, was a graduate of the Breslau Seminary, was, in all probability, the determining factor in my appointment; nevertheless, the selection itself was clear evidence that I was considered worthy of being entrusted with this important mission.

I must admit that this designation was very welcome to me. There was the honor directly involved which boded well for the making of my position in the Seminary firmer, and also it afforded me the opportunity of revisiting the scenes of my youthful studies and renewing the greatly esteemed associations and connections of those happy years.

Arriving in Breslau, my joyous anticipations were only partially realized, for there was much sadness mingled with the joy. Of my teachers, Professor Graetz and Doctors Rosin and Zuckermann had passed away, and Professor Freudenthal was no longer connected with the seminary. Rabbi Dr. Joel, my greatly beloved friend and mentor, too, was no longer in the land of the living. But Dr. Israel Lewy, the greatly revered and saintly Seminary Rabbi, was still there in person and also Doctors Horovitz and Braun, whom I had known and greatly esteemed in my student days. Most of my other friends were living, and they and I had great pleasure in meeting.

The celebration itself was a most impressive and noteworthy event. It consisted of two parts, a solemn and stately assembly in the seminary synagogue and a banquet and sociable gathering in one of the great halls of the city. Hundreds of visitors, former students and friends of Jewish scholarship, had come from all over Europe and from several non-European countries to take part in the exercises. There were, of course, several distinguished speakers at both occasions, but I think it can be fairly stated that Dr. Israel Lewy was the outstanding personality. There was something about his spare, ascetic figure and grave, soulful countenance that was arresting and compelled respectful attention. I was honored to deliver addresses, of course in German, at both gatherings. I brought the greetings of America, which I described as a daughter of Europe, and my chief thought was that, as a loving and grateful child, America, through my instrumentality, was bringing the tribute of gratitude and affection to the mother from whom it had received a priceless heritage of religion, civilization, and culture. I noticed with especial interest that a fine delegation of the Breslau city government, splendid, dignified men, was present and brought the official congratulations of the City of Breslau to the Jewish Theological Seminary. Their presence, and especially the tone of their addresses, which were extremely cordial and friendly, were clear evidence that in the Germany of that period anti-Semitism was unimportant. It undoubtedly existed as the ideology of individual bigots, but it certainly had no official sanction. After the celebration I remained in Breslau a few days enjoying the company of my old friends and then returned to America.

After my return, my first official act was to render to Dr. Schechter and the faculty a report of my visit to Breslau. It was received with apparent great interest. I then resumed my instruction in the Seminary and continued it as usual, to the manifest satisfaction and approval of the students. Not content, however, merely to continue my routine work, I felt an urge to contribute something to the scholastic standing and repute of the great institution of Jewish religion and learning among whose teachers I was numbered. After much reflection upon the nature and character of this contribution, I came to the conclusion that to publish some hitherto unknown or but slightly known work of medieval Hebrew literature, with appropriate historical introduction and commentary, would be the most suitable and valuable form that my contribution could take.

Accordingly, I began to rummage among the medieval manuscripts in which the library of the Jewish Theological Seminary was overflowingly rich. One day while thus engaged, without as yet having discovered anything that I deemed especially suited to my purpose, my attention was called by Dr. Alexander Marx, the learned and expert librarian, to a manuscript which had the merit not only of extreme rarity (being, indeed, a *unicum,* the only copy known to exist anywhere in the world), but also of high interest and great Jewish scholarly value. This was a manuscript containing an abstruse Talmudic discussion or controversy between two of the greatest and most renowned Talmudic authorities of the Middle Ages, Rabbi Abraham ben David of Posquieres in France and Rabbi Zerahiah ben Isaac Ha-Levi, originally of Gerona in Spain, and afterwards a resident of Lunel in France. The personalities of the parties to the controversy were in themselves sufficient to confer upon it the greatest scholarly value, but, apart from that, the discussion revealed the utmost Talmudic learning and acumen and there were also many matters of great philological and historical importance.

I no sooner saw this manuscript and gained some insight into its contents than I decided to study it closely and to publish it. Since the removal of manuscripts from the library was not permitted, I ordered a copy of it made, instructing the scribe to make an exact transcription, without corrections or alterations of any kind. He followed my instructions with the utmost faithfulness and exactness, as I convinced myself by comparing his copy with the original, and it was of this copy that I made a close and painstaking study. In this study I was assisted by Rabbi Nathan Hurwitz, who was at that time assistant rabbi, with the title of *Dayan,* in the Congregation *Zichron Ephraim,* and who was a deeply learned Talmudist.* We read together the text of the manuscript, which was in parts extremely obscure, and I found much of his interpretation invaluable. The actual literary work and the philological explanations were all done by me. I was engaged in this work for more than two years and finally published it in the year 1908. To my Hebrew commentary I gave the title of *"Hithgalluth Ha-Rib"* (Revelation of the Controversy) in allusion to the title of the work, *"Dibre Ha-Riboth"* (Matters of Controversy). Over two years of constant study and labor were required before the book was ready for publication. The printing I entrusted to Isaac Rachlin, a printer who was also considerable of a Hebrew scholar.

As soon as the work appeared, I made it my duty to present a copy personally with my compliments to Dr. Schechter. I expected, quite naturally so, I think, that my offering would be graciously accepted and that I would hear a few courteous words of appreciation of my effort to make a substantial contribution to the scientific work of the Seminary. To my intense surprise, my reception was entirely different. The learned head of the Seminary accepted my book most ungraciously, hardly said a word in acknowledgment thereof, and was unmistakably displeased. After a brief exchange of superficial remarks, I departed from his presence greatly bewildered, totally at a loss to understand what had happened. I never heard another word from the learned doctor in reference to my book, neither favorable nor unfavorable. It is idle to speculate, under these circumstances, what his reason was, especially as at the time when I presented the book to him he had no idea of its contents and could not, therefore, have formed any judgment concerning its merit or demerit. What I do know is that from that time on, and as long as I remained connected with the Seminary, I was *persona non grata*. It was a clearly evident and very uncomfortable fact.

---

* "Reb Noteh," as he was called, was a short, stocky, white-bearded, old-world scholar, who knew no English and delivered complex Yiddish *droshoth* on Sabbaths and some weekdays between afternoon and evening service for the more foreign and erudite worshippers at *Zichron Ephraim*. His son, the late Dr. S. T. Hurwitz became the founder of the *Jewish Forum Magazine*.—Ed.

The reception given to my book in learned Hebrew circles outside of the Seminary was a very different one. There it was decidedly favorable. A number of erudite rabbis and outstanding Hebrew scholars, mainly of the Russian-Polish element, among whom the love of Hebrew culture is keenest and the knowledge thereof most strongly developed, wrote me warmly appreciative letters.

Most of these letters have not been preserved but, as I write, I have before me one dated September 15, 1908, written by Simon A. Neuhausen, one of the most eminent of the numerous band of Eastern European Jewish scholars who flourished in New York in that period. The letter is written in beautiful and natural Hebrew and couched in the most laudatory terms. It extols, with the exception of a few minor criticisms, alike the merit of the work and of my preparation of the edition. A number of favorable reviews also appeared in the Jewish press throughout the world. Of these I best recall an especially excellent one written by George Alexander Kohut, son of the eminent Jewish scholar, Dr. Alexander Kohut, which appeared in *The American Hebrew*. There also appeared in *The Hebrew Standard* an excellent review and others elsewhere.

After the publication of my edition of the *Dibre Ha-Riboth* I continued my work at the Seminary as usual, and the time passed quietly and uneventfully. I saw little and heard less of Dr. Schechter. It appeared as though he had forgotten or decided to overlook his displeasure with me. Such was, however, evidently not the case, at least I may so infer from what happened toward the close of the academic year.

In 1909, I do not now recall whether it was before or after the summer vacation, I received an official letter from the board of directors of the Jewish Theological Seminary. It contained a notification that my appointment to the teaching staff was terminated and that my services would no longer be required. It was couched in courteous, almost apologetic terms and gave a reason for dispensing with my services. That reason was not dissatisfaction with the quality of my service, no allegation of lack of ability or scholarship, no imputation of religious or ethical shortcomings, but—listen and be astounded—*poverty!* There had been some sort of "slump" or financial depression in the country about that time, and the letter stated, in all seriousness, that the financial condition of the Seminary had been so gravely affected thereby that it would be unable to bear the burden of my salary. Why everything else in the Seminary was continued unaltered and why there was no suggestion of even reducing any other salaries was not explained.

In closing this chapter of my life history, I make no attempt to explain the action of the Seminary.* I may have my opinion or theory as to the reason or reasons at the bottom of it, but as no statement of any kind on the subject, as far as I know, was ever made by the authorities of the Seminary, except the manifestly absurd plea of poverty in the letter to me, I cannot be sure that my opinion is correct. In my inner consciousness I know that there was no justification on ethical or scholarly grounds for the action, that in so doing the Seminary departed far from the views of its sainted founder and first president, Dr. Sabato Morais, of blessed memory, and in that knowledge I proudly disdain it. That the treatment accorded me did not affect my devotion to Judaism or lessen my determination to do all in my power for its promotion need not be specially affirmed.

---

* Why the author so carefully avoided explaining his break with the Seminary and what that explanation may be, it is now difficult or impossible to guess. Unfortunately, the above narrative seems to suggest that it may all have been a personal issue of professional jealousy—an explanation which one cannot believe he meant to convey.

Far more plausible, and more creditable to both eminent scholars is another explanation, though, it must be stressed, nothing in this book tends to indicate it. Though Seminary authorities had never specifically found fault with him, he had, in the bosom of his family, often and bitterly lamented the emergence of new tendencies in its management. Its original character was that of an institution for the training of Orthodox rabbis. It had a compact faculty, a small group of students, and an intensive discipline as its course of study. Its graduates were few, but they were dependable. With the reorganization, all that began to change. The Seminary went in, apparently, for the kind of expansion that appeals to the public—and to wealthy contributors. Perhaps the latter influenced its policy directly. The new and "palatial structure," the higher-sounding title, the addition of great names to the Faculty were harmless expressions of this mood. but when pressure was applied to graduate large classes, over the protests of at least one teacher who had rated some of the students as failing, it could only mean that standards were being lowered. So too the teaching was, covertly and tentatively indeed, slipping away from genuine Orthodoxy.

This weakening of both Jewish loyalty and academic scholarship grieved him and caused him no end of anxiety. If he spoke up against it in Faculty conferences to a Board and President predetermined upon a fundamental change in policy, his insistence must have been painful. In getting rid of him, they were, then, "dropping the pilot," shaking off the voice of their own Orthodox conscience. In view of the Seminary's later development, as a "Conservative" institution not inhospitable to Reconstructionist tendencies, does not the above seem a probable explanation?—Ed.

Chapter Thirty

Working for Israel in Many Ways

FROM THE VERY BEGINNING OF MY CAREER AS RABBI I RECOGNIZED that, if I desired to live up to the ideals of that sacred office in any true sense, I must not be content to limit myself to the mere formal performance of its technical duties. That would be the easier and more comfortable way, but the true rabbi must be ready and willing to go the hard way, the way that is difficult and burdensome and laden with heavy responsibilities and which calls for the utmost energy and effort and courage. As the Roman poet said, "I am a man and I deem nothing human foreign to me," so the rabbi should say, "I am a Jew—indeed supposedly a leader of Jewry—and nothing that is Jewish—or indeed of general human interest or importance—should be beyond my purview or attention."

I conceived my vocation in this spirit. Therefore I turned my gaze and directed my chief efforts toward every domain of Jewish activity, spiritual, cultural, communal, and national. In all these domains my efforts were unceasingly directed toward one goal, spreading the influence of Judaism and causing it to be more upheld in Jewry and appreciated both in Jewry and the non-Jewish world.

Recognizing the importance of books and articles as a means of spreading views and doctrines, I early decided to be literarily active. I contributed many articles to the Jewish press and in the year 1899 published my first book.* This was a translation of a book by the celebrated rabbi of Frankfort-on-the-Main, Samson Raphael Hirsch, which he had written under the title of *"Neunzehn Briefe ueber Judentum"* and which I paraphrased in English as *"The Nineteen Let-*

---

* That is, leaving out of consideration my dissertation which I had published in Germany for the obtaining of the PH.D. This had only a scientific but no propagandistic purpose.—B.D.

ters of *Ben Uziel."* This was a book after my own heart. It was propagandistic in the finest and noblest sense of the term.

Hirsch was a great scholar and a profound thinker but, above all, a convinced and enthusiastic Jew. He wrote this book in his youth, in the early part of the nineteenth century, when the Jews, but recently released from the Ghetto, were coming into contact with the life and the culture of the Gentile world. His purpose was to show his co-religionists that they need have no sense of inferiority, that they were in possession of a great faith and a wonderful culture which they could uphold with pride and dignity in the sight of all men.

It seemed to me that very similar conditions prevailed in America and that work of the same kind was called for on this side of the Atlantic also. Here, too, the Jews, emigrating from the countries of the Old World, had come into contact with a new civilization and that this contact had given rise to an assimilatory tendency, which had expressed itself so strongly in the Reform movement. The work of the Frankfort rabbi seemed to me wonderfully adapted to combat this tendency and to bring about a better appreciation of the ancient faith, especially in the minds of the cultured youth. I, therefore, decided to reproduce it in the vernacular.

It was not an easy task. The German style of Rabbi Hirsch had many peculiarities and special expressions for concepts characteristic of his system, and to render these into idiomatic English required much thought and effort. It took me fully two years to complete my version, although the original is a comparatively small work.

It met with instantaneous success and a warm welcome in the English-speaking Jewish circles responsive to Rabbi Hirch's ideas. It is a classic of Jewish devotional literature in those circles at the present time (1943). The publishers of the first edition were the Funk and Wagnalls Company of New York. A recent edition has been brought out by the Bloch Publishing Company, also of New York.

After publishing the *Nineteen Letters* I decided that my next effort would be devoted to a lighter form of literature. While the value and the success of the *Nineteen Letters* were undeniable, I perceived that its profundity and abstruseness rendered it truly suitable only for persons of high intellectual caliber, but for those of a less intellectual type, literature in a lighter vein, such as tales and parables, would be more advisable.

The fruit of this recognition on my part was a book of tales, which appeared in 1905 under the title *"From the Heart of Israel,"* issued by the publishing house of James Pott & Company, New York. For the contents of this book I drew partly upon my own experience and observations and partly upon incidents of which I had heard or learned in various ways. The test of including a tale was that it should truly and illuminatingly present some aspect of Jewish character or life, and I strove to make my descriptions as pleasing and interesting in a literary sense as I was able. This book was successful and well received by the Jewish public and reviewers. A large sheaf of complimentary letters concerning it is among my souvenirs.

The tone of the reviews in the press, both Jewish and general, was on the whole very appreciative. Candor compels me to admit that there was one exception to the general chorus of approval. That was just in a Jewish paper, *The American Hebrew*. The reviewer in *The American Hebrew* did not like my book at all. He did not deny the literary value of the tales but said they were "reeking with piety." In other words, he objected to the Jewish life of the Diaspora being represented, in accordance with the historic truth, as being pervaded with a profound conviction of the truth of Judaism and a passionate loyalty to it. I wrote a letter to *The American Hebrew,* pointing out the error of the reviewer's point of view. My letter was printed, but no answer appeared.

Two other books have appeared in print, one a study of the history of Neo-Hebraic literature in America, which appeared in connection with one of the early biennial reports of the Jewish Theological Seminary, and the other a study of American problems which appeared in 1934 under the title of *"Looking at America."** In the last-mentioned work I departed from my usual course of considering topics of a religious, philosophical, or Hebrew scientific nature and treated subjects relating to political and economic life. I had certain views concerning the proper methods of solving the many and difficult problems which affect the successful realization of the ideals

---

* Published by G. P. Putnam's Sons.

Within the Sanctuary. Dedicated September, 1890.

Rabbi Dr. Bernard Drachman

Delegates to the World Congress of Sabbath Observers
Berlin, 1930

Hadassah L. Drachman

which are America, and I felt that, as an American, and despite the restrictions of my calling, I had not only the right but also the duty to contribute whatever I could to their solution. I have never regretted my decision, although I fully realize that my contribution to the solution of America's problems must necessarily have been very small.

Most of my literary activity has been in the form of articles or essays on themes of Jewish interest. These have been quite numerous and have appeared in many and varied publications, Jewish and non-Jewish, although I must confess that I have been very careless as regards preserving them, and of many of them do not even possess a copy. It would not be possible for me to give here anything like a complete list of these articles. I will, therefore, name only a few, some fifteen, as I recall them, which will, however, suffice to show what a wide range of important topics these essays cover.

(1) IS MATERIALISM A SATISFACTORY EXPLANATION OF THE MIND?
(2) ORTHODOX JUDAISM AND MODERN THOUGHT.
(3) ASSIMILATION.
(4) THE PROPER METHOD OF DEVELOPING THE NEO-HEBRAIC.
(5) AMERICANISM, THE TRUE AND THE FALSE DOCTRINE.
(6) HAS JUDAISM A FUTURE?
(7) JUDAH HA-LEVI, POET AND PHILOSOPHER.
(8) ZIONISM AND THE JEWISH PROBLEM.
(9) ANTI-JEWISH PREJUDICE IN AMERICA.
(10) THE SABBATH.
(11) THE BOUNDARIES OF PALESTINE, FROM THE VIEWPOINT OF THE JEWISH NATIONAL HOME.
(12) POETS AND POETRY OF THE KARAITES.
(13) THE JEWS OF GERMANY.
(14) LIFE AND MANNERS IN ANCIENT PALESTINE.
(15) ABSTRACT AND PHILOSOPHIC TERMS IN BIBLICAL HEBREW.

There was a society devoted to the cultivation of Hebrew learning, organized in New York toward the end of the nineteenth century, to be exact, in 1894, and which continued its activity during the early years of the twentieth century, in which I took considerable interest. It bore the name of *Ohole Shem* (Tents of Shem), a symbolic title indicating that it was devoted to Semitic studies. Its membership consisted mainly of Russian Jewish scholars, many of whom, although their names were hardly known in university circles, were deeply learned in Hebraic lore. It conducted monthly meetings from September to May, at which lectures were delivered by the members on themes drawn from everywhere in the vast field of Semitic, mainly Jewish, scholarship, and it also published for several years a Hebrew magazine entitled *Yalkut Maarabi* (The Occidental Bag).

I was a not infrequent lecturer before the meetings as well as a contributor to the magazine. For instance, at the meeting of the third of June, 1901, I lectured on one of the most interesting incidents of medieval Jewish history, the conversion of the Chazars to Judaism. On a subsequent occasion I lectured on a theme of a totally different nature but even more absorbingly interesting to lovers of the Hebrew language, *Abstract and Philosophic Terms in Biblical Hebrew*. In both of these lectures I employed the Hebrew as my vehicle of expression. The second lecture was published in the magazine of the society, the *Yalkut Maarabi*, and also appeared in English in the *Jewish Review* of London. These will serve as samples of a great many more.

Among the members of the *Ohole Shem* were two who possessed unique abilities, and who held positions of great public importance. Herman Rosenthal had been actively engaged in the establishment of colonies for the Jewish refugees from Russian persecution and was at this time in charge of the Slavonic department of the New York Public Library. He was a man of great dignity and the president of the *Ohole Shem,* a post for which his Hebrew attainments eminently qualified him. Abraham S. Freidus was the librarian of the Hebrew department of the public library. His knowledge of Hebrew literature was phenomenal. It was said of him that he knew by heart the names and contents of all the thousands of works which make up the vast Hebrew literature, medieval and modern, and that if an intending writer on a Jewish topic, even of the most recondite kind, would apply to him for aid, he would at once mention all the sources from which the prospective author could derive assistance. Other members whom I recall were Dr. Talmai, a practicing physician but devoted to Hebrew studies, and N. T. London, a Hebrew scholar of the good, old-fashioned Russian Jewish type. I am also of the impression that Gerson Rosenzweig, a Hebraist, noted for his extraordinary knowledge of the ancient tongue and author of a famous Hebrew satirical treatise about America, *Massecheth America,* if not a member of the *Ohole Shem,* was an occasional visitor at our meetings and that he addressed us. The usual meeting place of the *Ohole Shem* was the old Jewish Theological Seminary, at 736 Lexington Avenue. I do not recall whether it ever met in the new building of the Seminary.

In the years 1906-1907 a gigantic Jewish literary enterprise was launched in which I had a part, albeit a modest one. This was the *Jewish Encyclopedia,* which, with the exception, perhaps, of the Babylonian Talmud, was the greatest work or series of works devoted to Jewish subjects that has ever been published. As a financial venture it was unquestionably the greatest of all. It owed its realization to a Christian firm, the great publishing house of the Funk and Wagnalls Company of New York. As a Jewish enterprise it could probably never have been launched or, if it had been, would not have been carried out on the scale and completeness with which it was accomplished. As so often happens, the Gentile firm had more faith in Jewish ability and Jewish enthusiasm than the Jews themselves. Dr. Isaac Funk, the senior partner, or head of the corporation, had that faith, both in the value of the material which the proposed encyclopedia would contain and in the response of the Jewish people, which would justify the expenditure of the vast amount of money which it would require. I had something to do with giving Dr. Funk that faith.

The project itself was put before Dr. Funk by Dr. Isidore Singer, an Austrian Jewish scholar whom the exigencies of European life had exiled to America. He is entitled to great credit for the vision which enabled him to see the merits and the possibilities of the idea of a great Jewish encyclopedia in the English language, and for the courage and the persuasive ability to carry it to successful realization.

I had already made the acquaintance of Dr. Funk through the

"Nineteen Letters of Ben Uziel" which had been published by the Funk and Wagnalls Company, and I have reason to believe that the sentiment of Dr. Funk toward me was one of real friendship plus faith in my judgment. Dr. Funk was a fine and spiritually exalted character, a sincere believer in Christianity, but not of the type which leads to bigotry. Especially was he free from that pernicious malady of the non-Jewish world, anti-Semitism. On the contrary, his very Christianity seemed to create a sympathetic tendency toward the adherents of Judaism as the modern representatives of the ancient people of the Bible. This sympathetic sentiment had shown itself in connection with the publication of the *"Nineteen Letters."* When I submitted my manuscript to Dr. Funk for consideration, the reader to whom he turned it over for judgment handed in an unfavorable report. The gist of his opinion was that, while the book was written in good English and a not unattractive style, it contained old-fashioned Jewish doctrines, quite out of touch with modern science and culture, which rendered it untimely and unsuitable for publication. Calling on Dr. Funk to learn the fate of my book, he informed me of the opinion of his reader.

"But," he added, noticing my expression of disappointment, "this does not end the matter. While such an opinion by our reader, who is an able and scholarly man, would usually suffice to bring about the rejection of a book, it will not have that effect this time. I shall read your manuscript myself, and I will follow my own judgment as regards its publication by our house."

The result of Dr. Funk's perusal of my manuscript was that the Funk and Wagnalls Company published the *"Nineteen Letters"* in 1899. In informing me of his favorable decision, Dr. Funk gave expression to some extremely laudatory views of Samson Raphael Hirsch's ethical and spiritual concepts and of my manner of presenting them in English. The effect of this incident was to create a very sympathetic relation between Dr. Funk and me.

While the proposal to publish a Jewish encyclopedia was before the Funk and Wagnalls Company, Dr. Funk asked me what I thought of the project. My answer was dictated by mingled enthusiasm and caution. I said that the project in itself was magnificent, that the history and literature and religion of the Jews were overflowingly rich in instructive and inspiring matter, and that the encyclopedia, properly carried out, would serve a most useful purpose in supplying authentic information concerning the Jews and refutation of the many erroneous ideas prevalent in regard to them. As regards the financial side of the venture, I said that it was impossible for me to make any definite statement but that I thought it not improbable that the splendid undertaking would be greeted with enthusiasm by Jews and by all friends of enlightenment, of all races and creeds, and, despite the vast sums needed for its realization, would prove financially lucrative. I believe that my views were not without influence in bringing about the publication of the *Jewish Encyclopedia*.

When the editorial board was organized I was made a consulting editor, which constituted a certain measure of recognition, and a contributor, in which capacity I wrote a number of articles for the encyclopedia.

As contributor I had an experience which revealed to what depths of dishonesty persons of high station may sink and also how outspoken and courageous resistance to wrong may secure the rights which have been invaded. I was asked to write an article on a certain Biblical subject. The department to which this subject belonged was at this time in charge of a very prominent Reform rabbi, head of a great congregation in a Western city. When the writing of the article was assigned to me, I determined to prepare as thorough an article as was possible. I consulted several Biblical encyclopedias and found the articles extremely brief and superficial. I then made a thorough study of the subject in all available Biblical commentaries and treatises on Biblical archeology, including the Talmudic sources. I finally evolved an article far more detailed and complete than any in the existing cyclopedias. I then handed it, in the regular course of procedure, to Mr. Frank H. Vizetelly, secretary of the editorial board of the Jewish Encyclopedia, for insertion in the encyclopedia. Mr. Vizetelly, incidentally, was a regular employee of the Funk and Wagnalls Company, to whom this secretaryship had been assigned because of his excellent qualifications for the post—an English gentleman of Italian descent, as his slightly Anglicized Italian name shows. Too, he was a great authority on the English language.

In order to understand what follows one must know the procedure in regard to the writing and inclusion of articles in the encyclopedia. The contributor would submit his article, which was then put before the editor of the department to which the subject of the article belonged, for reading, and approval or rejection. If approved, the article was then tentatively printed in a form called the "galley" and returned to the author for correction of errors, after which it was ready for final printing. This procedure usually required only a few days. No article of mine had ever been rejected, and I had always received the galley in the normal short time.

This time a week or more passed, and the galley did not reach me. Much wondering at this, I decided to call on Mr. Vizetelly and find out the reason for the unusual delay. Putting the question to Mr. Vizetelly, I was unspeakably shocked to hear from his lips that Dr.— (naming the person in charge of the department) had rejected it.

"Why did he do that?" I asked.

"That I don't know," answered Mr. Vizetelly. "I have no technical knowledge of these subjects, and Dr. — gave me no reason."

A very definite suspicion began to rise in my mind. "Give me back my article," I said. "It is mine and I am entitled to it, if it is not going to be printed."

Mr. Vizetelly saw no objection to this and, searching among his papers, found my article and returned it to me. Across its front page was stamped, in bright red ink, the word "killed."

"Has any arrangement been made for another article on this subject?" I asked. Mr. Vizetelly answered in the affirmative.

"Who is going to write it?" I asked.

Mr. Vizetelly hesitated for a moment and then said, "Dr.— himself has already written one."

"In that case," I said, "I demand to see that article."

Mr. Vizetelly was extremely loath to comply with my desire, but I insisted firmly that, under the circumstances, I had an undeniable right to see the article which was to supplant mine. He finally yielded and produced it. My suspicions were completely justified. It was an almost literal copy of my article. A few superficial details had been added, but not enough to alter this fact. I showed the two articles to Mr. Vizetelly. He could not deny that the action of Dr. — was a piece of plagiarism. My indignation knew no bounds. I declared that

I must have justice, that this action must be undone and that, if justice were refused me, I would create a scandal that would shake the city and the whole scholarly world. Mr. Vizetelly said he was powerless in the matter and suggested that I see Dr. Funk. This was a logical suggestion, and I acted accordingly. Dr. Funk listened to me attentively and gravely. It seemed to me that he was deeply affected by what I had told him but he gave no verbal expression to his reaction. When I had finished my passionate denunciation of the wrong done me, he said to me in a very serious manner:

"Dr. Drachman, I will take this up with the editorial board, and I will see to it that proper action is taken."

A few days later I received a letter from the editorial board to the effect that since it appeared, after an examination of both articles, that both Dr. — and I had contributed to the article in its final form, they had decided it would appear with both signatures appended. This was only a partial remedy of the injustice done me, but by this time my indignation had begun to cool down, and I decided to make no further protest. In my desire to avoid scandal, I have not mentioned the name of the contemptible betrayer and plagiarist nor the title of the article, but should any of my readers desire to know them, I will be pleased, as long as I am in this world, to furnish, if asked, the desired information on both points.

It can easily be imagined that, under these circumstances, my relations to the *Jewish Encyclopedia* or, rather, to the leading personages in its literary preparation, were not exactly cordial. That fact did not, however, blind me to its great importance in Jewish history. I recognized it as a monumental literary achievement, the greatest Jewish work, with the exception of Bible and Talmud, ever issued, and an invaluable source of authentic information for the inquirer, Jew or Gentile, desirous of knowing the facts about Jews and things Jewish. I rejoiced that such an outstandingly important work had come into existence and that I had had some share, however modest, in its preparation.

Thus intensely engrossed in the activities derived from my office and my vocation, it would seem that I could have no time available for extraneous activities, especially not for politics. I was far too busy with the normal work of my vocation to be able to devote any of my precious time to other causes. Besides, I was opposed, as a matter of principle, to the active participation of the clergy in politics. Nevertheless, I departed once from my rule and took a very active part in a political campaign. It was a very important campaign, too, when Hon. Seth Low sought the mayoralty of New York in 1901 as the Fusion candidate against the Tammany machine. How and why did I get into it? To explain that I must take the reader back a few years.

In 1890 Mr. Seth Low became president of Columbia University. He was an alumnus of the university of the year 1870, a gentleman of noble ethical principles, very wealthy and a most generous benefactor of his alma mater, to which he had donated in one sum the princely gift of a million dollars. Shortly after his accession to the presidency, the first group of Seminary students became mature and advanced enough to require university tuition. The money required for university tuition fees, a couple of hundred dollars annually for each student, was lacking. In this emergency I remembered that I was a graduate of Columbia and a classmate of Dr. (then Professor) Nicholas Murray Butler. I thought of consulting Dr. Butler and asking him whether he could not think of some way by which the students of the Seminary would be admitted to the university without payment of fees, or at reduced rates. I communicated my idea to the board of directors of the Seminary, who gladly approved it and bade me go ahead.

Accordingly, I visited Dr. Butler and sought his aid in the matter. He was sympathetic and introduced me to President Low. Mr. Low was kind and affable in the highest degree. He said he would look into the matter and do what he could to meet my wishes. Very shortly thereafter I received an official communication from the university, informing me that it had been decided to place the students of the Jewish Theological Seminary in the same status as the students of the General Theological Seminary and the Union Theological Seminary, that is, that they would be admitted to Columbia University without payment of fees. Thus the problem of the university education of our students had been most satisfactorily, indeed, gloriously, solved. Needless to say, we were very grateful to Columbia University and particularly to President Low.

In 1901 there was a determined Fusion movement in New York City, resolved to overthrow the corrupt government of Tammany Hall. Seth Low was recognized as a most highly qualified candidate to head an anti-Tammany movement. He received the nomination for mayor. His candidacy was greeted with enthusiasm, and there was every indication that he would lead the anti-Tammany forces to a splendid victory.

Tammany was at a loss how to avert its threatened defeat. In its extremity, it resorted to the expedient which has been the reliance of tyrants and reactionaries in all ages, anti-Semitism. The "Jewish vote" in New York City is very important, amply sufficient to decide a close election. Tammany calculated that if the Jews could be induced to think that Seth Low was their enemy and to vote against him he would surely be defeated.

Of a sudden, the newspapers began to publish articles accusing Seth Low of being an anti-Semite and stating that Jewish students in Columbia University were subjected to various discriminations and disabilities. These articles appeared not only in the general press but in the Yiddish press of the East Side as well. They were cunningly worded to rouse strong antagonism to Seth Low on the part of Jews and liberal-minded Gentiles and were practically certain to unite the Jews in opposition to him, which would spell sure defeat.

Reading such an article in my morning newspaper and knowing from my own experience how shamefully false and calumnious it was, I was filled with indignation and also apprehension that the accusation might find credence on the part of gullible Jewish readers and bring about his defeat. I saw at once in what direction my duty lay, that this was a case where I must give up my habitual disinclination to mingle in politics, that I must do all in my power to prevent this foul plot from succeeding. I recognized that this was my duty alike as a patriotic American and a sincere Jew. I lost no time in taking action. That very morning saw me in the office from which Seth Low's candidacy was directed.

After explaining the purpose of my visit, I was at once admitted into the presence of the campaign manager. That gentleman and several of his associates, who were present during our interview, were very much impressed by my account of the magnanimous and prejudice-free action of President Seth Low in the matter of the application of the students of the Jewish Theological Seminary for free tuition in Columbia University. They gave it as their opinion that these facts were a complete refutation of the charge that Mr. Low was an anti-Semite and that, coming from me, they would be accepted as unquestionably true by the entire Jewish community and would deprive Tammany of any advantage which it had hoped to gain from these false accusations.

The campaign manager, whose name, to my regret, I no longer remember, proceeded at once to take the necessary steps to secure adequate publicity. Communications were sent to the press, both general and Yiddish, denying in vigorous terms and in my name the charge of anti-Semitism launched by Tammany against Mr. Low. Trucks bearing signs in Yiddish, and in huge letters, were driven through the streets of the Jewish quarter of the lower East Side, so that whosoever ran, or walked, through those teeming thoroughfares might read and know the truth. I also atended a number of meetings, mainly in Jewish districts, and delivered addresses in favor of Mr. Low. These tactics were completely successful. The backbone of the attack by Tammany on the candidacy of Seth Low was broken and he was triumphantly elected mayor.

This was the one and only time that I ever departed from my lifelong principle of not participating actively in political contests, and I was more than pleased with the action itself and with its result.

Chapter Thirty-one

New Synagogue Connections

AFTER A NUMBER OF YEARS SPENT IN THE SERVICE OF THE CONGREgation *Zichron Ephraim,* I began to feel that it did not give me sufficient opportunity for the employment of my energies. I will not say that I was right in this feeling. After all, the congregation included a goodly number of members and seatholders, our *Talmud Torah* was attended by upwards of two hundreds boys and girls. We maintained all the normal activities of an Orthodox Jewish congregation, and I might well have assumed that there was abundant possibility of concentrating and intensifying my energies in its service and thus raising it to ever higher levels of power and influence in the cause of the ancient faith of Israel.

But, somehow or other, I did not feel that way. I saw that significant changes had taken place in the distribution of the Jewish population of the great American metropolis, that Yorkville was no longer the important center of Jewish residence that it had been, that it had, indeed, sunk into a position of relative unimportance while other sections of the city, such as Harlem and Brownsville, had taken its place and, like a modern Jewish version of Alexander of old, I longed for "new worlds to conquer."

I did not desire either to sever my connection with Congregation *Zichron Ephraim* or to become openly a candidate for another position. Toward the end of 1907, however, an unexpected opportunity to accomplish my desire presented itself. The Harlem section was then developing into a great Jewish residential district, but was very imperfectly provided with synagogue facilities. There was, indeed, not a single synagogue of large and impressive proportions dedicated to the traditional Jewish worship.

Under these circumstances, naturally, various groups organized movements for the erection of synagogues. One such group applied to me about the end of 1907 or in the early part of 1908 to guide and assist them in the organization of a congregation and the erection of a synagogue in Harlem, with the understanding that I was to be the spiritual leader of the new organization. It was not a large group, only fourteen or fifteen men, as I recollect, but they were all substantial business men, not extremely wealthy but quite well-to-do, and their plans were ambitious. They desired to erect a large and beautiful house of worship, to be conducted in strict accordance with the traditional Jewish laws and usages and in harmony with modern concepts of decorum. Their ideas agreed with my concept of Judaism, therefore I consented to associate myself with them in the carrying out of their plans. No request was made to me in regard to the relation between my position in the new congregation and that in the Congregation *Zichron Ephraim* and it was tacitly understood that the matter was to be regulated in accordance with my own desire and decision.

The leading spirits in this new group were a Mr. David Rogow, the outstanding leader, Mr. Jacob Samuelson, Mr. Weinstein, and Mr. Levy, the latter two being partners in the great clothing firm of Weinstein and Levy.

At first everything seemed to go well. A considerable sum of money was put together. Mr. Rogow alone contributed five thousand dollars and the others a thousand or several hundred dollars each. A fine piece of property covering a space of eighty by a hundred feet, in One Hundred and Twenty-third Street between Lenox and Seventh Avenues, was purchased. A down payment was made, the exact amount of which I do not remember but which was approximately twenty thousand dollars. The rest of the cost of the property and the synagogue building—more than one hundred thousand dollars—was to be raised by subscriptions of new members and by a mortgage which would be gradually amortized and paid off in subsequent years. This is the usual method followed in the erection of synagogues in America—not a very wise or prudent financial policy, it must be confessed, but one which has been successful in many instances. The members of our group were very sanguine and had not the slightest doubt that their enterprise would be carried to the wished-for conclusion. Their confidence went so far that they engaged an architect, whose name, I recall, was Cobb, to draw up the plans for the intended synagogue. These plans were submiitted to me for approval. They provided for an edifice which would be not only architecturally beautiful but would also be supplied with rooms and accommodations required for the social and educational work carried on by modern congregations.

In the midst of these joyous anticipations our dream palace collapsed. A "slump," or financial depression, swept over the land, attended by its usual sequences of commercial calamity and economic catastrophe. It became impossible to secure new members. A mortgage could not possibly be obtained. Our people, who had suffered the same economic blows as those from which the community in general was suffering, could not themselves contribute the large amount required for completing the purchase of the land and the erection and furnishing of the building.

Under these circumstances, no choice was left but to abandon the enterprise. Regretfully and sorrowfully but yielding to unavoidable necessity, this was done. The money paid on the purchase of the lots was lost. There was a relatively small amount, a few thousand dollars, left in the treasury, and this, in a final display of Jewish idealism, was not returned to the members but was distributed among charitable institutions.

Thus ended a melancholy but, to a certain extent, inspiring episode in my life history. I hold my associates in this unsuccessful effort in affectionate remembrance. Their purpose was true and sincere, and I mourn the malevolence of fate or, let us rather say, the mysterious working of Providence, which did not permit it to ripen into fruition. Under normal conditions our group, I am convinced, would have developed into a great congregation.

Hardly had this melancholy episode ended than a cheerful and promising opportunity took its place. The First Hungarian Congregation *Ohab Zedek,* which had maintained for many years* a large synagogue in Norfolk Street on the lower East Side of New York, was now engaged in erecting a new structure in One Hundred Six-

---

* Founded in 1873.—Ed.

teenth Street between Fifth and Lenox Avenues, only a few blocks from the spot which had been the scene of the unhappy endeavors of our group, but under circumstances which protected it from the unfortunate outcome of that ill-starred venture. This happier condition was due to the circumstances of its origin and the nature of its composition. Its membership consisted of Jews of Hungarian birth or descent, who had been resident on the lower East Side and who now, following the movement of population taking place at that time, were transferring their abode to the upper West Side. There were several hundred members upon whom the congregation could draw for assistance, a considerable number of whom were generous supporters of their beloved congregation. Besides, it had already secured its inevitable and indispensable mortgage so that, while financial worries were not altogether absent, there was no danger of failure. Their problem was of a different nature. They had a learned and profoundly pious rabbi, like themselves of Hungarian nationality, Dr. Philip Klein, who officiated in the synagogue in Norfolk Street. In the course of years, however, they had become largely Americanized, so that for the synagogue in One Hundred Sixteenth Street they desired an American, English-speaking spiritual leader.

In the year 1909, in the month of May, this great congregation extended a call to me to accept the position of rabbi to them. I accepted with genuine joy. I felt that, in this outstandingly important assembly of my brethren, I should be able to serve the historic cause of Israel to a degree which had not been hitherto possible. My relation to the senior rabbi was that of parity. Neither of us was to be superior or inferior to his colleague. I assured the committee who discussed the terms of the rabbinate with me that I knew how to honor an elder colleague and that I should not be lacking in the respect and deference due to his age and renown.

It was also understood that I was not expected to sever my connection with the Congregation *Zichron Ephraim*. I was to be rabbi of both congregations and to preach on alternate Sabbaths in each synagogue. I remained rabbi of the First Hungarian Congregation *Ohab Zedek* until the year 1922. It was, on the whole, a most happy and satisfactory period in my history.

The Hungarian Jewish element which constituted the main membership of the congregation was ideal material for the proper functioning of an Orthodox Jewish synagogue. The congregation was not composed exclusively of Hungarian Jews. Any adherent of the Jewish faith was, as a matter of course, accepted as a member, and a certain number of Jews of non-Hungarian origin was enrolled in its ranks. At one time, in fact, a co-religionist of Russian origin and English birth, Mr. Henry Glass, incidentally, a true gentleman as well as a loyal Jew, was elected president and remained in that office for several years.* But the majority of the congregation was of Hungarian origin. The Hungarian Jewish type was omnipresent, and the Hungarian Jewish customs and usages were all prevalent in its conduct and management. The other members accommodated themselves good-naturedly to the prevailing conditions, and there was not the slightest conflict or friction on that account.

Our Hungarian brethren, as I had already come to know them through the Hungarian students in the Breslau Seminary and as I grew to know them more intimately in the Congregation *Ohab Zedek,* are unquestionably one of the best elements in world Jewry. They have succeeded in accomplishing the synthesis of modern Occidental culture and etiquette with ancient Jewish learning and piety better than most other elements of Jewry. This synthesis is, as a rule, absent or imperfectly accomplished in other elements. The Jews of Westen Europe have assimilated themselves thoroughly to their non-Jewish environment, but Hebrew culture is rare among them, even among those who are religiously observant. The Jews of Eastern Europe, on the other hand, are steeped in Judaic lore, but Occidental culture is the possession only of rare individuals. Among Hungarian Jews the possession of both of these cultures with remarkable completeness is quite usual. It was surprising to me to observe that while their Judaism was, in almost all respects, identical with that of Poland, their secular culture was that of the Western world. Though the Yiddish dialect is spoken, to some extent, by Hungarian Jews, it is only the idiom of the lowly and uncultured class. Those of higher social and intellectual standing invariably speak a correct and gram-

---

* It is interesting to note, as an example of the contrary aspects of modern Jewish life, that Henry Glass was the brother of the well known dramatist and writer, Montague Glass, a man of a totally different type and not at all an orthodox Jew.—B.D.

matical German and usually also the Magyar idiom of their native land.

My senior colleague, Rabbi Dr. Philip Klein, was an excellent example of this cultural duality. In Talmudic erudition he was a rabbi of the old ghetto type, on a par with the great Talmudists of Poland and Russia, but he was a university graduate as well. In his sermons and addresses he employed a high and classic German, so high and classic, indeed, that many of his less cultured congregants complained that he spoke above their heads and they could not understand him.

The higher circles of Hungarian Jewry, as I observed them, are not only cultured, in the Occidental sense, but also refined and courteous in bearing and manner and actuated by a strong sense of personal honor. While these qualities are all inculcated by Judaism, directly enjoined, indeed, by Talmudic dicta, I believe they are, in this instance, more directly due to the influence of their Magyar environment and the traditions of their native land.

There were special reasons why the Jews in Hungary should have become thoroughly Magyarized. Pre-Hitler Hungary was a truly free and liberal country and the position of the Jews was especially favorable. The Magyars, though giving the national character and tone to the land, were never the majority of the population, which consisted of various ethnic elements, all of whom jealously preserved their linguistic and cultural identity and refused, as groups, to be Magyarized. The Jews were the only group who entered wholeheartedly into the Magyar nationality. This they could easily do because preserving Judaism meant preserving Jewish identity.

The result was that they were cordially welcomed by the Magyars and acquired the status of Hungarians of the Jewish faith, differentiated from other Hungarians only by their religious allegiance. They attained to the highest positions in the Hungarian state and became nationally and most patriotically Hungarian. The reflection of these conditions I saw in the Congregation *Ohab Zedek*. Incidentally, the Magyars seem to be very similar to the Spaniards. The same feeling of *grandezza*, the same courtly manners and the same delicate sense of honor, are characteristic of both nations, and their Jewish elements have acquired them with remarkable fidelity from their Gentile co-nationals.

It was highly interesting, as well as surprising, to me to observe how very Jewish these Hungarian Jews were in their manifestation of Judaism. Most of them had a very fair knowledge of Hebrew and the traditional Hebrew culture; a not inconsiderable number were deeply learned in Talmudic lore.

Dr. Klein was accustomed to deliver *derashoth* or Talmudic discourses twice a year, on Sabbath *Ha-Gadol* (the Sabbath before Passover) and on Sabbath *Shubah* (the Sabbath between the New Year and the Day of Atonement). These discourses, customarily delivered by Talmudically learned rabbis, are extraordinarily profound and complicated. Only a real Talmudist can understand them, and to the ordinary layman they are absolutely unintelligible. Yet they were always attended by comparatively large gatherings, forty or fifty persons, whose expression of face showed that they followed the rabbi's train of thought. I delivered such addresses a few times, but, as a rule, this domain was reserved to Dr. Klein. I was accustomed to deliver one such discourse annually, on Sabbath *Ha-Gadol,* in the synagogue of Congregation *Zichron Ephraim,* where I had an audience smaller than those in *Ohab Zedek* and of less Talmudically erudite listeners. Still, they were sincerely appreciative.

The pronounced ghetto Jewishness of these Hungarian brethren was even more emphatically shown in their attitude toward another domain of Jewish religious life, that of *Chazanuth,* the traditional chanting of the synagogue service. Everyone acquainted with the ideology of the old-time ghetto dwellers knows that they were dearly fond of a "good Chazan," that is, of a synagogue cantor able to chant the ancient ritual with sweet melody and to touch the hearts of the worshippers by his sometimes joyous, sometimes pathetic rendition of the prayers. To have "a *Chazan* for Sabbath" was the highest delight of the old-time Jew in his secluded and unworldly habitation. Listening to those melodious outpourings, he forgot all about the hard realities of the unkind present and felt himself transplanted to a holy realm, in the company of the saints and sages of Israel's past and, as he fondly believed, wondrous future.

The people of *Ohab Zedek* were no less fond of *Chazanuth,* perhaps not with the olden unquestioning faith but with real and sincere love. The extent of their appreciation of the art of the cantor was convincingly shown by the fact that they paid their *chazanim* far higher salaries than they did their rabbis, although the ecclesiastical rank of the rabbi is, of course, far exalted above that of the *chazan*.

During the time of my connection with Congregation *Ohab Zedek* it had three or four *chazanim*, all of whom were considered masters of the musical part of their vocation. Of these, unquestionably, the greatest was Joseph Rosenblatt. He received an annual salary of ten thousand dollars, for which he was not obliged to officiate on every Sabbath and holy day but was privileged to be away during a great part of the year, which time he utilized for traveling about the country and officiating and giving concerts in various cities and towns, from which he derived a large additional income.

The congregation fairly idolized him. Whenever he officiated, the synagogue was filled to the doors, and on the high holy days not a seat remained unsold. The income of the congregation from this one source, which was mainly attributable to the popularity of the *chazan*, was very large, indeed, approximately twenty-five thousand dollars a year.

In this matter of *chazanuth* I did not see eye to eye with my congregants. Not that I do not appreciate music.* On the contrary, I agree wholeheartedly that stately and solemn chanting is very effectual in bringing out the significance of a devotional composition and in stirring religious emotion and that music is entitled to be considered an integral part of the worshp of the Most High. Since the days of David, "the sweet singer of Israel," and earlier, singing and playing musical instruments have been an indispensable part of Jewish worship, in the Temple on Zion's height and in other religious gatherings as well. The chanting of the psalms was, perhaps, the chief function of the Levites. But what I object to is the exaggerated role assigned to *chazanuth* in the East European synagogues. The voice of the cantor is often strained to quite unnatural heights. Words and

---

* The author maintained a particular interest in music all his life and frequently played the piano and sang for his own enjoyment and that of friends. He eagerly collected all sorts of Jewish melodies and loved to demonstrate them. He also composed a number of songs, notably "*Eretz Hemdah*" ("Beauteous Land, a Song of Exiled Israel") and "*Hail, Joyous Day!*", a wedding song. However, his musical taste was definitely Occidental, and he preferred traditional hymn-tunes and congregational singing to the complicated trills and quasi-Operatic arias characteristic of a certain class of *chazanim*.—Ed.

whole passages are repeated endlessly. The service is unduly prolonged, and the entire effect is wearisome in the extreme to one not accustomed to this manner of chanting the ritual. Worst of all, this manner of rendition tends to deprive the service of its religious character and to make it a purely musical performance. Even in the case of Joseph Rosenblatt, who was a sincerely devout Jew and strictly observant of the Law—which not all *chazanim* are—his high repute was not due to his conscientious piety and religious loyalty but purely to his musical ability.

I made no secret of my antagonism to this perversion of the musical part of the service. I preached openly against it and did not hesitate to condemn it.

On a certain Sabbath, which was also the first day of the new month, a *chazan*—it was not Joseph Rosenblatt—was conducting service. In the ritual of the new month occur the words, "And because we have sinned before Thee, our city is destroyed," a reference to the cruel and sacrilegious act of the Roman emperor Titus by whom, together with his co-emperor Vespasian, the holy city Jerusalem and the Temple were destroyed. Titus is remembered in Jewish history as *Titus Ha-Rasha,* "Titus the wicked." To the pious Jew he typifies the summit of human depravity. To his Roman contemporaries he was *"delicium generis humani"* ("the delight of the human race"), a striking example of the differing judgments which differing viewpoints can bring about.

When this *chazan* came to the words which I have quoted, he repeated them *no less than eight times,* each time in a different tone of lamentation and threnody. His object was, of course, to stress the horror and gruesomeness of the deed, in itself and at the right time a perfectly proper action but, it seemed to me, it was exaggerated and in poor taste especially as the new month is not, in the Jewish concept, a time of sorrow and lamentation but rather of joy. My reaction to this manner of chanting, on this occasion, was one of impatience and disapproval. After the service, one of the members, a great admirer of *chazanim* and *chazanuth,* came to me to wish me good Sabbath and good month. He asked me, incidentally, how I liked the *chazan.* I could not restrain the mischievous impulse which came suddenly to my mind.

"That *chazan*," I replied, "I think he is worse than Titus *Ha-Rasha*."

"How do you mean that?" asked my interrogator, in a tone of horrified surprise.

"Very simple," I replied. "Titus *Ha-Rasha* destroyed Jerusalem, but he did it only once, but this *chazan* destroyed the Holy City and the Temple eight times."

The Congregation *Ohab Zedek* also maintained a male choir of trained singers under the leadership of musically educated choir leaders. Generally speaking, the same criticism applies to the choirs as to the *chazanim*.

The Congregation *Zichron Ephraim* also had an excellent *chazan*, named Moses Lublinski, and later one named S. Fine, and maintained a choir, under the leadership of a thoroughly musical choir leader, named Kantrowitz. The musical part of the service was conducted, largely owing to my influence, not only in accordance with the traditional Jewish methods but also in harmony with modern Occidental musical taste.

Apart from the question of *chazanuth*, I found myself in thorough accord with the religious spirit prevailing in the Congregation *Ohab Zedek*. It was a model Jewish religious body in its attachment to the traditions of Israel and in its loyal maintenance of them, unaltered and undisturbed. It was free, however, from extremism or fanaticism. Not all the members were personally strictly observant. It was an open secret that some of them belonged to the congregation because they were Hungarian rather than because they were Orthodox, but they were all united, without a dissenting voice, in the view that it was to be maintained on the basis of Orthodox Judaism. Not one would have even suggested the idea of Reform.

I have already stated that among the members were a number who were well learned in Talmudic lore. I particularly recall two, Mr. Rappaport and Mr. Liebowitz, who, judged by their Talmudic learning, would have been qualified for the rabbinical post. They were what is called—or was called—in Germany *"Privatgelehrte,"* "learned laymen," but without any aspirations for professional utilization of their knowledge. For a time Mr. Liebowitz and I read Talmud together and I enjoyed his interpretations very much. Others interested in Talmudic study were organized in a *Chevrah Shass* ("Society for the Study of the Talmud"), and met at regular intervals for that purpose. One of the members, presumably the most learned among them, led the instruction, and the others listened or particpated by the occasional asking of questions. When the point or points involved were knotty, as was frequently the case, the resulting discussion was apt to become exceedingly lively.

The zeal with which the great majority of the people attended service was quite remarkable. All the services were exceedingly well attended, even the weekday early morning services, which, in many congregations, only attract a mere handful of worshippers. I customarily attended these services and I cannot recall a single instance in which a *Minyan* was not present. This zeal was particularly in evidence during the penitential season, the period beginning with the Sunday before New Year and lasting until after the Day of Atonement. During this period the *Selichoth* services, devoted to earnest expression of repentance of sin and prayer for Divine pardon, take place. They begin with a solemn midnight service, and it was a thrilling spectacle, in the synagogue of Congregation *Ohab Zedek*, to behold the vast edifice thronged, at dead of night, with devout worshippers, male and female, all listening with rapt attention to the sacred liturgy of the penitential season as it poured forth from the lips of the *chazan* and his choir.

Although I was in complete sympathy with the religious attitude of the congregation and felt thoroughly at home in their midst, I did not become intimate with many of the individual members. This was not due to aloofness on my part but rather to the Hungarian-Jewish concept of the relation between clergy and laity. The typical Hungarian Jew is imbued with profound respect, even reverence, for his rabbi, his spiritual guide and mentor, but the very earnestness of this sentiment precludes anything like close association and intimacy. The rabbi is like a being from another sphere, an honored and revered being indeed, to whom one comes in distress or when in need of counsel and guidance, but who is not expected to mingle with *hoi polloi*, except for reasons of especial religious or other significance and importance. Some modern, especially American Jews, would not understand this concept. It would certainly not agree with the views of a certain congregation in the wild and woolly West who, in advertising for a rabbi, stated that "he need not be a Talmudist but he should be a good mixer." In itself it is a noble, an admirable concept. It is in harmony with the Talmudic dictum: "If the rabbi is like an angel of the Lord of Hosts, they shall seek Torah from his mouth, and if not, they shall not seek Torah from him" (*Moed Katan*, 17).

Like many other ethically noble and beautiful precepts this, too, can be exaggerated. The middle course is, in all relations of life, the best and most advisable. While, therefore, the rabbi, as a teacher and example of Judaism, should stand upon a lofty ethical and spiritual level, he should not permit this to estrange him from the people, to make him unapproachable. Such has always been, and is, my conviction. When I first took up my rabbinical duties in the Congreggation *Ohab Zedek* I acted in accordance with this view, but I soon found that it was neither appreciated nor expected. I began to visit my flock and was, of course, always courteously received, but I could not help perceiving that, in most instances, the people seemed surprised.

Once while I was visiting one of the families of the congregation, the head of the household moved uneasily upon his seat as if disturbed by some inner thought. Finally he said to me, "Rabbi, might I ask what you wish me to do? I know you would not come here unless you expected something from me. Kindly let me know what it is, and I will be glad to do it if it is in my power." When I explained to him that I had no special purpose whatever, that I had not come to ask anything of him but merely to visit him and his family as members of the congregation, he breathed a sigh of relief mingled with an expression of intense surprise. After that I made no more visits except on occasions which really called for them, such as *Bar Mitzvoth* or betrothals or to request cooperation in some religious or charitable undertaking. Nevertheless, I did not hold myself aloof but encouraged approach on the part of my people as far as opportunity offered. Thus my relations with most of the people, while not closely intimate, were friendly and cordial.

Despite my cessation of visits to the homes, there were many occasions which brought me together, outside of the formal meetings for worship, with larger or smaller groups of the people. There were the weddings, a goodly number of them. There were the synagogue weddings at which I merely officiated at the ceremony and which did not lead to any better acquaintance or closer friendship with the parties concerned. And there were the private weddings, the ceremonies of which took place either in the synagogue or in a hotel or hall. In such case I remained, by invitation, at the wedding feast. At these functions I was expected to pronounce grace and to deliver an address. They were delightful affairs, these good, old-fashioned, traditional Jewish marriages, where innocent, heartfelt rejoicing and merrymaking combined with the best of food and drink to create a few hours of undiluted happiness for bride and groom, their families and their guests. If anyone sincerely believes, as some of our enemies do, that Judaism is a bleak and gloomy faith and its customs and usages productive of a cheerless and melancholy concept of life, let him attend a typical Jewish wedding and he will be speedily cured of his misconception. The addresses at the wedding feast are expected to be in a vein of humor. Dr. Klein was frequently associated with me on these occasions and, although he was a very devout and pious rabbi and extremely serious-minded in his view of life, at weddings he unbent, and his speeches at the feasts were delightfully humorous.

And then there were the occurrences on the other side of human existence, the sad and sorrowful gatherings when death had invaded a happy home. It was in connection with the sad and inevitable termination of man's earthly pilgrimage that I came closest to my people and made true and abiding friends of many to whom I might otherwise have remained almost a stranger. The services and observances enjoined by Judaism for funerals and the subsequent days of mourning, while simple and unpretentious, are peculiarly touching and adapted to fill the heart of the mourner with solemn emotion. While Judaism does not favor extreme and excessive grief and lamentation, considering them an impugnment of the justice of God, it does demand that full honor be given to the departed and earnest and reverent attention to the problem of death and immortality. This note of reverent and thoughtful solemnity pervades all the services. It begins in the home or funeral parlor, continues at the cemetery where all that is mortal of the dear departed one is laid to rest and during the *Shivah*, the seven days of confined mourning. The mourners do not stir from the home and they and their friends assemble three times daily, morning and afternoon and evening, to join in worship to the Most High, to recite the mystic *Kaddish* prayer, and to listen to the words of instruction and comfort of the Sages, as expounded by the officiating rabbi. I endeavored to the utmost to fill my service with this spirit. I succeeded in great measure in bringing comfort to many a sorrow-laden heart and reconciliation to the mysterious ways of the Almighty. Through these sad activities I acquired many sincere and enduring friendships.

There were also other occasions in the lives of individual members of my flock which brought me nearer to them. People would come to me when in trouble and difficulties, when bowed down by trials and problems, for counsel and guidance, sometimes also when disputes and antagonisms had arisen among them, for decision and reconciliation. To all of these my services were freely and gladly given as the occasion required. To be sure, I gave the best counsel I could render, at times by clearly pointing out where truth and justice lay, at other times by obtaining actual, even material aid and assistance. In all these efforts my one aim was to promote peace and harmony and happiness. Thus, although the intimacy of personal relations was lacking, many a valued friendship was acquired.

There was one exception to this otherwise universal rule of non-intimacy. There was one man in the congregation whose sympathetic understanding of my sentiments and aspirations led to a close association which continued long after the cessation of my connection with Congregation *Ohab Zedek*. Morris Engelman is his name. He possessed something better than mere riches or scholarly attainments —intense love of Judaism, profound respect for those who teach and expound it, and an overwhelming desire to serve the cause of the Jewish faith and people. When I think of Congregation *Ohab Zedek* and the years I spent in its midst and at its head, it is a very happy memory. It is a memory of a large and important group of co-religionists devoted to the upholding of the unaltered and undiminished precepts of Traditional Judaism, a memory of friendly, kindly, and sincerely God-fearing Jewish men and women, a memory of many occasions of joy joyously and happily celebrated and of occasions of sorrow observed with general sharing of grief and sincerest sympathy.

My stay with the Congregation *Ohab Zedek* was not destined to be permanent, but I shall always remember, as long as breath is within my frame, with respect and affection the many noble men and women in its ranks and the splendid service which they rendered to the cause of the ancient faith of Israel, a service some portion of which I may, without exaggerating, not unjustly attribute to my efforts.

Chapter Thirty-two

I Am Called Abroad

IN THE YEAR 1912, THE POST OF CHIEF RABBI OF THE UNITED SYNAgogue of London had become vacant through the passing away of its then incumbent, the Very Reverend Doctor Hermann Adler. It was a great and most important post, in all probability the greatest and most important rabbinate in the world. The authority of the Chief Rabbi was acknowledged not only in London but throughout Great Britain and all its colonies and dominions. Whether this was through full and legal election or merely through the tacit acquiescence of the scattered congregations this writer does not know, but, as a matter of fact, the Chief Rabbi of London was Chief Rabbi of the British Empire.

This was a position unrivaled for dignity and power anywhere among the Jewries of the world. It was not because of the great number of persons subject to its ecclesiastical authority. The Jewish population of the British Empire, even today (1944) probably does not exceed half a million* and was then even less, and there were countries in both Europe and America with far greater numbers of Jewish inhabitants, but nowhere else was there such an excellent, well ordered organization and nowhere else was rabbinical authority so firmly established and generally recognized.

This exalted post being now vacant, it, of course, became necessary for the United Synagogue to select a successor. The choice of the successor was not an easy matter. Whoever was to be chosen must, of course, possess all the usual qualifications of an Orthodox rabbi or

---

* This figure is, of course, exclusive of Palestine, not truly a part of the Empire.—Ed.

chief rabbi: thorough knowledge of Biblical and Talmudic lore, giving him the ability to decide questions of Jewish law, sincere faith in and loyalty to Traditional Judaism, endowing him with the spiritual authority required of the leader of an Orthodox Jewish community, an impressive personality, enabling him to arouse respect for his exalted post and the faith which he was to represent among both Jews and non-Jews. In addition to all this he must possess complete familiarity with the English language and literature, an indispensable prerequisite of a great public official in an English-speaking empire. This last requirement excluded from consideration the many hundreds of learned and pious rabbis in the countries of Central and Eastern Europe, possessing the other qualifications in fullest measure but devoid of English culture. It is true that the first of the Adler family to occupy this post, Chief Rabbi Dr. Nathan Adler, father of Dr. Hermann Adler, who had been called to his place of dignity and power in the year 1845, was a non-English-speaking foreigner, a German, who had afterward acquired a good knowledge of English. But conditions had changed since those days, and the authorities of the United Synagogue did not consider it advisable to repeat the experiment.

Under these circumstances the list of available candidates was extremely limited. The number of English-speaking rabbis, possessing the requisite qualifications, was very small indeed. Only three rabbis were considered as logical candidates for the vacant post. They were Rabbi Dr. Moses Hyamson, then Chief *Dayan* of the United Synagogue, who had been assistant to Dr. Hermann Adler, Rabbi Dr. Joseph Herman Hertz, who had headed a congregation in Johannesburg, South Africa, and was at that time rabbi of the Congregation *Orach Chaim** of New York, and myself.

In the early summer of 1912 I received an official letter from the United Synagogue, formally inviting me to come to England and preach in various synagogues with a view of becoming a candidate for

---

* This is the same congregation mentioned above as existing some twenty-five years earlier. In the interval it had moved to a new building at Ninety-fourth Street and Lexington Avenue and has grown in numbers and influence. Dr. Hertz became its rabbi, succeeding the late Joseph Mayer Asher, only after a short and apparently fruitless visit to London in connection with his candidature for the Chief Rabbinate. —Ed.

the chief rabbinate. I received this communication with mixed feelings. On the one hand was the realization that a very great honor was being conferred on me in being so considered. On the other hand and more important yet, this high post offered an unequaled opportunity of rendering great and enduring service to Judaism and the Jewish people. But crowding out these happy thoughts was another less happy—if I should be the chosen one, I should be obliged to tear up my roots, to forsake my native land and my kindred, and to pass the rest of my days on foreign soil, among those whom I had never before known.

The material benefits which the position would bring had no attractive power. My financial position was such that I was under no necessity of seeking a place for the purpose of earning a living. I felt myself an American in every fiber of my being. At the possibility of leaving home and country forever, America loomed up before me. America, loved and cherished above all lands! The glorious and irreplaceable home of liberty, beauty, and happiness, the loss of which could not be compensated for by all the treasures of earth. My beloved wife looked upon the matter in the same light. Although she made no audible objection, deeming it improper to seek to influence my decisions in matters connected with my vocation, I could see that the prospect of leaving America and her family was very distasteful to her. My children, it is true, felt differently. The glamor of the exalted post of Chief Rabbi of the British Empire fascinated them, and they would have been delighted to see their father occupying it. For me, the matter was the choice between duty and inclination.

I decided to follow the call of duty. That does not mean that I took it for granted that I would be chosen for the post. I knew very well that I was only one of several candidates who would be considered and that it was not at all certain that I would be the successful one. I decided, however, that should the choice fall upon me, I would disregard considerations of personal convenience or preference and would dedicate whatever abilities I might possess to the service of this great community of Israel. Accordingly I answered the letter of the United Synagogue expressing thanks for the invitation and stating that I would come to England after the fall holy days.

In the month of October, 1912, I arrived in London. I was accompanied on my trip by my daughter Beatrice. Omitting all inconsequential details, I will only say that I carried out in its entirety the program which had been arranged for me. I spoke at the Sabbath services at several synagogues in London. I attended and addressed gatherings at a number of Jewish institutions, among them one great *Talmud Torah*. When I had completed my program in London, I visited several cities in the provinces—by which term is meant in England all the country outside of London—among them Birmingham, Leeds, Manchester, and Liverpool, and addressed everywhere the congregations at the Sabbath services and also other meetings.

The first place in which I appeared publicly in London was the Great Synagogue in Duke's Place, often referred to as the "Cathedral Synagogue" on account of its great size and its importance in the history of the English-Jewish community. This had been selected by the committee of the United Synagogue as the most appropriate synagogue in which to begin my speaking tour. It was the third Sabbath after the holy days of the year 5673, and I had selected as the basis of my sermon themes suggested by the portions of the Law read on all three Sabbaths. I had, therefore, given the sermon the title of "The Trilogy of Judaism."

The occasion had received ample publicity, and the sermon appeared in full, *verbatim et literatim*, in the issue of *The Jewish Chronicle*, the most widely read Jewish newspaper in London and the official organ of the United Synagogue. Incidentally, the arrangements for publicizing my movements and my utterances were of the first order. Huge placards in front of the synagogue at which I was scheduled to speak announced that fact to all passers by, and *The Jewish Chronicle* not only printed advance notices of all occasions on which I was to appear but also stenographic reports of all sermons or other addresses which I delivered. It also published several editorials dealing with my candidacy and my person, all of them in the most friendly and appreciative tone. I had the privilege of becoming well acquainted with its editor, Mr. L. J. Greenberg, a typical English gentleman and a loyal Jew, whom I hold in affectionate remembrance. *The Jewish World,* another important Anglo-Jewish newspaper, and the Yiddish press reported fully concerning my movements and actions.

My emotional reaction toward the task which I had set myself was clearly indicative of my inner attitude and sentiment over against the whole undertaking. I was at first, and in a lesser degree during my entire stay in England, in a state of extreme nervous tension and agitation. It was not that I did not respect and think highly of much of what I observed in England and in its Jewish community. In particular I admired and profoundly esteemed the august institution of the Chief Rabbinate and thought regretfully of its absence in America. But I felt, and could not rid myself of the feeling, that I did not belong in that country and environment, that only a rigid sense of loyalty to duty could induce me to remain there and accept the post of chief rabbi, should it be tendered me.

On the night before my appearance in the Duke's Place synagogue I had a severe nervous attack in my room at the hotel in which I was staying. My heart palpitated violently, a fit of trembling seized upon me, and everything seemed dark around me. I do not know whence I derived the strength, but I resolved that, come what might, I would not reveal my plight to anyone nor call upon anyone for help. I lay upon my bed trembling and with palpitating heart, and sleep came to me only in brief, intermittent fits and snatches. When the morning light appeared, the palpitation had somewhat abated, but a great weariness had come over my whole body. I disregarded utterly my physical condition and wended my way to the synagogue, where I arrived, with the first comers, at the very beginning of the service. I answered all greetings pleasantly and gave no intimation to anyone of the sufferings I was enduring.

At last the time came, after the conclusion of the Reading of the Law and before the *Musaph* or Additional Service, when I must deliver the sermon. To comprehend what a strain and trial this meant for me, one must realize that preaching in the Duke's Place synagogue was attended, even for a person in perfectly normal condition, with no slight difficulty. The synagogue was constructed in an old-fashioned manner. The pulpit was extremely high, approached by a long, winding staircase. As I left my seat and proceeded to ascend the staircase, I hardly saw what was before me. I felt as though I might collapse at any moment. But I did not collapse. I ascended to the pulpit and faced the vast congregation. I delivered my sermon with perfect self-possession, without the slightest indication of the pain that was racking my frame. My sermon was a phenomenal success. After the service I was the recipient of numerous enthusiastic congratulations, and, as already stated, the *Jewish Chronicle* published my sermon in full.

The other London synagogues in which I preached were the Bayswater, the St. Petersburg Place, the St. John's Wood, the Poets' Road, and the Stepney. There is nothing special to report from any of these occasions except that everywhere I preached the synagogues were crowded and I was received with the utmost respect. When I would enter, in order to participate in the service, the congregation would arise and remain standing until I had taken my seat. In the Stepney synagogue an incident occurred which at first puzzled and disturbed me greatly but which was afterward explained and cleared up in a perfectly satisfactory manner. My theme was "Prayer," and the line of thought of my sermon was that the fixed ritual of the synagogue is not at all contrary to the true devotion of worship but quite the reverse, that it is filled with the loftiest religious sentiments and that, if read or recited with the proper concentration of attention and thought, it is certain to raise our souls to true communion with the Most High. I condemned the views of those who hold that a fixed ritual is mechanical and lifeless and stated that such a concept of the sublime ritual of the synagogue is narrow and superficial.

I noticed that my sermon seemed to produce considerable amusement, that there was much smiling among my auditors. The observation both puzzled and angered me. I saw no reason for even slight hilarity. I had delivered a serious address on a perfectly serious subject, and I objected to its being received as though my object had been to stir the risibilities of my listeners. After the service, one of the officers of the congregation approached me and congratulated me on having delivered a very instructive and inspiring sermon.

"Your members don't seem to agree with your view," I said. "I noticed they were smiling while I was speaking."

"They were not smiling at your remarks," he said. "On the contrary, they were greatly impressed and entirely agree with your presentation of the subject. You see, last Sabbath our minister* preached on the same theme and treated it in an exactly contrary manner. He severely condemned our ritual and said that true prayer must be entirely spontaneous and the product of momentary emotion. Many of our members were greatly aggrieved by his views. When they heard your eloquent and convincing treatment of the subject, it seemed as though your were intentionally refuting our minister. That, naturally made them smile."

During my sojourn in London I came into contact with most of the leading personalities of the Jewish community, both clergy and laity. Of the clergy the one who impressed me most was Dr. Moses Gaster, the *Haham* or chief rabbi of the Sephardic Jews. I had received *Semichah* or rabbinical ordination at his hands and had become acquainted with his charming family on a previous visit to London, so that I had at once a most cordial welcome to his home. His wife was the former Polly Friedlander, daughter of Dr. Friedlander, at that earlier time (1885) principal of Jews' College.

Through Dr. Gaster I became acquainted with a number of the leading members of the Sephardic community. Outstanding among these were the Sassoons, the famous Anglo-Indian family, enormously wealthy, on which account they were frequently referred to as "the Rothschilds of Asia." Their charitable generosity, especially to Indian-Jewish communities and causes, was commensurate with their wealth.

I was a guest of the Sassoon family on several occasions and was much impressed by their unique combination of European culture, Oriental dignity, and Jewish piety. The most interesting and impressive member of the family was, without question, Lady Solomon Sassoon. She was not only an English lady, a Hindu aristocrat, and

---

* The term "*minister*," as applied to a Jewish clergyman, calls for the following explanation. Any Jew who knows how to read Hebrew is permitted to conduct services, this function not being reserved to the rabbi. The term "*rabbi*" is really an academic degree, signifying that its possessor has a scholarly command of theology and is competent to decide questions of religious law. Many synagogues, even in America, do not have rabbis, the service being chanted by a *chazan* or read by any layman. In England, the position of "*minister*" (with the title of "Reverend") is assigned to the clergyman in charge of a synagogue. If he has undertaken advanced study, he obtains the title of "Rabbi," but his office remains that of minister. . . . After his English visit, the author altered his own designation of "Rev. Dr." to "Rabbi Dr.," in accordance with Anglo-Jewish usage.—Ed.

a loyal Jewess, but also—and that was most astounding in the case of a woman—a profoundly learned Hebraic and Talmudic scholar. Her father, a leading member of the great Indo-Jewish family, had given her, as a girl, the opportunity to acquire a complete Hebrew education, and she had taken the fullest advantage of it.

As an illustration of her great erudition, the following story was going the rounds in London at that time, and I must admit that I heard it with amazement. A certain Sephardic family was involved in a dispute concerning an inheritance of large proportions which they had submitted for adjudication to the *Dayanim* of the Jewish community—the rabbis entrusted with the decision on all questions of Jewish law, including civic matters. When Lady Sassoon heard of the decision which they had rendered she declared, and proved from the *Hoshen Mishpat*, the Jewish code of civil law, that their decision was erroneous. When one considers that practically no laymen and even very few rabbis are acquainted with the *Hoshen Mishpat*, since the Jewish civil law is rarely invoked in modern Jewish life, especially in the Occident, one can realize what this little incident means.

During my stay in London, a wedding took place in the Sassoon family. A daughter, whose name I do not recall, was married to a Mr. Ezra, of the well known Ezra family of Calcutta, India. The ceremony took place in the beautiful Lauderdale Avenue Sephardic Synagogue and was performed by *Haham Gaster*, assisted by the *chazanim* of the synagogue. It was a wonderfully beautiful and impressive celebration, made doubly so by the rich floral decorations of the synagogue and the melodious chanting of the Sephardic marriage ritual by the *chazanim* and the robed choir. Dr. Gaster delivered the wedding address with great dignity and eloquence. The ceremony was followed by a reception and dinner in the palatial and lavishly decorated residence of the bride's family. I was a guest in the synagogue and also at the reception and dinner. All the arrangements were on the most magnificent scale and in scrupulous conformity with Jewish tradition. The company present was a cross-section of the highest London society, both Jewish and Gentile.

On the following morning I called on Dr. Gaster. My visit was not in any way related to the wedding of the previous afternoon and evening, but we naturally touched upon it. Quite casually I said to

Dr. Gaster, "I presume you received a fine fee." And here I learned something about conditions in London, at least in its Jewish segment, which may well have had its good reason and justification but which was certainly very surprising to me. As I put the question to Dr. Gaster, his face assumed a quizzical expression. "How large a fee do you think I received?" he asked.

"I have no idea," I answered. "From such a wealthy family probably a hundred pounds or more."

"Not even a hundred buttons," answered Dr. Gaster. He thereupon explained to me that it was not customary in London to remunerate synagogue officials for personal services rendered to individuals, such as marriages or funerals, that the minister, rabbi or cantor was in duty bound, as a part of the obligation of his ministerial office, to render to all his congregants, whether rich or poor, whatever religious service they might require, without emolument or remuneration, and that his salary (which, incidentally, was paid in weekly installments and not, as is our custom in America, in monthly amounts) was his sole and entire compensation for all services rendered by him. I did not discuss the subject further with Dr. Gaster, but I afterwards learned, from other sources, that great dissatisfaction existed among the Jewish clergy with this custom, that most of them considered themselves entitled to compensation for services to individuals, especially when these latter were well-to-do. I learned, too, that certain congregants did not abide by the custom but compensated officiating ministers for services rendered and that their action was much appreciated. The ancient rabbis did not receive salaries but for centuries supported themselves by practicing trades and handicrafts while their rabbinical functions were exercised without money and without price.

Such is the ideal, the beautiful theory. In actual practice it does not work out so well, especially not under modern conditions. A minister has financial obligations as well as a layman and he, too, is under special obligation to meet them honestly and completely. Few congregations pay salaries sufficiently large to enable him to live in a manner consonant with the dignity of his vocation, especially when, as in Judaism, he is expected to marry and there may be a more or less numerous family looking to him for support. The income derived from personal services may be a valuable aid in enabling the minister to solve his financial problem. The receipt of adequate compensation does not detract from the spiritual purity of the minister's devotion to his sacred task. On the contrary, it may increase it by freeing his mind from material worries. In America and Germany both I had occasion to observe that the English theory is rejected. Yet no one can say truthfully that the character of the American or German ministry has suffered by these arrangements.

In connection with my candidacy for the chief rabbinate a special interview with Lord Rothschild, President of the United Synagogue, was arranged for me. The interview took place in his Lordship's office in the city, and no other person was present. My meeting with this distinguished representative of Anglo-Israel, member of the most prominent and probably most wealthy Jewish family in the world and head of the Jewish community of the British Empire, made a deep and unforgettable impression upon me. In his presence any thought that my co-religionists were a weak and humble minority seemed absurd. A people headed by a gentleman of this exalted type must necessarily, it seemed, be a highly respected and honored group among the families of earth.

Lord Rothschild, a handsome and distinguished-looking elderly gentleman, spoke to me with the utmost courtesy and friendliness. He complimented me on the favorable reports which he had heard of my sermons—he had not been able to be personally present—and inquired closely into my past history and into Jewish conditions in America generally.

He also asked me concerning my concept of the chief rabbinate, listened attentively to my answers, and seemed much pleased by them. The interview lasted about an hour, and I left with the impression that, as far as Lord Rothschild was concerned, my election as chief rabbi was certain.

I also had the privilege of being received in his home by Lord Swaythling, the second bearer of the title, son of Sir Samuel Montagu, who had been raised to the peerage as the first bearer of the title. The first Lord Swaythling had been a most zealous adherent of Orthodox Judaism, not only personally strictly observant thereof but also ardently desirous of promoting its observance among the rank and file of the Jewish people. For this purpose he had established and generously supported the Federation of Synagogues, an organization designed to bring within the ranks of the community the poorer elements of English Jewry, especially the many thousands of foreign Jews who had immigrated into England. His son, I understood, was walking in his paths and continuing his good work. My visit to Lord Swaythling and his charming family was most pleasant and his good will to me was manifest.

As candidate for the chief rabbinate I was in constant touch with the gentlemen who constituted the board of deputies, or administrative council, or whatever the title was, of the United Synagogue. They were all splendid examples of English gentlemen who took their duties as officials of the United Synagogue very seriously. In order to assure themselves of my fitness for the exalted post of chief rabbi, they arranged an evening conference in one of the homes—I do not recall in whose home it was—in which I was to answer questions concerning my views on the manner in which the chief rabbinate should be administered.

I was subjected to a rigorous questioning on all conceivable matters concerning my standpoint in Judaism and my concept of the relations which should exist between Jews and the non-Jewish world. In all matters save one there was perfect approval of all that I said and even on that point there was agreement that my attitude was fundamentally correct. I was asked whether I considered cremation permissible from the viewpoint of the Jewish law. In order to appreciate the significance of this question it must be premised that it is a very serious problem in a densely populated country like England.

The Jewish law prohibits the slightest mutilation of the human body and, *eo ipso,* its complete destruction, as takes place by cremation. But land is scarce and expensive in England, and its increasing absorption by cemeteries is also an increasing encroachment upon the rights and needs of the living. The former chief rabbi, Dr. Hermann Adler, had, therefore, felt himself impelled to permit cremation and the interment of the ashes of the cremated in the consecrated soil of Jewish cemeteries. I answered that I could not declare cremation permitted, but that, in view of the special circumstances existing in England, I would abstain from any pronouncement on the subject.

Of the leaders of the United Synagogue two stand out in my memory with especial distinctness. They were Sir Adolph Tuck and Mr. Herbert Bentwich. This is not said in disparagement of the others, for, as already stated, they impressed me as splendid gentlemen and very earnest in their fulfillment of their official duties. But there was something about Sir Adolph and Mr. Bentwich which set them apart and marked them as especially noble, both as English gentlemen and as Jews.*

Another aspect of the rabbinate, in regard to which the leaders of the United Synagogue were very anxious to know my views, was my attitude toward the Yiddish-speaking Jews. This they considered a matter of high importance, inasmuch as there was a large number of this element in London, mostly more or less recent immigrants from Eastern Europe and resident in the East End, which corresponds, in a general way, to the lower East Side of New York. They were very desirous that these people should be integrated into the general Jewish community or, at least, should not be estranged from it and, for this purpose, they deemed it essential that the chief rabbi should be on terms of close intimacy with the co-religionists of Yiddish idiom and be revered by them as their spiritual head. They asked me whether I could speak any Yiddish and whether I would be willing to go to the East End and address its Jewish inhabitants in their ancestral tongue. I answered that I would be very glad to visit the East End and do everything in my power to make our Yiddish-speaking brethren feel that they were indeed our brethren and co-religionists in the fullest sense of the words, but that, although I understood it, I should not care to use the Yiddish as the language of my sermons.

At this they were greatly astonished and asked me, "Why not?"

I answered, "I do not consider Yiddish a language, in the true sense of the term. It is, at best, a dialect of the German. It is an

---

* Sir Adolph Tuck and Mr. Herbert Bentwich later came to America as a special committee to view the candidate in his home environment. They attended service in the *Ohab Zedek* synagogue and were dinner guests at the home. During the subsequent election maneuvers, both strongly urged the author's election, as did Dr. Gaster. . . .Sir Adolph was the head of the toy firm of S. Tuck and Sons. Mr. Bentwich was a distinguished barrister, whose son, Norman Bentwich, later became Attorney General of Palestine.—Ed.

incorrect and ungrammatical German. Since I can speak a correct German, I see no reason why I should myself corrupt and spoil the language I speak."

At this there was great shaking of heads and dubiousness of countenance. "But the people of the East End will not understand you," they remonstrated. "They do not know the real German."

"I have no fear on that score," I answered. "In New York there is a great Yiddish-speaking element, much larger than in London. I have addressed many meetings on the East Side, at which I have never spoken Yiddish. I have addressed them in German, not, of course, in a high, classic style, but in a simple language, abstaining from the use of rare and obscure terms. There was never any difficulty on account of my language. I was always perfectly understood."

There were some misgivings on the part of the committee, but my view prevailed. A meeting was arranged for me in some great hall in the East End. An immense crowd attended. I addressed them in a simple but grammatical German. My theme was Samson Raphael Hirsch, and I pictured the man and his influence on Orthodox Judaism. There was not the slightest indication of any difficulty in understanding me, and my address was received with great enthusiasm. Neither was there any evidence of estrangement on the part of the Yiddish-speaking Jews. On the contrary, they were even more wholeheartedly in my favor than their English-speaking co-religionists, and the Yiddish press came out with articles warmly endorsing my candidacy.

I have already mentioned that I attended and spoke at a public meeting of a great London Hebrew and religious school. It was the Dalston School, and the occasion was the annual distribution of prizes to especially meritorious pupils. There was a great gathering of ladies and gentlemen present to witness the exercises, far more than would be likely to assemble on a similar occasion in America. The chairman or presiding officer was Mr. Evelyn De Rothschild, a scion of the distinguished family of that name. He was a handsome young man, fair-complexioned and with pleasant, affable manners. I found it very significant that a young man of such distinguished family and social standing should be willing to preside over a strictly Jewish communal gathering of this kind.

I was also a guest, together with my daughter Beatrice, at several dinners and other social functions in the highest circles of London Jewish society, but as these affairs, though very pleasant and possibly valuable from the purely social point of view, are of no intrinsic importance, I shall not devote any space to describing them. Beatrice found them very enjoyable and was also much pleased with several other social connections which she made. As for myself, I shall only mention that, at one of these affairs, I had the honor of leading in to dinner Mrs. Herbert Samuel, the wife of Herbert Samuel, at that time, I believe, postmaster general and afterwards the first High Commissioner of Palestine, after the assumption by Great Britain of the mandate for the establishment of the Jewish national home. The custom of leading another man's wife in to dinner is one of the British customs which struck me as, to say the least, peculiar. I presume, but do not know, that the idea of this singular custom is to promote general sociability among the guests.

I was the guest of honor at one dinner which I did not enjoy, which did not run off pleasantly and which may have had an important influence upon the outcome of the campaign for the chief rabbinate. I was invited by the Reverend A. A. Green, minister of the Hampstead Synagogue, to meet a number of other ministers and laymen at dinner at his home. I was not happy to receive this invitation for the very good reason that I had been informed by two or three persons whom I considered trustworthy that this gentleman did not observe the dietary laws.* That would make it impossible for me to partake of flesh food in his home. How it was possible for a non-observer of the dietary laws to officiate as minister of an Orthodox synagogue is another question, for which I will attempt no answer. I would gladly have avoided accepting the invitation but could not think up a plausible excuse.

The evening of the dinner arrived, and I was present, together with fourteen or fifteen other guests, two or three of them clergy and the

---

* The Reverend A. A. Green, one of the most prominent Anglo-Jewish clergyman of the period, was the leader of a group with attitudes favorable toward Reform. Doubtless this unquestioned fact gave rise to the rumor, possibly exaggerated, which produced the social calamity of the dinner. . . . He was, incidentally, a cousin of the late Rabbi Maurice H. Harris, of Temple Israel in New York.—Ed.

rest laymen. As the guest of honor, I was seated at the head of the table, next to my host. I endeavored to be particularly amiable and conversational, so as to prevent the fact being observed that I was merely toying with the food but not eating, at least nothing the permitted character of which could be in doubt. My stratagem did not avail. After a few moments of this non-participation or semi-participation, my host said to me in no very gentle voice:

"Why aren't you eating?"

I answered that I had no appetite, but that he should not mind that and not permit it to disturb the enjoyable character of the evening. This answer did not please him at all. He frowned and said, in the same ungentle voice:

"I presume you are not eating because you think my food is not kosher. I assure you it is as kosher as the board of *Shechitah* permits it to be."

I assured Mr. Green that I was not insinuating that the meal was not kosher, and no further reference was made to the subject. But the atmosphere had become distinctly chilly, and when I left I felt that the Reverend Mr. Green could hardly be numbered among my friends. That feeling did not particularly disturb my equanimity, but I reproached myself for having permitted myself to be involved in a controversy, be it ever so slight, or brought into a position which could be considered compromising. I also said to myself that, if questioned in regard to my action, I would answer that, under the circumstances, it was perfectly justified—that, after all, a prospective chief rabbi of an Orthodox Jewish community must be guided by the Talmudic injunction, "Keep far from that which is sinful and *that which seems to be.*" However, I was not questioned about the matter and, indeed, heard nothing further of it during the rest of my stay in England—which does not at all mean that it was not discussed in private in certain circles or was without influence on the course of events.

One other recollection of my stay in London I desire to chronicle before closing this chapter. Unlike the experience just described, this was entirely unofficial and of the pleasantest nature. On Saturday evening, the ninth of November, 1912, I lectured before a meeting of "The Hebraists," an organization devoted, as its name indicates, to the study of Hebrew language and literature. The society included, I was informed, most of the leading Hebrew scholars of the British metropolis. I had been invited to address the society in a letter couched in the most beautiful and expressive Hebrew, by the secretary, Mr. H. M. Lazarus. The meeting took place in the residence of Dr. Adolf Buechler, 27 College Crescent, Swiss Cottage, N.W. Dr. Buechler was at that time the principal of Jews' College, having succeeded Dr. Friedlander, who had been the principal at the time of my first visit to London.

I took for my theme a philological subject on which I had previously lectured before the *Ohole Shem* in New York but which had as yet not been published and was unknown in London. Its title was "Abstract and Philosophical Terms in Biblical Hebrew." The audience was an ideal one before which to lecture on a recondite theme of this kind. They listened with closest attention and with evident perfect comprehension of everything that was said. The atmosphere was one of pure, undiluted faith in and love of Jewish, particularly Hebrew, culture.

When I concluded and the customary discussion from the floor took place, the comments were many and enlightening. But there was little disagreement with my views and interpretations; on the contrary, the audience, Hebrew scholars of the first order, practically all of them, gave their unqualified approval. It was a wonderful and most enjoyable evening of its kind, the memory of which is indelibly stamped upon my mind. Indeed, in all probability, it is the most precious and inspiring of all my experiences in England. Love for Hebrew culture may be, probably is, an acquired taste, but it is very real and very sweet to those who have acquired it.

Chapter Thirty-three

My Trip Through the Provinces

Return to London and America

Decision in the Issue of the Chief Rabbinate

THE JEWISH COMMUNITIES IN THE PROVINCES, NATURALLY, ALSO desired to see and hear the candidates for the chief rabbinate. Therefore, as one of those considered for the post, I visited a number of the chief cities of England outside of London, preached in the synagogues and met the clerical and lay representatives of the local Jewish communities.

I made this trip about the middle of November, 1912, after the conclusion of my speaking tour in London, and I visited the cities of Birmingham, Leeds, Manchester, and Liverpool. These four cities are, of course, only a small fraction of the towns and other places in England, to say nothing of Scotland and Wales, in which communities of the adherents of Judaism exist. But it was manifestly impossible for me to visit all these places, especially in view of the limited time at my disposal, since I planned to return to America toward the end of December. Since these cities are all places of importance and their Jewish communities well representative of English provincial Jewry, the committee in London felt that it would be sufficient for me to visit them and that the provincial Jews would be satisfied that their desires had been adequately considered.

My trip was interesting in the highest degree, both to me and to my daughter Beatrice, who accompanied me. I found the provincial Jews of England splendid members of the general Jewish community of that country. They were very similar to the Jews of London, and yet there was about them an indefinable something which was different. While some of the clergy of London impressed me as not entirely sincere in their adherence to Orthodox Judaism and as secretly lust-

My Trip Through the Provinces

ing after the flesh-pots of Reform, I derived no such impression from the provincial Jewish ministers whom I met. All the latter appeared to me thoroughly sincere and wholehearted in their devotion to the traditional faith of Israel.

Everywhere I preached in the synagogues, I met the clergy and representative laymen of the communities, and I discussed with them the problems of Jewry, particularly of English Jewry. Together with my daughter I enjoyed the hospitality of leading personages and their families, which was very cordial and lavish indeed. I can truthfully say that the reception given to my adddresses and the expression of my concept of the place and function of the chief rabbinate in English-Jewish life was very favorable. It would be no exaggeration to say that it was enthusiastic. According to all indications, the provinces were solidly united in their demand that I should be the next chief rabbi. An evidence of this general favorable sentiment was given by an incident which occurred in Birmingham. There was a meeting of communal leaders in the home of the gentleman with whom I was staying, Mr. Samuel Mordecai Levi, for the purpose of meeting me and of discussing with me the problems of the rabbinate.

Among those present was a Rabbi Bloch, a spiritual leader of high standing among the Yiddish-speaking immigrant Jews in the city. Rabbi Bloch was noted for his, to put it mildly, negative attitude over against the native, English-speaking Jews, both clergy and laity. He approved neither their learning nor their piety; indeed, he considered them *Amme Ha-Aretz,* which is the Talmudic term for persons devoid of both culture and religious trustworthiness, and he had given open and unrestrained expression to his views.

But Rabbi Bloch was enthusiastically in favor of me. He addressed the meeting, applying to me the saying of the Talmud, "The words of the Torah are poor in one place and rich in another," interpreting them as signifying that Judaism is poor in England but rich in America. I assume no guarantee of the correctness of his interpretation. Indeed, personally I disagree with it completely, but the effect produced by his address was very great. I was, of course, an English-speaking rabbi; I had even declined to use the Yiddish in a public address in the East End of London. For a Yiddish-speaking rabbi to endorse me publicly and in the enthusiastic manner in which Rabbi

Bloch had done was a matter, therefore, of extraordinary importance.

The English provincial cities impressed me as being quite different one from the other; as having each a specific character, one might almost say, a special personality of its own. Birmingham seemed to me a quiet, genteel, refined country town. Leeds was a busy, bustling manufacturing and working-class center, with the labor element exceedingly conspicuous. Manchester was a great commercial and industrial city, with energy and enterprise written all over it. Liverpool was a magnificent city, almost a metropolis, with fine streets and avenues and, no doubt owing to its direct connection with the New World through its being the point of departure of the trans-Atlantic steamers, strongly suggestive of a prosperous American city. These characteristics were reflected in the characteristics of their inhabitants, including the Jewish communities thereof.

My host, Mr. Samuel Mordecai Levi, represented in his person the qualities of Birmingham. He was a most courteous gentleman, quiet and soft-spoken and of evident refinement and culture. It was extremely interesting to me that Mr. Levi, though thoroughly English in language and demeanor, bore such an outspoken Hebrew cognomen. It was as though he defiantly threw his Jewishness into the face of his Gentile environment and said to them:

"Do you want to know what I am? Hear my name and you will know. I am a Jew."

But I must remark that Mr. Levi was not alone or even exceptional in this regard. He only followed the practice of a great portion of the English Jews—for which I pay them my tribute of appreciation—of bearing unmistakable Jewish names. It is an evidence of their self-respect and their consciousness of an assured position in British citizenship, which will not be affected by the unafraid asseverance of their ethnic origin and religious affiliation.

Mr. Levi was a widower with one daughter, a comely and well mannered maiden named Edith. The household was in charge of a housekeeper, an elderly lady, by name Miss Myers. It goes without saying that the household was conducted in strict accordance with the dietary laws and other Jewish precepts. Beatrice and I enjoyed several days of the most charming hospitality in the Levi home. Mr. Levi did all in his power to promote my comfort and enjoyment, and

Edith and Miss Myers devoted the same attention to Beatrice.

After dinner on Sabbath, Mr. Levi accompanied me for a stroll through a considerable part of the city. On this stroll I beheld a remarkable sight, which gave me an insight into some of the principles which are potent in shaping the economic life of England and make it comprehensible that the English people, in their great majority, are conservatively inclined and free from subversive or revolutionary desires.

Walking through the clean and well kept streets of Birmingham, thoroughly urban in their appearance, we suddenly entered a district of a totally different aspect. We saw before us a thoroughly rustic scene, cultivated fields and grassy meadows of considerable size, cattle peacefully grazing, farm houses or cottages with unmistakable rural inhabitants—in every way a genuine farming village. It seemed like the heart of the country, a hundred miles or more removed from the city through whose streets we had just been strolling. I gazed with amazement at the sight before me and expressed my wonderment to Mr. Levi.

He smiled and gave the explanation. It seems it was an ancient village and had existed for many centuries, before the city of Birmingham had grown to its present proportions. Its land and the land on which Birmingham stood belonged to the Dukes of —. Its people were tenant farmers, paying rent to the ducal proprietor in each generation. Of course, if the farms were converted into urban properties, as the duke had a perfect, legal right to have done, the income derived from them would be far greater. But the ducal family pursued a humane and considerate policy toward the village tenants. No tenant was evicted, and rents were not raised, at least not to the level of rents paid by urban tenants. As long as villagers remained in their homes and tilled their soil and paid the moderate rent of their farms, they were undisturbed in their tenancy. Only in the rare instances in which a farm became vacant through the dying out or the removal of the entire family did the duke resume his ownership rights and convert the farm into urban property, cutting streets through and erecting city buildings upon the land. And thus came about the anomaly and anachronism of *rus in urbe,* an old-time country village in the heart of a modern city.

Mr. Levi assured me that the villagers were well content with their lot and that the citizens of Birmingham, although the ducal policy interfered somewhat with the progress and prosperity of the city, nevertheless warmly approved of it, on grounds of both humanitarianism and political wisdom. He did not need to give me that assurance. I recognized at once that this was the sort of policy which makes for a contented people, which discourages subversive and revolutionary tendencies and increases respect for, and attachment to, national traditions and established institutions.

From Birmingham Beatrice and I directed our steps to Leeds. Overlooking the details of the formal and very deferential reception which was accorded me, one incident stands out conspicuously in my memory as especially interesting and instructive. Rev. Moses Abrahams, minister of the chief congregation of the city, who was one of the members of the reception committee, undertook to look after me during my stay in Leeds. Rev. Abrahams, incidentally, belonged to a family of great importance in English Jewry, his father, Barnett, having been *Dayan* or assistant rabbi of the Sephardic community and principal of Jews' College in London, and one of his brothers, Israel, a Hebrew scholar and author. Of his lofty concept of his vocation and the moral courage and sturdiness of his character, the incident which I am about to narrate will give interesting evidence.

We were seated in his office on the Friday before the Sabbath on which I was to speak in the synagogue, discussing matters connected with my visit to Leeds. While we were thus engaged, the telephone rang. Taking the receiver to his ear, Mr. Abrahams began to converse with his interlocutor at the other end of the wire. From the remarks of Mr. Abrahams, I could understand the substance and bearing of the conversation. Most interesting and surprising it was. A Mr. Lionel Rothschild, a member of the famous family though not the only bearer of the name Lionel, was at the other end of the wire. He had come to Leeds in the interest of a candidate for Parliament, a Mr. John Gordon, who was with him. He desired to hold a meeting in the synagogue for the purpose of recommending the election of Mr. Gordon to the Jewish voters of Leeds. He, no doubt, expected immediate compliance with his request and was probably even more surprised than I at Mr. Abrahams' answer.

My Trip Through the Provinces

"I am very sorry, Mr. Rothschild," said Mr. Abrahams in a firm and decisive tone, without the slightest hesitancy or temporizing. "I could not think of permitting the use of the synagogue for such a purpose. The sole purpose of the synagogue is for prayer and religious instruction, and that is the only purpose for which I would permit the synagogue over which I preside to be used. A secular hall is the only proper place for a political meeting, and that is where you should have your meeting. But since you have come to Leeds as a Jew and with the object of influencing the Jewish voters, I would suggest that you come to synagogue tomorrow morning. I would be pleased if Mr. Gordon would come with you. Neither of you would make any address, but your presence would attract the attention of the people to the purpose of your visit and would probably increase the attendance at your meeting."

Mr. Abrahams ceased and there was a brief pause, after which he said, "Very well, Mr. Rothschild, I shall be pleased to greet you and Mr. Gordon in synagogue tomorrow morning."

On the following morning Mr. Rothschild and Mr. Gordon, who was not a Jew, came together to synagogue. They sat side by side during the service, but no reference whatever was made to the reason for their presence in Leeds. Mr. Rothschild was called to the Law in the customary manner. After the conclusion of the service, they both joined the throng of those who congratulated me on my sermon.

I do not know whether the meeting in favor of the candidacy of Mr. John Gordon was successful or not. But I do know that I was filled with admiration—I might say reverence—for the courageous and genuinely religious manner in which Mr. Abrahams had met his problem. I recognized in him a true servant of God and a brave defender of Judaism and of the respect which is its due.

Our next visit was to Manchester, a great commercial and industrial city, very important in Jewish life as the seat of the second largest Jewish community in England, some twenty-five thousand souls or more. It is very important also in English-Jewish history because of the distinguished men who have graced the Jewish pulpit there: Dr. Schiller-Szinessy, Professor Theodores, and one very well known in America, Dr. Gustave Gottheil.

My reception here was similar to that of the other provincial cities which I had visited, if possible even somewhat more enthusiastic. I was received by a large and representative delegation and hospitably entertained, together with Beatrice. One of the delegation, apparently one of the less important members thereof—whose name I have forgotten—insisted urgently that I must dine at his home and would not take no for an answer. At the meal he explained his insistence by saying that he desired to have in later years the privilege of saying that he had been host to the chief rabbi. For that reason he had invited all three candidates to be his guests so that, no matter which of them was successful, he would have accomplished his purpose. I must admit that, although it was an excellent meal, his explanation made the viands taste rather less palatable.

I had abundant opportunity to observe what a great and busy commercial city Manchester is. A small committee of the delegation took us in a carriage around the city to show us its sights. To mention only one of these noteworthy sights, we visited the Exchange or Chamber of Commerce. I shall never forget the sight of its main room. It was of tremendous extent and it was completely filled with brokers and dealers, so that hardly a square foot of its floor was unoccupied. There must have been thousands of men gathered together, and one could realize how tremendous must be the volume of business there transacted in order to require the services of such a throng.

I found the Jewish life of Manchester very vigorous and purposeful. In addition to the numerous synagogues, some thirty or more, there were quite a number of institutions, both charitable and cultural. I delivered an address before the Young People's Society—I do not know whether that was its exact title. I was really surprised by the mighty throng of young men and women who attended and who were evidently all animated by warm and earnest Jewish sentiment. A Dr. Dulberg was the leading personage among them.

One of my treasured memories of Manchester is a visit to Rabbi Dr. B. Salomon, rabbi of the main synagogue. I found him a learned and dignified spiritual leader, of Danish birth, I believe. I passed a couple of very pleasant hours in his company and that of his good wife.

As an American it was very interesting to me to learn that our President, Woodrow Wilson, was connected by ancestry with Man-

My Trip Through the Provinces

chester. His father had been a minister in Manchester and I was shown the church in which the Reverend Mr. Wilson had officiated for a number of years. In connection with this incident I noticed, as also on other occasions, that the British have a strong feeling of kinship with America and Americans. Several times in conversation with English people they referred to Americans as "brothers" or "cousins" and they were almost as proud of the President of the United States as if he had been their President. All who happened to mention the subject were unanimous in condemning George the Third as a stupid and pig-headed monarch, whose obstinacy and lack of vision were responsible for tearing off from the British Empire what might have been its greatest, richest, and mightiest dominion.

Manchester may be a great commercial city and its Jewish community an impressively earnest and loyal body of adherents of Judaism, but it certainly has a wretched climate, at least in the time of year when I was there. Throughout our stay the weather was raw, chilly, and damp, and so dark that lights burned all day in many of the houses. On the Sabbath morning when I was to preach in the synagogue, it was as dark as midnight. The street lights were burning everywhere. By myself I would never have been able to find my way to the House of God, but fortunately the congregation sent a special messenger to the hotel, who guided me with perfect ease to my destination through a maze of dark and gloomy streets. None of the people with whom I spoke referred to the weather or seemed to find anything extraordinary or even worthy of comment in it.

My sermon and addresses in Manchester were received very favorably, and there seemed to be unanimity of sentiment that I was to be the next chief rabbi. Indeed, this sentiment seemed to have preceded my arrival, presumably based on reports from London, and to have even reached some circles of the Gentile population. When we visited the Exchange, the official who acted as guide said, in a tone of deep respect, to the committee who accompanied me," This, I presume, is the gentleman who is to be your chief rabbi." Indicative of this feeling among the Jews of Manchester is a letter, which I still have, written to me, just previous to my departure for America, by a Mr. Jacob Cohen, a much respected member of the Manchester community, from his home, Smedley Villa, Smedley Lane, Cheetham,

Manchester, in which he expresses himself as follows:

"I shall be delighted to have the early opportunity of seeing you again in Manchester, no doubt as our Chief Rabbi, which, from my personal observation, is the unanimous feeling of Manchester Jewry." He concludes with the words, "Best wishes for a safe journey and a speedy return to England as our revered Chief."

Before taking leave of Manchester I must not forget to mention that there is resident there a quite numerous community of Sephardic Jews, originating mainly from Morocco and other parts of North Africa. I had the privilege of being a guest of Mr. Hamwee, their lay head, I believe, and I found him and his family typically refined, well mannered, and sincerely religious Sephardic co-religionists.

From Manchester Beatrice and I wended our way to Liverpool. There is little that I can say of any special interest to my readers concerning this beautiful city, the chief seaport of Great Britain. As in all the provincial towns, my reception by the Jewish community was most cordial, and my sermons and addresses were heard with evident approval. Mr. Herbert Levey, the head of the reception committee, looked after our comfort most solicitously. The suite which he secured for us in the Hotel Adelphi was the acme of beauty, comfort, and luxury. Beatrice was delighted with it.

One little incident of our stay will serve to show the friendly sentiment toward my candidacy which prevailed in Liverpool. Beatrice and I were guests at a social gathering in the beautiful home of one of the most prominent members of the Liverpool Jewish community, at which a Mr. Cohen, said to be the head of a chain of great department stores, was present. This gentleman, who was of a somewhat humorous disposition, spoke to Beatrice and urged her to use her influence to persuade me to accept the post of chief rabbi. (In some way it had become known that I was not very eager to be chosen for the august position.)

"My dear Miss Drachman," Mr. Cohen said, "do, pray, induce your father to remain here with us as chief rabbi. You see, if he remains here and you, of course, remain with him, you will not have to leave your native land."

"Why, what do you mean?" asked Beatrice, astonished at this enigmatical remark.

"Very simple," answered Mr. Cohen. "You see, if you stay here, you will surely be in the *United State*." Not a very witty remark, perhaps, but the friendly sentiment underlying it was clearly manifest and pleasing.

In Liverpool I had the privilege of visiting a most exceptional Jewish school. It was kept by a Dr. Fox, and the language of instruction was Hebrew. At the time of my visit a class was learning *Mishnah,* and the lads explained the text in beautiful Hebrew, far more classic than the language of the *Mishnah.* Liverpool was the limit of my tour of the provinces. From there, we returned to London.

In London the sentiment, on the whole, continued overwhelmingly favorable to my candidacy. This sentiment found its expression in the press, both Jewish and non-Jewish. The *Westminster Gazette* devoted an entire article to the selection of a successor to Dr. Hermann Adler. While giving full justice to the scholarship and ability of the two other candidates, it described me in an especially favorable manner. It referred to me as "a divine of attractive charm and an author of high repute." Continuing, it described me in terms of which I could, by no means, completely approve but which, undoubtedly, seemed to its English readers the highest praise. "Dr. Drachman is quite without even a taint of Americanism, either in the pulpit or outside of it; his flow of pure English rendered in the easiest and readiest manner, yielding the most rapt attention, led the large congregation in the Great Synagogue to quite a pitch of admiration." In describing me as "without even a *taint of Americanism,*" the *Westminster Gazette* referred only to my use of the English language. In any other sense I would, of course, emphatically reject any such praise. In thus expressing itself the *Gazette* said what I had already heard several times from some of my auditors who expressed surprise that my English was free from the Yankee twang which they seemed to think characteristic of all Americans. The Jewish press, both that in the English language and in Yiddish, also wrote most appreciatively concerning me. They appeared to take it as self-understood that I would be the next incumbent of the Chief Rabbinate.

But there were not lacking indications of a contrary sentiment. Already in Birmingham I had received a letter, marked "private and confidential" from Mr. L. J. Greenberg, editor of *The Jewish Chronicle,* informing me that "certain gentlemen connected with a certain institution"—he did not describe them more recognizably than that, but I had an idea as to whom he referred—had expressed themselves as feeling that my principles were *too orthodox.* Mr. Greenberg intimated that he intended writing a strong editorial on the subject and seemed to imply that he would like my views in reference thereto. In my answer I wrote that I was not desirous of becoming the object of a public controversy, that I preferred to have the matter settle itself. Also the Reverend Isaac Samuel, a very worthy and dignified representative of the English-Jewish clergy, with whom and whose good lady I had the privilege of dining and passing a pleasant afternoon and who was, I understand, the father-in-law of our own Rev. Meldola De Sola, of Montreal, Canada, informed me, in the course of our conversation, that he had heard that some few people considered my religious views too strict. Mr. Samuel condemned such an idea as intrinsically absurd and said it was a good reason, not for rejecting, but for preferring me as chief rabbi.

"What is the purpose of a Chief Rabbi?" asked Mr. Samuel, "if not to maintain and defend the Jewish faith? And how can he do this better than by himself giving an example of sincere and conscientious observance of its laws and precepts?" Which certainly is logical reasoning, although it did not appeal to the objecting minority.

Whatever opposition existed did not become articulate during the brief time that Beatrice and I remained in London before our return to America. All those persons with whom we came into contact were extremely courteous and friendly. I did not deliver any sermons or addresses during this period. From the treasurer of the United Synagogue, a very courteous and pleasant gentleman whose name I believe was Emanuel, I received a check of three hundred pounds in defrayment of the expenses of my trip. About the middle of December, 1912, we boarded the ship and, after a stormy voyage of approximately a week, we landed in New York.

Returned again to my native land, I found that interest was general, among Jews and to a considerable extent among non-Jews, in the outcome of the election. This took place in January, 1913. It was conducted by means of a college of electors, whose membership consisted of delegates chosen by the congregations belonging to the United Synagogue, who were endowed with the full power of electing the Chief Rabbi. The exact nature of the proceedings at the meeting of the college of electors, especially of what went on behind the curtains, is not known to me, but, from the information which reached me, I believe that what happened was about as follows.

There was a strong sentiment in my favor among the electors, indeed a clear majority was warmly desirous of electing me, but certain legal difficulties, or ostensible difficulties of a legal nature, made it impossible for them to carry out their will. The electors opposed to my election, though only a small minority, made skillful use of these difficulties to prevent my election. As I have stated, I was not a direct candidate for the position. My attitude was that I was not seeking the appointment but that, if I were called by the Jewish community of Great Britain to stand at its head, I would, as a matter of duty, of religious obligation, accede to the call. This attitude, as my readers know, corresponded to my true feelings.

My opponents secured a ruling from the legal counsel of the United Synagogue, a Mr. Algernon Sidney, if I recall correctly, that such a call could not be issued. The constitution of the United Synagogue, Mr. Sidney ruled, did not provide for such a call but only for selection of a Chief Rabbi from candidates who had applied for appointment. As I had not made any such application, he decided, my name was not before the College of Electors and therefore choice must be made between the two other gentlemen considered, Rabbi Dr. Moses Hyamson and Rabbi Dr. Joseph H. Hertz. The College of Electors saw itself obliged to bow to this decision. Thus the subsequent division resulted in the election of Dr. Hertz.

The reaction to this result in America was a diversified one. Among the general public it was one of surprise. The reports coming from England had all been to the effect that my election as Chief Rabbi was practically certain. The contrary result, therefore, naturally aroused great wonderment. Many of my friends were grievously disappointed. They had thought that selection of me for this exalted post was a well merited distinction and they were grieved and, to some extent, resentful at this unexpected outcome of their hopes. My children belonged to the disappointed ones. My parents-in-law and their family felt mainly great relief. They had not wanted me, and especially not their daughter and sister, to leave them and remove to a far-distant land. But mingled with their relief was considerable resentment.

My dear wife's reaction was one of unconditional relief. She would have accompanied me, had I been chosen for the post and accepted, without a word of objection or complaint—such was her loyalty to her concept of wifely duty—but now that the sacrifice was not to be required of her, she was frankly happy. She bade me "forget it," dismiss the matter from my mind, and resolve to be happy with her in our own dearly beloved America, our precious native land.

As for my own reaction, it was also mainly one of relief. There was, naturally, a certain degree of humiliation in the thought that I was apparently a defeated candidate. But when I reflected upon the manner in which my rejection had been brought about, that it had not been the result of a straight, direct vote but of a mere legal technicality, and when I reflected further on the reasons which actuated my opponents, that they found no fault either with my character or ability, but did not want a Chief Rabbi of firm and uncompromising devotion to the principles of Orthodox Judaism, I came to the conclusion that my lack of success, instead of being a dishonor, was really a tribute of honor and high esteem.

One result my failure to reach the Chief Rabbinate did not have. It did not embitter me in the slightest. I felt that the English-Jewish community had honored me signally in inviting me, without any solicitation on my part, to become a candidate for the highest position in its power to confer and I was sincerely happy that I had had the opportunity to get in touch with this great community of Israel, to observe its workings from within, and to make the acquaintance and, in many instances, gain the friendship of so many noble men and women of its members. I felt that my life was greatly enriched by this experience. Neither did my experience in England lessen or weaken my desire to do what I could in behalf of my brethren and faith on the west side of the Atlantic.

I saw that fate, or, let us rather say, the workings of Providence, had decided that my field of activity was to be America, and I resolved that whatever strength or ability I possessed should henceforth be devoted, primarily and mainly, to the service of my Jewish brethren and their ancient faith in that portion of the globe in which my eyes had first beheld the light of day.

Chapter Thirty-four

Back Again to America

Activities of a Strenuous Career

HOME AGAIN IN MY BELOVED LAND, I TOOK UP THE TASKS OF MY vocation with even greater energy and devotion than before, if that were possible. Relieved of the nightmare of possible transportation to the foreign land beyond the sea—for a nightmare it had been, despite its external brilliance and undeniable importance—I felt within me fresh zeal and renewed determination to render the best service within my power to the sacred cause of Judaism.

The accustomed tasks of my vocation seemed to me doubly pleasant after an absence of several months. I preached with intenser zeal and higher eloquence in both synagogues and looked after the educational welfare of both *Talmud Torahs* with keener interest than before. The people in the congregations noticed this, and some remarks were made to the effect that my trip to Europe had heightened my love for America. I threw myself with especial zeal into the service of the Jewish Sabbath Alliance of America. In my renewed dedication to the cause of Orthodox Judaism in America, I felt that the Sabbath was the one most important element requisite for the perpetuation and strengthening of the ancient faith in the New World and that it was entitled to my most earnest thought and most strenuous endeavors.

Shortly after my return to America I had the privilege of celebrating, together with my dear wife and our children, the youngest of whom, Theodore Solomon, was in his ninth year, the significant event of our silver wedding. On February the eighth, 1913, a quarter century had passed since Bernard Drachman and Sarah Weil were joined in holy wedlock. On Sabbath, February eighth, the happy event was celebrated in the synagogue of the First Hungarian Congregation *Ohab Zedek* in 116th Street and was followed by a dinner at our residence, 128 West 121st Street. This dinner was essentially a family affair, being attended, except for the presence of the trustees of both congregations, only by the families on both sides. In the afternoon of the following Sunday there was a public reception and in the evening a large dinner, at which the two rabbis who had officiated at our marriage twenty-five years previously, Drs. H. Pereira Mendes and Moses Maisner, and my senior colleague in the *Ohab Zedek* congregation, Dr. Philip Klein, were present. The rabbis made appropriate and appreciative addresses. Dr. Klein's address was in unusually felicitous vein and marked by delicately humorous and sarcastic references to the ineptitude of the United Synagogue of London in failing to secure me as its spiritual head and America's gratitude for its omission.

There were also addresses by several of the laymen present, including one by Mr. Jonas Weil, president of Congregation *Zichron Ephraim*, my worthy father-in-law. The Congregation *Ohab Zedek* presented me with a beautiful silver loving-cup, and similar gifts, of smaller dimensions, were presented to me by the Sisterhood and the children of the *Talmud Torah*.

The interest shown by the members of the two congregations was very great. They thronged the afternoon reception, as did many friends who were not members, and were most profuse and cordial in their congratulations to my dear wife and me. My dear Sarah would have preferred no celebration. Crowds and publicity were embarrassing to her modest and retiring nature. But she bore herself with simple dignity, responded to all greetings with unaffected cordiality and, in her own gentle and unassuming way, was undeniably happy. I had written a poem in honor of the occasion which has not been preserved.

It is rather difficult to describe all the various forms of Jewish activity in which I was engaged during this period, and the previous and following years which are linked with it in "the spinning of history." They are so numerous and so varied that it is difficult to make a choice, especially as I have not kept a chronological record.

Perhaps my efforts at securing legislation favorable to conscientious observers of the seventh-day Sabbath are entitled to priority of narrating. If the stress and strenuousness of endeavor which I put into my efforts to promote the cause of Sabbath observance are to be the criterion of priority, then that is entitled to precedence. The effort to secure favorable legislation required greater intensity of preparation and exertion than any other form of activity. I cannot claim that all this effort was rewarded with any success, unless the approval of one's conscience be such. What I did gain was a first hand knowledge of the methods of politicians, which for "ways that are dark and tricks that are vain" greatly resemble the characteristics of the "heathen Chinee," as described by Bret Harte. I also gained a keenly disappointing, indeed, a heart-sickening realization of the fact that, under the fair surface of American democracy and liberality of sentiment, there lurks an astonishing mass of bitter prejudice and bigotry.

At many sessions of the Legislature of the State of New York I appeared, in my twofold capacity of President of the Jewish Sabbath Alliance of America and of President of the Union of Orthodox Jewish Congregations of America, to plead with the legislators to grant elementary justice to the conscientious observers of the seventh-day Sabbath, Jewish or Gentile, by granting them exemption from the Sunday law. On these occasions I was always accompanied by large and impressive delegations of representatives of Jewish and non-Jewish seventh-day Sabbath-observing congregations and organizations. Our opponents also appeared in large numbers, and we were obliged to listen to arguments of the most superficial and illogical kind, when considered from the viewpoint of a free and democratic state, and also to occasional outbursts of open anti-Semitism, even to condemnation of the Jew for daring to demand the rights of American citizenship.

I was several times the recipient of "left-handed" compliments. Some of the representatives of the other side would come to me, after the close of the hearing, and compliment me on my address, but they never said that my arguments had convinced them and that they were converted to my view. On one occasion one of the opponents, the paid agent of a Sunday observance society, approached me and said to me bluntly, "Dr. Drachman, you've delivered a very fine speech, but it's no use. You're on the wrong side." I leave it to my readers to criticize the ethical quality of this point of view. As for the members of the legislature, they never said anything unless they were cornered and asked point blank for an expression of their views and their intended course of action. Then they would hem and haw, express high regard for the nobility of my sentiments and the justice of my aims but, with the exception of a few individuals, carefully avoid committing themselves.

The outcome was always the same, defeat for our side. One year the Assembly would pass the bill permitting seventh-day Sabbath observers to attend to their secular business on Sunday, and the Senate would reject it. The next year the process would be reversed, but the result would be the same. The history of these experiences and their emotional effect upon me are perhaps most clearly revealed in a letter which I addressed to *The Tribune* on April 10, 1913, and which appeared in that paper a few days later. I give it here in full.

SEVENTH DAY SABBATH BILL

A Plea Is Made for Its Passage as a Matter of Justice

To the Editor of The Tribune.

Sir:

On Wednesday, the 2d inst., the bill introduced in the Legislature at Albany at the request of the Jewish Sabbath Association by the Hon. Aaron J. Levy, permitting persons who observe the seventh-day Sabbath to attend to their business on the first day of the week, was rejected by the Assembly. This, if the undersigned mistakes not, was the sixth time that a bill to this effect had been introduced into the Legislature and defeated.

Its history is a wearisome account of fair promises and partial successes, ending invariably in final defeat. When introduced for the first time it passed both Assembly and Senate and was vetoed by Governor Odell. On other occasions it passed one House and was defeated in the other. While the Republicans were in power, Democratic Representatives told our society that nothing else could be expected from the Republican party because of its narrow and illiberal views. Now the Democratic party is in the saddle and has meted out to seventh-day Sabbath observers the same inconsiderate and unsympathetic treatment as its predeces-

sors. We have always been loth to put this matter in the foreground of public attention, thinking that it is not a matter of particular consequence to the community in general whether those persons who rest on the seventh day shall be permitted to attend to their secular business on the first day or not, and that there was no need to create public excitement on this account. But the constant disheartening experience through which we have gone convinces us that our policy has been a mistaken one, and that it is necessary to enlist public opinion in our behalf if we would succeed.

We are, therefore, now appealing to our fellow-citizens of New York and, in particular, to the recognized leaders of public opinion, the press, the clergy, and public-spirited citizens in general, to consider this question and to give expression to their views thereon. The question is a simple one and seems to us one of elementary justice and American citizenship rights. There are in this state several hundred thousand citizens, Orthodox Jews and Seventh Day Baptists and Adventists, who strictly abstain from all labor and business from Friday evening to Saturday evening, observing that period as the Sabbath and holy time. Nevertheless, these conscientious and religious people are prevented by the Sunday law from attending to their secular business on Sunday, and are put to serious disadvantage and loss, being deprived of one-sixth of their time without compensation. Only sincerely religious and conscientious people suffer under the law, for those of easier principles violate the Sabbath and care nothing for it.

Shall this disability continue? To us it seems almost inconceivable that the Legislature of a free American state should subject a most worthy element of its citizenship to such disadvantage. Twenty-four states of the union, among them our neighboring states of Connecticut and Rhode Island, grant this exemption, and no harm has resulted therefrom. How strange that in New York, where the Seventh-Day observing element is much more numerous, it can obtain no consideration for its needs and justified wishes!

The Jewish Sabbath Association
Bernard Drachman, President

New York, April 10, 1913.

This appeal, I regret to say, fell flat. It did not evoke a single response. Whether this negative result was due to active disinclination to accord recognition to the needs and desires of seventh-day observers or simply to ignorance or indifference on the part of the public, I have no means of deciding. Possibly the second assumption may be the case.

I was a frequent writer of letters to the general press, not only in regard to the Sabbath question but also in reference to many other matters. Whenever it was necessary to correct errors concerning Jews or Judaism or to defend their fair name against misrepresentation, I did not hesitate to address the journal in which the objectionable statement had appeared and I usually had no difficulty in securing the publication of my communication. I also was a not infrequent correspondent in regard to questions not of specific Jewish import and I also had little or no difficulty in having my missives published, usually with the notation that the views expressed were derived from a Jewish source.

Thus as far back as 1905, one of these letters to the *New York Sun* was a protest against the statement: "Of Jews alone in this city there are now as many as the population of native parentage." I insisted that a Jew born in America is, of course, a native American. Long before that, indeed during the Spanish-American war, a newspaper statement told of how Captain Jack Philip restrained his men from cheering with the words: "Don't cheer; they're dying!" and called his action truly Christian. In this case, the basis of my protest was a *Midrashic* story of how while Pharaoh was drowning in the Red Sea, the Holy One, blessed be He, hushed his angelic choir, saying, "My creatures are drowning, and would ye sing a song!" My letter said, "It is hardly fair to claim, as specifically Christian, teachings and sentiments demonstrably derived from Hebrew sources." In both cases, as in many others, the newspaper wrote sympathetic editorials in response to these communications.

The year 1913 was a very busy year for me. I do not know whether the fact that I had been in England as a possible incumbent of the Chief Rabbinate attracted more general attention to me than previously, but, whatever may have been the reason, I had become the cynosure of all eyes in the Jewish community of America. I was approached from the most varied quarters in regard to the most diversified matters.

Congregational duties kept me extremely busy. I preached regularly on Sabbaths and holy days in both synagogues, on one Sabbath or holy day in the synagogue of Congregation *Ohab Zedek* in West 116th Street and on the following such occasion in the synagogue of Congregation *Zichron Ephraim* in East 67th Street. As our home was in 121st Street, between Lenox and Seventh Avenues, and it is forbidden by Jewish law to travel by vehicle on Sabbaths or holy days, that meant that I had to make the journey on foot. After service I returned to my home in 121st Street, also, of course, on foot. The distance between West 121st Street and East 67th Street is approximately three miles—probably more, rather than less—so that my Sabbath journey, when I preached in *Zichron Ephraim,* was at least six miles. But I was comparatively young and vigorous. Besides, my summer walks at Sharon Springs had made me a good "hiker," so I did not mind the long walks but, on the contrary, I rather enjoyed them. I timed myself and found that, walking leisurely, I could make the trip in a little over an hour but that, if I hastened, it required only fifty-four minutes.

I was called to many family religious ceremonies, such as weddings and funerals, occasionally, also, to silver or golden wedding celebrations. I was kept extremely busy by engagements of this kind. The extent of the demands which were made on my time and energy by these engagements may be realized when I relate that, on one *Lag B'Omer*—the thirty-third day between Passover and the Feast of Weeks—when, after many weeks when marriages are prohibited, the prohibition is temporarily suspended, as a consequence of which there is a great rush of weddings on that day, I officiated at five marriages in four towns, two in Manhattan and one each in Brooklyn, Jersey City, and Lafayette, New Jersey. I began my officiations at one p.m. and concluded at eleven p.m. I admit that when I was finished with my last engagement I did not need to be rocked in a cradle in order to sleep soundly that night. In all these private ministrations, especially when the grim messenger, death, had brought grief and sorrow into a happy home, it was my earnest effort to adapt my services to the character and the condition of the people to whom they were rendered, and was rewarded by the multitude of grateful and appreciative letters which I received.

In the spring of 1913 I had quite a violent controversy with Professor Gotthard Deutsch, of the Hebrew Union College of Cincinnati, Ohio, in regard to the significance of the term *Orthodox*, as applied to adherents of Judaism. Professor Deutsch was unquestionably a Hebrew scholar of great attainment but a strong opponent of Orthodox Judaism. On April 3, 1913, there appeared in *The American Israelite* of Cincinnati, the organ of Dr. I. M. Wise, founder of the Reform Jewish movement in America, an article by Professor Deutsch in which he launched a violent attack on the Orthodox Judaism of America.

He declared, in the article, that the Orthodox Jews of America did not deserve to bear that title, that they could, at best, be styled *neo-Orthodox*, that is to say that they practiced a new form of Judaism to which they gave, unjustifiedly, the name of *Orthodox*, that, in effect, they "sailed under false colors." He defended this statement by saying that the so-called Orthodox Jews of America differed greatly from the genuine and undeniably Orthodox Jews of Eastern and Central Europe whom he had known in his youth, that these latter wore a special Jewish costume, long, untrimmed beards and ear curls, that they spoke only Yiddish, and entertained various superstitious beliefs, and that since American, supposedly Orthodox, Jews did none of these things, they could not be described by the same religious designation.

In an article published in *The Hebrew Standard* of New York on May 30, 1913, I vigorously refuted these views. I pointed out that Professor Deutsch entirely misconceived the concept of Jewish Orthodoxy. I showed from history and the Jewish sources that there is room for wide divergence of practices and views within the framework of Orthodox Judaism and that such divergence is, by no means, tantamount to heterodoxy or reform. Othodoxy and piety, I maintained, are not identical. The former means acceptance of Bible and Talmud and Rabbinical Codes as authoritative, the latter signifies personal zeal in fulfilling the precepts. There never was a time when all Jews were equally observant or agreed completely in their concept of the doctrines, but the authorized and universal faith of Israel was Orthodox Judaism. Reform was the misbirth of the nineteenth century, the period of misunderstood emancipation and assimilation. I concluded by showing, from the Rabbinical Codes and responses, that the great rabbinical authorities of Eastern Europe, themselves scrupulous observers of the traditional usages of the countries of their residence, did not ask or expect their Occidental co-religionists to conform to all the details of these usages. Thus I completely corroborated my point of view.

My article made a profound impression and I was assured by a number of qualified judges that I had completely demolished the logical basis of Professor Deutsch's views. The professor, in a brief letter to *The American Israelite* of June 3, 1913, tried to refute my article, but as his communication was a mere repetition of his already expressed idea, without a single new thought, I ignored it.

In the same year I was the recipient of two calls to the rabbinate by congregations, both situated in the city of Cleveland, Ohio. One was the Congregation *Bne Jeshurun*, the other *Knesseth Israel*. The first named was a great and wealthy congregation. The second was smaller and, naturally, less wealthy, but they were both of great importance and splendid fields of activity. I was obliged, for several reasons, to decline both calls, but it was with real regret that I did so.

The manner in which the *Bne Jeshurun* called me could not have been more flattering or attractive. A delegation of five or six prominent members came to New York for the special purpose of inviting me to become the spiritual leader of their congregation. They were splendid gentlemen, of Hungarian birth but thoroughly Americanized, and very courteous in their demeanor. They told me, through their spokesman, that they knew all about me and, therefore, did not ask me to submit any credentials or to come for a trial sermon. All they desired of me was an answer in the affirmative, and they were prepared to give me at once a contract of election. As for the salary, that was a matter entirely for me to decide. Whatever amount I considered necessary for a proper living and for properly maintaining the dignity of my office they were gladly willing to pay. It was as honorable and pleasing a call as any rabbi could possibly ask, but, as already stated, I felt obliged to decline it. There was a religious reason, into the nature of which I need not go, which would have made my acceptance inconsistent with my duty as a leader of Orthodox Judaism. But I must admit that it was with a real pang that I gave my answer in the negative.

The call from the other congregation came in quite a different manner but one which was also pleasing and honorable. In June of 1913 I had determined to make a trip, together with a few of my colleagues from the board of directors of the Union of Orthodox Jewish Congregations of America, to a number of cities for the purpose of endeavoring to induce the Orthodox congregations in those cities to join the Union. In pursuance of this intention, I addressed a letter to the Congregation *Knesseth Israel* in Cleveland, Ohio, requesting permission to address the congregation for the purpose mentioned. Early in July, I received a letter from the secretary, J. Rothman, written in beautiful Hebrew and with the flowery and highly laudatory phraseology in which it is customary, in Hebrew, to address distinguished rabbis, acceding to my request and designating a Sabbath on which I should appear in their synagogue. On the date designated I was with them and succeeded completely in the object of my visit. Without waiting for the meeting of the congregation, which would take official action on my request, several of the most prominent members assured me that they would join the Union and make a suitable annual contribution.

I had come to Cleveland, as stated, only for the purpose of gaining the adhesion of the *Knesseth Israel* congregation to the Orthodox Union, with no thought of a personal nature in my mind. But, as it happened, the position of rabbi in the congregation was vacant, and such was the enthusiasm aroused by my address that a number of my auditors spontaneously conceived the idea of tendering the post to me. One of the most enthusiastic of these was Mr. Isaac Feigenbaum, in whose home I was staying during my visit to Cleveland, and whom I remember as a most sincere and devout Jew, who was rearing his lovely family of sons and daughters in the true spirit of Traditional Judaism.

Immediately after our return from the synagogue he broached the subject to me. He was very sanguine concerning the future of the congregation under my guidance. He assured me that, if I would consent to be their spiritual leader, he was certain that there would be such a great and rapid accession of new members of the best type, that, in a short time, *Knesseth Israel* would be the greatest Jewish congregation in Cleveland, far surpassing the *Bne Jeshurun*, of whose munificent offer to me he had heard. He told me that, although the congregation was not in a position just then to pay me a salary commensurate with my standing, they would give me an amount sufficient to support my family and myself in comfort and would supplement it by presenting me with a cottage for our residence. On the following day, Sunday, he took me to see the cottage. It was really a very presentable building, roomy and in good condition and situated in an excellent residential section.

The prospect thus opened to me was embarrassing, rather than attractive. Since the call extended to me by the *Bne Jeshurun* congregation, my views on the matter had changed. Not that I did not respect and esteem the *Knesseth Israel* group, for I certainly thought highly of that fine body of loyal Jews and Jewesses. However, sober second thought made me realize that I was already located in the metropolis of America, the queenly city to which people desire to come from all over the hemisphere, and that nowhere could be found a larger or better field for Jewish activity than where I was. I did not feel justified in flatly rejecting the offer, but I gave my host an evasive answer.

A few weeks later, to be exact on July 30, 1913, in Sharon Springs, where my family had taken up their residence for the summer, and whither I had gone immediately after concluding my engagement in Cleveland, I received simultaneously two letters. One was an official communication from the secretary of the Congregation *Knesseth Israel* informing me that I had been elected rabbi of the congregation and stating the terms and conditions of the appointment. The other was a personal letter from Mr. Feigenbaum, containing the same information and expressing his desire and hope that I would accept the election.

Very regretfully but in accordance with the decision which I had reached, I answered both letters, expressing my thanks and appreciation for the honor which the congregation desired to confer upon me but that I had no intention of leaving New York or the congregations in which I was officiating.

I had several interesting correspondences in 1913 with learned Talmudists on abstruse questions of rabbinic law. I shall merely mention a few, in order to show how variegated were the activities which engrossed my attention.

In April, 1913, I had such a discussion with Dr. S. T. Hurwitz, of the Jewish Department of the New York Public Library. I have still preserved in my records one letter from Dr. Hurwitz which shows his great erudition and the vast extent of his reading in the rabbinic field. Dr. Hurwitz was a very young man, the son of Rabbi Nathan Hurwitz, who was at that time associated with me as *Dayan*, or assistant rabbi, in Congregation *Zichron Ephraim*. Dr. Hurwitz died a few months later, and in his untimely demise Israel lost a learned teacher and a most loyal adherent.

Another such correspondent was Rev. David Rudofsky of Utica, New York, whom I met in Sharon Springs in the summer of 1913. Rev. Rudofsky was not a rabbi. I believe he was the cantor of a congregation in Utica, but he was a Hebrew scholar and Talmudist of the first order, as his letter, written to me under date of August 13, 1913, amply demonstrates.

In June, 1913, I received from Rabbi Dr. S. Pick, of Strasburg, West Prussia, his book (in German), *"Judentum und Christentum in ihren Unterscheidungslehren"* (Judaism and Christianity, in their Differentiating Doctrines). This is a profound and truly scientific study of the doctrinal differences between Judaism and Christianity, written with objective frankness, but which has not been properly appreciated. Dr. Pick and I had an interesting correspondence in reference to his book, the agreeable character of which was increased by the fact that the learned doctor was a former fellow-student of mine in the Breslau Seminary. That it was possible to publish such a book in Germany without fear of consequences is a proof of the spirit of liberty and tolerance which prevailed in that country at that time.

In 1913, I read with great appreciation and satisfaction a letter which had probably reached my New York home about the beginning of 1912 but which had been overlooked, undoubtedly on account of my great press of engagements at the time and my preoccupation with preparations for my trip to England. It was from Dr. Leopold Wintner. Dr. Wintner was the rabbi of a Reform congregation in Brooklyn, but he had undoubtedly received a thorough old-time

Hebrew training in his native land—Hungary, I believe—for he was a fine Hebrew scholar and a lover of the traditional rabbinic learning. In the summer of 1911 he had been in Sharon Springs and visited me in my cottage. I presented him with a copy of my Hebrew work, *Dibre Ha-Riboth,* and he told me he would read it carefully through and would then write me his opinion. He did not write me until December of that year and, as stated, I did not see it until 1913.

His opinion of my book, conveyed in a fine and very expressive Hebrew, was highly laudatory. But it was not that circumstance in itself which gave me satisfaction. It was the fact that his criticisms were to the point and showed that he had read the book with close attention and thorough understanding. From that circumstance his favorable judgment derived a special value.

In July, 1913, I was the recipient of a proffered honor which I felt obliged to decline with thanks. I was asked to permit a biographical sketch of me to be inserted in a German "Who's Who," entitled *Das Deutsche Element der Stadt New York* (The German Element of the City of New York). The publisher, Otto Spengler of 352 Third Avenue, New York, explained, in an accompanying circular, that persons of German ancestry, but born in America, would be included and as I was of German descent I was eligible for inclusion. I did not consider myself German merely because my mother had first seen the light on German soil, and I declined, politely but firmly. But my father-in-law, Mr. Jonas Weil, who was, of course, a native of Germany, born in Emmendigen, Baden, accepted, and his biography, together with his photograph, was printed in a conspicuous place in the collection.

In the light of later happenings this incident must seem extraordinary. But it was not. Germany was then a civilized country, and the Germans of that period acted in accordance with the standards prevailing among civilized nations. Would that the events which have stained the name of Germany with indelible shame and disgrace had never occurred, and that Germany of 1933 or 1943 still stood on its ethical and political level of 1913! Then would the greatest tragedy in human history be non-existent and the world would still be a peaceful and happy place in which to dwell.

Chapter Thirty-five

A Great Calamity Comes Over the World

Our Attempt to Relieve It

THE REMAINDER OF THE YEAR 1913 AND THE FIRST HALF OF 1914 passed in comparative quiet and calm. I pursued the even tenor of my way, carrying out the routine activities of my vocation and other activities to promote the welfare of Judaism and the Jewish people. That does not meant that, to speak with Solomon in the *Book of Proverbs,* I could "sleep and slumber and fold my hands to lie down." Far from it. My duties as rabbi of the two congregations *Ohab Zedek* and *Zichron Ephraim* and as president of the Jewish Sabbath Alliance of America, the Union of Orthodox Jewish Congregations of America, and the *Ohole Shem* Society, provided me with more than sufficient occupation for my time and energy. I had also at this time been appointed to a preceptorship in the Rabbi Isaac Elchanan Theological Seminary and was teaching there several times weekly.

Some time in this period—I have not preserved the article and, therefore, cannot state the exact date—I published in the magazine *The Forum,* of New York, an article entitled *"Anti-Jewish Prejudice in America."* In this article I dealt, for the first time in America, I believe, in an objective and scientific manner, with the question of the prejudice against Jewish people.

This article attracted wide attention and was commented on and criticized from coast to coast. I received many letters in reference thereto, most of them favorable, some unfavorable. The majority of the unfavorable criticisms expressed the view that, by openly referring to anti-Semitism, I was increasing it, that it would have been better to ignore the subject altogether, trusting to the democratic institutions of America to prevent any anti-Jewish tendencies from becoming dangerous. In other words, they advocated the so-called "hush-hush" policy, the futility of which has been demonstrated time and again.

At the time my family and I were at our summer home in Sharon Springs. The atmosphere of the beautiful village that summer did not have the peaceful and reposeful quality usually characteristic of it. Since June 28th, on which date the Austrian Archduke Franz Ferdinand and his wife had been assassinated at Sarajevo, Bosnia, by the fanatical Serbian patriot Gavril Prinzip, dark and sinister reports of impending war between the great powers of Europe had been flashed over the cables, and at last the dread conflict had burst forth. It is hard to describe the devastating effect of this event upon public sentiment in America. No war between major European powers had occurred since the Franco-German war of 1870, almost half a century previously, and the general feeling had been that such wars would not occur again.

I, myself, held this view. Since I had seen in Europe the tremendous armaments of the great nations and had realized what frightful destruction a war between them would entail, I was confident that no responsible statesmen could be willing to incur the guilt of bringing about such a catastrophe. I also imagined that civilization had progressed to such a degree and the ethical precepts of mercy and kindness and respect for human life had been so universally recognized as binding upon civilized nations that nevermore would they resort, for the settlement of international disputes, to the fierce and cruel arbitrament of war. The pacifist movement which seeks to outlaw war completely as an instrument of national policy had found many and eloquent advocates in that period and seemed to be growing, even in militaristic Germany, where Baroness Von Suttner, in her book, *Die Waffen Nieder* (Down with the Weapons), had given the world one of the most eloquent and touching pleas against war ever written.

The realization that all these promising indications of a better time, these glittering presages of a happier future, had been based upon a mere delusion, came as an indescribable shock to all well-wishers of humanity. To us Jews the shock came with especial intensity. Sad experience had taught us that, although our brethren were in no way concerned with or responsible for the quarrels between the nations, they would be the first, in case of war, to feel the fury of the contending powers. The rabbis of the Talmud had told us, "There is no vessel so laden with blessing for Israel as peace," and all Jews, even the unbelievers, who, in most things, rejected the authority of the rabbis, felt that that statement was incontrovertibly true.

With uneasy minds and hearts filled with grave apprehensions, we in Sharon Springs passed the summer, hoping against hope that this time would be the exception that proves the rule, and that no special evil would come to our brethren of the house of Israel because of the war raging in the lands in which it was their misfortune to dwell.

While in this restless and uneasy state of mind there came on August sixth the sad news from Washington, D. C., that Mrs. Woodrow Wilson, wife of the President, had passed away. In my capacity as president of the Union of Orthodox Jewish Congregations of America, I sent, from Sharon Springs, a message of condolence to the President. On August 24th I received the official answer of the President expressing his thanks for the message of sympathy sent him.

The news from Europe did not improve. The reports from the Eastern European war zones told the sad tale that the Jews residing in those regions, at that time the main center of Jewish population in Europe, were beginning to suffer terrible hardships, alike from the ravages of the warring hosts and from the hostile regulations of unfriendly authorities, mainly Russian. It became clearly evident that these suffering people would need help and that there was practically no source from which such help could be derived except from their co-religionists in America.

About the beginning of September my family and I returned to New York. I immediately began conversations with my colleagues and others, who might be expected to sympathize with the plan, as to taking steps for forming an organization for the relief of the Jewish sufferers from the war in Europe. On September 28th, as president of the Union of Orthodox Jewish Congregations of America, I sent telegrams, countersigned by Albert Lucas as secretary, to eighty Orthodox congregations to appeal on the evening of Yom Kippur for offerings in aid of the Jewish war sufferers. Such an appeal was made, under my direct supervision, on Yom Kippur evening in *Ohab Zedek* synagogue. Judge Otto Rosalsky made the chief address. Offerings of fifteen hundred dollars were made. Thus began the great relief fund.

On October 1, 1914, the first meeting for the organization of such relief took place. It was held in the home of my senior colleague, Rev. Dr. Philip Klein, in the presence of the following rabbis: Dr. H. Pereira Mendes, Dr. Moses Hyamson, M. Z. Margolies, and the present writer; laymen present were Morris Engelman and Albert Lucas. Of these, Drs. Klein, Mendes, and Hyamson and Mr. Engelman are already known to my readers. Rabbi Margolies was an elderly rabbi of Lithuanian origin, widely known and greatly esteemed for piety and learning. Mr. Lucas was an English Jew of Sephardic descent, fervently attached to Orthodox Judaism and an ardent worker in its behalf. Of the members of the committee, none, except Dr. Klein and Rabbi Margolies, could be called elderly, but all were equally imbued with a zealous desire to promote the cause which they had undertaken.

This small gathering was the beginning of a movement which was destined to culminate in the organization of the Central Relief Committee and the Joint Distribution Committee, through whose combined instrumentality approximately one hundred and fifty million dollars were raised, and immeasurable help brought to the greatest of all war sufferers, the Jews of Central and Eastern Europe. On October fourth the Central Relief Committee was formally organized in the office of Mr. Leon Kamaiky, editor and proprietor of the *Jewish Morning Journal.*

Despite the troubled conditions in Europe, my normal work went on about as usual, although necessarily affected thereby. Among my scanty records I find a few interesting communications and statements in reference thereto. Thus, under date of July 8, 1914, I received a letter from Jacob H. Schiff, expressing sympathy with my work in the Jewish Sabbath Alliance—at that time still known as the Jewish Sabbath Association—and enclosing a not ungenerous contribution. This incident is interesting because it shows that Mr. Schiff, although an adherent of Reform Judaism, did not interpret it in such a way as to deprive him of all interest in the traditional institutions of the Jewish faith. Jacob H. Schiff was a great philanthropist, a most generous supporter of charitable causes, but he did not think that charity was the be-all and end-all of Judaism. The Sabbath was close to his heart, and the knowledge of that fact deserves to be preserved as an additional cause of honor to his memory.

On December seventh I lectured before the Menorah Society of the College of the City of New York on the theme *"Chassidism."* The Menorah Society was a society of Jewish students of the City College, interested in Judaism and desirous of increasing their knowledge of it. The lecture was one in a series on Modern Jewish Movements, conducted under the leadership of Moses H. Gitelson. I remember yet the eager, intelligent faces of the youths as they sat before me, listening with closest attention to my words. After the lecture there were, as usual, a number of very intelligent questions. I considered it a Jewish duty of the highest importance to do all in my power to interest and enlighten the adolescent Jewish youth concerning the faith and people to whom they were born.

In October and November of 1914 I had some pleasant social contacts with two interesting personages of significant qualities. They were Mr. and Mrs. Harry Houdini. Harry Houdini is a name which, in its time, possessed world-wide fame. Its bearer had uncanny power to perform deeds which were far more than mere tricks. He mystified all observers, and he baffled the police of both hemispheres. He would permit himself to be fastened with chains or placed within a locked box or trunk, and in a few minutes he would cast off the chains or emerge smiling from the trunk.

Whence he derived these mysterious powers, no one had the faintest conception. There was nothing in his antecedents or rearing to explain it. "Houdini" was, of course, not his real name. He had adopted it for professional or stage purposes. His family name was Weiss, his first name, I believe, Jacob, and he was the son of a rabbi of Hungarian birth, Dr. Mayer S. Weiss. Despite the nature of his vocation, he had a profound reverence for the Jewish faith and deep-seated filial affection for his parents and reverence for their memory. His father had held a rabbinical position in a Western city, and when he retired he moved to New York. Jacob, or Harry, was then a young boy. He became a pupil in the *Talmud Torah* of Congregation *Zichron Ephraim,* together with a sister and a brother.

In later years Harry Houdini always looked upon me as his teacher and respected me as such. He traveled over a great part of the world, and from the most distant places he would write me, telling me of his experiences. How great his reverence for his parents was, the following incident will show. Shortly after the family settled in New York, about 1890, they were financially embarrassed. Dr. Weiss called on me and asked if I could be of aid to him. I answered that I would be glad to render any aid in my power. I asked him whether I should give or lend him some money, or recommend him to some generous persons for financial help. He declined these proposals, but said he would be grateful if I would buy some of his books. I agreed to his suggestion and visited him in his apartment for that purpose. He had a large and excellent Hebrew library, and I selected a fine set of the *Codes of Maimonides,* for which I paid the price he asked.

Years later, when Dr. Weiss had gone to his eternal reward and Harry had become a world-renowned and wealthy man, I undertook to raise a fund to pay off on the mortgage of our synagogue. I thought of Harry Houdini as a possible contributor. I called on him to ask him to assist me in my effort. He smiled a most friendly smile and said:

"Certainly, Dr. Drachman, I will be glad to assist your synagogue. I will give five hundred dollars toward your fund, but I want you to do me a favor too."

"Why, certainly, Harry," I answered. "What is it you wish me to do?"

"You remember that set of Maimonides you bought of Father (*selig*)? I would like to keep it in his memory."

I returned the books to Harry, and twenty-four hours later I had his check for five hundred dollars. (It cost me forty dollars to replace the set of Maimonides, but I never mentioned the fact to the congregation.) Incidentally I may mention that I collected at this time in all some ten thousand dollars, which amount served to diminish the mortgage to that extent.

I considered it an extraordinary act of filial devotion on the part of Harry Houdini that, although his Hebrew attainments were extremely weak, and he could not read the code of Maimonides, he desired to keep it out of respect for the memory of his father.

Another tribute of filial respect was given in the year 1916. In that year Harry Houdini erected a most elaborate and beautiful memorial structure over the graves of his parents. It was not a mausoleum and did not, therefore, contravene the Jewish law, but in beauty and dimensions it surpassed any similar structure that I have ever known of in a Jewish cemetery. Its cost was, naturally, very high, forty thousand dollars, I understand. There may be two views as to the necessity or propriety of such elaborate monuments to the dead, but as to the genuineness and fervor of Harry Houdini's filial affection and reverence there can be no difference of opinion. In the letter of invitation to me to officiate at the unveiling, on October 1, 1916, Harry Houdini refers to the memorial structure as an "exedra-monument" and signs himself "your old scholar."* Rabbi Tintner also spoke at the unveiling, in behalf of the mother, at whose funeral he had officiated, in my absence.

Mrs. Harry Houdini was a woman of a deeply spiritual nature. She was not a born Jewess, but from remarks which she made during the dinner at my home in November, 1914, it was to be inferred that she considered that, through her marriage to Mr. Houdini, she had joined her husband's faith. I did not comment on this view, for which, indeed, Talmudic support may be found.

As the year 1915 began, the shadow of the war hung heavily over all my thoughts and deeds. It was not easy then to decide on which side to direct one's sympathies, especially not for American Jews, citizens of a neutral nation, with co-religionists and, frequently, relatives in both of the contending hosts. The issue was far from being as clear-cut and definite as it has, unfortunately, become in recent years. Germany still enjoyed the reputation of a highly civilized and fundamentally liberal country, with anti-Semitism present only in negligible measure among the civilian population and entirely unapproved of officially, while, on the side of the Allies was Russia, with the bitterly anti-Semitic tradition of Czaristic days.

Under these circumstances it seemed to me that the only logical

---

* The author also composed the Hebrew inscription for the monument.—Ed.

attitude for American Jews, as for Americans generally, was to observe strict neutrality in thought and deed, to refrain completely from taking sides and to hope for a speedy and just peace, which would leave all the nations basically uninjured and make possible a new period of progressive and universally beneficial civilization.

When, therefore, the famous novelist, Mr. Israel Zangwill, toward the end of 1914, permitted an interview with him to appear in *The New York Sun,* in which he gave it as his opinion that it was the duty of all Jews, without distinction of country of residence or national allegiance, to espouse the cause of the Allies, I felt it my duty to oppose his views. My article appeared in *The Hebrew Standard* of January 1, 1915, and expressed, in full detail, the ideas to which I have given expression above. I pointed out that modern Jews did not constitute a political entity and could not be expected to act in one manner.

I do not know what Mr. Zangwill thought of my article, as he never answered it or gave any indication, as far as I am aware, that he knew of its existence, but Mr. J. P. Solomon, the learned and literarily gifted editor of *The Hebrew Standard,* must have thought very well of it indeed, for he did all in his power to give it the utmost possible publicity.

It is hardly necessary for me to state that the attitude over against Germany to which I have given expression above was mine only as long as America remained neutral. As soon as our beloved country found it necessary to enter the war on the side of the Allies, it became a self-understood matter of patriotic duty to uphold the cause of our country. I did so with all my heart and soul. I will not deny that it cost me harsh pains and cruel pangs to suppress all consideration for the ties of love and the tender memories which bound me to Germany, but patriotism demanded the sacrifice and I made it sincerely and completely.

In the summer of 1915 I was staying in Sharon Springs with my family, enjoying my customary summer vacation, when Mr. Morris Engelman arrived. He came with a bold and far-seeing plan for obtaining aid for the Jewish war sufferers, which plan at once gained my approval and promise of cooperation. It was that we two, of our own accord and without being officially delegated by any organiza-

A Great Calamity Comes Over the World

tion, should make a trip over the entire continent, visit a number of the most important cities and towns, and endeavor everywhere to obtain contributions among the Jewish inhabitants for the relief of the European war sufferers. We were then to form committees for the purpose of continuing the work after our departure.

Mr. Engelman was so filled with the desire of bringing aid to the multitudes of sufferers and so sanguine in his expectation of the success of his idea that he told me all he desired of me was my cooperation and that he would defray all the expenses that the trip would involve. I might have been willing to share the expenses with him, but he was so eager to have the merit of this good deed that I would not deprive him of his *Mitzvah* (meritorious action). The project aroused great interest in Sharon Springs and met with general approval.

On July 22nd Mr. Engelman and I left Sharon by automobile on our errand of mercy. Our first stopping place was Buffalo. On the very next day, July 23rd, a public meeting of the Jewish community took place, which I addressed with an earnest plea for generous contributions for the relief of the Jewish war sufferers. On account of the hastiness of my journey, I am unable to name any of those who participated in the meeting, but I recall that there was a great throng. A splendid spirit of sympathy and cooperation prevailed, and generous offerings were made. Mr. Engelman and I left Buffalo well pleased with the first results of our trip.

We next directed our steps to Youngstown, Ohio. The same warm sympathy and earnest desire to help prevailed as we had already encountered and our meeting was eminently successful. Indeed, it was the condition which we found in every place we visited in the course of our trip. The Jewish heart showed itself everywhere profoundly stirred by the reports of the dreadful sufferings of our persecuted brethren in Europe and eagerly desirous of mitigating the pain and binding the wounds. I had always known that my Jewish brethren are, as the Talmud calls them, "the compassionate children of compassionate parents," but I had never seen that truth so convincingly demonstrated as during this journey of mercy. My recollections of Youngstown are somewhat clearer than of the trip hitherto. I recall the names of two earnest and energetic members of the committee, Mr. Max Schagrin and Mr. M. A. Frankel.

Our visit to Youngstown was rendered particularly noteworthy by an interesting family event in which we were privileged to participate. The young and earnest spiritual leader of the Youngstown Jewish community, Rabbi Isidore M. Davidson, had just become the father of a boy. The *Brith Milah* (or Feast of the Circumcision) took place while Mr. Engelman and I were in Youngstown, and we were among the guests. Let me say here that Rabbi Davidson, who later became and is at present (1944) the spiritual head of the Jewish community of the neighboring city of Wilkes-Barre, Pennsylvania, is one of the noblest representatives of the younger members of the American rabbinate. He has succeeded in making Wilkes-Barre one of the most truly Orthodox Jewish communities in America.

Our next visit was to Cleveland. Here we had the same cordial reception and generous response to my appeal. Here we were the guests of Mr. Solomon Engelman, an uncle of the Mr. Engelman who accompanied me on the trip. He insisted on our staying at his home and he proved himself a most friendly and hospitable host.

Our next goal was the great metropolis of the State of Illinois—Chicago. It was not the first time I had been in Chicago. I had visited it many years previously as a representative of *The Jewish Encyclopedia* to rouse interest among the Jews of Chicago in that monumental Jewish work. But the difference in appearance of the Chicago of my first visit and the Chicago of my second visit was stupendous and filled me with amazement. What had seemed like an immense village rather than a city, wild and raw, characteristic of a Western frontier settlement, had become a magnificent metropolis, with splendid avenues and wonderful buildings and all institutions which go to the making up of a great, progressive, modern city. It was no mean rival of New York. Corresponding changes had also taken place in Chicago's great Jewish community, which, while not to be compared with that of New York, was, nevertheless, of impressive proportions, several hundred thousand souls.

The Jews of Chicago welcomed our mission with the same warmhearted cooperation as our brethren everywhere. Generous offerings were made and a permanent committee organized, and in later years a great part of the amounts raised for the war-relief work came from the warm-hearted citizens of Illinois' great metropolis. During our stay in Chicago Mr. Engelman and I were the guests of Rabbi Moses Fischer, the most hospitable spiritual head of a Hungarian congregation, who would not hear of our going to a hotel.

From Chicago we took our way to Denver, Colorado. On the way thither we began to realize the existence of a great American desert, although the main portion of that vast arid expanse lies farther west between Denver and California. Few Americans, at least of those who live outside the desert area, have any idea how great a part of our country is taken up by desert. The sight of the far outstretched expanse of dull, sandy-colored or brownish soil, almost completely devoid of vegetation, with the exception of stunted sagebrush, is almost terrifying. But it is a tribute to the courage and the ingenuity of Americans that, even amidst these arid wastes, scattered habitations are to be found and, here and there, prosperous and progressive cities. Denver is such a city. There are compensating advantages which go far to counterbalance the disadvantage of proximity to the desert. Its fine climate, in particular its remarkably mild and pure air, make Denver an ideal spot for persons afflicted with lung trouble and has brought about the existence of several great institutions, two of them Jewish, for the treatment of pulmonary sufferers. The great silver mines which exist in its vicinity have brought much wealth to the city and are also responsible for a great growth of population.

We arrived in Denver at 7:20 a.m., July 27, 1915. Early as the hour was, a committee was at the railroad station to receive us. It consisted of Rabbis C. H. Kauvar and Halpern, Mr. I. J. Kolinsky and Drs. Zederbaum, Hillkowitz, and Spivak of the Jewish Consumptives Relief Sanitarium. The reception was made especially cordial, and interesting to me, by the fact that Rabbi Kauvar, of the largest congregation in the city, was a former pupil of mine in the Jewish Theological Seminary. At first we were taken to the Sanatorium, where breakfast was served, after which Mr. Engelman and I were conducted on a tour of the Sanatorium and its spacious grounds and were shown the fine and thoroughly modern arrangements for the care of the patients. I was delighted to find among the resident physicians Dr. Levin, also a former pupil of mine in the Jewish Theological Seminary. From the Sanatorium we were taken on a visit of inspection of the *Talmud Torah*. It was situated in a large building of its own and attended by several hundred pupils, who were evidently receiving very thorough Hebrew instruction.

Although Denver is a typically American city, its Jewish district was very similar to an Eastern European Jewish town, such as might have existed in Russia or Poland. Yiddish signs were on the front of all the shops, and the Yiddish dialect was heard on all sides.

After our visit to the *Talmud Torah* we went at once to the office of the Jewish Consumptives Relief Society, where a well attended meeting of Jewish citizens, which had been previously arranged, was assembled, waiting to hear our message. In the usual manner I addressed the gathering, describing the dreadful condition of our co-religionists in the war zones of Europe, and called for offerings in their aid.

My appeal, assisted by the remarks of other speakers, had the usual effect. Generous offerings were made and a committee was appointed to continue the collection. The meeting concluded, Rabbi and Mrs. Kauvar conducted us to their home and entertained us at a very excellent dinner, and we passed a few very agreeable hours in their company. We then bade them good-bye, with cordial thanks for their kind hospitality and earnest cooperation.

Before leaving the subject of Denver, where our reception, though short, was the most friendly and cordial of any place on our journey, owing, no doubt, mainly to the presence and efforts of Rabbi Kauvar, I will make bold to put before my readers a statement of the impression produced upon the Jewish public opinion of Denver by my visit. The statement is taken from a report of the visit of Mr. Engelman and myself, appearing in the issue of July 30, 1915, of the *Denver Jewish News*...

This fulsome description is the uninfluenced expression of opinion of someone unknown to us and unrelated by kinship or friendship.

Rabbi Drachman in Denver

One of the most eminent rabbis in the world came quietly to Denver Tuesday morning and left in the afternoon. Rabbi Bernard Drachman is one of the rare specimens of humankind of whom the Yiddish speaking Jews would say that he possesses *"dem siebenten chen,"* "the seventh grace." All who behold Dr. Drachman are attracted to him. He left a strong impression upon all who had the good fortune to come in contact with him.

Our next destination was Los Angeles, California, which we reached after a rather tedious trip of, if I recall correctly, two nights and one day mainly through apparently unending stretches of dull, monotonous desert country. The contrast, when we crossed the border and entered the State of California, was nothing less than glorious. The bright green expanses of luxuriant grass, the variegated and vividly colored flowers and the richly foliaged trees, with golden-hued fruit gleaming between the leaves, delighted the eyes and refreshed the spirit. It seemed to me that as I felt then, thus must my ancestors, the Children of Israel, have felt, only in higher degree, when, after their many years of wilderness wandering, they were permitted to enter the Promised Land, the land "flowing with milk and honey."

In Los Angeles we had a meeting which was successful, as all the previous meetings had been. Generous offerings were made, and a committee was appointed to continue the work of collecting contributions for the war sufferers. I made several interesting observations in Los Angeles. One was that there existed there a group of Hebrew scholars, mainly of Russian and Polish origin, who were interested in Hebrew as a vehicle of modern literary expression. They desired to use it to describe the new things and scenes by which they were surrounded in the Far Western world, and they asked me to assist them to find Hebrew terms for these new objects for which they knew no equivalent in Biblical or rabbinic Hebrew. Among other questions I was asked for the proper Hebrew rendition of "surf" and "canyon." I was able to give them the proper terms, and their naive rejoicing thereat was delightful to witness.*

My outstanding recollection of Los Angeles is that I met there Reverend Isidore Myers. I had met him in the East where he had held, I believe, a ministerial post, before removing to Los Angeles,

---

* I am not giving the exact Hebrew terms involved in this discussion as I believe it would be going too far in this narration. Should any of my readers desire to know the exact terms, I will be glad, on request, to furnish him with the desired information. —B.D.

where he was now living in retirement. Reverend Myers was an exceptionally gifted man, although, for some reason or other, he did not attain much publicity, and his light "shone under a bushel." He was a native of Poland but had been a Jewish minister in England, where he had acquired a thorough knowledge of English. His main love, however, was for the Hebrew, which he employed with skill and fluency and in which he had written several booklets, mainly poetical in nature. I met him several times in Los Angeles and enjoyed his bright and witty conversation.**

Our next stopping place was San Francisco, which we reached after an overnight railroad trip. In that great and historic city we found a most important Jewish community, which responded sympathetically to our mission and took the usual appropriate steps to carry out my appeal. All wings of Judaism were represented in the community, but the Reform element seemed to predominate. We came into contact with the leading rabbis and lay representatives of all elements. Of these I recollect Rabbi Meyer Hirsch, the leading Orthodox rabbi, a dignified spiritual leader of the East European type, Martin A. Meyer, rabbi of Temple *Emanu-El,* a handsome and courteous gentleman, and Jacob Nieto, rabbi of Temple *Israel,* a son of Rev. Abraham H. Nieto, for many years the *Chazan* of the Spanish and Portuguese congregation *Shearith Israel* in New York. Of laymen I recollect Otto A. Wise, brother of Rabbi Stephen S. Wise of New York, who was practicing law in San Francisco, and Mr. S. Diller, a well-to-do business man of Eastern European birth, a man with a big Jewish heart and considerable learning and sincerely loyal to Traditional Judaism. All these and many others, whom, to my regret, I no longer recall, were most sympathetic to the purpose of my visit and very helpful in carrying it out.

I also made an appeal at a luncheon meeting of the Rabbinical Association. This took place on Sabbath afternoon, and I was much distressed to observe the rabbis present not only smoking but partaking of forbidden food. I knew, of course, that, in the theory of Reform Judaism, the so-called ceremonial laws are supposed to be

---

** His daughter, Carmel Myers, was a dramatic star of the old silent motion pictures, distinguished both for her art and because no breath of scandal ever touched her name.—Ed.

superseded, but this was the first time I had ever seen the theory carried into practice by *rabbis*. In New York we have a Board* of Jewish Ministers to which clergymen of all the schools of Jewish thought, Orthodox, Conservative, and Reform, belong, but there is a tacit understanding that, whenever a question involving ritual law occurs, the practice follows the Orthodox code. Whenever, therefore, we have a gathering at which food is served, it is of the permitted kind. Nevertheless, I presented the matter which had brought me to San Francisco. My words were received with the utmost cordiality, and a resolution to support the War Sufferers Relief Fund was passed unanimously.

My arrival in San Francisco attracted considerable public attention. The leading newspapers sent reporters to interview me concerning the purpose of my visit. These reporters were cheerful, sprightly young women, evidently thoroughly familiar with all the details of their vocation, who submitted me to a searching cross-examination. They not only wanted to know everything about my personal history and likes and dislikes but also my political views, regarding both domestic and foreign politics, and the war. I answered all their questions patiently and in considerable detail. I considered that if the San Francisco public was interested in having this information—and the reporters, being in touch with public sentiment, were presumably aware if such was the case—I had no right to withhold it.

During my stay in San Francisco I attended to another matter of high importance. I delivered an address before the Fourteenth International Lord's Day Congress, which was in session at Oakland, just across the bay from San Francisco, from July 27 to August 1, 1915. My address was devoted to a defense of the Jewish Sabbath. More specifically, it was a defense of the right of the Sabbath-observing Jew to be exempt from the provisions of the Sunday laws and to be free from any legal interference or molestation when attending to his secular work or business on the first day of the week.

The congress was, of course, dedicated to the strengthening and glorification of Sunday observance, so it may seem strange that a Jewish rabbi was given the opportunity of expressing his contrary

---

* B.D. was President of the Board for several years, now called Board of Rabbis.—Ed.

views. It was, indeed, an exceptional privilege, and it would not have been accorded to me but for the courteous efforts of one of the leading personages of the congress, Dr. Duncan J. McMillan.

I had met Dr. McMillan, a sincere Christian and a courteous and broad-minded gentleman, in New York City and in Albany, N. Y., where we had both appeared before the Legislature on opposite sides of the Sabbath Bill. But although we opposed each other in matters legislative, that fact did not prevent us from entertaining sentiments of mutual respect and friendship. Dr. McMillan was truly appreciative of my Jewish viewpoint, although, in accordance with the policy of the organization which he represented, he was in duty bound to oppose it. In private conversation with me, he said that the Jewish point of view should be better known to Christians. After the close of the legislative session of 1914-1915 he communicated with me, informing me of the Lord's Day Congress to be held in Oakland and stating that, if I could make it possible to attend, he would see to it that I should receive the opportunity to present my views. I answered, thanking him for his courtesy and broad-mindedness, and assuring him that, if at all possible, I would be present and prepared to plead the Jewish cause.

It was a happy coincidence that, at the time when the congress met, I was in San Francisco. Thus I was easily able to take advantage of the opportunity open to me to reveal the sentiment of Israel to a representative gathering of adherents of the majority faith. My address was scheduled for July 30th, and on that day I went to the congress. As I entered the hall where the congress was in session, I must admit that I was greatly impressed. I saw before me a numerous assemblage of dignified and refined-looking gentlemen, whose seriousness of purpose was at once manifest. I was especially impressed by the great number of those who wore full beards, so that it almost seemed as though the gathering were one of Orthodox rabbis of the olden type.

The gist of my argument was that since Orthodox Jews observe the Sabbath enjoined by their own faith, by abstaining on it from all work and business, they should not be compelled by state law to observe also the Sabbath of another faith. This was along the familiar line in which Jews and other seventh-day Sabbath observers are accustomed to protest against being subjected to the restrictions of the Sunday law.

I departed from the mere legal aspect of the question and made a plea which had the double merit of both realism and novelty. I suggested that, in view of the practical impossibility of getting both Sunday and seventh-day observers to agree on the observance of one day and also in view of the need, especially for the younger people, of a weekly day of recuperation, both Saturday and Sunday be made days of rest, one to be observed as holy time and the other to be used for the secular purposes of refreshing, health-giving recuperation.

This was, to the best of my knowledge, the first time that the proposal of the two weekly rest days, or the five-day working-week, was publicly made. As my readers undoubtedly know, the plan met with much favor a few years later and was adopted by many industrial and commercial establishments. It has been found to work very well. So far as I know, I was the first to make the suggestion in a manner adapted to call public attention to it.

There was no discussion of the address and, shortly after concluding it, I left the hall. As I walked down the aisle I was greeted with friendly smiles and nods, and many of the delegates, especially the older, full-bearded ones, said to me, "God bless you, brother!" My address had evidently made a good impression and helped to increase the respect for Israel and Israel's faith. While this was not all that I had hoped, it was a result not without value.

The addresses delivered at the congress were subsequently published in book form, under the title *"Sunday the World's Rest Day."* My address is included in the collection under the title *"The Jewish Problem of the Sabbath in a Christian Land."* This is not the title I had given it. I called it *"The Jewish Sabbath in Its Relation to the General Question of Sabbath Observance,"* which title also appears at the place where the address is printed, page 516.

After San Francisco and Oakland our way led homeward, but our task was not yet fully accomplished. We stopped at a number of towns on the return trip and brought before the Jewish communities the urgent need of helping the war sufferers. The pattern of all these visits was the same and we met everywhere with the same sympathetic response and cheerful cooperation. I shall merely mention a few of the interesting experiences of our return trip.

Our first stop after leaving San Francisco was at Albuquerque, New Mexico. This was on the southern or Santa Fe route and brought us into the heart of the Indian and Mexican and cowboy country, the Wild West of the moving pictures. It is the only section in all our great country, I believe, which still retains that character. It was, unquestionably, the most interesting part, scenically and picturesquely, of all our trip.

Fiendish heat prevailed from the moment we left California until we reached Albuquerque and in the town itself. We seemed to be immersed in an ocean of intense, boiling and sizzling, relentless and pitiless heat. Heat, however, did not seem to mean anything at all to the residents. Albuquerque, despite its tropical climate, had, as far as I could observe, no protection whatsoever against the heat. There were no shade trees nor do I remember seeing any awnings. The blazing rays poured down upon an open town, exposed to all the fury of the celestial conflagration without any protection whatsoever. But the inhabitants of Albuquerque paid no attention to it. They would stand on the sidewalks of the open street and converse together as though the temperature were as cool and pleasant as could be desired.

Early the next morning the local rabbi, who was a very presentable and courteous gentleman of early middle age, called at the hotel. He welcomed us to Albuquerque and told us that he would arrange a meeting at the temple for that evening.

At the meeting, which was well attended, I made some discoveries that were both interesting and surprising. I learned that there was an important Jewish community in Albuquerque, not very numerous nor strictly observant, but filled with a strong sense of Jewish brotherhood and warm-hearted and charitable. The surprising part was that they were nearly all of Alsatian origin, the relatives and country people of Alsatian Jews who had settled there many years previously. Their Alsatian origin was easily recognizable to anyone acquainted with European Jews. As I gazed at the assemblage, I was reminded of the pleasant combination of French and German characteristics which I had observed in my student years in the people of Alsace and Lorraine, those border provinces which have been for centuries the bone of contention between Germany and France. This, too, despite the fact that the atmosphere of America dominated the meeting and English was the only language employed in the proceedings. Despite the intense heat and the swarms of huge and bloodthirsty mosquitoes that filled the air, nobody seemed to mind, and the results of the meeting were eminently satisfactory. The people heard my appeal with complete approval. They pledged themselves not only to immediate generous donations but also to continue to work in the future for the relief of the war sufferers.

We were glad to leave Albuquerque the following morning for regions with more civilized temperature conditions. In taking leave of it, however, there is a tribute of acknowldgment which I must pay. Despite its abominable climate, it was otherwise interesting in the highest degree. The sight of its Mexicans, its Indians, and its American cowboys, and the constant hearing of the Spanish language, gave it an unforgettable, exotic character unparalleled in any other region of the United States. We were pleased also to observe that the relations between Jews and Gentiles were of a simple, natural, friendly nature and that there was no trace of the artificial plague called anti-Semitism. I had feared that in a region where such a great proportion of the population was of a wild, hot-tempered sort, it might be different. One pleasant evidence of this was a sign which I saw in front of a store. It bore the inscription *"La Tienda de Solomoncito"* (The Store of Little Solomon). The pleasing inferences which may be drawn from this inscription are obvious.

On our return trip we stopped in Tulsa, Oklahoma, in Kansas City, in St. Louis, in Cincinnati, and in Pittsburgh before returning East about the end of August. My goal was Sharon Springs, and Mr. Engelman went on directly to New York. Everywhere the object of our visit was successfully accomplished. In Tulsa we found an unusual and very important Jewish community. It consisted of Jews of strong Orthodox convictions, men of wealth, some of high culture, both Hebrew and secular, and filled with a warm desire to serve the cause of Traditional Judaism. Of this group, though of a later date, was Dr. Bernard Revel, who became the head of Yeshivah College in New York. In Cincinnati we were the guests of the Manischewitz family, the celebrated manufacturers of *Matzoth*. We visited their great *matzah factory,* the greatest and most wonderfully conducted establishment of its kind in the world.

We concluded our trip with the comforting consciousness that we had rendered real help to our suffering brethren, that, too, we had started a movement destined to bring relief and rescue to millions.

Chapter Thirty-six

Some Typical Incidents

The War Comes to America

THE YEAR 1915 WITNESSED OTHER INCIDENTS BESIDES THOSE HITHerto narrated and other activity on my part, not without interest and importance from the point of view of my rabbinical career and the history of Judaism in America. I wish first to record a gracious act by a friend, Mr. Philip Gotthelf, a gentleman of culture and refinement and imbued with a warm affection for Judaism and things Jewish. Mr. Gotthelf, proprietor of a business known as Elite Styles, wrote me on March 17, 1915, asking me to send him a dozen copies of my book *"From the Heart of Israel."* He had taken a strong liking to the book and, not satisfied with enjoying it himself, he desired that others should enjoy it also. The twelve copies which he ordered from me were intended for relatives of his, most of whom resided in Australia.

I was obliged to tell him that I was not in a position to fill his order, as the first edition was now entirely exhausted and there was no immediate prospect of a second edition. His answer was characteristic of the man.

"Very well, Dr. Drachman," he said. "You may have another edition published and charge it to me." Thus it came about that the second edition of *"From the Heart of Israel"* represents the Jewish enthusiasm and generosity of Philip Gotthelf.

In the fall of 1915 *The New York Herald* invited me to contribute a Thanksgiving sermon to its columns. My sermon, together with my picture and a biographical sketch, appeared in *The Herald* on November 28th. In accepting the invitation of *The Herald* I attached little importance to the matter, but I was surprised by the warmth of appreciation which my sermon evoked. I was the recipient of quite a number of letters from readers, both Jewish and non-Jewish, expressing great admiration for my thoughts and my manner of conveying them. One of these letters was so exceptional in its warmth and friendliness and depth of spiritual sentiment that I feel I should reproduce it here, especially as its writer was a non-Jew, a cultured and profoundly religious Catholic gentleman, Mr. Xavier Roth, whom I had met in connection with the sale of the Ursuline Convent property to the Lebanon Hospital Association.

Briarcliff Hotel
White Plains, N. Y.
December 6th, 1915

Rev. Dr. Bernard Drachman
128 West 121st Street, N. Y. C.
Reverend and Dear Doctor:

Permit me to express my congratulations for that most beautiful, as well as edifying, Thanksgiving sermon which I read over and over again, as I clipped it from the N. Y. Herald. *I carry it with me and have read it to others or had them read it. One and all agreed with me as to the beauty and the lofty sentiment expressed therein. I trust you are enjoying most excellent good health, that you may praise and bless the good God for many years here below, and at last join in the everlasting praise and thanksgiving with the Saints and the Angels in the heavens above.*

With sentiments of high esteem,
Yours very truly,

Xavier Roth.

Such appreciation and personal friendliness by a devout Catholic for one who was technically a heretic is certainly convincing proof that human attachments may break down the barriers erected by theological distinctions and antagonisms.

About this time—I do not recall the exact dates—it was my privilege to initiate some work which has been of enduring importance in the charitable and institutional life of the Jewish community of New York. It may help in fixing the dates when I state that the events I am about to narrate occurred while Commissioners Kingsbury and

Coler were, in succession to each other, at the head of the Department of Charities of the City of New York. To the best of my recollection these events began in 1915 and continued until 1919.

Jewish employees of the City Hospital on Blackwell's Island, of whom I recall best Mrs. Lizzie Gold, a very sincere and well meaning woman, visited me in my home and called to my attention that there were aged and chronically ill Jewish men and women in the hospital who were very unhappy because the food which they were obliged to eat was not kosher. They were religious Jews and Jewesses who, when they were well and self-supporting, had always avoided the eating of non-kosher food and, now that they were gravely ill and facing eternity, they felt themselves especially burdened in their consciences at being obliged to violate this fundamental precept of Jewish practice.

An appeal of this kind was, to me, irresistible. I promised to do whatever was in my power. Forthwith I applied to Commissioner Kingsbury for an audience, which was readily and courteously granted. I found the commissioner most approachable and understanding. He agreed at once with my view that the city should not inflict any avoidable hardships upon its pensioners and gave his ready consent to the establishment of a kosher kitchen on Blackwell's Island. That the observant Jewish inmates of the City Hospital were greatly rejoiced needs no special statement. The incident also aroused considerable interest in the city, especially in observant Jewish circles. It was a novel experiment in the city administration and was naturally looked upon and criticized from various points of view.

For a few years—if I recall correctly, as long as Commissioner Kingsbury remained in office—the experiment worked very well. I gave particular attention to the religious part and saw to it that everything was carried out in strict conformity with the Jewish law, to the great satisfaction and delight of the poor inmates. The city paid the bills. The cost of kosher food is, it is true, higher than that of ordinary provender but no one raised the point, at least not in an unfriendly spirit, and there was no difficulty on that score.

In the course of time and in accordance with the vicissitudes of politics, Commissioner Kingsbury lost his position, and Commissioner Coler then took his place. With the advent of the new commissioner, a different wind began to blow *in re* kosher kitchen. I was first notified that the city would no longer pay the excess of the cost of kosher food over that of the non-kosher and that, if I desired to maintain the kosher kitchen, I must obtain the funds for the excess expenditure from other sources. That did not seem to be an unfair demand, and I undertook to do as requested.

It was not a petty task, for the difference in cost between the two species of nutriment went into thousands of dollars. However, I took up the task with energy; I had hundreds of letters written to persons likely to sympathize requesting financial assistance, and I made many personal calls for the same purpose. I succeeded in my quest and I was able to satisfy the demand of the commissioner.

In this manner I continued to maintain the kosher kitchen for a considerable time. But the troubles did not cease. The commissioner found new difficulties and raised new objections from time to time, the details of which I have forgotten, and I came to recognize that the maintenance of an institution with kosher dietary laws under city auspices did not harmonize with his views, even if the city was not obliged to defray the entire expense. The only satisfactory solution of the problem would be to remove the Jewish patients from the City Hospital and to care for them in a separate institution entirely under Jewish religious control, in which religious requirements of the Jewish faith would be provided as a self-understood matter.

Fortunately, while this problem was occupying my thoughts and agitating me not a little, I happened to come in contact with Rabbi Abraham Alperstein and his good wife. Rabbi Alperstein was the spiritual leader of a congregation on the lower East Side of New York City, a rabbi of the good old Russian-Polish type, a profoundly pious, yes, a saintly man. Mrs. Alperstein was an ideal helpmeet for such a Jew, sharing his piety and spiritual aspirations in the fullest degree. They had a daughter, a Mrs. Wittenberg, who had inherited a great measure of their spirit and was gladly willing, indeed, eager to assist her parents in their religious and charitable work.

To these good Jewish people I revealed my difficulties. Their response was instantaneous and enthusiastic. They saw the problem just as I did, and they agreed with me as to its solution. Rabbi Alperstein said that to remove these conscientious, God-fearing Jews and

Jewesses from the City Hospital and to place them in a religious home of their own was a *Mitzvah* comparable to that of *Pidyon Shevuyim*, the Redemption of Captives, which our ancestors were so often called on to perform in the dark days of the Middle Ages.

To make a long story short, Rabbi and Mrs. Alperstein undertook to bring about the organization of a society which would establish an institution to which the Jewish patients of the City Hospital could be transferred and in which they, and other similarly circumstanced unfortunate Jews and Jewesses, would receive adequate care and proper treatment. They worked at their task with extraordinary zeal and were remarkably successful. The result of their efforts may be seen in the *Beth Abraham*—named after Rabbi Alperstein—*Home for Incurables*, housed at present (1944) in a fine, roomy building on Allerton Avenue, the Bronx, in which a large number of aged and chronically invalid Jews and Jewesses are lovingly provided for and find most excellent care for all their physical and spiritual wants.

In this period a new development in the Jewish life of America, particularly of New York City, took place, which interested me greatly and in which I participated to a certain extent. A new element appeared on the American Jewish scene. It consisted of Sephardic Jews, mainly immigrants from the Balkan countries but partially derived also from North Africa.

There had been, it is true, a Sephardic contingent in the Jewry of America since the earliest days. Indeed, the first Jewish arrivals in America, those who aroused the displeasure of the Dutch governor of Nieuw Amsterdam, Peter Stuyvesant, were Sephardim. But the proportion of the Sephardic element to the totality of American Jewry was so small as to be insignificant. By and large the Jewish population of America was overwhelmingly *Ashkenazic*.

But now Sephardim came in their thousands and, though they remained a comparatively small minority of the Jewish community, it was a minority large enough to be conspicuous and to attract attention. The number of new Sephardim in New York was estimated at from forty to fifty thousand. As is the custom of all Jewish elements, they speedily developed their own spiritual and cultural life. They had their own synagogues, their own charitable and benevolent societies, and their own newspapers. These journals were printed in

Español or *Ladino*, a dialect of medieval Spanish, which their ancestors, expelled from Spain by Ferdinand and Isabella, had brought with them and which their descendants continued to speak in the lands of their residence.

I was greatly interested in these new brethren. I admired their Jewish loyalty—their great majority was strictly observant of their religious traditions—I respected the devout and decorous manner of their worship, I loved their sonorous and melodious pronunciation of the Hebrew and their dignified and courtly demeanor suggestive of the Orient and, remotely, of medieval Castile. Indeed, one of the motives which had induced me to study Spanish was that the knowledge of it would enable me to converse with these co-religionists, if the opportunity offered.

I took an active interest in their communal undertakings, attended many of their meetings and became personally intimate with a considerable number of their leading personages. On one occasion I surprised them by delivering an address in Spanish. I do not know whether my pronunciation of the Spanish was quite that to which they were accustomed, but they not only seemed surprised but also pleased. At all events, they were too polite to indulge in any unfavorable criticism, so that, if my effort did not impress them favorably, I had no opportunity of knowing it. They certainly understood what I said, and that is, after all, the chief consideration.

Among the chief personages of this group with whom I became intimately acquainted was Señor Mosheh Gadol, editor of the Spanish Jewish journal *"La America."* Señor Gadol was a native of Bulgaria, a man of considerable Hebrew and other culture and warmly devoted to the promotion of Jewish interests, particularly—but not exclusively—those of his own Sephardic brethren. Señor Gadol discussed with me many Jewish problems and asked me many questions concerning Jewish religious law. In so doing, he assured me, he acted as the representative of his community, who had the utmost faith in me.

A letter, which I have fortunately preserved, from Señor Gadol to me, is interesting in itself and as a corroboration of the above statement. It is in Spanish but, as a concession to me, written with Latin letters, instead of Hebrew, with which the Sephardim are ac-

Some Typical Incidents 359

customed to write their language, just as the Yiddish-speaking Jews customarily write the Yiddish with Hebrew script. Señor Gadol wrote me under date of January 1, 1917. I quote only the essential parts of his letter.

> *Muy estimado Señor y Reverend:*
> *En mi puder su estimada lettra del 23 November y rogo de escusarmi por el retardo de responder. Profitando de esta occasion rogo de hacer la favor y solvir la cuestion que se presenta en el puerto de San Michael Portugal. Nuestros immigrantes Sefardim de Turkia aviendo passado por este puerto ondi fueron calorosamente recibidos por los 9 coreligionarios Sefardim que se encuentran en esta ciudad. Ellos cargaron nuestros immigrantes de enformarsin exactamente de un Rabbi competente si ellos puedrian acceptar por Minian para sus oraciones de cadadia como el deceno un minor hijo en edad de 9 años. Siendo en esta ciudad se encontran solamente 9 Judios majorentes y un minorente y encuentran dificultad por obtener el de 10 ajustar.. Minian. Nos hemos enformado de muchas partes por esta cuestion todavia ningun Rabbino pudo darnos una repuesta logica.. ..y satisfaciente en acuerdo con las tradiciones de nuestros Sabios como obrar en asi un caso excepcional y raro.*
>   *Sinceremente el vuestro*
>   M S Gadol

TRANSLATION

Much esteemed and reverend sir:
    I have in my possession your esteemed letter of November 23rd, and I beg you to excuse my delay in answering. Taking advantage of this occasion I beg you to do the favor of solving the question which came up in the port of San Michael, Portugal. Our Sephardic immigrants from Turkey having passed this port where they were warmly received by the nine Sephardic coreligionists who were found in this city, they (the Jews of San Michael) charged our immigrants to inform themselves exactly from a competent rabbi whether they could accept for Minyan (the number of ten adults required for public worship) as the tenth a minor, a lad of nine years of age. Since in this city there are only nine Jews and one minor, they have difficulty in obtaining the ten for arranging Minyan. We have sought information from many quarters concerning this question but no rabbi was

able to give us a logical and satisfactory answer in accordance with the traditions of our Sages how to do in such an exceptional and rare case.

Sincerely yours,

M. S. Gadol

I was much pleased to receive this letter. The sincere, unquestioning faith in Judaism and the earnest desire to fulfill its precepts which it revealed, touched my heart. The dignified, albeit simple and almost naive terms in which the question was couched, were respect-inspiring.

It was a little puzzling, to be sure, to find the question described as an extremely difficult one, to which none of the rabbis whom they had previously consulted, had been able to give a satisfactory answer. I knew that the case was explicitly referred to in the Talmud and rabbinical codes, accessible to any rabbi worthy of the title. However, it was gratifying to find myself looked upon as a *"rabbino competente"* and my decision accepted without question as authoritative. I answered, in accordance with the rabbinic sources, that if there are nine male Israelites above thirteen years of age in the synagogue, a lad under thirteen, who knows the significance of prayer, may be accepted to complete the number of ten required for congregational worship. My answer was written in rabbinical Hebrew, which is the language of the sources from which it was drawn. Señor Gadol published it in his newspaper, *"La America,"* just as I sent it in.

This was not the only inquiry concerning a point of religious law which I received. Nor were the inquiries all from laymen. I was frequently consulted by rabbis in regard to questions concerning which they hesitated, or felt themselves unable, to reach a decision alone. These questions were, of course, of an especially difficult or delicate nature, involving issues of far-reaching importance. I shall tell of two of these inquiries but shall not mention the names of those who inquired, since they addressed me in confidence and under the impression that their communications would be treated as strictly private.

The first inquiry related to the acceptability of a Negro as a convert to Judaism. The rabbi putting the question stated in his letter that a young Negro had applied to him to become a member of the

Jewish faith. The young man seemed to be thoroughly respectable and well educated and had declared that his only motive was a sincere belief in the truth and Divine origin of Judaism. The rabbi, however, was strongly opposed to accepting him into the Jewish fold and doubted whether he was authorized to do so under the Jewish law. I imagine that the rabbi was not ignorant of the Jewish law, which is truly universal and makes admittance to Judaism dependent only upon sincerity of sentiment, without consideration of racial origin, but that he was actuated by an underlying racial sentiment which made him feel it improper to add a person of black-hued skin to the House of Israel.

I answered that his attitude was entirely unwarranted by Jewish law, that he could not forbid what the Torah permitted and that it, the Torah, looked only to the heart of an intending proselyte but not to his or her complexion or other physical characteristics, and that since the young man in question had remained steadfast in his desire to enter the fold of Israel, despite the words of discouragement addressed to him in accordance with Talmudic precept, he, the rabbi, had no choice in the matter except to yield to his desire. I added that, in accepting into Judaism a person with a black skin, the rabbi would not be doing anything strange or unprecedented, inasmuch as there already existed, and had existed since time immemorial, in various parts of Asia and Africa, communities of devout and loyal Jews, the color of whose skin was as black or almost as black as that of the Negro race.*

The other inquiry was also in reference to a case involving the relation of Gentiles to Judaism, a case far more unclear and unpleasant than the one just mentioned. The rabbi making the inquiry was the spiritual leader of one of the oldest and wealthiest congregations of the city. He indicated in his letter that he was utterly at

---

* The author of these memoirs took a particularly keen interest in the work of Jacques Faitlovich, a Jewish explorer of French citizenship, who had discovered, or rediscovered, the *Falashas*, a tribe of black Jews in Abyssinia. These primitive coreligionists, who trace their origin to Hebrews of Solomon's time that returned to Ethiopia with the Queen of Sheba, practiced a crude form of Judaism, and were ignorant of the Talmud and of later Jewish thought, but spoke a Semitic dialect. Faitlovich obtained aid and teachers for them, through the help of American and European Jewries. The author energetically assisted in this work and maintained cordial personal relations with the explorer.—Ed.

a loss as to what course to pursue, or what counsel to give the parties in the case which had come before him.

A certain Jew had become a convert to Christianity and had married a Christian woman. Three children, a boy and two girls, were the fruit of this union. The children were, at this time, in their early "teens." This man had now repented of his action in going over to another religion. He desired to return to Judaism and that his wife and children should also become Jewish. His wife had no objection to his returning to his original religion and was willing also that the boy become Jewish but, for herself, refused to give up her Christian faith and insisted that the girls, too, remain Christian. Neither husband nor wife desired divorce. The rabbi was in doubt as to whether he could accept the man into Judaism, under these circumstances, and altogether as to what he should advise these people to do.

I answered that the case was, indeed, a most difficult and complicated as well as a very sad one, but that the Jewish law relating to the questions involved was clear and definite. The first point to be considered was that the Jewish law does not permit marriage or marital relations between a Jew and a woman not of the Jewish faith or *vice versa* and that, therefore, it became automatically impossible for this man to continue to live in marital relations with this woman, if he intended to be a Jew and she persisted in her refusal to become a Jewess.

On the other hand the Jewish law recognized the validity of the marriage as a civic obligation, in accordance with the Talmudic principle *Dina de Malchutha Dina*—"The law of the state is law." The man was, therefore, in duty bound to support his wife and the children to whom she had given birth even if he could not live with the woman as husband and wife. It was permitted, I wrote, for the rabbi to take the man back into the Jewish fold, in accordance with the principle, "Even if he has sinned, he is still of Israel," provided he would agree to abide by these injunctions.

As for the children, they were to be considered as Gentiles since, according to the Jewish law, children have the status of the mother. The mother in this case being Gentile, the children were also Gentile. Neither could they be arbitrarily pushed around and told to be Jewish or Gentile without their own desires being consulted. The

Some Typical Incidents

Jewish law specifically provides that if a Gentile child has been converted to Judaism, he or she may, on reaching the age of majority, that is, on becoming thirteen years old, renounce this act and opt to remain a Gentile. The most advisable course for the rabbi, I wrote, would be to exercise no pressure of any kind on the parties concerned, to point out clearly how the law affects them, and to leave the action to be taken to their own uninfluenced decision.

All this spiritual and rabbinical activity was carried on while war raged on the other side of the Atlantic and dark war clouds hung threateningly over America. In April, 1917, the die was cast and our beloved country decided to enter the titanic world conflict.* In the summer of that year we were again at our cottage at Sharon Springs, but there was little or nothing of the usual calm and restful enjoyment of the vacation season. The dreadful uncertainties and the necessary preparations for the impending mighty struggle occupied all minds. My three oldest sons were just of military age and were assigned to various activities made necessary by the exigency. My eldest son, Edgar, became a religious and welfare worker for Jewish troops, my second son, Julian, was assigned to the Medical Department of the Army, and my third son, Albert, was sent to a farmer in Sullivan County New York State, to assist in increasing the production of food for the armed forces and the civilian population of the nation. I recall one occasion when the spirit moved Edgar and he delivered a sermon in the synagogue at Sharon Springs on America's duty in the war, although, to the best of my recollection, he had never preached before, and a rousing, eloquent oration it was.

Now that war had come to America, the Jewish community, as has always been the case in Jewish history, fulfilled its patriotic duty with zeal and complete devotion. The young men of military age enlisted or were conscripted into the armed forces of the nation and performed their task as soldiers with courage and fidelity. Those who could not serve with weapons in their hands helped by the purchase of bonds or by whatever other service was in their power.

One of the ways in which this patriotic zeal manifested itself was

---

* Jonas Weil died on April 11, 1917, a few days after the declaration of war.—Ed.
summer of that year we were again in our cottage at Sharon Springs,

the organization of the Jewish Board for Welfare Work in the United States Army and Navy, known as the Jewish Welfare Board. This became a very powerful nation-wide organization with branches in all the states and large cities of the Union. Its object was to work among the Jewish men in the armed forces, to comfort and encourage them in their arduous task, and to show them and their families in every possible way that they had the sympathy and cooperation of their brethren-in-faith in the inevitable trials and tribulations of war.

From its very inception I took an active part in the organization and work of this truly well named Welfare Board. I belonged to the boards of directors of both the national organization and of the New York State branch.

The greatest national Jewish organizations took part in the formation of the Welfare Board, and a splendid array of public-spirited Jews constituted its board of directors. I shall name them both in full. The knowledge of who they were and what they did is an indispensable contribution to the American Jewish history of that period.

The organizations were:

The Central Conference of American Rabbis;
The Council of Y.M.H.A. and Kindred Associations;
The Jewish Publication Society of America;
The Union of American Hebrew Congregations;
The Union of Orthodox Jewish Congregations of America;
The United Synagogue of America.

The board of directors consisted of the following gentlemen:

Col. Harry Cutler, Providence, R. I., Chairman;
Dr. Cyrus Adler, Philadelphia, Pa., Vice-Chairman;
S. S. Rosenstamm, New York, N. Y., Treasurer;
Samuel A. Goldsmith, New York, N. Y., Secretary;
Dr. Leon W. Goldrich, Field Secretary;
I. W. Bernheim, Louisville, Ky.;
Dr. Bernard Drachman, New York, N. Y.;
J. Walter Freiberg, Cincinnati, Ohio;
Louis Kirstein, Boston, Massachusetts;
A. D. Lasker, Chicago, Illinois;

H. H. Lehman,* New York, N. Y.;
Simon Miller, Philadelphia, Pa.;
Dr. William Rosenau, Baltimore, Maryland;
Israel Unterberg, New York, N. Y.;
Rabbi George Zepin, Cincinnati, Ohio.

The Welfare Board laid great stress upon its spiritual work, upon bringing the message and the comfort of religion to the soldiers. An essential part of this work was the preparation of a suitable abbreviated prayer book. It was recognized at once that men engaged in active war service, in the midst of the constant alarms and peril of daily combat, could not be expected to use the full ritual of the Jewish order of prayer.

In the preparation of the abbreviated prayer book I took a leading part. Some of the more orthodox members of the board were in doubt as to whether it was permissible to shorten the order of service. I showed them that the *Mishnah* makes express provision for this contingency. It ordains (*Berachoth, Cap IV, 4*): "He that goeth in a place of danger shall offer up a shortened prayer." The inference is natural that there is no greater "place of danger" than an army in time of warfare. There was no further objection to the abbreviated prayer book, and it was duly prepared.

The testimony is unanimous that it proved of the utmost value to the men in service. It enabled them to offer up their devotions to their Maker in a few brief moments. It strengthened and fortified them in the dread hours of battle that try men's souls. It preserved in their hearts and minds the knowledge of their religious adherence, the remembrance of their allegiance to the faith of Israel.

---

* Later the brilliantly successful Governor of New York State and Director-General of United Nations Relief and Rehabilitation Administration (UNRRA), at that time a banker with philanthropic leanings.—Ed.

Chapter Thirty-seven

During the War and After

I Leave the Congregation Ohab Zedek

THE JEWISH CLERGY CANNOT ESCAPE THE OBLIGATIONS OF SPECIAL wartime service any more than the clergy of the other denominations. And so I, as a member of the clerical or spiritual class of the Jewish people, did my duty to the fullest extent of my power. It was not my privilege to participate directly in the war as a chaplain on the very field of combat, but what I could do on the home front I did. I met many soldiers and gave them my blessing and words of encouragement and comfort before their departure for the war. I went to camps and gave the men there assembled whatever inspiration my words could convey. By sermons and addresses in the synagogue and at meetings I strove to rouse the spirit of patriotic devotion to our noble America and its righteous cause.

I was myself deeply moved by the manly bearing and gallantry of the youths who came to me for my blessing. Never once did I hear a word of complaint or discontent with their hard lot which made them risk their lives in deadly conflict. Almost invariably they said that they realized that they were being put to the test as Jews and that they were resolved to show their Christian comrades, their "buddies," that they were not lacking in love of country or inferior in courageous loyalty.

One such instance is particularly stamped on my memory. A handsome youth, about to depart for the war, came to me for my blessing. His family name was Rubel, his first name, I believe, Edward. After I had pronounced over him the Priestly Blessing, we conversed a little. I said to him that I hoped that he would go safely through the perils of battle and return in health and well-being to his dear ones.

He said to me, "Thank you, Dr. Drachman, for your prayer and good wishes. I hope they will be fulfilled. But believe me, if I knew with certainty that I was to die, I would go to the war just as cheerfully and as willingly. We Jews owe a great debt of gratitude to America. America has done very much for us. It is now up to us to show what we can do for America. If it takes the lives of thousands of us to keep America safe and free, it is not too high a price to pay."

Alas, he did not return. I am proud to know that his simply expressed but noble and profoundly sincere sentiments of patriotic devotion to America are shared by practically all American Jews.

Amidst war's alarms and despite the additional burdens which it placed upon me, the work of both congregations continued without the slightest deviation. The daily and Sabbath and holy day services and the *Talmud Torahs* were kept up with the same unfailing regularity as in the piping days of peace. I also continued without interruption my alternate sermons in the synagogues of both congregations. I was also able to gain supporters of my work in Congregation *Zichron Ephraim* from outside sources, persons not members of the congregation.

Mr. Adolph Lewisohn, one of New York's greatest Jewish philanthropists, was especially appreciative of my work. Already in 1914 he had presented me with a massive silver loving-cup as a token of his personal appreciation of my services to the Jewish community of New York. On May 1, 1918, he addressed a letter to me informing me that he had designated, through Federation, for Congregation *Zichron Ephraim* an annual subvention of five hundred dollars. Mr. Lewisohn kept up this generous annual donation to Congregation *Zichron Ephraim* for upward of twenty years.

The war ended, happily with the complete victory of the Allied and Associated Nations. For me the return of peace meant chiefly the opportunity to continue my work for Judaism, undisturbed by extraneous matters. I did so with renewed vigor and assiduity. It is difficult for me to tell of all the different forms of activity in which I engaged as the years rolled on. They were very numerous and I have kept no exact chronological record. I shall, therefore, tell of them only in rambling fashion, as they recur to my memory.

I recall now with great pleasure the class of girls with whom I read Bible and *Mishnah* in the original Hebrew. I conducted this class at my home in West 121st Street on Monday evenings. It began in 1918 and continued for seven or eight years. The work we did was worthy of professional theological students. We read *Pentateuch* with the commentary of *Rashi, Psalms* and *Mishnah* with the commentary of Rabbenu Obadiah Bertinoro, to all of which I added my personal exegetical interpretation. The girls read the Hebrew texts fluently and followed my interpretations with perfect comprehension. It was an ideal class, in which was fulfilled the Talmudic prayer of the teacher, "May my pupils rejoice in me and I in them!"

After severing my connection with the Jewish Theological Seminary, I entered the service of the Rabbi Isaac Elchanan Theological Seminary, afterward known as Yeshiva College. I forget the exact year when I began this service. I believe it was in the early "teen" years of the twentieth century, and I remained connected with the institution until 1940. When I began my service, the Rabbi Isaac Elchanan Seminary was a very poor institution, located in humble quarters on the lower East Side of New York, but I was privileged to remain with it after its financial condition had experienced a new birth of prosperity and it had moved into the fine edifice which it occupies at present on Amsterdam Avenue, from 186th to 187th Streets. During this long period of service, upwards of thirty years, I had acted in various instructional capacities. These included most of the Hebrew subjects, with the exception of the Talmud and related branches.

I have never looked into the question of why no Talmudic subjects were assigned to me. Of course, I knew that our Russian and Polish co-religionists, to whom most of the supporters of Yeshiva belonged, look upon Talmudic scholarship as the special domain of their rabbis and are inclined to consider Occidental, and most especially American, rabbis as inferior in this regard. But no intimation that this view was extended to me ever reached me, and I cannot, therefore, say that this was the reason in my case. However, I considered all Hebrew subjects valuable and essential and, therefore, accepted without question whatever subject Dr. Bernard Revel, the president, or rector, of Yeshiva College, assigned to me.

Dr. Revel presided over the Yeshiva in its downtown quarters and was its first president in its splendid uptown building and was identified with Yeshiva College as no president before him and as probably none after him will ever be. He maintained Yeshiva College spiritually and materially. He filled it with his remarkable spiritual interpretation of Traditional Judaism. When the initial prosperity, to which the fine new building owed its erection, seemed to fail and the sources of income to grow dry, he—and he practically alone—despite fragile health and growing weakness, found the means to maintain the Yeshiva, its teaching staff, and its stipendiary students.

His material aid was indispensable, but the spiritual impetus which he gave was even more valuable. Yeshiva reflected his personality, which was a rare combination of saintliness and scholarship. Although a native of Russia, he was a master of pure and classic English. His sermons and addresses are models of exalted and inspiring exhortation. Humility and gentleness were leading traits of his character, resembling, in this regard, his master and ideal, Moses, of whom Scripture testifies that he was "the meekest of all men." If Orthodox Judaism in America is destined to a future of dignity and importance, it will be largely as a heritage of Bernard Revel.

One of the forms of my activity in connection with Yeshiva College was to officiate at the installation of rabbis in out-of-town congregations or at the celebrations of out-of-town institutions. On these trips I was usually accompanied by Mr. Samuel Sar, who was a sort of general representative of the Yeshiva. The following letter was written after the return of Mr. Sar and myself from Toronto, Canada, where we had attended the dedication of a *Talmud Torah*.

The Rabbi Isaac Elchanan Theological Seminary
301-303 East Broadway, New York
January 10th, 1922

Dr. B. Drachman
128 W. 121st St.
New York City.
My dear Dr. Drachman:

Mr. Sar has informed me of the great **Kiddush Ha-Shem** *(Sanctification of the Name, i. e. conferring of honor on Judaism) which you have caused during your stay in Toronto. I wish to express my deep appreciation and hope that in the future we* will, p. G., co-operate more closely for the sake of our holy Torah and the ideals of true Judaism. With kindest personal regards, I am,

Sincerely yours,

B. Revel

I not only instructed in the Hebrew subjects but for several years I was a member of the Department of German* as a colleague of Dr. M. Lipzin. In this connection I had an interesting experience which I deem worthy of being recorded here. It is a striking demonstration of the broadmindedness, under trying conditions, of Yeshiva students and is instructive in more than one way. It occurred after Hitler had come to power and had begun his barbarous persecution of the German Jews, presumably in 1934 or 1935.

It had occurred to me that, in view of the cruelties visited upon the Jews by the Germans, my students might not care to continue the study of German, a point of view which I would have found entirely justified. Before speaking of any arrangements for the coming term I therefore made the following prefatory remarks:

"It may be that, considering how terribly the German government is persecuting our Jewish brethren at present, you may not wish to study the language of that cruel nation. If you feel that way I certainly would not condemn you, and I would be glad to take up with you some other subject instead of German. In order to find out your sentiments on this question, I will ask all of you who wish to keep up the study of German to raise your hands." To my great surprise, every one of the boys raised his hand.

"This is indeed surprising," I said. "I would have expected, under present circumstances, a different result. Since you desire to keep up your study of German, you must have a reason for your wish. Who will tell me a reason for desiring to know the German language?"

Again the hands went up. I selected one of the youths, and he spoke thus:

"I think, Dr. Drachman, that we should not confuse cultural and political matters. The Nazis, it is true, are savage and brutal, and

---

* B.D. also conducted classes in the history and principles of education. His official title was "professorial lecturer."—Ed.

their persecution of the Jews is unpardonable. But the German language and culture are not to blame for that. There is a wonderful literature in German, such authors as Goethe and Schiller and Heine and many others. If we do not know the German language, we deprive ourselves of the knowledge of this literature. It would be very foolish to do that."

"That is a very excellent reason," I said. "Who can give me another and, if possible, even better reason?"

A second boy spoke as follows:

"We must not forget that much valuable and important Jewish literature exists only in German. Some of our greatest Jewish scholars, such as Graetz and Fuerst and Samson Raphael Hirsch, have written in German. We cannot be real Jewish scholars without knowing their works, and, in order to do so, we must know German."

"That is also a most excellent reason," I said, "and of special importance to us as Jews. But, as the German saying puts it, '*Alle gute Dinge sind drei*—All good things come in threes,' so I think there must be a third reason. Who can give me a third reason?"

A third boy spoke up and said, "I think, Dr. Drachman, if we Jews are to stop studying the languages of all the nations that have persecuted us, there won't be any languages left for us to study." At this there arose general laughter, in which I joined, whereupon I remarked, "You, —, have given the best reason of all."

In the early post-war period my work for Orthodox Judaism attracted attention not only everywhere on the American continent but in Europe and the Near East and other regions as well. I was the recipient of many communications from Jewish communities and rabbis and lay individuals in all parts of the world asking for information or cooperation in matters of Jewish importance. To all of these communications I gave painstaking attention and whatever assistance was in my power. Brief reference to a few of these will suffice to show what varied service I was called on to do for Israel.

On January 8, 1919, I received a letter on official paper of the Commonwealth of Massachusetts, House of Representatives, from Mr. Philip J. Feinberg, Representative of District 5, Boston, of which I give an extract to show the nature of the request made to me.

> ...*I am seeking information on the question of permitting those who conscientiously believe Saturday to be the Sabbath and close their places of business from Friday at sundown to Saturday sundown to keep their places of business open on Sundays. I have presented such a bill for legislation in the Massachusetts Legislature. I should be very much obliged to you if you can forward me such information. By so doing you will greatly assist me as well as the Jewry of our community.*

In response to this letter I wrote Mr. Feinberg, supplying the information desired and offering to appear before the Legislature of Massachusetts in support of his bill, should he so desire. On January 25th I received his response thanking me for my cooperation. But I was not asked to appear before the Legislature, and I never learned what happened to his bill.

On December 6, 1919, I received a lengthy letter from the *Rabbinaat der Nederlandisch Israelitisch Hoofdsynagoge te Amsterdam* (Rabbinate of the Netherland Israelitish Main Synagogue, in Amsterdam). It was an official communication of the chief rabbi, Abraham Cohen Onderwyzer, written in beautiful Hebrew and signed by him personally, asking for my cooperation in bringing relief to the Jewish war sufferers in Eastern Europe, especially to the rabbis, many of whose congregations had become utterly impoverished. In a postscript the rabbi informed me that a *gett*, or rabbinical bill of divorce, which had been prepared, at his request, under my supervision had been forwarded to Amsterdam. It had reached him and would be delivered to the woman as soon as the legal proceedings for the civil divorce were completed.

Early in 1921 it became my duty and my privilege to take an important, perhaps a decisive, part in an issue which had arisen in American Jewry. In order to understand the issue and my part therein the narration of a little American Jewish history will be necessary. The issue centers around the person of Mordecai M. Kaplan.

Mordecai M. Kaplan was a graduate of the Jewish Theological Seminary. He had been one of the students under my tuition and had received his rabbinical degree from a commission of which I was a member. He was the son of a Russian rabbi of great Talmudic attainments and of unquestioned orthodoxy. His antecedents and training were, therefore, such as apparently to guarantee that he, too, would walk upon the path of Traditional Judaism.

His first steps after graduation seemed to indicate that such would be his course. He became the rabbi of the Congregation *Kehillath Jeshurun* in East Eighty-fifth Street, Manhattan, a prominent and strictly Orthodox congregation and, after a short term in its service, of the Jewish Center in West Eighty-sixth Street, an even more prominent and more zealously tradition-minded group. He also became the head of Teachers' Institute, the institution for the training of teachers of religion of the Jewish Theological Seminary.

The incumbency of two such posts would seem to be a clear indication that their incumbent was a sincere, indeed, a zealous upholder and champion of Traditional Judaism. In the case of Dr. Kaplan it was certainly no such indication. Early in his career he began to reveal, in published articles, views which were radically at variance not only with the doctrines of Orthodox Judaism but even with the basic concepts of religion. His articles permitted the inference that he was a disbeliever in the existence of a personal Deity, in a hereafter, in miracles, and in Divine revelation. His concept of the great figures of the Bible was most offensive to those who had been reared in reverence for them as exalted personages pervaded with the spirit of the Most High and charged with sublime messages of righteousness and holiness to all the inhabitants of Earth.

To him, they were merely primitive human beings, and their "ideology" was merely that of their primitive and undeveloped age. When it became generally known that such was the concept of Judaism entertained by the rabbi of the Jewish Center and the head of the Seminary Teachers' Institute, a great shock pervaded the entire Jewish community. It was felt that this was a far graver assault on Traditional Judaism than that emanating from Reform or Conservatism. While the views of some of the radical Reformers might have been substantially identical with those of Dr. Kaplan, they had never propounded them with such crass directness. The Reform wing of Judaism had never officially declared its adherence to such views. As far as the general Jewish public knew, the difference between Reform and Orthodoxy was limited to the ceremonial laws, the Orthodox being strict observers and the Reformers non-observers. As for the Conservatives, it was considered that they were very close to Orthodoxy both in doctrines and practices.

Despite the general recognition of the un-Jewishness of Dr. Kaplan's views, the reaction to them was singularly weak. It is said that, when the impropriety of permitting a man of Dr. Kaplan's views to stand at the head of a teachers' institute and poison the minds of the teachers of the coming generation was pointed out to Dr. Cyrus Adler, President of the Seminary, the latter answered, "To dismiss Dr. Kaplan would be persecution, and the Seminary cannot persecute."*

This view is utterly incorrect. No institution can be expected to retain a person in its service who acts contrary to the principles of that institution. To dismiss such a person *is not persecution*. On the contrary, it is the duty and sacred obligation of those who lead the institution to keep it faithful to its principles. If the Seminary is an Orthodox Jewish institution, as it is supposed to be, neither logic nor tolerance require it to retain in its service a man whose avowed beliefs are utterly contrary to those which it was established to maintain. If, therefore, Dr. Adler made the statement attributed to him, he took an attitude justified neither by a logical view of the situation nor by his Jewish loyalty.

The reaction in the Jewish Center to the utterly unorthodox views of their supposed spiritual leader was at first hesitating and uncertain. There can be no doubt that the great majority of members, especially those best qualified to be considered true representatives of Orthodox Judaism, were deeply offended and aggrieved that their rabbi should take such an attitude over against the faith they loved and revered. But Dr. Kaplan's reputation for learning was so great, and his articles were so full of apparently profound erudition, that they felt unable to oppose him. And there was also in many hearts the lingering fear, to which Dr. Cyrus Adler had given expression, that opposition would be persecution. The general Jewish community, too, was strangely silent. Even from Orthodox rabbinical circles hardly a whisper of opposition was heard.

---

* An interesting viewpoint, in the light of the events of 1909, with reference to the author of these memoirs.—Ed.

Under these circumstances, I felt that I could not remain inactive at the side lines. I realized that this was a critical time in American Jewish history, perhaps in the history of world Jewry. If strong action to counteract such a destructive movement were not speedily taken, there was no telling to how great an extent it might spread and what havoc it might wreak upon the historic edifice of Traditional Judaism. I felt that I must obey the summons of the Psalmist, "It is time to do for the Lord; they have made void Thy Torah" (*Psalm cxix, 126*), that to refrain from obeying this inner summons would be sin and that nothing should prevent me from doing all in my power to ward off this dastardly attack on Israel's sanctuary.

I decided that the best, indeed, the only proper method to repel the attack would be a calm and dispassionate but thoroughly scientific and critical analysis of the views of Dr. Kaplan, exposing their falsity and superficiality and demonstrating, as thank God, is quite easily possible to those who really know Judaism, that the ancient faith of Israel stands upon such a lofty ethical, intellectual, and spiritual level that it may be unhesitatingly and wholeheartedly accepted by the most cultured and enlightened human beings. Accordingly I prepared such an article, devoting much thought and effort to its careful and convincing elaboration, and submitted it for publication to Mr. Isaac Rosengarten, editor and proprietor of the *Jewish Forum,* who accepted it gladly. It appeared in the *Forum* in the issue of March, 1921, under the title *"An Examination of Prof. Mordecai M. Kaplan's Views on Judaism."*

I may truthfully say that my article made a profound impression on the Jewish community, particularly on the Orthodox and observant elements, and contributed materially to counteracting the evil influence of the Kaplan movement.

Here are two of the many letters which were addressed to me in connection therewith, written by two honored co-religionists, both of them men of culture and sincerely Orthodox Jews, whose views may be taken as representative of those of observant Jewry in general. The first letter is by Mr. Joseph H. Cohen, an American Orthodox Jew of the finest type, a leading member of the Jewish Center. Mr. Cohen had been greatly troubled by the Kaplan movement and had called on me in reference thereto shortly before I published my article, and I had permitted him to read my manuscript. His letter follows:

February 16th, 1921

My dear Dr. Drachman,

I thank you most sincerely for your kindness in sending me the manuscript of your article which is to appear in the next issue of the Jewish Forum, entitled "An Examination of Prof. Mordecai M. Kaplan's Views on Judaism."

I read the article very carefully and I am bound to say that, while you treat the subject in a most temperate manner, laying emphasis on the point that your opposition is "to the book, not the author," your arguments are nevertheless most thorough and logical and will, I am sure, appeal not only to the believing and observing Jew, but to the skeptic as well. Would that we had more such able, valiant and ready advocates of Jewish principles and ideals in the defense of which, to quote from your article, "countless numbers of men and women have made the supreme sacrifice and died as martyrs."

Very truly yours,

Joseph H. Cohen

The other letter is from Dr. Joseph Bieber, a prominent physician and a sincerely Orthodox Jew, a member of the First Hungarian Congregation *Ohab Zedek.*

March 7th, 1921

My dear Dr. Drachman

Having just finished reading in the last issue of the Jewish Forum *your reply to Prof. Kaplan's articles, with which I am familiar, I cannot help giving vent to my deep appreciation of your masterful way of combating those malicious views. To those of us who believe in, or, at least, incline to Orthodox and Traditional Judaism, Prof. Kaplan's agnostic and sophistic opinions had a terrible effect. I especially dread the effect of those articles on the susceptible minds of the educated Jewish youth. For this reason I deem it a blessing that your article has come forward with arguments so convincing as to leave no room for doubt even to the uneducated mind. I do hope that your article will receive the widest publicity among all classes of Jews* in general and our own congregation in particular. Permit me, as your humble friend, to congratulate you upon your efforts and success.

Very respectfully yours,

Joseph Bieber

Shortly after the appearance of my article, which he made no attempt to answer, Dr. Kaplan withdrew from his position in the Jewish Center. The inner history of this withdrawal, whether it was a voluntary resignation or a compulsory departure, is unknown to me. Reports, however, have come to me, which seem not devoid of probability, that the majority of the members of the Jewish Center, encouraged and strengthened by my article, notified him unequivocally that his Orthodox leadership had become insupportable. As a consequence, Dr. Kaplan saw himself compelled to renounce his post.

The severance of Dr. Kaplan's connection with the Jewish Center did not, unfortunately, mean the end of the disruptive movement which he had originated. He had a considerable following of wealthy and influential persons in the Center, some relatives, some non-relatives, who withdrew with him and established a new congregation, to which they gave, what I must consider the arrogant and presumptuous title of "Society for the Advancement of Judaism." In this organization his views and theories are, presumably, carried out without let or hindrance and not, according to the concepts hitherto prevalent in Israel, for the advancement of Judaism but quite the reverse.

The scope of this narrative does not demand, or even permit, a full consideration of the significance and implications of what Dr. Kaplan audaciously designates as the Reconstruction of Judaism. But before taking final leave of this subject, a brief consideration of one aspect of the matter, at which many have wondered, appears to be necessary.

Among the followers of Dr. Kaplan are a considerable number of persons whose mode of life and apparent views would indicate that they are sincere adherents of Orthodox Judaism. How is this possible? How can sincere believers in Traditional Judaism accept the leadership of a man whose views are utterly opposed to the historic standards of Jewish faith? The answer, I think, is twofold. First, ignorance. These persons, led away, perhaps, by his eloquence and scholarship and not understanding the full significance of his words, do not realize how utterly antagonistic to true Judaism his theories are. Secondly, Dr. Kaplan, it is reported, conducts himself, in some measure, according to the external characteristics of Orthodox Judaism. It is said that he is personally observant of the dietary and other ritual laws. That there is little or no religious value in these practices if not based on faith in them as Divine ordinances is a thought which might not occur to "the man in the street."

Throughout this crisis, all usual activities continued. I frequently addressed meetings of young people on questions of Jewish importance. Just at this time, when the Kaplan controversy was absorbing so much of my energy, I lectured to the Hebrew Cultural Society of De Witt Clinton High School on "The Future of Judaism"—one of many such functions remembered now because of a letter of appreciation from the society's president.

The year 1922 saw also the end of my connection with the First Hungarian Congregation *Ohab Zedek*. This happened in such an unexpected and casual manner that to this day I occasionally find myself wondering that it happened at all.

I believe it was a case of, as the Talmud puts it, "Tobias has sinned, and Zingad is punished." There had been some misunderstanding between the senior rabbi, Dr. Philip Klein, and the president of the congregation, Mr. Moritz Neuman, in consequence of which the latter had grown very angry and had ceased to attend the services in the synagogue. I was not involved in any way in this dispute and knew nothing of its cause or the matter at issue. All I knew was that it was highly improper and very regrettable that the relations between the venerable senior rabbi and the lay head of the congregation were so very strained. It seemed to me a real scandal.

Actuated by these sentiments, I deemed it my duty to endeavor to persuade the president to desist from his hostile conduct over against the senior rabbi and especially to resume his attendance at service. In pursuit of this intention I called on Mr. Neuman in his place of business. He was in the leather trade, and his office and shop were in one of the lower downtown streets, if I recall correctly, in Front Street. Mr. Neuman received me in a friendly manner, and at first we conversed on indifferent subjects. Before I could come to the real matter which had brought me there, he made a remark which appeared to be a personal reflection. I was shocked, I was proud, and I was not diplomatic. I might easily have answered evasively. Instead I said to Mr. Neuman, "Very well. I have no desire to remain where I am not wanted. Tomorrow you will have my resignation."

That night I wrote my resignation and mailed it. The text is a matter of indifference. A few days later a sparsely attended congregational meeting took place, to which my resignation was presented. The few who were present, so I am told, seemed dazed, and the resignation was accepted with hardly the semblance of a regular vote.

I retained my post as rabbi of the Congregation *Zichron Ephraim* and continued my rabbinical activity in that capacity. Although my official relations with *Ohab Zedek* had now terminated, the ties of friendship which had bound me to so many of the members and their families did not terminate. I remained on terms of sincere intimacy with them, continued to be, so to speak, their unofficial rabbi and spiritual counselor. I was frequently called to officiate in their families on occasions of both joy and sorrow. These amicable relations have persisted, more or less, to the present day (1944) and my recollection of my term of service to the First Hungarian Congregation *Ohab Zedek* is, despite the rude and inexplicable manner of its termination, by and large, unclouded by any shadow of resentment and truly pleasant and agreeable. I shall always treasure the memory of the many true and fine friendships which I was privileged to make among the members of that congregation as that of a sweet and precious experience in my life.

Chapter Thirty-eight

Continued Activities for Judaism

A Testimonial Dinner

AFTER RETIRING FROM THE FIRST HUNGARIAN CONGREGATION *Ohab Zedek,* I devoted myself to the rabbinical care of Congregation *Zichron Ephraim* with intenser energy since it was no longer necessary to divide my attention with another organization. I did not, however, discontinue the work which I had been doing in behalf of general Jewish interests. On the contrary, because of greater leisure I was able to devote more time and effort to the promotion of the general welfare of Judaism and the Jewish people.

In 1921 we disposed of our cottage at Sharon Springs and ceased to be summer residents of that beautiful rustic borough. For nineteen years we had made our home there during the summer months and had witnessed its growth from a village with hardly a Jewish resident to a real Jewish town, during the summer months only, of course. I had become thoroughly identified with the place and, although my real status was only that of a summer resident, I had become, to all intents and purposes, rabbi of Sharon Springs.

I was in exclusive charge of the synagogue. I saw to it that it and the surrounding grounds were kept in clean and presentable condition. Too, I preached on Sabbaths and special occasions. I was called upon to decide questions of *Kosher* and *Trefah* and to perform other rabbinical functions, as well as to lead in matters of charity.

It was with feelings of real regret that I bade good-bye to Sharon and our cozy and comfortable cottage, but circumstances had made it necessary and there was no other choice. The synagogue I turned over, free and clear, to a committee of the Jewish hotel keepers with the understanding that it was to continue to be used for its holy purpose.*

About then, too, I witnessed a Jewish event, the like of which Israel had not known during all the centuries of the Diaspora. I refer to the great Jewish parade which took place in New York City after the League of Nations had recognized the historic right of the Jewish people to Palestine and had entrusted Great Britain with the Mandate over that country and charged it with the duty of establishing the Jewish National Home.

Words cannot describe the wave of emotion which swept over the Jewish masses, over all Jews who had preserved Jewish feelings and Jewish thoughts in their hearts and minds, when these world-stirring announcements became known to them. It seemed to them that the apparently unending Jewish exile had finally reached a glorious termination, that the sufferings and persecution and misery which had seemed the inevitable accompaniment of Jewish history had now vanished into the abyss of the past. It seemed, indeed, that the days of the Messiah (or if not the actual Messianic days, at least the preparatory and introductory period leading thereto, the *Ikba Di-Meishicha*, "the footsteps of Messiah") had arrived. This overwhelming tide of emotion had created the parade. It forced the throngs of rejoicing and ecstatic Jews out of the tenement houses and the back streets of the Ghetto on to the highways and avenues of the metropolis, where almost spontaneously they organized and marched to celebrate in triumph the coming of their national redemption.

I understood those feelings and felt them myself, and so I was also among the throngs of spectators, incidentally, not all of them Jews, by any means, who stood on the sidewalks of Fifth Avenue, and saw the great Jewish parade march past.

---

* After the disposal of the Sharon house, part of the family took advantage of the opportunity thus afforded by spending the summer of 1922 in a European tour. They visited England, France, Switzerland, and Germany. In England, the author of these memoirs was cordially received by his former pupil and one-time rival, Chief Rabbi Hertz, and also renewed other associations of his earlier visit. In Germany, the Drachmans were guests of several groups of relatives. While in Schweinfurt, where they stayed with Rabbi Dr. Solomon Stein and Adolph Stein, he lectured before the *Juedische Kultus-Gemeinde* on "The Wonders of America!" Most of the tour, however, was spent in nothing more important than "sight-seeing" and social recreation, which, no doubt, explains its absence from the body of these memoirs.—Ed.

The parade was most interesting and impressive, first of all, from the mere point of view of its happening, of its actual taking place. A public parade of Jews in a non-Jewish city was a startling thing, which was probably occurring for the first time in thousands of years. Jews in the Diaspora have always shrunk from publicity, have avoided obtruding themselves on public notice as much as they could. They had abundantly good reasons for this. The fact that they now came out in the open, parading and rejoicing in the sight of all men, was a proof that times had changed, that the ages in which Israel withdrew from the world and lived in seclusion and obscurity had passed away forever. Whether the change was for good or evil could not then be told. The parade was especially remarkable because of the evident deep emotion which pervaded all the participants. Epoch-making events rouse great emotion in the hearts of all people. The triumphant ending of a great war will naturally rouse the enthusiasm of the citizens of the victorious nation or nations. But victory or national triumph does not mean to the *Ummoth Ha-Olam,* the Gentile peoples of the world, sweet though it be, what *"geulah,"* redemption, means to the homeless, helpless Jew, a wandering exile for century after century. And so his emotion, his joy and gladness when redemption comes, as those poor people thought it had come at that time, are infinitely deep and potent.

The parade was remarkable because of the very appearance, the physical types of the people composing it. Anyone who thought that the Jews are a homogeneous race, of one fixed "Jewish" type, only needed to look at that parade to recognize his error. There were people of the most diverse ethnic types marching in that parade. Some of the men resembled, in complexion, features, and bodily build, Slavs or Teutons, others were strongly suggestive of Arabs or other Orientals, and a few were practically identical in appearance with the swarthy natives of Africa. But they were all Jews, most earnestly and enthusiastically so. What better proof could there be that not physical but spiritual and ideological characteristics are the determining factors of nationality, that not the hue of the skin or the shape of the skull but the beliefs and ideals and aspirations of a man decide to what human group he must be considered as belonging!

I noticed these facts, and they confirmed in me the views which

I had always held on this much disputed subject. This is perhaps the right place for me to speak of my attitude toward Zionism or the Zionistic movement, to which I have not hitherto referred in this book. In my very boyhood, before the organized movement now known as Zionism had ever come into existence, I already adhered to the basic concepts of that movement. These are, to state them in a nutshell, that Judaism is a religion, or rather, *the* religion; that the Jewish people are, or were, a nation and may become such again, and that Palestine is the land designated by Divine fiat for the national life of Israel. There are many details of significance in these doctrines which cannot be fully elucidated here, as the subject of this writing is merely biographical but not explicatory of all subjects touched upon in the course of the narrative. Suffice it to say, therefore, that what may be called the Zionistic concepts of Judaism do not imply that Judaism is limited to the descendants of one race or people, that it is what Goldwin Smith sarcastically called a "tribal cult."

It was given historically to a nation descended from a common ancestor or ancestors, but it is, in the fullest sense, a universal religion, adapted to satisfy the spiritual needs of all human beings and open to all human beings who desire to enter. Neither does the nationhood of Israel imply that those Jews who are citizens or subjects of non-Jewish states nevertheless belong to a Jewish political national entity. As far as the diaspora is concerned, Jewish nationality is a matter of theory, or rather, of religious faith. Politically the Jews of the diaspora are nationals only of the nations to which they owe political allegiance.

I did not take any active part in the political workings of Zionism. Nor did I remain entirely outside of Zionistic activity, but my participation was in accordance with my concept of my task, spiritual and cultural.

I frequently stressed the Zionistic concepts in my sermons. I addressed a number of public gatherings in behalf of the movement, and I wrote several articles on Zionistic themes. One of the best known of these articles was entitled *"The Boundaries of Palestine from the Viewpoint of a Jewish National Home,"* which I read first as a lecture before the Jewish Academy of Arts and Sciences in New York and which was published in *Israel's Messenger* of Shanghai,

China, in 1933.* I also contributed to the *Jewish World* of London an article entitled *"Why the Mizrachi?"* explaining the reasons for the existence of the *Mizrachi* as a separate Zionist body, and an article on the same theme for the souvenir volume published in commemoration of the twenty-fifth anniversary of the *Mizrachi* organization of America.

I deviated somewhat from my attitude toward Zionism by becoming one of the founders of the American Mizrachi and accepting membership on its board of directors. But that was for a very special reason. The general Zionists looked upon the movement too much in the light of a secular undertaking. They did not give sufficient consideration to the fundamental importance of the religious element.

The Mizrachi Organization was formed for the express purpose of preserving the religious character of Zionism. The difference between the two organizations is shown by the difference between their two mottos or slogans. The slogan of the general Zionists is, "The Land of Israel for the People of Israel." That of the Mizrachi is, "The Land of Israel for the People of Israel in Accordance with the Torah of Israel." My views were so completely in accord with those of the Mizrachi that, although I retained my membership in the general Zionist body, I felt it my duty to assist in the organization of the Mizrachi and to accept official position in it. But I never became really active** in its affairs nor a leader in its councils. My relation to the Mizrachi was and is that of sympathy and agreement but not of active participation.

Toward the close of 1923 a committee, headed by Mr. Gustavus A. Rogers, was formed to tender me the honor of a public testimonial dinner. Mr. William Rosenberg acted as secretary of the committee.

---

* The author used to receive "*Israel's Messenger*" regularly, and he read it faithfully and with enthusiastic interest. It seems that there was a large and prosperous community of Jews, mostly Sephardic, in the Chinese city. At one time, the newspaper published some correspondence with the Rev. Dr. D. De Sola Pool of New York. The family thus discovered, indirectly and with amazement, that the Shanghai community had asked Dr. Pool to sound out Rabbi Drachman with a view to his serving as their spiritual leader. Dr. Pool had replied, as reported in the paper, that, as Rabbi Drachman had "a large family of small children," his removal to the Orient was out of the question. His deduction was, of course, correct.—Ed.

**An understatement, as he was at one time President of the American Mizrachi.—Ed.

Continued Activities for Judaism

The dinner took place at the Hotel Astor on the twenty-first of January, 1924, and was attended by a goodly throng, among them a number of persons, both Jewish and Gentile, of prominence and importance in the community. Others, who were unavoidably absent, indicated their participation by telegrams. The addresses of the speakers have not been preserved, but a few of the letters of acceptance and of the telegrams are still extant and will show the spirit of the participants.

The following letter came from the president of Columbia University, Dr. Nicholas Murray Butler.

November 14, 1923

My dear Mr Rosenberg
I have your letter of November 13 and am very glad indeed to learn that a movement is on foot to make public recognition of the long and devoted service to religion and to humanity of my friend and collegemate, the Rev. Dr. Bernard Drachman. I shall, of course, be happy to serve. . . .
Very truly yours,
Nicholas Murray Butler

The following letter of acceptance was sent by Joseph Barondess. Mr. Barondess, as those New Yorkers who remember the history of the American metropolis in those years will recall, was the outstanding Jewish labor leader of the period and a man of high culture and great ability.

November 10th, 1923

My dear Mr. Rosenberg
Nothing in the world will give me greater pleasure than to be able to serve in my humble capacity, to do honor to Rev. Dr. Bernard Drachman. I know of no rabbi in the City of New York, and, for that matter, in this country, who has rendered greater service to the cause of true Judaism and Jewish scholarship. I know of no rabbi who has done the Jewish people greater honor by his pure and honorable life, by his unselfish service to the cause of Judaism, in general, and humanity, at large, than did Dr. Drachman.
It will, indeed, be an honor and a privilege to serve in any

capacity that I can, to do ourselves honor by honoring Dr. Drachman. With best wishes for the success of the undertaking, I beg to remain,

Very cordially yours,

Joseph Barondess

There were numerous others—from Mr. Bernard Downing, then Democratic leader in the Senate of New York State, from Professor Richard Gottheil, from Mr. Adolph Lewisohn |("Dr. Drachman deserves the greatest admiration for the splendid work . . ."), from Dr. Revel ("Sabbath, the greatest gift of Judaism to humanity . . . , has in Dr. Drachman its greatest exponent . . ."), from Rev. Dr. Samuel Schulman ("I join in the community's recognition of Dr. Drachman's scholarship, spiritual leadership and distinguished service to God and Israel"), and many more.

As the central figure of the occasion it was, of course, incumbent upon me to make fitting response to the addresses and other expressions of appreciation and good will extended to me. I did so in a formal address, an abstract of which has been preserved. It gives an excellent picture of my sentiments on this occasion and is also my only public statement of my concept of the work to which I had dedicated myself. It shall, therefore, be recorded here.

ABSTRACT OF REMARKS BY REV. DR. BERNARD DRACHMAN AT THE TESTIMONIAL DINNER TENDERED TO HIM AT HOTEL ASTOR, JANUARY 21, 1924.

My very, very dear Friends:

I am deeply grateful to you all for the friendship and kindly sentiments towards me which your presence here this evening denotes and to the speakers in particular for the sympathetic and flattering words which they have spoken. I cannot feel that these kind words of appreciation have any relation to my personality as such, but only to the work in behalf of Judaism and humanity which I have been privileged in some slight measure to perform. I am vividly conscious of the fact that whatever I have been able to do in furtherance of the spiritual and ethical interests of mankind in general and Israel in particular has been most insignificant over against the tremendous vastness of what should and might be done. Even the little I have done could not have been accomplished but for the earnest and faithful cooperation of many sincere and unselfish co-workers.

I want to pay here my tribute of gratitude and appreciation to these loyal and untiring co-laborers in the cause of Jewish ideals and the betterment of human relations. And I want to pay my particular tribute to my beloved wife, whose unswerving attachment and friendly counsel have been a source of strength and encouragement in many an hour of despondency, when the task I had taken upon myself seemed hopeless and impossible of fulfillment. I do not want to speak of myself, or what I have or have not accomplished. But I do want to speak of the things in which I have been and am interested, for I feel that they are of vast and fundamental importance within and without the Jewish pale, that they are things which we should all desire to see realized.

To state it briefly, I have always been deeply impressed by the Talmudic saying, "On three things the world stands: on the study of the Law, the service of God, and the doing of acts of benevolence." Expressed in modern phrase, this means that three things are the moral basis of human society: education, religion, and charity. In these three things I have always been deeply interested. They are the things which make men truly human, which make Jews truly Jewish. Education is the first requisite in raising men above the level of the beast; only as men acquire scientific knowledge can they control the forces of nature and develop civilization; only as they acquire spiritual and ethical knowledge can they control their animal instincts and savage cravings. Religion raises human character to its finest and loftiest heights, fills our souls with the purest emotions of unselfish love and loyalty and with sublime aspirations for union with the Divine. Charity is the tender sentiment of sympathy with the needy and afflicted, of altruistic realization of the sufferings of the unfortunate which causes the prosperous to assist those less happily situated and makes life on earth possible and endurable for myriads.

In the realization of these three ideals lies the totality of Jewish duty. I have done what I could in my humble way to promote and further them, to disseminate Jewish education, to strengthen Jewish faith and observance, and to bring about a response to the cry of the needy, which alas in our time is so intense and urgent. Realizing, alas, that the workers for religion are so few, I have felt it my especial duty to labor in its behalf.

That is why I have devoted so much time and effort to the promotion of Sabbath observance, which is the heart and central feature of Jewish observance.

In all my efforts I have always realized that I am an American and that we American Jews owe a special debt of love and gratitude to our dear America. But there is one thing I must say before concluding and that is really my message to my brethren to-night. It is that we American Jews need unity. The three ideals which I have pictured to you to-night can only be properly carried out if the vast Jewish community of America works together. I think such united action is possible, despite the differences which exist in our ranks. The Federation shows the possibility of such united action, but the Federation is limited to one task, charity. I believe that the other two great domains, education and religion, can be included in the scope of one vast Federation, if we approach the task in the spirit of fairness, mutual tolerance, and brotherliness. May all Israel be speedily united in the task of carrying out the ideals which devolve on all Israel!

The audience, by generous applause, showed its approval of the sentiments which I had expressed. After the conclusion of the banquet a number of guests spoke to me, to express their individual agreement with my views and their good wishes for the continued success of my work, and the affair was amply reported in the press.

In 1924 I contributed to an international work of Jewish scholarship of great importance. This was a collection of essays describing the achievements of Jews in all the various fields of human endeavor. The work was gotten up in London under the supervision of H. Newman. Each essay was written by an authority on that particular topic. The Chief Rabbi, Dr. Joseph H. Hertz, contributed a Prefatory Note and the Foreword or Introduction was written by Israel Zangwill.

My essay was on the theme *"The Jew and Philosophy."* I treated my theme historically, describing the role of philosophic thought in Israel from the earliest times up to the present. The work appeared early in 1925 under the title *"The Real Jew."* For thoughtful readers it certainly supplied ample evidence of the important part which Jews have taken in the upbuilding of civilization.

It is desirable, therefore, that such books as *"The Real Jew"* be written and published and disseminated as widely as possible. If circulated to anything like the extent to which the scurrilous and calumnious writings of the anti-Semites are, they would serve a most useful, indeed, an indispensable purpose, by refuting these calumnies and spreading a just appraisal of the Jewish people—that is all the Jews ask—everywhere on earth.

Chapter Thirty-nine

Tragedy Comes to Me

A Glance at Canadian Jewry

THE YEAR 1925 WAS FOR ME A YEAR OF TRAGEDY. EARLY IN THAT year, in the month of February, the Angel of Death made his fell visit to our happy home and took the apple of my eye, the treasure of my heart, my beloved wife. Words are utterly impotent to describe the greatness of my loss, the intensity of the tragedy which befell me. To portray in some measure the vastness of my affliction I must quote the words which the prophet Jeremiah uses to picture for Israel the downfall of the Temple and the Holy City: "For great as the sea is thy breach; who can heal thee?" As the sea, which, in the view of the ancients, was without end, and like a sickness for which there is no healing, so was the sorrow of Israel when that which was most precious in his national existence was taken from him. And so was my sorrow when she who had been the crown of my head and the joy of my life closed her gentle, loving eyes forever.

We had been married thirty-seven years. In all that time there had never been a quarrel or dispute of any kind between us, no unfriendly interchange of words, not even, as far as I can recall, the slightest misunderstanding. She had presented me with eight children, six sons and two daughters, all of whom (with the exception of our first-born, a boy, who died as an infant of four months) grew up, thanks to her loving care and devotion, in health and vigor. As they came, unlike many American mothers who cannot tolerate the idea of a large family, she greeted them all with the same unvarying love and tenderness. Her eighth child was as dear and precious to her as her first.

Her end was startlingly sudden and utterly unexpected. She had always been exceptionally well and strong. Never, to the best of my remembrance, had she suffered a day's ill health, previous to her last and fatal illness. Since she was my junior by four years, I had no other thought but that she would survive me. About the beginning of February she began to suffer from listlessness and sudden attacks of weakness. She did not believe she was ill and tried to attend to her household duties in her accustomed manner. I as well as the other members of the family besought her to go to bed and have a physician called, but she insisted her weakness would pass away of itself, and refused.

On the eighth of the month her weakness increased to an alarming extent. We then insisted that she must go to bed, while we summoned our family physician, Dr. Carl Goldmark. She yielded to our importunities. No sooner did her body touch the couch than she fell into a deep coma, from which she did not again emerge.

Three days she lay in coma, and on the eleventh of February her pure soul departed from its earthly habitation. Dr. Goldmark had associated with him two or three other physicians, whose names I no longer recall. They gave their utmost efforts to her case but were helpless. Frankly, it baffled them. They were unable to state with positiveness what the disease was. To the best of my understanding from their words, they thought it some form of pneumonia.

I will omit the details of the funeral and the "shivah," the seven days of confined mourning. When it was all over, a dreadful sense of loneliness and forlornness overcame me. My only consolation was in my religious faith. I recognized that all human beings are in the hands of a Higher Power, that just as we cannot decide the time of our entrance into earthly existence, so also we cannot fix the time of our departure therefrom and that our only fitting attitude is one of uncomplaining submission to the decrees of the Higher Power. But the recognition and the submission did not diminish the pain nor remove the sense of loneliness and forsakenness. Whenever I entered a place where she had been accustomed to be, in our home or synagogue or anywhere else, I would imagine that she was there, and the discovery of her absence and the realization of its reason would come to me as a sudden shock. I began to shun the places where we had been so happy together and from which her dear presence was forever departed.

Under these circumstances the thought of accepting another position and removing to another city, a thought which I had hitherto always rejected, seemed not only acceptable but even desirable. Just about this time, in the early spring of 1925, there came to me a communication from the Hebrew Congregation of Toronto, the second largest city of Canada, inviting me to preach in their synagogue, with a view of becoming their rabbi. In the then state of my feelings this invitation was very welcome. I secured permission from the board of trustees of the Congregation *Zichron Ephraim* to absent myself over the two opening days of the Passover festival and I went to Toronto in accordance with the invitation. As I did not desire to travel alone, I was accompanied by my youngest son, Theodore.

My experience in Toronto was most agreeable and had, indeed, a great effect in diverting my thoughts into other channels and thus diminishing, though not utterly dispelling, my sorrow. The congregation is a large and important one and worshipped in a correspondingly large and fine synagogue, and the officers and leading members did all in their power to make my stay and that of my son as pleasant as possible. They did not permit us to stay at a hotel but assigned us to the hospitable care of Mr. Nathan Smith, a prominent member of the congregation, and his charming family. The Smith family occupied a roomy and beautifully furnished private house on St. George Street, Number 124, I believe. They placed two comfortable rooms at the disposition of Theodore and myself, providing, of course, also for our meals.

The family consisted of the father, Mr. Smith, who was a widower, and several sons and daughters, all of them cultured and refined and sincerely devoted to Traditional Judaism. Of the children I recall best the oldest son, Dr. Rupert, a prominent physician in Toronto, Meyer, active in his father's business, a very gentle and lovable character, and Lillian, deeply interested in Jewish social work and prominent in the Jewish Girl Scouts of Toronto. It may also be mentioned that the Smith family, a very wealthy one, possessed a beautiful summer home and estate at Poplar Hill on the shore of Lake Ontario, where they exercised a gracious and charming hospitality.

At the *Seder* home service on the first two evenings of Passover, at

THE TRUSTEES OF COLUMBIA UNIVERSITY
IN THE CITY OF NEW YORK
TO ALL PERSONS TO WHOM THESE PRESENTS MAY COME GREETING
BE IT KNOWN THAT
Reverend Doctor Bernard Drachman
HAS BEEN AWARDED
THE UNIVERSITY MEDAL
IN ACCORDANCE WITH THE PROVISIONS OF THE RULES OF THE
UNIVERSITY GOVERNING SUCH AWARD
IN WITNESS WHEREOF WE HAVE CAUSED THIS DIPLOMA TO BE SIGNED
BY THE PRESIDENT OF THE UNIVERSITY AND OUR CORPORATE SEAL TO BE
HERETO AFFIXED IN THE CITY OF NEW YORK ON THE *Third*
DAY OF *June* IN THE YEAR OF OUR LORD ONE THOUSAND NINE
HUNDRED AND FORTY *One*

Certificate Accompanying the University Medal

Columbia University Medal

Obverse

Reverse

which all the family were assembled, Mr. Smith requested me to conduct the service, which I did with the assistance of Theodore. They were much impressed and pleased, indeed delighted, with our rendition of the *Seder* ritual, especially with our chanting of the hymns, the melodies of which were quite unknown to them. On the two mornings of Passover, I addressed the congregation in the synagogue. The sacred edifice was filled to capacity, and my sermons were very well received.

On leaving Toronto on the morning of the day after the festival, a large delegation of the congregation was present in the railroad station to see me off, and I was assured that the matter of my election would be taken up in the meeting of the congregation, which would take place in *Chol Ha-Moed,* on one of the intermediary days of the festival.

They were as good as their word. A few days after the festival I received in New York an official communication from the Toronto Hebrew Congregation informing me that I had been elected their rabbi for a term of years and at a handsome salary. But now my point of view had changed. Despite my sorrow at the loss of my beloved wife, or rather, because of it, I felt that I must not leave the place which it seemed that Providence had assigned to me for my life work. My children were now in the years of early manhood and womanhood or of adolescence. They had more or less found their way in life and would not be able to accompany me to a new region. They would be left entirely to themselves, and the separation might bring about a certain degree of estrangement.

I felt, therefore, that I could not take a step which might entail such consequences. Regretfully indeed, because Toronto and its Jewish community had made a very favorable impression upon me and I was confident that I would find there a most fruitful field of activity, I yielded to what I conceived to be the duty of the hour. I answered the congregation, thanking them for the honor they had desired to confer upon me but regretting that circumstances made it impossible for me to accept it.

Before leaving this theme, I desire to record briefly some of the impressions which Toronto and Canadian Jewry in general had made upon me. First, the congregation whose guest I had been was, in many respects, an ideal Jewish congregation. It combined splendidly loyal adherence to the traditions and due consideration of the requirements of the modern age.

There were many individuals and families of the type of the Smith family, whose outstanding qualities I have already described. For example, there was the Pullan family, who were living demonstrations of pure, sincere and vivid Judaism. Mr. Pullan, the father, was a true Hebrew patriarch, dignified, soft-spoken and quiet, but highly intelligent in speech. He conveyed in all his words and actions the impression of lofty ethical and spiritual ideals and utter sincerity. His family of sons and daughters, pervaded with the same spirit, were worthy scions of such a progenitor. From some of the Toronto people, not from Mr. Pullan himself, I heard that he was not only very greatly in favor of calling me to the Toronto rabbinate but had also the plan of uniting the Canadian congregations into one community and making me their head as chief rabbi, after the British model. My admiration of Mr. Pullan was not due to that circumstance, but it undeniably added to the keenness of my regret that it was not my privilege to live with and labor among such sincere and noble Jews.

Canadian Jewry impressed me mainly through the circumstance that, although such close neighbors of the United States, they were greatly different from our American Jewry. They are really what they are officially supposed to be, a segment of the Jewish community of Great Britain. The division into three fragments, Orthodox, Conservative, and Reform, to say nothing of the host of those unaffiliated with any form of Jewish religion, which is the sickness and misfortune of the Jewry of the United States, is practically unknown in Canada. There are a few Reform congregations and radical groups, whose existence is due to the inevitable influence of Canada's huge neighbor. By and large, however, Canadian Jewry adheres to the example set by the parent community of Great Britain and is unswervingly loyal to Traditional Judaism. It is a dignified, loyal, and energetic branch of what Professor Schechter used to call "Catholic Israel." I was very happy to see such a splendid and valuable contingent of adherents of our ancient faith on this side of the Atlantic. I could not help wishing, with a pang of regret in my soul, that the same spirit had pervaded our great community in the United States.

Then there would be practically no limit to the blessed influence which American Jewry could exercise on Judaism and Jewish conditions the world over.

The British influence is also recognizable in the speech, manners, and appearance of Canadians in general, including the Jews. Canadians, generally speaking, look, speak, and act like their British cousins. But here there is the counteracting influence of the United States, and so, while the resemblance is close, it is not perfect. In the last analysis, Canadians are not only British. They are also Americans.

The year 1925 marked the completion of thirty-five years since the organization of Congregation *Zichron Ephraim*. The congregation decided to commemorate the event by a fitting celebration. The celebration took place in the month of March. Religious services in the synagogue were followed by a banquet in Vienna Hall, a very popular hall in those days, situated at the corner of Lexington Avenue and Fifty-eighth Street. A large gathering of members and friends attended. I was in doubt at first as to whether I should attend, in view of my recent bereavement, but finally decided that, as spiritual leader of the congregation, it was a matter of official duty for me to preside at a congregational celebration of this kind. I did my duty to the fullest extent of my power, but it was, naturally, impossible for me to enter into the full spirit of the occasion, and therefore, while the congregation rejoiced in the auspicious event and I participated with them, in reality my feelings were the reverse of joyful. It was, however, a cause of satisfaction to me to notice the ready willingness with which members and their families participated in the celebration and their evident pride and delight in their congregation. That was ample compensation for many an hour of doubt and uncertainty and of strenuous toil and effort.

Chapter Forty

A Trip to the Holy Land

The Mizrachi Conference in Antwerp

IN 1926 I CARRIED OUT A PLAN WHICH I HAD LONG CHERISHED, TO visit the land which had witnessed the birth of Israel and Israel's faith, Palestine. The fulfillment of this hope was undoubtedly hastened by the demise of my dear wife and my increased awareness of the uncertainty of mortal existence. I determined not to put off any longer the fulfillment of my ardent desire to behold with my own eyes the land where the cradle of Judaism had stood, where the prophets and sages of Israel had performed their sublime work, and where the stirring events recorded in Biblical and post-Biblical history had occurred. To this I subsequently added the plan of attending the world conference of the *Mizrachi* organization at Antwerp as germane to a trip to Palestine.

I decided, therefore, to devote the nine weeks of my summer vacation to these purposes. Nine weeks are a rather limited time for such a double purpose. Aerial travel, which makes the most distant places unbelievably near and the time of travel unbelievably short, was not yet known. I was, therefore, obliged to select the quickest possible route for my journey, although that meant considerable exertion. Accordingly I sailed on June 30, 1926, by the steamship *Mauretania* for Cherbourg, thence to Paris, and thence, by a twenty-six-hour railroad trip, to Trieste in Italy. There we, my son Theodore and I, took the Mediterranean Lloyd Triestino steamer *Vienna* to Alexandria, Egypt, thence by train to Cairo, and on the following day we traveled by train to Jerusalem, which we reached on the morning of July 14th.

By taking this route, although it lasted fifteen days, we saved about a week. The direct ocean trip from New York required, at that time, approximately three weeks. On the *Mauretania* were two fellow-travelers of great importance in the Jewish development of Palestine, Rev. Dr. D. de Sola Pool, who held for several years an official position in the Zionist organization in Jerusalem, and Mrs. Sol Rosenbloom, widow of the lamented and unforgettable Sol Rosenbloom of Pittsburgh. Mrs. Rosenbloom was the donor of the largest individual gift to the Hebrew University in Jerusalem, the princely sum of half a million dollars.

We utilized the brief time at our disposal in Egypt for a visit to the pyramids, the Sphinx, the Cairo Museum, and the historic Cairo synagogue. Egypt, too, makes a profound impression upon the thoughtful Jewish visitor. The wonderful relics of Egyptian antiquity. visible in the land and preserved in the museum. show conclusively that the civilization of ancient Egypt was of a very high order. It is striking, also, to reflect that this great empire, perhaps the mightiest empire of its time, has been utterly obliterated and extinguished, and that its ancient glories are a mere memory, while Israel, the weak and humble shepherd band whom the haughty Pharaohs despised and enslaved, still exists and is, in all probability, about to enter upon a new period of national existence in its historic homeland. Recalling that this tiny people has exercised a most extraordinary influence upon humanity in general and that its book of sacred lore has become the revered Bible of the civilized world, one is forced to the conclusion that a Divine Power has upheld Israel in its manifold tribulations, has saved it from the apparently insuperable perils which so often threatened its very existence, and has preserved it for some great and wondrous destiny.

Early in the morning of July 14th our train reached the southern district of Palestine, and I at once began to recognize those characteristics which distinguish this land from all others. There appears to be no doubt that the present Arab inhabitants have preserved in many ways the ancient features of the land. The animals so familiar from Biblical narratives are still its typical fauna. Caravans of camels loaded with all sorts of freight still traverse its roads. Sheep, goats, and patient little donkeys abound everywhere. The Arab *fellah* still plows his field with a primitive plowshare and is frequently guilty of violating the Biblical precept. "Thou shalt not plow with an ox and an ass together." Replicas of Rebecca at the well may be seen at every village.

To the visitor who knows his Bible, especially in the Hebrew original, a visit to Palestine is most illuminating. He sees the actuality of that which he had only half comprehended through Bible reading. As I traveled through the land, Bible verses which I had never properly understood became intelligible. The evidences of the new period which were manifest also created a profound impression. The Hebrew language is one of the three official languages of the land, the other two being English and Arabic. The railroad stations bore signs giving the names of the places in all three tongues. The Hebrew terms used are derived from the Bible and Jewish antiquity, and it seemed most extraordinary to read station names like En-Sorek, Lud, and Bethar. I realized, as never before, that here lived a great nation and that ties of the most intimate kind bind all Jews and, indeed, all people whose faith is built upon the Bible, to the life which was lived here when Israel was young. Years and centuries lose their significance.

But the sights were not all pleasing. This section of the country is quite bare and arid. The mountains of Judah, through which the train now pulled, are bleak and rugged with very little green upon their stony sides, and I realized that I was in a land which has been almost as much persecuted as the people belonging to it, upon which the Romans wreaked their insensate fury and which Turk and Arab did little to improve. But now the train entered the station of Jerusalem, and my eyes and thoughts were directed to the contemplation of the Holy City of the world.

Jerusalem! What a glamor lies in that name! With what words can I describe the emotions of a Jew whose feet, for the first time, stand upon that sacred soil! In vision he beholds again the Temple standing upon Zion's height, the priests and Levites conducting its solemn services, the vast multitudes of Israelites thronging its outer courts, the kings of Israel sitting upon their royal thrones, and the sages and lawgivers assembled in the sessions of the Sanhedrin! The contrast of former glory with the present condition of Jewish suffering and humiliation in so many countries of the *Galuth* is, of course, most painful. My heart throbbed and my eyes filled with tears, as these thoughts came rushing to my mind.

I found Jerusalem full alike of relics of Israel's great past and of the strong, vigorous, pulsating Jewish life of the present.

The chief surviving structure of Jewish antiquity is the *Kothel Maaravi,* the West Wall of the Temple, or "Wailing Wall" as it is known to the non-Jews, whither our brethren repair on Fridays before Sabbath and on other occasions. I was in Jerusalem on *Tishah Be'av,* the ninth of Ab, the anniversary of the destruction of the Temple, and never will I forget the sight which my eyes then beheld. A dense throng, estimated at from twenty to thirty thousand, filled the narrow space before the West Wall, the majority evidently brought there by deep sorrow for Israel's downfall, others by historic sentiment or curiosity. Unable to force myself through the throng, I went for services to the historic synagogue of Judah He-Chasid, also known as the Churvah Synagogue.

Present-day Jerusalem is a hive of Jewish activity, religious, charitable, and Zionistic. There are numerous *Yeshivoth, Talmud Torahs,* and other schools, hospitals, homes for the aged and infirm and other institutions, both of the old *Yishuv* and of the new. I shall not single out any for special mention in order to make no invidious distinctions. They certainly all appeared to be doing excellent work and to be really indispensable. I shall, however, narrate an incident which occurred in one of the hospitals which I visited, not in order to describe that particular institution, which shall remain unnamed, but because of the element of involuntary humor contained in the incident or perhaps the lesson which it may teach.

The hospital in question is a fine institution, maintained by a great American-Jewish organization and conducted in accordance with the most modern scientific and hygienic principles. The nurses are as fine a group of young women as I have seen anywhere, clad in snow-white uniforms, and evidently thoroughly acquainted with their profession. The language used in the hospital is the Hebrew, and everyone connected appeared to speak Israel's ancient tongue with perfect fluency.

The superintendent placed one of the nurses at my disposal to show me around the hospital. She conducted me through the various wards and rooms and, as we walked, she explained everything to me in Hebrew. I asked a number of questions in the same tongue, and she gave me full and explicit answers in a clear and almost classical Hebrew, which, I believe, our ancestors would have understood very well. Suddenly she stood still and, looking at me with an expression of surprise upon her face, said to me, "*Me-hechan kevodo yodea ledaber Ivrith?*" ("How does your Honor come to know how to speak Hebrew?")

"I am a rabbi," I answered. "Should not a rabbi be able to speak Hebrew?"

"Why, yes," she answered, evidently dissatisfied with my answer. "We expect that usually but not of an American rabbi." Such is the reputation which our American spiritual leaders enjoy in the Holy Land.

At the conclusion of our eight days' stay in Jerusalem, I hired an automobile, a chauffeur, and a guide, both native Palestinian Jews, and made a trip, accompanied by Theodore, through the entire country, almost literally "from Dan to Beer Sheba." We saw practically everything of importance, both from the historic and the modern points of view. This, of course, would have been impossible, in the time at my disposal, but for the use of the automobile. Incidentally, it may be remarked that automobiles were already abundant in Palestine, mainly in the possession of Jews, but the Arabs were already beginning to use them. There were also many good roads, largely of recent construction by the Jewish *chalutzim*. I visited even the specifically non-Jewish towns, such as Bethlehem, Nazareth, and Shechem. The last named, now known as Nablus, possesses Jewish interest, through the presence therein of the Samaritans.

My two attendants, under whose supervision and guidance I made the trip, were both interesting characters and gave a touch of the amusing to it. The chauffeur was a true son of Palestine, a fluent speaker of the Arabic and thoroughly imbued, although a Jew, with the native Arab characteristics. He showed his Arabism mainly by entering into violent controversies with most of the travelers whom we met on the road, in which both parties hurled at each other extreme objurgations and imprecations in choice Arabic.

One particularly emphatic instance was when we ran into a large caravan which filled the road and the leader of the caravan had difficulty in getting the camels out of the way of our automobile. This slowed our progress and filled our chauffeur with rage, who, thereupon, poured a shower of invectives upon the caravan head, who returned them with equal vigor and emphasis. This, I understand, is a favorite method of expressing differences of opinion among the inhabitants of the Near East. My Arabic was not good enough to enable me to understand what the quarreling parties were saying, but one of the imprecations which, I believe, our chauffeur hurled at his opponent was the reputedly traditional Arabic malediction *Yuddal dul Ummak,* "May thy mother's shadow grow thin!"

I was sorry for these controversies and saw no reason for them, but they were interesting to me for two reasons. First, they showed how thoroughly these immigrant Jews had become assimilated to their environment—our chauffeur, for instance, was the son of parents who had come from Russia—and secondly, his utter absence of fear was proof conclusive that the relations between Jews and Arabs were not so bad as some people reported.

The guide was of an entirely different type. He had acquired a considerable knowledge of English, which he was constantly endeavoring to air, and I think, although he did not say so, that he had a secret desire to get to America. His English propensity was a source of some embarrassment to me. Being in Palestine, I wanted to practice my Hebrew, but whenever the guide explained anything to us, he would do so in English and he would also answer in that tongue when I addressed him in Hebrew. However, he was otherwise a pleasant and well-mannered young fellow and we got on excellently together.

Thus we saw the work which the Jews have done in Palestine, and it is indeed wonderful. They do not as yet own a very large part of the land—only about seven or eight per cent—but the Jewish impress was already, at the time of my visit, very manifest. The agricultural communities then numbered upward of a hundred, and many of them, particularly the older ones, seemed to be doing very well. The beneficent influence of the generous, helping hand of Baron Edmond de Rothschild—the *Nadib* or "Princely Benefactor," as Palestinian Jews call him—was here very recognizable. The magnificent wineries at Rishon Le-Zion are an enduring memorial to his munificence and Jewish sentiment. Some of the settlements have developed into fair-sized towns. Pethach Tikvah, for instance, had, at that time, about seven thousand inhabitants.

Best of all, the presence of our brethren means everywhere higher culture and improved conditions. The Jews, to cite one instance, have introduced the eucalyptus tree, which has dried up, and thus has banished malaria from, thousands of acres of swampy land. Because of this the eucalyptus is styled by the Arabs *Shajar Al-Yahud*, "the Jewish tree." The contrast between Arab villages and Jewish colonies, as I saw it, was extraordinary. Here mud hovels, devoid of the most elementary comfort, unsanitary conditions, and slovenly fields; there, neat, though simple, homes with sanitary arrangements and modern improvements, well cared for, and smiling fields, gardens, and orchards.

A great development was then going on in the Emek—the valley of Jezreel—where a very large and fertile tract, about a hundred thousand acres in extent, had been shortly before acquired. The Zionists rightly stress the importance of agricultural development, but in some respects the town-building activity of the Jew is more remarkable than their agricultural colonization. In the older cities of the land, Jerusalem, Tiberias, and Haifa, new Jewish districts, composed of substantial stone houses and provided with excellent streets and parks and light and water supply, were being built.

Tel Aviv was already a fine modern city of about forty thousand inhabitants, with every prospect of speedily reaching the hundred thousand mark, which, as is well known, it has since greatly exceeded. To give employment and provide for the needs of the rapidly increasing population, a number of important industrial enterprises had been established, and more were planned.

Land values had risen extraordinarily, too high indeed, for the establishment of new colonies was rendered thereby increasingly difficult. A story told me by a Russian Jew whom I met in Safed shows this strikingly. This gentleman had been a wealthy merchant in Moscow before the war. He had not taken any particular interest in Palestine but had been induced to invest a few thousand rubles in the purchase of land in the colony of Migdal on the shore of Lake

Tiberias, more as a sign of sympathy with his brethren than as an act of Zionistic conviction. He put his deed aside and thought no more of the matter.

When the Bolsheviki came into power in Russia, they confiscated all his possessions. In one day, from a millionaire he became a penniless pauper. He then remembered that he owned some land in Palestine and decided to go there in the hope of being able to erect a humble home on his land, thus providing a roof over his head and the heads of his family. When, after considerable difficulty, he reached Migdal, he found that his land had so increased in value that he again became comfortably well off.

Ever since the inception of the Jewish National Home plan, reports had been current of the intense antagonism of the Arabs to the project and of their resultant hostility to the Jewish immigrants. I failed to discover any indications of such hostility. I cannot deny that when, in the course of my trip, I first entered an Arab village, I felt quite uneasy. It was only natural to apprehend that, if the reported Arab hostility to Jews really existed, the visit of a rabbi and two Jewish companions to an Arab settlement would be a matter of personal danger to the unwelcome visitors. But not even a scowl or a frown was visible. Everywhere we saw smiling countenances and heard friendly *"Salaams!"* and *"Shaloms!"* I personally was greeted with the utmost deference. The chief concern of the villagers seemed to be to sell picture postcards of their villages and other scenes of the Holy Land, and they did not worry about the religion or nationality of their prospective customers.

A number of Palestinian Jews, well acquainted with the conditions of the land, with whom I discussed this subject, assured me that the only Arab hostility to the Jewish settlement was on the part of the *effendis,* or wealthy landed proprietors, who, previous to the coming of the Jews, had been able to utilize the labor of the *fellahin* at absurdly low wages but were no longer able to do so. The poorer classes, on the other hand, I was told, recognized in the coming of the Jews a great benefit to themselves, that they now had better paid work and improved conditions in many respects. My own observations tended to confirm these statements.

Similarly unfavorable reports have been circulated concerning the religious conditions prevailing in Palestine under the new regime. It has been stated that religious laxity and the desecration of the holiest precepts of Judaism prevailed to a frightful extent. These evil reports have caused some of our sincerest and most loyal Jews to see in Zionism and in the new Jewish settlement in Palestine a grave danger to the Jewish faith.

While appreciating the sentiments of these loyal brethren, my observations did not permit me to share their apprehensions. I found the atmosphere of Palestine emphatically religious, or, let us say, Jewish. The Sabbath was universally observed. If there was Sabbath desecration, it was very little in evidence. I saw none of it. The Torah was earnestly studied in the *Yeshivoth* by disciples whose number must have amounted to many thousands. There were various religious elements ranging from the rigidly orthodox Jews of the old *Yishuv* to the utterly irreligious members of the radical *Kevutzoth*, but these latter were greatly in the minority. The overwhelming majority of the Jewish people of Palestine were unquestionably loyal to the ancient faith. However, it must be admitted that the radical groups make a most unpleasing impression upon all those Jews who consider Judaism an essential part of Jewish life. However, the influence of the Palestinian environment in bringing all those subject to it closer to true Jewishness is very strong. There is reason to believe that the radicals, or, if not they, their children, will yield to its spell. I was told that this effect of the *Eretz Israel* environment was already, to a great extent, noticeable.

Opinions may differ as to the religious conditions in Palestine, but there can be only one opinion, I think, concerning the revival of the Hebrew language and culture. This revival is magnificent, indeed, wonderful. It is a modern miracle, this springing to life of an ancient tongue, counted for centuries among the "dead" languages. It is the revival of the Hebrew language which gives the modern Jewish settlement of Palestine the aspect of a genuine national restoration. There are three official languages in Palestine—English, Arabic, and Hebrew—and the last-named appears to be fully as much in evidence as the other two. The signs of the railroad stations and all other public notices are in the three tongues. Jewish public meetings are conducted in Hebrew. Instruction in the Jewish schools is given in

Hebrew, and much private conversation is carried on in the ancient tongue.

The natural and fluent use of the Hebrew by the children is one of the most striking and pleasing signs of the restoration. I conversed in Hebrew with tots of four and five years of age, and the manner in which they laughed and jested while using the ancient tongue was the best evidence that it was perfectly natural to them, that it was, in fact, their native language. Another striking fact is that in Palestine, contrary to the condition prevailing in the lands of the Diaspora, the Hebrew is the language of the young rather than of the old.

I happened once to hear two old men conversing in Yiddish and took the liberty to rebuke them.

"Why do you speak a non-Jewish language in the Holy Land?" I said to them—in Palestine Yiddish is counted among the alien tongues. "Do you not know that in Palestine one should speak only the Holy Tongue?"

Thereupon one of them said to me, "What do you want of us old people? Go to the young people; they speak Hebrew."

Yet there are certain elements in the Palestinian Jewry, elements which consider themselves particularly pious and loyal, who do not share in this national revival of the Hebrew language. They hold every secular use of the Hebrew, as a Holy Tongue, irreligious, indeed, sacrilegious. The language of study in the *Yeshivoth* is largely, if not entirely, not Hebrew but Yiddish. This extreme standpoint is not, however, the view even of the majority of Jews of strictly Orthodox observance.

National sentiment is not the only, though it is, no doubt, the main impelling force which operates to bring about the use of the Hebrew as the vernacular of Jewish Palestine. Another great reason is the fact that there are many thousands of Oriental Jews in the country who do not know any Yiddish but are, more or less, acquainted with Hebrew. In conversation with them the *Ashkenazic* Jews are simply forced to make use of the Hebrew, as it is the linguistic medium which both can employ. In this manner, partly voluntary and partly through the force of circumstances, the ancient tongue of Israel has become the living speech of Jewish Palestine.

Summing up the results of my observations, my conviction is that

Palestine, the Palestine of the British Mandate and the Jewish National Home, possesses all the inherent possibilities for the development of a prosperous and numerically great Jewish commonwealth. Essential, however, for the realization of this hope is that the mandate be carried out in sincerity for the purposes for which it was given. Of the ardent desire of our brethren to build up in their ancestral homeland such an ideal Jewish commonwealth, which shall be in every way a model of a truly civilized and progressive state, and of their ability to do so if not hampered and hindered, there cannot be the slightest doubt. What they have already done is ample proof of what they can accomplish if their efforts are not thwarted and nullified by a mandatory power recreant to its sacred trust.

Unfortunately, and incomprehensibly, the actions of Great Britain indicate not a desire to fulfill its obligations under the mandate and to further the development of the Jewish National Home but, on the contrary, to prevent its realization. The facts which indicate this intention are patent to all and need not be stated here. Some of our good Zionists, loth to believe this of liberal and democratic and Bible-loving England conjecture that it is only a temporary policy. brought about by the exigencies of war. They believe that when the present dreadful struggle has ended in the complete overthrow of the Axis and the glorious victory of the Allied Powers, Great Britain will show its traditional liberality of sentiment and friendship for the Jews and will permit and even assist the Jewish people to reconstitute their National Home Land, in accordance with the terms of the mandate. Let us hope that these good friends are not merely indulging in wishful thinking and that the prayer may be fulfilled, "In our days may the Redeemer come to Zion and may Judah dwell in peace on the holy soil!"

After concluding our visit to Palestine, Theodore and I went to Antwerp, where I attended the Mizrachi Zionist Conference. It was a fine gathering, well attended by representatives of the Orthodox Jews of all countries, showing how strong was the conviction among the rank and file of Israel that the Jewish National Home must be built up upon the basis of the Torah, but there is little that I can write about it. It was occupied almost exclusively with practical matters, with the multifarious details of organization and finance,

The Mizrachi Conference in Antwerp

land acquisition and colonization, which are, of course, fundamental and indispensable to the work of the upbuilding but which do not fit into the framework of a narrative such as this.

The chief impression which I took from it—a very important and valuable impression—was that the religious Jews of the world were resolved that the Jewish National Home should not be permitted to be a merely secular state. They were determined to see to it that the New Judea, like the ancient Judea, should be erected upon the imperishable foundation of genuine Jewish tradition and Jewish faith.

I will, however, narrate one incident which occurred in connection with the conference because, while it is mainly of a personal nature, it raises some interesting questions of general Jewish, particularly Zionistic importance. Among the subjects discussed at the conference was the Mizrachi Bank, a chief financial instrument for promoting the colonization of Palestine in the spirit of Traditional Judaism. I am not concerned at present with this aspect of its functions, which is unquestionably of the highest importance, but with another matter altogether, a linguistic or philological question. The term *Mizrachi Bank* had been rendered into Hebrew, by whom I know not, as *Ha-Bank Ha-Mizrachi* and appeared thus in all Hebrew documents issued in connection with the conference. In other words, the term *bank* had not been translated at all but simply taken over in its non-Hebraic form and transcribed with Hebrew letters.

I took umbrage at this. To my Hebrew linguistic conscience this was a gross barbarism. I am not an extremist in regard to the purity of the revived Hebrew language. I recognize that, owing to the sad history alike of the Hebrew people and its national tongue, the latter was early arrested in its development and that it must be greatly enlarged and enriched with new terms before it can be fit to serve as the medium of communication and expression of a highly cultured and civilized modern nation. The classic tongue of the Bible, although it possesses a wealth of significant terms, which are far from having been adequately exploited, cannot be expected to cope with all the needs of modern speech. It must be greatly amplified in order to attain this goal.

But what I maintain is that this enlargement and amplification can be derived from its own resources, that there is no necessity for filling the Hebrew with a mass of incongruous foreign terms. To do so, is to destroy its beauty and genuine historic character, to make of it a new and very unlovely species of jargon. Whatever new terms are found necessary and desirable must be very carefully constructed from the ancient speech stock, must conform in every way to the spirit of the Biblical idiom. Then will the language of the revived Hebrew nation carry on the olden tradition and deserve to bear the honored title of Hebrew.

There is no specific term in ancient Hebrew for bank. Banks, as we know them now, were not known in antiquity. But there is a term for *banker* or *money-changer*. This is the term *shulchani,* formed in the Talmud from *shulchan,* a table, because the ancient money-changers were accustomed to sit in front of small tables at which they carried on all their financial transactions. I suggested to the directors of the Mizrachi Bank that, instead of employing the absolutely foreign and un-Hebraic term *"bank,"* they should call their financial institution by a collective or general term derived from the already existing Hebrew term for financier.

The term I suggested was *Shulchaniyah,* a direct and natural derivation from *Shulchani,* as well as an undeniably true and correct Hebrew term, which would be at once understood by any person acquainted with the Hebrew language. I was so enthusiastic in my advocacy of my proposal that, when I saw that my suggestion did not seem to appeal to them, I offered to donate to the bank the sum of five hundred dollars if they would agree to give it the Hebrew title of *Ha-Shulchaniyah Ha-Mizrachith.* In other languages the designation might remain the Mizrachi Bank or its equivalent.

Even this offer, which I think I may justifiably call munificent, did not seem to possess any attractive force. The directors answered me courteously that they would consider my proposal, but I received no further communication from them in the matter. I could only come to the conclusion that while the religious and national sentiments of the Mizrachists were truly Jewish and worthy of all appreciation, they were sadly deficient in their realization of the all-important part which the Hebrew language has always played in the cultural and spiritual life of Israel and of the urgent necessity that that language should not be permitted to degenerate in the new old land into a barbarous jargon but should be preserved in its pristine correctness and beauty.*

Apart from the Mizrachi conference, I found Antwerp most interesting from the Jewish point of view. Indeed, I was amazed by what I saw. Since Antwerp is a Western European city, far removed from the countries which are, or were, the centers and citadels of Traditional Judaism, I expected to find in it the sort of lukewarm, assimilated Judaism which we are accustomed to associate with the Occident. I found the direct opposite. The stamp of Judaism was over a great part of the city, and it was a strong, earnest, emphatic Judaism, the genuine heritage of Israel. Synagogues, Talmud Torahs, charitable institutions, and kosher restaurants abounded, these latter under the supervision of the rabbinate and unquestionably reliable. Many business establishments were closed on the Sabbath.

The reputation of the rabbis for learning and piety is sufficiently attested by the fact that one of their number, Rabbi Amiel, was called to a high rabbinical post in Palestine. I was greatly pleased to learn that the Belgian government was truly liberal, that it protected its Jewish citizens in the full enjoyment of their citizenship rights. Antwerp fully deserved to be called by the ancient and honorable designation "a mother city in Israel."

---

* I would like to state here that my proposal to derive a term for *bank* from the Mishnah term *Shulchani* was not entirely original with me, so as to be rejected as something utterly new and unheard of. In the book of travel, *Eben Saphir*, written in beautiful and expressive Hebrew by Jacob Saphir about the middle of the nineteenth century, in describing the occupations of the Jews of Alexandria, Egypt, the author employs an abstract term *Shulchanuth*, derived from *Shulchani* in the sense of "banking" or "finance." My proposal was really to accept a new linguistic form which had already been introduced.—B.D.

One of the author's life-long avocations was the development from classic Hebrew sources of terms for modern inventions or ideas. During his visit to Jerusalem, he lectured (in Hebrew, of course) before the *Vaad ha-Loshon* (Linguistic Council) on this theme.—Ed.

Chapter Forty-one

My Second Romance

BACK AGAIN IN AMERICA AND ENGAGED IN THE ORDINARY AND ROUtine activities of my vocation, there came over me a dreadful sense of loneliness. I felt with intensified force the absence of my beloved wife. While on my trip in Europe and Palestine, while new and vivid impressions were constantly rushing on my mind, that feeling had grown milder, and it had seemed to me that I might grow accustomed to solitude, to a lonely sojourn in this earthly vale.

But now I realized that this was self-deception. I perceived as never before the truth of the words of Scripture, "It is not good for man to be alone." I had enjoyed for so many years my dear wife's companionship that I felt I could not endure being utterly deprived of such companionship, even though I realized that no substitute could completely take her place.

At first I tried to repress this feeling. It seemed to me a sort of disloyalty to think of permitting any other woman to take the place which she had occupied. But after a while I began to ask myself, "What would have been her wish? Would dear Sarah, whose chief desire, during the many years of our marriage, had been to make me happy—would she have wished me to wander lonely and desolate through this earthly vale for as many or as few years as Divine Providence had assigned to me?"

Putting the question thus, I could only answer in the negative. From that time on I no longer rejected the thought of a second alliance as something outside the range of possibility. A true Jewish home is inconceivable without the presence therein of a God-fearing wife, who presides over it in the spirit of Judaism and conducts its affairs in strict conformity with the precepts of the Holy Torah. The Jewish wife is the *Akereth Ha-Bayith,* the basic essential and the indispensable pillar of the home.

It took me about a year and a half to reach this decision. Even when I had decided that such was the required course, I was in no hurry to put it into effect. I had been a widower for a little more than two years and grown accustomed to loneliness, when I began to hear casual references to a certain young woman, which attracted my attention.

People spoke of her as a most unusual person. She combined in a wonderful way, I heard them say, the finest qualities of Judaism and American culture. A native of this country and a model of American refinement in speech and deportment, she was at the same time enthusiastically loyal in her devotion to Traditional Judaism. She had conducted a summer camp for girls and had astonished all the patrons by insisting on the strictest Sabbath observance, even going so far as to forbid the entrance of automobiles into the camp on the Sabbath day. Although a teacher in the public schools and presumably in need of rest over the week-end, she had found strength and time to gather around her for instruction on Sunday afternoons a group of girls on the lower East Side, over whom her influence for good and especially for love of Judaism was said to be phenomenal.

These were not all the good things I heard told about her. All the reports were alike in that they showed her as a person in whom broad culture and refinement were combined with warm Jewish feeling and spirituality in a remarkable manner. Her name was Hadassah Levine, and she was the daughter of a highly respected and sincerely religious family.

I did not know the young lady personally. Strangely enough, I had never met her although, in view of the similarity of our views, it might have been expected that we would both attend Jewish public gatherings or other occasions of Jewish religious importance and thus become acquainted. The reports concerning her interested me greatly and I felt that I ought to become acquainted with such a kindred spirit. This was entirely because of her exalted Jewish qualities, and without any definite purpose.

The difficulty was as to how this acquaintance should be brought about. I resolved to take the bull by the horns and seek her acquaintance myself without the intervention of any other person. Accordingly, on the tenth of June, 1927, I addressed a letter to Miss Hadassah Levine, requesting the privilege of an interview, as I desired to see her on a matter of importance. A few days later—I do not recall the exact date—I received an answer, very courteously and graciously worded, according me that privilege. In response thereto I called at the residence of Miss Levine, and our conversation revealed to me a rare and genuinely ideal personage.

I do not desire to enter into the details of the growth of our acquaintance or of its final issue in my determination to seek her hand in wedlock. All I wish to say is that, reversing the words of Caesar, I could say of myself, "I came, I saw, I was conquered." Or, quoting the Queen of Sheba, after her visit to the court of King Solomon, I could say, "The half was not told me."

The reality far exceeded the reports. I saw before me a lady of charming presence, whose gentle and kindly countenance revealed high intelligence and spirituality, whose melodious and beautifully modulated voice uttered words of wisdom and ethical nobility. I led the conversation into Biblical channels, and she showed herself thoroughly familiar with Scripture. I brought up matters of Jewish ritual import, and her answers showed that she was a sincere observer of the precepts of Traditional Judaism. A ponderous Leeser Bible on her table and an equally ponderous Biblical concordance revealed the favorite subjects which occupied her attention.

When I left Miss Levine that evening I knew that I had found my ideal of a wife, the woman fitted to fill with dignity and grace the place left vacant by my dear Sarah.

The very next morning I addressed a letter to her, expressing some of the impressions which my visit to her had made upon me and formally proposing marriage. This was certainly hasty action. But it was not merely a case of "love at first sight." It was a case of "depth calling unto depth," of two kindred and related natures which, though as yet externally separated, were bound together by a thousand profound ideological and sympathetic ties. I was as certain of this, after that first interview, as though I had known the lady and met her daily for a quarter of a century. And so there was no thought of hesitation or of the need of further deliberation before committing myself definitely by the proposal.

Her reaction to my proposal was such as to increase, if that were possible, the high respect and esteem in which I held her. She neither accepted nor rejected it. Instead she let me know—I forget if it was through a letter or in some other manner—that she feared I had been over-hasty in my action. If such were the case, she did not desire to hold me to my proposal, as expressed in my letter, although greatly flattered and honored thereby, but released me from all obligation resulting therefrom.

In reply I stated that I had fully meant all that I had written in the letter, that I had not changed and had no intention of changing my view and that I purposed to visit her on the twenty-sixth of the month, in order to seek, formally and verbally, her hand in marriage and that I hoped for a favorable answer.

As it happened, the twenty-sixth was the wedding day of her brother Lionel, but the ceremony and the dinner had taken place in the afternoon and in the evening Miss Levine was at home awaiting my visit. She received me with a friendly smile and a few words of welcome, but there was about her, so it seemed to me, an unmistakable air of loneliness and melancholy. I was not surprised at this, for I knew that that day signified for her the end of a long period of comparative happiness and the beginning of a new and unknown future.

This will be understood when I point out that among the noble qualities of Hadassah Levine was a most rare and intense filial and family devotion. At the time when I made her acquaintance, she had been keeping house for her brother Lionel for upwards of ten years, and a very strong and unusual affection had grown up between them. And now he had married and the wonderful tie of brotherly and sisterly affection was sundered. She was to be, in a sense, all alone in the world. No wonder that her thoughts were sad and her feelings melancholy on that evening!

I doubt not that these melancholy feelings were strongly influential in inclining her to look favorably upon my suit—which was accepted with characteristic dignity.

The news of our betrothal, it is hardly necessary to state, created a great deal of interest among our relatives and friends.

On the twelfth of July our marriage took place. The ceremony was performed by the Reverend Dr. H. Pereira Mendes, who had officiated at my first marriage, and the words of his wedding address were pervaded with a true understanding and sincere friendship only possible to one who had been a friend of many years' standing to us both. We were both deeply appreciative of his wise and kind remarks.

On the following day we left by the steamer *New York,* of the Hamburg-American Line, on a European trip. By an interesting coincidence Miss Levine had already engaged passage for herself. She had taken her first sabbatical leave and had intended to pass several months of her free time in a tour of Europe. Naturally she had not had the faintest idea that she would make the trip as a married woman in the company of her husband. When she went to the office of the steamship company to change the cabin she had engaged to a more suitable one on account of the change in her status, the official concerned was greatly interested in her romance and did his utmost to provide us with suitable accommodations.

Of our European trip I will only say that it was most enjoyable, and I was able, through my knowledge of Europe, to make it much easier and pleasanter for my wife than it would otherwise have been. Our voyage across the ocean was saddened by the receipt of a wireless message informing us of the sudden passing of Mrs. Therese Weil, the mother of my first wife, of blessed memory. Like all the other members of dear Sarah's family, Mrs. Weil had taken a great liking to Hadassah, and had promised us that, when we returned from our trip, she would be a regular visitor at our home on Sunday evenings. We were greatly grieved by the sad news and especially by the fact that we were unable to pay our last respects.

In concluding this chapter I wish to say that all the hopes and expectations which I had placed upon Hadassah have been fulfilled in fullest measure. The manner in which I became betrothed may be condemned as rash and hasty, but the experince of my second wedlock has proved convincingly that my intuition was right and true. We are now (1944) in the eighteenth year of our marriage and dear Hadah, as we call her for short, has more than lived up to all the expectations concerning her. To me she has been an ideal helpmeet, looking after my health and welfare in every way, presiding over my household with grace and dignity, and participating sympathetically, to the extent of her power, in the movements and activities in which I am interested.

Her kindly and friendly and ever helpful ways have endeared her to my children, so that the name "stepmother," if applied to her, would be most inappropriate. Her friends are a host, and all of them love, indeed, adore her. As a *rebbetzin,* or rabbi's wife, she fills the part to perfection. She is scrupulously exact in the performance of her religious duties, regular in her attendance at service and a tower of strength to the Sisterhood of the congregation, in whose congregational and charitable work she takes, perhaps, the leading part. May our Heavenly Father preserve her in health and strength for many years and reward her for her noble deeds! That is the fervent prayer of him whose privilege it is to call himself her husband.

Chapter Forty-two

Houdini's Funeral

A Proposed Calendar Reform

My marriage made no difference in my Jewish activity. I performed my congregational duties and participated in public movements just as I had always done and, as stated, my dear Hadassah cooperated with extraordinary zeal and remarkable efficiency.

A few events of special significance stand out above the level of mediocre happenings. One of these was the passing of Houdini, which occurred, if I recall correctly, in the month of October, 1927.

It was my sad privilege to officiate at the funeral. His passing became the occasion for the widespread discussion of his personality and the extraordinary powers which he unquestionably possessed. His ability to free himself with astonishing swiftness from chains and padlocks and other means of restraint baffled all investigators.

What these powers were I, of course, know as little as anyone else, but they certainly were far exalted above the vulgar sleight of hand and tricks of ordinary so-called magicians. The Spiritualists claimed Houdini as one of their own and asserted that his escape from apparently insuperable means of confinement was due to his ability to dematerialize his body and thus pass through all physical restraints. Houdini himself denied that he was a Spiritualist medium—he was, indeed, an outspoken opponent of Spiritualism—and stated that his performances were strictly in accordance with natural law.

This statement, of course, left the matter as much of a mystery as before. The Spiritualists refused to accept Houdini's denial that he was a medium. They insisted that he was. They even tried to drag me into the controversy as upholding their contention. In my funeral address I had used the words, "Houdini possessed a wondrous power that he never understood and which he never revealed to anyone in life." These words are to be taken in their narrowest and most literal significance. All I meant was that Houdini possessed an extraordinary and mysterious power—and by that statement I am still willing to stand—the precise nature and quality of which was not clear even to him and that he had never taken anyone into his confidence nor revealed what his concept of his extraordinary gift was.

But the Spiritualists seized upon these words to draw from them the utterly unjustified inference that I considered Houdini a Spiritualist medium and that his extraordinary powers were derived from a super-mundane, non-material source. Arthur Conan Doyle, the well-known author and Spiritualist leader, interprets them to that effect in his book, *"The Edge of the Unknown."** Of course, I meant nothing of the kind. My statement was simply a recognition of his undeniably extraordinary power, concerning the nature of which I admit that I am just as ignorant as everybody else, including A. C. Doyle, neither more nor less.

However, it is not because of this aspect of his personality that I esteemed and respected Houdini and cherish his memory. My respect and, I may say, my love went to him, as a true friend, as a generous and unselfish character, as a loyal and truly filial son, and as a Jew with a warm Jewish heart. As such and for these reasons his name will ever be held in honor as a worthy son of Israel.

In the late twenties and early thirties of the twentieth century, the Jewish people, as a religious community, and the Jewish faith as a definite and established religious system, were confronted by a grave peril. Under the guise of an effort to reform the existing calendar, the system by which the chief civilized nations of the world have, for approximately twenty centuries, regulated the computation of time and all matters connected therewith, a movement arose inimical to Jewish religious life. If it had succeeded in attaining its objective, it would have dealt a practically fatal blow at Jewish religious life by bringing confusion into the observance of the traditional, Biblical seventh-day Sabbath.

The moving spirit in this movement was Mr. George Eastman, of

---

* Arthur Conan Doyle *"The Edge of the Unknown,"* G. P. Putnam's Sons, London, New York, 1930.—B.D.

Kodak fame. What his motive was can only be conjectured. It may have been merely a desire to bring about an improvement in technical, mainly business, conditions, or it may have been an anti-Semitic plot to strike, in this manner, a severe blow at Jews and Judaism. Some characteristics of the methods employed for furthering the scheme seem to indicate that the latter was the case. Whatever Mr. Eastman's motive may have been, it certainly was a very strong one, for the expense involved in pushing a scheme of this kind was unquestionably very heavy. Mr. Eastman, of course, did not stand alone in this enterprise. A group of sympathizers, of unknown numbers, gave their influence in favor of his plan. His chief assistants, presumably paid employees, were a Dr. Charles F. Marvin and a Mr. Moses B. Cotsworth. These two gentlemen were the joint authors of an ostensibly scientific treatise entitled *"Moses, the Greatest of Calendar Reformers."*

The purpose of this book was to furnish a supposedly historical and Biblical basis for the new calendar. The advocates of the new calendar declared that it would be a great improvement upon the existing system. The present calendar, they alleged, is full of irregularities and confusions and tends greatly to hamper business. The varying number of days in the months, thirty-one and thirty and twenty-eight or twenty-nine, they assert, makes bookkeeping exceedingly difficult and also increases the difficulty of comparing the business of one year with another. All this is remedied, they argued, by the beautiful uniformity, under the new system, of the year, which will consist of thirteen months of exactly twenty-eight days each, while every week and every month and every year will begin with Sunday and end with Saturday.

Whether there is any substantial merit in this claim of the lightening of business difficulties by the proposed new calendar is not for the writer, as a non-business man, to say. There is probably considerable exaggeration in it, as the bookkeeping systems of business establishments, as at present conducted, seem to be functioning very efficiently. All that I can really see is that the alleged increased easiness of bookkeeping would undoubtedly lessen the number of bookkeepers and accountants needed. While this would, of course, add to the profits of merchants and manufacturers, it would throw a considerable number of employees out of work. Under present economic conditions, this would be anything but desirable.

But apart from the question as to whether the proposed new calendar would be economically advantageous or disadvantageous, it is certainly gravely objectionable from the religious, particularly the Jewish, point of view.

Before considering the reasons for this, I will premise that the Jews, *qua* Jews do not object at all to calendar reform, if it can be brought about without harm or peril to Judaism. We maintain that it can, inasmuch as Judaism does not oppose true progress or antagonize anything that is essential to the welfare of the human race. All it asks is that the improvements suggested shall not tend to destroy or overthrow the sacred traditions of the Jewish faith.

But calendar reform, as planned, contains a feature which, in a totally unnecessary manner, would tend not merely to make it difficult to uphold the traditional Jewish life but to render it practically impossible. This feature is the so-called "blank day," "leap day," or *"dies non."* The reason for this device is to insure that all years, months, and weeks shall begin with a Sunday. It would be perfectly feasible to secure this result by several other methods, but the proponents of calendar reform obstinately insist on the "blank day" device and will listen to no other suggestions. Should it be adopted (which may Providence in mercy avert!), its effect on Jewish observance would be disastrous.

Consideration of its workings will at once show the truth of this statement. Since time immemorial the Jewish Sabbath has been coincident with Saturday. Jews and non-Jews are alike accustomed to this condition. Under the new system it would become a wandering day. Since Judaism has a traditional seventh-day Sabbath and does not accept fictions, it would not recognize as the Sabbath a seventh day falsely designated as such. Hence the Sabbath would in one year be on a so-called Monday, in another year on a Wednesday or Thursday and so on. The disastrous effect of this on Sabbath-observing Jewish business men is at once recognizable. It is difficult enough, under present conditions, for a Jewish Sabbath-keeping merchant to close his establishment on Saturday, although both Jews and Gentiles are accustomed to look upon that day as Sabbath. Should the

Sabbath occur on constantly varying days in different years, the resultant confusion would be extraordinary.

Under present conditions, the five-day working week, which is increasingly being adopted, is a blessing for Sabbath-keeping Jews. Should the new calendar be adopted, it would be a horror and a curse. Under it the Sabbath-keeping Jew would have only four days of the week in which to earn a living. The present five-day school week is very beneficial to Jewish teachers and pupils alike. Under the new calendar, they would be in a great quandary, as the Sabbath might occur on any of the school days.

As already stated, there are several ways in which the objective of calendar reform, the securing of perfectly uniform months of twenty-eight days each, always beginning with Sunday, could be attained without interfering with the fixity of the Sabbath or of the sequence of days. One way would be to wait five or six years, until the excess days would amount to a week, and then insert an extra week, or to wait until they amounted to a month and then insert an extra month. But, as we have seen, the sponsors of the calendar reform movement will not hear of any other device than that of the "blank day."

The leaders of Jewry, here and abroad, have not been blind to the threatening dangers, nor have they been inert. They have appeared before Congress in this country and before the League of Nations in Europe and protested vigorously against the "blank day" scheme. Special credit is due to Rabbi Dr. M. Hyamson of New York for his energetic and most effective efforts in this regard. In all of these efforts I have cooperated to the utmost extent of my power. Together we organized the League for Safeguarding the Fixity of the Sabbath. To this League we succeeded in securing the adherence of fifty-one of the most important Jewish organizations, thus impressively demonstrating that all Jewry was united as one man in opposing any tampering with Israel's sacred day of rest. Dr. Hyamson was elected president of the league and I became its vice-president.

We also appeared together before a committee of Congress in Washington in opposition to a bill which had been introduced to adopt calendar reform. It was undoubtedly due to our efforts that the bill was never reported out of committee. Dr. Hyamson, together with other European Jewish leaders, among them Chief Rabbi Dr. Joseph

H. Hertz of London, also appeared, in 1931, before the League of Nations in Geneva, in opposition to calendar reform. Their dignity and eloquence made a deep impression upon the assembled statesmen, and they were completely successful in their mission.

Thanks to the untiring efforts of these devoted leaders of Jewry, and to the blessing of All-Merciful Providence, the peril to the Holy Sabbath was averted. With the death of George Eastman, a few years ago, it seemed as though all danger had ceased to be. But, unfortunately, such was not the case. A woman, a Mrs. Achelis, was found ready to step into the place of Eastman and to devote her energy and her financial resources to the attainment of the same aim. It has been reported recently (1944) that the Calendar Reformers have reorganized, under the leadership of Mrs. Achelis, and are preparing to lay siege to the governments of all nations to bring about the adoption of their pet plan. It is evident, therefore, that the war for the preservation of the Sabbath has not been definitely and finally won.

Let us, therefore, arouse ourselves to the impending danger; let us unite and muster all our strength to defend our heritage! In this struggle we shall have the cooperation of a large section of the Christian world, many of whom recognize that the calendar reform movement is a danger to the integrity of their faith as well as to ours.*

With an intelligent and courageous effort, and the blessing of God Almighty, we shall defeat the second attack of our foes as we did the first. But we must not again be caught napping.

---

* I have before me, as I write, a booklet entitled "*Calendar Change Threatens Religion*" by Rev. Carlyle B. Haynes. The writer, evidently a Protestant clergyman, objects to a "wandering Sunday" just as Jews object to a "wandering Sabbath."—B.D.

Chapter Forty-three

A Visit to California in 1928

The World Congress of Jewish Sabbath Observers in Berlin in 1930

IN THE YEAR 1928, HADASSAH AND I DECIDED THAT WE OUGHT TO visit my daughters, Beatrice and Mathilde, residing in California. My sons, resident in the East, had all had the opportunity to become acquainted with Hadassah, and we decided that it was only right that the daughters should have the same opportunity.

We left New York on our westward trip toward the close of June after we had made all necessary preparations on a generous scale. We took with us, as our travel guest, our much esteemed housekeeper, Mrs. Bertha Kahn. She had been a devoted and invaluable household assistant. We were glad to afford her this opportunity of a pleasant vacation. I knew, besides, that her presence would be useful and agreeable to my dear wife.

A letter written on board "The Gold Coast Limited" by my dear Hadassah to my sons in New York gave a graphic description of our week-end stay in Chicago, of our attendance at Sabbath service in the Orthodox Synagogue, of my being called on unexpectedly to deliver a sermon, of our search for a kosher restaurant and of other details of our stay.

It was a simple, natural and I might say a chatty missive, yet it revealed my dear Hadassah (or Hadah) in all aspects of her quality as woman and wife and showed that she measured fully up to the highest standards that can be applied to a woman in her position.

She wished wholeheartedly to enter completely into the life of my family, to be on the sincerest terms of friendship and love to the children, already mature men and women, to whom she now became what the cold customary phrase calls "stepmother." She did not wish to be considered in that light but as their older sister and friend and to take, to some extent, the place of their dear, unforgettable mother.

We were on the way to meet the sisters in California and the letter was written to the brothers in New York. It is axiomatic that second wives often do not display these tendencies toward their new relations. It revealed the sincere Jewess, interested in the synagogue, in the kosher dietary and—self-understood—in the ethical and spiritual precepts of Judaism. Add to this that she supervises her household with marvelous efficiency and has even developed into an expert in the culinary art, I know not aught that is lacking from the concept of the perfect housewife as the wise Solomon describes her. In short, if I had been able to create miraculously a wife after my own ideals I could not have created a different one.

We had looked forward with eager anticipation to our visit to Yellowstone Park. We discussed in advance the wonders of nature for which that most extraordinary region is famous. We promised ourselves a most interesting and enjoyable experience. Alas, it was to come otherwise. Hadah met with an accident which resulted in a broken arm, a wild and terrifying ride in an ambulance through the blackness of the night, and several days' stay in a hospital.

From Yellowstone Park we went directly to California, where my dear daughters, Beatrice and Mathilde, had rented a cottage for our accommodation at Lake Tahoe, where they were staying for the summer. Our meeting was thrilling to all of us. It was thrilling to me to meet my daughters, whom I had not seen for several years and to whom I was bringing a new mother; it was thrilling to my daughters to meet her who had taken the place of the beloved parent who had given them birth; it was, of course, thrilling and deeply moving to dear Hadassah. But the strain was very brief. The mutual good will and affection of all of us and especially the natural cordiality and sincere amiability of dear Hadassah speedily broke down whatever differences had existed and in a few moments we were chatting as familiarly and unrestrainedly as though we had always known each other and had never been separated.

On the whole we spent a very pleasant summer at Lake Tahoe. But one Friday a forest fire started a number of miles away from our cottage and, as the wind was blowing in our direction, there was danger that our cottage might fall a victim to the flames. In fact, we were told that the conflagration might overtake us at about evening. All the men of the town were summoned to fight the flames. As Friday evening coincides with the incoming of the Sabbath, that added another most disagreeable possibility to the impending danger. We consoled ourselves with the thought that, as our cottage stood on the very edge of the lake, we would be able to save ourselves by taking refuge in its waters. Most fortunately, however, a few hours before sunset the wind changed and drove the flames in the opposite direction. Some fifty cottages used by lumber men and a huge quantity of piled wood were destroyed, and several lives were lost.

In the year 1930 an event of great significance in Jewish religious life took place in which my dear Hadassah and I both participated. A World Congress of Jewish Sabbath Observers took place in Berlin which we attended as representatives of the Jewish Sabbath Alliance of America.

The Congress was in session from August Twenty-third to August Twenty-eighth, inclusive. It was called by the *Verband der Sabbat-Freunde** and was attended by Sabbath-keeping Jews interested in the preservation of the Sabbath and representing practically all parts of the world. It was a most representative Jewish gathering. It was indeed interesting to observe how these Jews and Jewesses coming from such different surroundings and apparently actuated by the most various ideas were nevertheless united in religious harmony through their common love for the Sabbath and their desire to strengthen and perpetuate its observance.

The meetings took place in two great halls, *Der Saal des Bruder-*

---

* League of Friends of the Sabbath.—Ed.

Columbia University Commencement — June 3, 1941
Award of Citation by Dr. Nicholas Murray Butler

The Patriarch

Photograph taken for the
Golden Anniversary
December, 1940

vereins and *Siegersfest Saal*. The latter was the greater of the two, but both were attended by large and very representative gatherings. It was impressive to observe the great interest existing in the world metropolis of Berlin for the cause of the ancient Hebrew day of rest.

The most representative rabbis and prominent men of Jewish faith, not only of Germany but of other countries as well, were present. The addresses were on a very high plane of ability and earnestness. Among those whom I recall were Rabbi Dr. Meyer Hildesheimer, Rabbi Dr. Jacobus, Rabbi Dr. Samuel Grueneberg, Rabbi Meyer Berlin, prominent in the Mizrachi Organization, and a number of the most distinguished and prominent laymen of Poland and Russia. An especially interesting personage was Dr. Angelo Pacifici, who, as he was not sufficiently fluent in the German, delivered his address in Hebrew—a very classic and beautiful Hebrew at that. Both my dear Hadassah and I were among those who addressed the gatherings. We both delivered our addresses in German. My theme was the *Fünf Tag Arbeitswoche*—Five-Day Working-Week—and Hadassah's *Die Juedische Frau als Foerderin der Sabbatheiligung*— The Jewish Woman as Promoter of Sabbath Sanctification. Hadassah's address. which was delivered before a special gathering of women, was greeted with much enthusiasm. but my dear wife was more than surprised when, after delivering her address, it was commented on by several of the ladies in excellent English.

I must take occasion here to remark upon the extraordinarily high cultural standard of all the men and women who delivered addresses at the Congress—those of German and Western European origin were splendid examples of the harmonious combination of Jewish and Occidental culture and of sincere devotion to Judaism, and the rabbis and other persons representing Eastern European Judaism were very impressive in their quaint, traditional way.

It fills one's heart with melancholy to think that the brutal sadistic fury of the Nazi savages, only a few years later, should have been able almost completely to obliterate and exterminate the splendid communities represented by those gathered in conclave then at Berlin.

We were privileged to meet in the course of the Congress with

Herr and Frau Strauss. Frau Badt-Strauss was the daughter of Professor Badt* and his wife, the former Martha Gutmann of Breslau, who had been friends of mine during my student years in Breslau. She was a most charming personality, and to meet her and her cultured husband revived in me most pleasant memories of my youth.

There is no doubt that this Congress, a most worthy representative of Jewish religious sentiment, would have had a great effect upon Jewish religious life all over the world but for the cruel fate which was destined to overwhelm European Israel so shortly after. As it was, I was greatly encouraged thereby in my own work as president of the Jewish Sabbath Alliance of America for the cause of our ancient day of rest in the new world.

In the following spring, I learned with sorrow of the death of an old friend, a Sephardic Jew from Jerusalem, named Nissim Behar. He was a very modest person and worked almost in privacy, but he was a Jew of outstanding and noble character, greatly devoted to Judaism and to the Jewish people, and, above all, kind-hearted and benevolent in the highest degree. He did all in his power to be of help to his fellow-beings not only of Jewish origin but others as well, and his concept of Judaism may truly be called universalistic.

On learning of his death, I felt it my duty to show him the honor which was his due. Accordingly I arranged a memorial service for him in the synagogue of *Zichron Ephraim*. Without going into details, I can say that the memorial service was worthy of his memory. A number of speakers who had known and appreciated him, among them myself, paid due tribute to the deeds of modest virtue, religion, and benevolence to which his life had been dedicated. A few days after the memorial service, I received the following letter from his son.

---

* Dr. Hans Badt, the son of this couple, was Minister of Aviation in the cabinet of the German Republic. In this capacity, he came to America on the first voyage of the *Graf Zeppelin*. As he was an observant Jew, the great airship carried a supply of Kosher food, and its return voyage was delayed several hours from the time originally set, which was on a Saturday, until after sunset. . . . At the Sabbath congress, Dr. Heinrich Bruening, the last Chancellor of the Republic, delivered an address of welcome.—Ed.

25 Mawhinnery Street
Pittsburgh, Pa.
August 22, 1931

Dear Dr. Drachman:

From Professor Naron I have just received a long letter telling about the beautiful Memorial Service last Sunday. While he commends all the speakers, he quotes verbatim only from your address, which therefore must have been memorable. I regret all the more the cruelty of circumstances which have so reduced my financial resources as to make a trip to New York beyond my means.

Judging from Professor Naron's letter, you were among those rare Orthodox rabbis who really understood Nissim Behar the man, who thoroughly understand his teachings, and who therefore are eminently fitted to interpret him and his transcendent universalism.

It would ill become me to thank you on behalf of Judaism or on behalf of the disciples of Nissim Behar, for I am not a Jewish leader, and the mantle of Nissim Behar has not fallen on my shoulders; but as the son of Nissim Behar and as his appointed spokesman on many occasions, I cannot refrain from expressing the affection and gratitude of

Yours respectfully

Manoel Behar

I was greatly touched by the receipt of this communication. I was distressed that a young man whose letter showed that he was a person of high intelligence and fine character should have been unable to attend the last testimonal of honor to his distinguished father on account of financial reasons. Had I been aware that such was the case, I would have seen to it that he would have been with us on that occasion. However, I treasure this letter not only because it preserves the memory of Nissim Behar bright within me, but also because it revealed to me the existence of another Jew, secluded and unknown to publicity, but who nevertheless was a possessor of those fine spiritual and ethical attributes which are the true fruit of Judaism.

With this I interrupt the chronological description of my life record. I shall here devote several pages of this autobiography to the description of various forms of my activity without regard to chronological order.

Chapter Forty-four

Conversions to Judaism

IT IS A WIDELY DISSEMINATED IDEA THAT JUDAISM DOES NOT ACCEPT converts and that, if it did, the desire would be useless, inasmuch as no non-Jew would wish under any circumstances to enter the ranks of Judaism. Both views are entirely mistaken.

Judaism does not, it is true, *seek* converts, inasmuch as it does not make salvation dependent upon membership in the Jewish fold. In accordance with the psalm, "The Lord is good to all, and His tender mercies are upon all His works," and also in accordance with the Talmudic adage, "The righteous of all nations shall have a portion in the world to come," it teaches that there is no logical necessity for so doing. However, it does not prohibit the entrance of non-Jews into the Jewish fold, if they so desire. On the contrary, the rabbis earnestly enjoin upon their followers to extend the kindest and most cordial welcome to non-Jews whose heart impels them to ally themselves with Israel.

A beautiful Talmudic parable tells of a flock-owner to whose flock there once came a deer from the forest, and the owner of the flock constantly adjured his shepherds to pay the utmost attention to the deer and see that he was well provided with all his needs. The shepherds remonstrated with the owner and said to him, "Master, you have so many sheep and so many cattle, and you do not point out to us our duties to them, but only stress that we should care for this newly arrived deer. Why is this?"

The owner answered, "The sheep and cattle are accustomed to the restraints and confinement of the pasture and the farmyard, but this new arrival comes from the freedom of the broad open country and the forest; it would, therefore, be natural that he would find the restraint of the farm and pasture unpleasant and hard to endure. You must therefore do all in your power to make it pleasant and agreeable for him to stay with his companions of the flocks and herds."

The application, of course, is that the convert to Judaism comes from the liberty and the absence of restraint of the non-Jewish life, while by entering the Jewish fold he takes upon himself the unaccustomed restrictions of the Jewish law. There is also a special prayer in the Jewish ritual asking the blessing of God upon the "Proselytes of Righteousness," by which term is meant those non-Jews who seek admission into Judaism because of a sincere belief in the righteousness of its precepts and a desire to be affiliated with its historic adherents and upholders—the Jewish people.

Nor is the number of such persons by any means small. In various parts of the world whole groups of non-Jews have entered Judaism. Without going into the description of these events and tendencies, it may be said that the alleged antipathy of non-Jews, apart from professional anti-Semites is largely a delusion and that, should the authorities of the Synagogue ever resolve to launch a campaign for conversion in the manner of the missionary efforts of other religions, there would not be the slightest difficulty in securing a great number of new adherents. I have had abundant opportunity in my experience to become aware of this willingness on the part of many non-Jews to enter the Jewish fold. It must however be stated here that there is a class of converts whose motives are far from spiritual. There are those who consent to enter Judaism in order to be able to contract a marriage alliance with a Jew or Jewess.

Judaism accepts these converts if they have gone through the requisite ceremonies. Some Jewish young people of religious families, on the verge of entering an intermarriage, persuade the intended spouse to join the Jewish fold. Some rabbis accept these proselytes without raising any further questions. Such has not been my policy. I haver never consented to accept such a proselyte without the consent of the Jewish family involved. Knowing how greatly God-fearing Jews grieve, if members of their family marry outside of the faith, and also what little value they attach to conversions of this nature, I have never been willing to bring such grief and sorrow into a family of Israel. Unless, therefore, I receive the assurance that the parents of the Jewish party consent to the marriage and consider it, under the circumstances, desirable, I do not entertain such a request at all. Still, it must be admitted that in many cases non-Jewish women entering into Judaism under these circumstances have been more observant than some born Jewesses.

Contrasted with these, the "proselytes of righteousness" are worthy of the highest admiration and respect. It means for them a complete revolution in their lives. It means defying the prejudices of their environment and the non-Jewish world in general. It means following the dictates of their consciences and remaining loyal thereto, whatever be the cost or sacrifice involved, and these are frequently very hard and heavy indeed. Their number, naturally, under the prevailing conditions of anti-Jewish prejudice, is not great. No action in which there is not involved some kind of a material motive is ever very popular, and it is hard to think of any action less popular and less attractive than to forsake the ranks of the vast majority and to ally oneself with a humble and persecuted minority.

It has been my good fortune in the course of my career to come into contact with a few of such pure and exalted spiritual characters, and it has given me a new respect for the sincerity and loyalty to principle and conviction of which the best and purest human souls are capable. I will tell of only one such instance, and since it occurred about the turn of the century and is therefore already rather remote in the past I shall mention the name of the person. Miss Anna Ottilie Goepp, a lady from Philadelphia, applied to me to be accepted as a convert to Judaism. I shall quote a few lines from her letter which show the utter sincerity of her desire. She wrote:

> *I am most anxious to be made a Jewess and it has been my dearest wish for three years at least. Do not think that I am not fully alive to the solemnity of this step. I can think of nothing else. Among my favorite books is your translation of "Ben Uziel's Letters." It interests me deeply.*

In the personal interview which followed, I pointed out, in accordance with my rabbinical duty, that there was no need for her to enter the ranks of Israel in order to be assured of salvation in the world to come, that God would not reject the most insignificant of His creatures as long as they adhere to the dictates of righteousness and virtue.

Her answer was, "I am happy to hear this, but it only increases my desire to become a member of the faith which inculcates such broadly humane and merciful teachings."

I then asked her how it was that she came to desire to join Judaism. She answered that she had been a Bible student for many years, and her studies had convinced her that the true revelation of God was contained in the so-called Old Testament, while the New Testament was no genuine or logical supplement thereto. I then stressed the fact that Judaism did not seek converts and that therefore it might be as well if she remained in her present status. To this her answer was that she could not possibly worship in a church, inasmuch as her view had become that of the Jewish people, and, if I rejected her application, it would merely mean that I was casting her out into the spiritual wilderness and that she would have no place that she could call her religious home. This appeal I was, of course, unable to resist. She was therefore duly inducted into Judaism and remained a most loyal and zealous Jewess. The synagogue which she attended was that of the Portuguese Congregation in Philadelphia, and from time to time she sent me religious questions which revealed the profundity of her attachment to Judaism.

I will conclude this narration with a quotation from the letter which she wrote me after she knew that she would be accepted as a sister in faith. No born Jew or Jewess, even if possessed of the profoundest understanding of Jewish teachings, and the sincerest desire to uphold them, could have a truer or finer conception of the significance of Judaism and the role of the Jewish people as its upholders and defenders.*

> *Your consent to accept me as a Jewess fills me with joy. I am not worthy to join your glorious band who have been witnesses*

---

* This story is only one of many such, each with its own peculiar human interest. There was, for example, a man who, on becoming a Jew, removed with his family to Palestine. The following year he notified the author of the *bar mitzvah* of his son, and, *the year after that*, of the boy's wedding!—Ed.

to the truth, and so cruelly persecuted since the beginning of history. But since you will really bestow this high honor upon me, I shall try to be a good Jewess. Looking forward with joyous anticipation to the holy ceremony which will make me one of the sacred band of Israel, I remain with deep and sincere respect,

Yours earnestly and faithfully,
Anna Ottilie Goepp

Chapter Forty-five

Lighter Side of the Rabbi's Vocation

THE VOCATION OF A MINISTER, OF WHATEVER FAITH HE BE, IS NATurally one of solemnity, and to a certain degree, of sadness. Yet while my duties have for the greater part been of a serious and solemn nature, there have not been wanting mirth-provoking incidents. I shall tell in this chapter of a few of them. Among our Russian and Polish co-religionists it is customary for many of the guests at a wedding to carry burning candles during the marriage ceremony. This is not a custom enjoined by Jewish law but has probably been derived from the custom of the Greek Church, at whose marriage ceremony many candles are borne in this manner.

At first I did not object to this custom, although it is attended with manifest danger, but it happened once that this danger was so great and so threatening that I resolved in the future not to permit any more candles at a marriage ceremony than the regulation two. The marriage party was assembled under the canopy, the bride and groom were facing me, and the parents of the bride and groom as well as a number of the other guests stood around carrying burning candles in their hands. Suddenly the mother of the bride turned around, and her candle came into contact with the bride's veil, which instantly burst into flames. Without a moment's hesitation, I seized the veil, tore it from the bride's head, cast it to the floor, trampled upon it, and extinguished the flames. I then proceeded with the ceremony as though nothing had happened. After that I no longer permitted the carrying of lighted candles by guests.

Lighter Side of the Rabbi's Vocation

Shortly after this experience I was called upon to officiate at a wedding the parties to which were both of Eastern European origin. They were well-to-do people and strictly observant of traditional customs. In accordance with my new resolution, I notified all concerned that I would not permit the carrying of burning candles. I had concluded all arrangements for the ceremony and was standing under the canopy waiting for the arrival of the bridal couple and their attendants, who were assembled in a room at the end of the hall. To my surprise, they did not come.

After waiting some time, I went back to the room to see what was the trouble. There I found the mothers of the young couple lying upon a sofa weeping and wailing bitterly. Shocked at the sight, I asked the reason. I was informed that the two mothers had each prepared a beautiful and elaborate candle, and that they considered me a cruel tyrant and enemy of Judaism, who was endeavoring to destroy their ancient and sacred custom. In choice Yiddish they were denouncing me vehemently. Some of the other people explained to me that the mothers did not object to my forbidding the carrying of candles by the other guests. But they considered that under no circumstance should they as mothers be deprived of that privilege.

I hastily explained that my motive was merely one of safety, that I had no intention of interfering with their religious practices, and would consent to the carrying of candles by the mothers provided that they would exercise the utmost care to avoid any accident. The wailing ceased, smiles took its place, and the ceremony was carried to its conclusion in peace and harmony.

I once was called upon to officiate at a ceremony at which the groom was a Mr. Cohen from the wild woods of Arkansas. He was a typical Westerner, breezy, cheerful, and utterly devoid of any consciousness of respect or deference. He addressed me as "Doc." After attending to the necessary papers, he clapped me familiarly on the back and said:

"Doc, I want to tell you something. I want a short ceremony; it mustn't last over ten minutes. I'm going to give you twenty-five dollars, but for every minute over ten, I shall deduct one dollar, see?"

That time I did something which I had never done before and have never done since. I took out my watch and placed it on the table before me. I concluded the ceremony in nine and one half minutes. After the ceremony the groom came to me, thanked me for the way I officiated, which he said was "swell," and handed me twenty-five dollars and fifty cents.

"Thank you," said I, "but what is the meaning of the extra fifty cents?"

"Why, you see," he answered, "you did the job in nine and a half minutes, and you are entitled to the fifty cents for the half minute which you saved." I saw the point.

Among the co-religionists with whom I associated in the early years of my ministry in Sixty-seventh Street Synagogue was one elderly gentleman who was an interesting personality. He was a little man, married to a tall and stately wife. He was of Russian birth, but his wife was of French origin. They had one daughter. Despite his short stature he was full of energy and ruled his household with absolute domination. But he was also a man with a sense of humor and respect for the rabbinate, as the following story will show.

In due course his daughter became betrothed, and I was engaged to officiate at the marriage. There was nothing unusual about the ceremony. I did my duty in the customary manner, and, after the conclusion of the ceremony, the bridegroom handed me an envelope containing a check for fifteen dollars. I had no complaint. Fifteen dollars, it is true, is not a large amount, but neither is the amount unduly small, and I thought nothing further of the matter.

I did not see or hear of the parties again for some four or five months, when as it happened I officiated at another wedding at which they were present. I was glad to see them and greeted them cordially. After the ceremony, the aged father of the bride at the previous marriage called me aside and said that he wished to speak with me on an important matter. He began by apologizing to me most deferentially.

"I hope you will excuse my son-in-law," he said. "He is an inexperienced young man and does not know what is due to a rabbi of your standing."

I was puzzled by these remarks. "Oh, I don't know," I said. "Mr. — has never done any wrong to me. He is a very fine young man."

"That is very nice of you to say so," said the father-in-law, "and

Lighter Side of the Rabbi's Vocation

I thank you for your kindness, but still I know that he did not treat you right and I have wanted to make amends all along, but I am an old man and slow to act, and that is why I have neglected it, but now I am happy to meet you here and I am going to do the right thing."

Wonderingly, I asked, "What did Mr. — do to me?"

"It was very wrong of him to give you only fifteen dollars," was the answer. "I consider that an insult, so now I will make up the difference, and I hope you will accept it." With that he drew forth his pocketbook and extracted therefrom seven five-dollar bills and handed them to me, saying, "I hope you will accept this and not be angry at the delay."

I need not say that this most unexpected windfall was a most pleasant surprise. Rabbis, too, are not unappreciative of recognition in substantial form.

The exaggerated fear of the old gentleman was, of course, rather amusing, but that he made amends in such substantial fashion did honor to his understanding of the proprieties of the case.

Among the members of Congregation *Zichron Ephraim* was one who was not only impelled, no doubt, by religious sentiment but had also a keen eye to business. He was a coal dealer. Of course, as our member, he supplied the coal for heating the synagogue. He was also a member of four or five other congregations to all of which he rendered the same service. He was jestingly referred to as the coal-member, which suggests the Hebrew word *"Kohol,"* signifying *"congregation."* In course of time his daughter became betrothed. Naturally I expected that as the rabbi of the congregation with which he considered himself most intimately connected and whose synagogue he regularly attended, he would engage me to officiate. To my surprise, several months passed without his doing so. He sent me an invitation, but he did not formally ask me to officiate. The wedding was to take place in the Harlem Opera House in 125th Street. Coming there, I met a varied group of rabbis from all the congregations with which he was affiliated, among them the Chief Rabbi Jacob Joseph, Rabbi Dr. Lustig, and Rev. Henry S. Jacobs. I thought, of course, that one of these rabbis was to perform the ceremony. I was curious to ascertain which one it was.

I put the question first to Chief Rabbi Jacob Joseph. *"Rebbi,"* said I, *"seid ihr der Mesader Kiddushin?"* ("Rabbi, are you the one who will perform the ceremony?")

He answered, *"Ich weiss vun nisht."* (I know nothing of the sort.)

I asked Rabbi Lustig, who spoke a pure German, *"Herr Doktor, Werden Sie die Trauung vollziehen?"* (Doctor, are you to perform the ceremony?)

Shrugging his shoulders, he answered, *"Nicht dass ich wuesste. Ich bin bloss geladener gast."* (Not to my knowledge. I am merely an invited guest.)

I put the same question to Rev. Jacobs, whose language, as a native of London, was pure English. He answered with a smile, "No, I am not present in an official capacity."

I was puzzled, but the solution of the puzzle came immediately after.

The canopy was set up, and the father of the bride asked all the rabbis and also a cantor to take part in the ceremony. Now the matter was clear. He had calculated on having the ceremony performed by all the rabbis, which would obviate the necessity of engaging and remunerating any particular one.

The wedding party stood under the canopy and the cantor had recited the initial prayer, when suddenly a snag arose. It was discovered that no *Ketubah,* or marriage document, without which no marriage ceremony is valid, according to Jewish law, had been provided. The father of the bride had overlooked that apparently petty detail!

The question now arose as to what should be done. Someone suggested that the bridal couple should leave the canopy and wait until a *Ketubah* could be obtained. The question as to whether this was permissible was submitted to the chief rabbi and was decided in the negative. When the betrothed couple stand under the canopy and the ceremony has begun, he decided, they must not leave the canopy until it is concluded.

The only recourse left was to send a special messenger to purchase and bring a *Ketubah,* and in the meantime the rabbis would deliver wedding addresses in order to give the ceremony a presentable appearance until the messenger should return.

As the nearest Hebrew bookstore where such a document could be obtained was situated, at that time, in Canal Street, a distance of five or six miles from Harlem, the delay involved can be imagined.

The rabbis set bravely to work to perform their allotted tasks. Each one spoke a half hour or more amid a scene of indescribable confusion.

Some of the guests were indignant and protested loudly; others were highly amused.

The poor bride and groom stood there as though they wished the floor would swallow them up.

I was the one selected to deliver the concluding address. I preached bravely against time. I spoke and spoke and spoke. At last I decided I had said all that I cared to and more, that I would leave the young couple to their fate. But, just then, lo and behold, the messenger arrived bearing the precious *Ketubah*. Approximately three hours had passed since he set forth on his mission, but the rest of the proceedings hardly required more than three minutes. Needless to say, the father of the bride was ashamed to show his face for many weeks.

One day in the month of June I was sitting in the vestry room of our synagogue in Sixty-seventh Street, when a young man entered and asked me to officiate at his marriage, which was to take place in August in a small town in New Jersey. I informed him that at that time I would be away from New York, therefore I could not take an engagement. He seemed disappointed and went away without saying anything further. The next day, about the same hour, he returned and urged me to accept the engagement. He told me that both his family and the family of the bride were very anxious that I should be the one to solemnize the marriage and said that, for their sake and in order not to disappoint them, I should make an exception and come from Sharon Springs to their home in New Jersey to perform the marriage ceremony. I could not resist this appeal. He added that I would receive a substantial fee—one hundred dollars and traveling expenses.

When the day arrived, I left Sharon with the midnight train from Palatine Bridge and reached New York City at about seven A.M. I then left for the New Jersey town, arriving there at about two P.M. I found that it was a pleasant town of four or five thousand people, among them five or six Jewish families, and that the ceremony was to take place in the Opera House.

The auditorium was crowded with guests, of whom the Gentile residents of the town constituted the great majority. In the course of conversation, I discovered that the Jewish residents of the town were all Orthodox and Sabbath observers and that they were on the best of terms with their Gentile neighbors. This made it necessary for them to have the ceremony in the town. They would have preferred to go to New York for that purpose, but that would have offended their non-Jewish friends, who were their customers as well. I also discovered that in a nearby watering place two Yiddish-speaking rabbis from the East Side of New York were passing the summer and that it would not have been necessary at all to engage me to perform the ceremony.

Before the ceremony took place, a little incident happened which showed the friendly disposition of the non-Jews toward their Jewish neighbors and their courteous consideration for their Jewish customs. In accordance with traditional usage, the Jews wore their hats, while the Gentiles had their heads uncovered. I noticed a little conversation among the guests, and then four or five approached me.

"Rabbi," said the spokesman, "your people have their heads covered. Shall we also wear our hats?"

"It is not your duty," I answered, "as you are not members of the Jewish faith, but if you care to do so, we would appreciate it as a courtesy."

The committee returned to their people, and in a moment every head was covered.

The ceremony then took place, and I was happy to find that it aroused universal satisfaction among Jews and Gentiles alike.

The father of the bride then called me aside and gave the fee, at the same time thanking me warmly for my services. But I was curious. Something had puzzled me, and I wanted to know the explanation.

"Tell me, Mr. —, why did you go to the expense and trouble to bring me all the way from Sharon Springs when you knew I did not want to come, especially when two Orthodox rabbis were nearby who could have performed the ceremony according to your wishes?"

Lighter Side of the Rabbi's Vocation

"Ah, Rabbi," he answered, "I could never have done without you. My Christian neighbors and I are the best of friends, but naturally they do not understand Yiddish, and the ceremony would have meant nothing to them. Some time ago, one of our people married off a daughter and brought a Yiddish-speaking rabbi from the East Side of New York to officiate. Between the Yiddish and the Hebrew, my Gentile neighbors did not understand one word. You are the only Orthodox rabbi I know who not only conducts the Hebrew ceremony beautifully but delivers an impressive address in English, and my neighbors are all delighted. I simply could not have gotten along without you."

"Well," said I, jestingly, "I could have charged you five hundred dollars."

"Yes, you could," answered he, "and if you had, I would have paid it."

I will close this chapter with a story of a similar nature, but not of my own experience. It was told me by Dr. Gustave Gottheil, of Temple Emanu-El.

He once had a marriage ceremony, the parties to which belonged to the upper ten of New York Jewry. It took place in the palatial residence of the bride's parents, which was gorgeously decorated in honor of the festive occasion. The rarest flowers and plants filled the house from basement to roof. The floral decorations alone cost thousands of dollars. The ceremony was followed by a Lucullian repast.

When the dinner was over, the best man, a son of one of the wealthy families at the wedding, accompanied Dr. Gottheil to the door and, with an air of great importance, handed him an envelope. The rabbi then entered a carriage to ride home. He told me he was not accustomed to open the envelope in which his fee was contained until he had reached home. But this time, in view of the great wealth and high social standing of the parties concerned, his curiosity overcame him and, as soon as he was seated in the carriage, he opened the envelope. Who can describe his amazement when he saw in it a *one-dollar bill!* He could hardly believe his eyes, but there it was—*one dollar*—and no amount of looking and staring could make it any more. When he reached his residence, there was standing at the curb a poor woman who begged for a dole. With indescribable scorn and contempt, he handed her the dollar and said:

"Here, my good woman. It is a wedding fee given me by my millionaire friends."

The memory of this inexplicable act remained in his mind, but his pride and self-respect forbade making any inquiries.

In the meantime, the young couple had gone on their wedding trip, and nothing was heard or seen of them for several months.

A few months later, Dr. Gottheil chanced to meet the groom riding uptown in the Madison Avenue trolley. He greeted the doctor most cordially and sat at his side. They indulged in a pleasant conversation. All this while Dr. Gottheil was thinking "one dollar"—but did not put his thoughts into words.

Then the young man asked him, "Did you enjoy my wedding?"

The doctor answered, "Yes, indeed. It was a very wonderful affair, and I enjoyed it very much."

"And were you satisfied with the fee?" asked the young man.

This made it possible for the doctor to express his feelings. "You ask me whether I was satisfied with the fee," he said. "How can you expect me to be satisfied with a fee of one dollar for my services at a luxurious wedding such as yours?"

"What do you say?" asked the young man, startled in the highest degree. "You received a fee of one dollar? I placed in the envelope a thousand-dollar bill, with instructions to my best man to hand it to you."

"I do not doubt your word at all," said the doctor, "but the envelope when I opened it contained a single one-dollar bill."

"I will look into this matter," answered the groom, "and I will see to it that it is rectified."

The solution of the matter, which the groom wrote to Dr. Gottheil a few days later, at the same time enclosing his check for one thousand dollars, was as follows:

The best man, although the son of a very wealthy family, was just at that time short of funds. He had looked at the fee and could not withstand the temptation to take it. His idea was to substitute for it a smaller amount which would, nevertheless, be satisfactory. Unfortunately, however, he had no cash with him at the moment except a one-dollar bill, and that was what he placed in the envelope. Had he inserted a hundred-dollar bill or two or three hundred dollars, the doctor would have been perfectly satisfied and would have answered to that effect if asked the question.

The best man received a most emphatic reprimand, but in view of the high social standing of his family, the matter was hushed up, and no further consequences followed.

Chapter Forty-six

Golden Jubilee

IN THE YEAR 1940 A HALF CENTURY OF THE EXISTENCE OF CONGREgation *Zichron Ephraim* and of my connection with it as rabbi was completed.

As the completion of the half century drew near, the people of my congregation began to think of celebrating it in a fitting manner. Early in 1940 a committee of arrangements was organized, headed by Mr. Benjamin J. Weil, son of the founder of the congregation. It was decided that the celebration should be in three parts, a dinner at the Hotel Commodore, a Jubilee Fund, and a Golden Jubilee Souvenir Volume. The celebration was to be ushered in by a religious service to be held in the synagogue of the congregation. The entire program was carried out with great solemnity and impressiveness. All branches of the Jewish and lay community were represented, both at the service and at the dinner. The service took place on Sunday evening, December first, 1940, and the banquet one week later, Sunday evening, December eighth.

The festive throng assembled at the hotel, and the celebration was especially graced by a most beautiful souvenir volume prepared under the auspices of the Journal Committee, headed by Abraham Pollack, but the chief spirit of which and the one responsible for its beauty and success was my own dear wife, Hadassah L. Drachman, with whom it was truly a labor of love.

The presiding officer of the banquet was Benjamin J. Weil, who performed his duties not only with considerable eloquence but also with charming wit. The main other speakers were Rabbi Herbert S. Goldstein, spiritual leader of the Institutional Synagogue, Rev. Dr. Samuel Goldenson of Temple Emanu-El, Rabbi Dr. Jacob Hoffman

Golden Jubilee

of Congregation *Ohab Zedek*, Honorable Samuel Dickstein, member of the Congress of the United States, and Assemblyman Samuel Mandelbaum, all of whom paid more glowing tributes to my achievements in Jewish and public life than I felt that I deserved. I, myself, was the concluding speaker.

The main tone of my address was gratitude, gratitude to the Giver of All Good who had preserved me in life and health during the fifty years of my service and enabled me to accomplish the many tasks that had devolved upon me, gratitude to the congregation who had stood loyally by me during all that lengthy period, gratitude to the numerous friends and sympathizers in the outside community who had apportioned to me a full measure of understanding and cooperation, and last, but by no means least, gratitude to my beloved wife, Hadassah L. Drachman, whose true loyalty and sympathetic cooperation had lightened my burden to a greater extent than I could express in words.

Particularly pleasing and very unexpected were the tributes which had come to me in the form of letters and telegrams from many of the highest personages in the life of the nation and of the Jewish community, excerpts from which were printed in the Souvenir Journal. Among the senders of these messages were President Franklin D. Roosevelt, Governor Herbert H. Lehman, Mayor Fiorello H. La Guardia, the Very Reverend Dr. Joseph H. Hertz. Chief Rabbi of the British Empire, the Honorable Wendell Willkie, the President of Columbia University, Dr. Nicholas Murray Butler, Supreme Court Justice Felix Frankfurter, the rabbi of Congregation *Orach Chaim* Dr. Moses Hyamson, the rabbi of the Jewish Center, Dr. Leo Jung, and the rabbi of Congregation *Kehillath Jeshurun*, Joseph H. Lookstein, and many others.

I quote just three or four.

President Roosevelt wrote:

I trust that for long years to come you may be spared in health and strength to exemplify the highest ideals of the ancient teachings of Israel.

Governor Lehman wrote:

> *It is a wonderful thing to have served actively in the rabbinate for half a century and to have had such great and lasting influence not only on the members of your own synagogue but on the community as a whole.*

The Very Reverend Dr. Hertz wrote:

> *I gladly learn of the golden jubilee of the rabbinical activity of my beloved and revered teacher. He has remained a valiant champion of historic continuity in Jewish life, as scholar, preacher, and leader and rendered lasting services to every religious, humanitarian and patriotic cause.*

And one tribute coming from a former pupil whom I had almost forgotten touched my heart especially because of its tone of personal devotion and appreciation.

Oscar I. Janowsky, at present professor of history in the College of the City of New York, wrote:

> *Twenty-five years ago I sat at your feet as a disciple. Your profound and illuminating comments of the prophetic books of the Bible still serve as an inspiration.*

As I listened to the addresses and read the expressions of sentiment from so many honored and distinguished personages, I felt that my services to the cause of Judaism and humanity had not gone unrewarded.

I will include here a most touching and affectionate tribute, written by my son Julian, which appeard in the Golden Anniversary Journal and which was read at the banquet that evening.

JUBILEE ODE
All things must change. In half a hundred years
   What changes have we seen!
Winters, Springs, Summers, white earth, brown, and green,
Laughter and tears—
The old, soft sorrows, always fresh and dear,

The long parade of joys, kindly and small,
Discoveries looming suddenly, sharply clear,
    Heaped-up successes—we remember all.

All things must change. Since first these gates swung wide
    How has our city grown!
The streets have stretched, stone upon towering stone
In swelling pride—
What rich machines pierce swiftly through the night,
    Under the ground or high in upper air,
And from them bursts the unimagined might
    To wreck our world and drench it in despair.

Must all things change? . . . One thing has ever stood—
    The Everlasting Voice
    Still thundering as from Sinai, "Make your choice,
Evil or Good.
Stand and be counted." And this holy shrine,
    A Rock secure amid the floods of change,
Stands, a firm testimony and a sign
    Of hope and home where all is rough and strange.

Once these doors opened. They are open still.
    Ye everlasting gates,
Lift up; behold! the King of Glory waits
To enter, bringing peace from the Holy Hill.

And one here like a second Moses stands,
    Having heard from the burning bush the Voice that spoke.
Gently he bears the Law in shielding hands.
    Freely he offers his own chief wealth—God's yoke.

For fifty years unresting he has striven,
    Father and friend,
    To plant that heaven-on-earth good men intend,
Taught freely, labored, generously given
Counsel, help, love, and loyalty, and truth.
    Now, when the outer world is steeped in night,
Bravely he tends, with undiminished youth,
    Here on this altar the undying light.

In 1941 Columbia University honored me by conferring on me (at the Commencement on June third) the University Medal for Excellence and also the engraved University Diploma to that effect. The President of the University, Dr. Nicholas Murray Butler. in a brief but eloquent discourse pronounced the citation. It was thrilling indeed to stand in that wonderful, vast, open space in front of the majestic buildings of the university and to feel one's self the center of all eyes of the thronging thousands assembled for the Commencement. I was informed that this was the first time in the one hundred eighty-six years since Columbia was founded that such a distinction had been conferred on a Jewish rabbi.

In 1942 the sixtieth year of the class of 1882 of Columbia College was completed. In honor of this rare event. Dr. Butler, with his accustomed gracious hospitality, invited the surviving members to dinner at his home on Morningside Heights. I was one of those invited. There were only nineteen survivors of the original class, of whom seven were unable to come, so that the number present, including the host, was only twelve.

It was a most enjoyable reunion, mainly devoted to reminiscences of our college days, although a touch of pensiveness was added by the reflection that we would probably never again meet in the same numbers, in the same way.

I had taken upon myself to write a poem dedicated to the occasion and, as its meter was the same as that of the well known song *"Maryland, My Maryland,"* it was easy for us to sing it, which we did with a vim. As it may interest some of my readers, I give here the text.

TO THE CLASS OF 1882
OF COLUMBIA UNIVERSITY

ON THE SIXTIETH ANNIVERSARY
OF ITS GRADUATION

BY BERNARD DRACHMAN

Melody of "My Maryland"

I

O, Eighty Two, O Eighty Two!

Golden Jubilee

From our heart's depth we sing to you.
We sing the happy days long past,
   To whose bright mem'ries we hold fast.
Ne'er from our minds they'll fade away,
   While on this earth in life we stay.
O, Eighty Two, O Eighty Two!
   From our heart's depth we sing to you.

II

Within Columbia's ancient walls,
   A merry band we trod its halls.
With sportive jest and mighty voice
   In youthful glee we did rejoice.
No shade of care our spirits paled.
   The future as our own we hailed.
O, Eighty Two, O Eighty Two!
   You surely were a jolly crew.

III

And when we went forth into life,
   Columbia armed us for the strife.
Great store of wisdom old and new
   From learned teachers' lips we drew.
In the great world our mark we made,
   Each one where'er his path was laid.
O Alma Mater, sweet and dear,
   We love thee more each passing year.

IV

And now though we've grown gray and old
   Our friendship's glow has not grown cold.
For those dear classmates passed away,
   We shed a tear of grief this day.
Preserve us, Lord, yet many a year,
   To meet again in health and cheer.
O, Eighty Two, O Eighty Two!
   God's choicest blessings rest on you.

V

Our glasses to our host we raise,
   With meed of honor, thanks and praise.
His deeds have made his name renowned,
   With fame and glory he is crowned.
We share the glory of those deeds,

Through him our class Columbia leads.
Nick Butler, here's great love to you
From your old pals of Eighty Two.

The next day, the following letter reached me:

COLUMBIA UNIVERSITY
IN THE CITY OF NEW YORK
President's Room

May 14, 1942

The Reverend Dr. Bernard Drachman
242 East 72nd Street
My dear Drachman:
  Those verses of yours were quite charming and most interesting.
  Unfortunately, you gave me only one copy. Could you supply a few more? I want particularly to put one into Columbiana *for.. permanent preservation in the University Library.*
  We had a good time last night and I greatly enjoyed the gathering.
      Faithfully yours,
        Nicholas Murray Butler

At this point I will conclude this chronicle.

I have sought to give my readers an adequate picture of what I have stood for and what I have sought to accomplish in the years of activity which a Merciful Providence has allotted to me. I believe that whatever I have been privileged to accomplish has taken place essentially and fundamentally during those years. I am grateful for whatever additional sojourn on this earth our Heavenly Father may vouchsafe me but I do not believe that it will bring new deeds or new achievements worthy of perpetuating. I shall be satisfied and grateful if the opinion of those who read this record will be that the world and Jewish life are at least a little better because of that which it was given me to do.

My aims, I trust, are not too difficult of attainment. If it has been my privilege, at least in some measure, to demonstrate that Judaism is an unfailing light to those who permit themselves to be guided

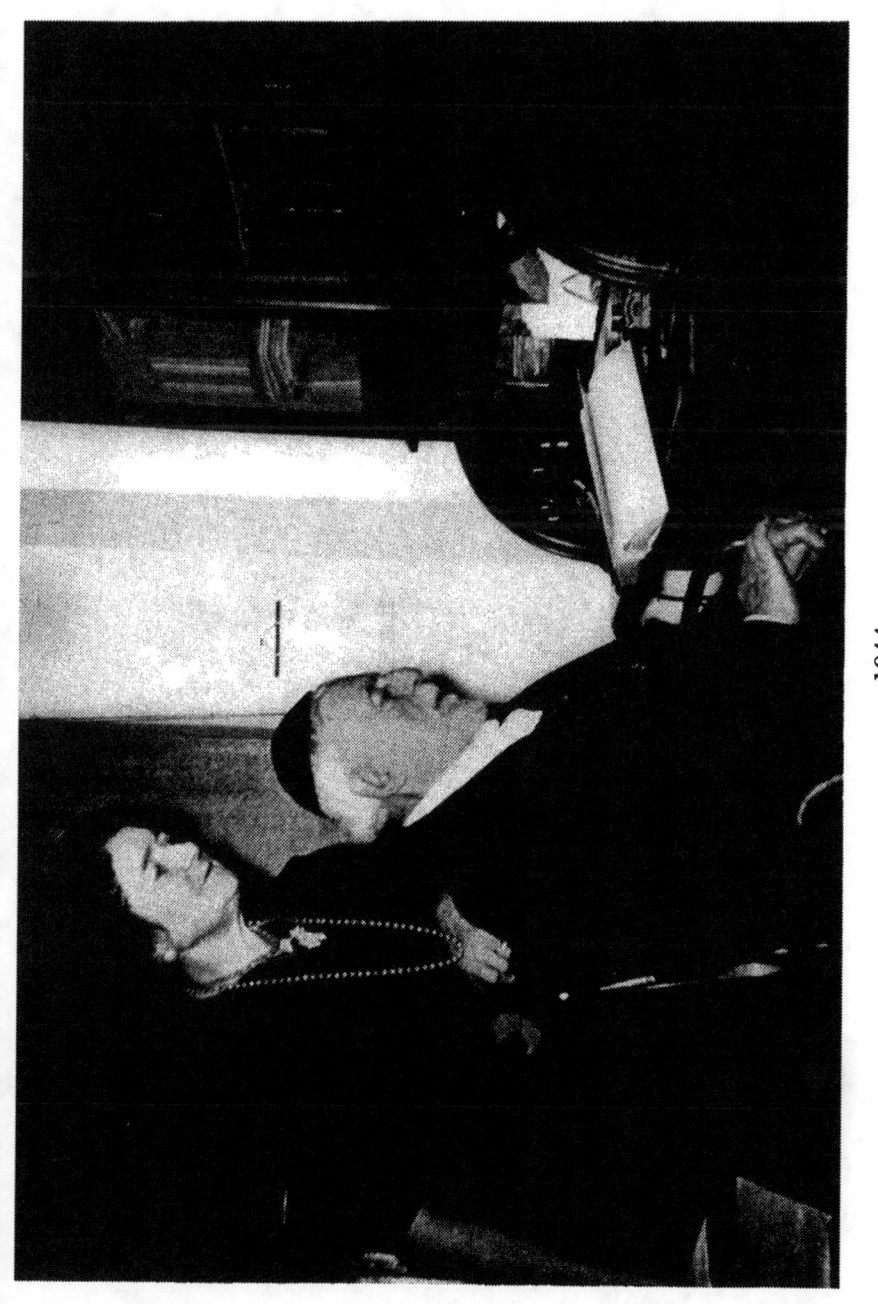

1944
Home Scene — A Corner of the Study at
245 East Seventy-Second Street

thereby, and if what I have written will aid in disseminating a fairer and juster appraisal of Israel's ancient faith and a realization that it is perfectly compatible and in harmony with the finest achievements of modern civilization and particularly of Americanism, I shall feel that the time and effort which I have devoted to this book have not been spent in vain.

In this consciousness I shall find an ample reward.

INDEX

Abraham ben David of Posquieres, 258
  See also: Posquieres
Abrahams, Moses (Rev., of Leeds, 310, 311
Abramowitz, Herman, 184, 216
Achelis, Mrs. (Elizabeth), 421
Adler, Cyrus, 374
Adler, Hermann (Dr., Chief Rabbi)
  157, 158, 290, 300
Adler, Samuel, 40, 42
Agudath Am Israel, 228
Ahavath Chesed Synagogue
  (See also Congregation *Ahavath Chesed*)
Alexander, Professor, 47, 50
Albany, N. Y., 44
Albuquerque, N. M., 350, 351
Alperstein, Abraham (Rabbi) 356
American Hebrew, The (publication), 264
Americanism, 12, 13, 17, 21
"American Hebrew" (publication), 353
Anglo-American culture, 46, 47
Amiel, (Rabbi), 409
Anglo-Jewish clergy, 42, 296-9
Anti Semitism, 9, 36, 37, *rishus* 42, 43, 51
Antwerp, (Belgium), 409
Arabic language, 107, 400, 401
Arabs, 397, 402, 404
Armstrong, Rev. Mr., 251
Arnstein, Emanuel, 208, 213
Arnstein, Max, J., 213
Arnstein, Samuel, 213
Arnstein, Sigmund, 213
Articles (list of), 265
Asher, Joseph Mayer, 254
Ashkenazim, 29
Ashaway, R. I., 239
Austria, 29
Austro-Hungarian Empire, 12, 132
Baden, 189
Badt, Benno, 114
Baptists (See: Sabbatarians)
Bar Mitzvah, 12
Barnard, Dr. (Pres., Columbia College), 47
Barondess, Joseph, 385
Barton, George H., 32, 34, 36, 38, 39, 40
Bavaria, 12
Bay Shore, L. I., 242, 243
Behar, Nissim, 426
Behar, Manoel, 426
Ben Sira (text from Cairo *Genizah*), 253
Bentwich, Herbert, 301
Bentwich, Norman, footnote 301
Berlin, 118 ff, 422 ff
Berlin, Meyer, 425
Bernheim family, 234
Beth Abraham Home, 356, 357
Bible, 41, 269
Bieber, Joseph, 376
Birmingham (England), 308
Blizzard of '88, 195, 196
Bnai Brith, 29
Bohemia, Bohemian Jews, 41
Bondy, Bernard, 249
Blumenthal, Joseph, 208, 224
Braun, Julius, 214
Breslau, 88-96, 257
Breslau Seminary
  See: Jewish Theological Seminary of Breslau
Breslau University, 97

British Empire, 290 ff
Brody, (Galicia), 126, 141
Bronco, 238
Bronx, The, 218
Buechler, Adolf (Principal, Jews' College, London), 305
Butler, Nicholas Murray, 52, 53, 272, 385, 448
Cahn, David, 186
Cairo, 394
Calculus, burning of, 49
Calendar reform, 418 ff
Canada and Canadian Jewry, 392-5
Cantor (*Chazan, chazonim, chazanuth*)
  28, 134, 173, 174, 281-4
Castle Garden, 20
Central Relief Committee, 336
Chalutzim, 399 ff
Chandler, Professor, 47, 48
chazan (See *Cantor*)
Chazars
  (See also: *Cusari*)
Cheder, 27
Chicago, 342
Christian Endeavor Society, 225
Clement, Alfred C., 35
Cleveland, (Ohio), 328 ff
Cohen, Joseph H., 375, 376
Coler, Bird S. (Commissioner, Dep't of Charities), 355, 356
Collegio Rabbinico, (Florence, Italy), 141
Columbia Classmates: N. M. Butler, Wm. O. Wiley, D. Murphy, J. B. Niles, 57
Columbia College, 46
  Old buildings, 49
Columbia Law School, 24
Columbia University, 44
Congregation *Adath Israel*, 188
Congregation *Ahavath Chesed*, 176
Congregation *Beth Israel Bikur Cholim*, 187, 188, 193, 197-204
Congregation *Bne Jeshurun* (Cleveland), 328
Congregation *Kehillath Jeshurun* (Syracuse), 373
Congregation *Kehillah Kedoshah Isaac Ephraim* (Jersey City), 27-30
Congregation *Knesseth Israel* (Cleveland), 328
Congregation *Ohab Zedek*
  See: *Ohab Zedek*
Congregation *Oheb Sholom*, Newark, 169, 170 ff, 175, 185
Congregation *Orach Chaim*, 188, 291
Congregation *Shaarey Zedek*, 226
Congregation *Zichron Ephraim*, 205, 216
  Constitution of, 208
Conkling, Roscoe (U. S. Senator), 196
Conservative Judaism, 177, 178
Coe, Dr., 242
Cotsworth, Moses B., 418
Cracow (Poland), 131-9
Curry's Woods and "The Hill," N. J., 4, 5, 30
Cusari, 42, 106
Davidson, Gabriel, 226
Davidson, Isidore M. (Wilkesbarre), 342
De Sola, Meldola (Rev., of Montreal), 178, 316
Deutsch, Gotthard (Cincinnati), 327
Deutsch's *Hebrew Grammar*, 36
Deutschredender Amerikanische Buerger, 12
Dickstein, Samuel, 447

Index

Diller, S., 346
"*Dibre ha-Riboth*, 258 ff
Doyle, Arthur Conan, 417
Drachman, Benjamin, 11-15
Drachman, Mathilde, 15-20
Drachman, Holger, 14
Drachman, Professor A. B., 14
Drachman, Bessie, 22
Drachman, Emily, 24, 25
Drachman, Fannie, 26, 27
Drachman, Gustave S., 23, 24
Drachman, Louis, 21, 22
Drachman, Albert, 363
Drachman, Beatrice, 293 ff, 423
Drachman, Edgar, 363
Drachman, Julian, 363, 447
Drachman, Mathilde, 244, 423
Drachman, Myron
Drachman, Theodore
Drachman, Hadassah L., 411-415, 422, 423, 444, 445
   (See also: Levine, Hadassah)
Drachman, Julia Raunheim, 24
Dukas, Julius, J., 213, 214
Eastman, George, 418, 421
East Orange, N. J., 53
East Side, 439
Effendis, 403
Egypt, 396
Ehrenreich, Bernard, 184
Ehrlich, Arnold B., 41
Eichler, Michael M., 184
Elmaleh, Leon M., 184
Emanu-el Theological Seminary Association
   (See: *Hebrew Preparatory School*)
Emanu-El, Temple
   (See: Temple Emanu-El)
Emmendingen, 387
Employment Bureau, Jewish Sabbath Alliance, 229
Engelman, Morris, 288, 336, 340, 341
England, English Jews, 29, 42
English language, 32
Faitlovich, Jacques, (footnote) 361
Feigenbaum, Isaac (Cleveland) 329, 330
Feinberg, Philip J.
Fellahin, 403
First Hungarian Congregation *Ohab Zedek* 278, 284, 289, 378, 379
Fischer, Kuno (Heidelberg), 153
Fischer, Moses (Chicago), 343
Five-day Working Week Proposal, 349
Forensic Society, 36-8, 51
Frankel, Jonas, 99-102
Frankel, Martin, 99-102
Frankel, Zacharias (Breslau), 67, 103
Frankfort-on-the-Main, 24, 123
Freidus, Abraham S., 266
Freudenthal, Jacob (Breslau), 68, 103, 105, 257
Fried, Michael, 184
Friendlander, Israel, 253
Friedlaender, Michael (Principal, Jews' College, London) 157-9
Friedman, Max, 214
"From the Heart of Israel" (publication), 353
Funk and Wagnall Company, 263
Funk, Isaac, 267, 268
Fusion Movement, 273
Gadol, Moshe (editor *La America*) 358-60
Galicia, 25, 128, 129
Gaster, Moses (Dr., *Haham* or Chief Rabbi), 296, 297
Geiger, Abraham, 100
Genizah, 253
German Language and literature, 12, 35, 41, 371
Germans, 5, 90 ff
Germany, 15-18, 29, 42

Ginzberg, Louis, 253
Gittelson, Moses, 337
Glass, Henry (Pres., *Ohab Zedek*), 278
Gleiwitz, 144
Goepp, Anna Ottilie, 431-3
Goldberg, Israel
Goldenson, Samuel, 444
Goldfarb, Israel, 184, 226
Goldstein, Herbert S., 444
"good neighbors"
Gordon, John, 310, 311
Gottheil, Gustave, 40, 42, 43, 311
Gottheil, Richard J. H., 43, 44, 386
Gotthelf, Philip, 353
Graetz, Heinrich (Breslau) 68, 103, 157, 158, 257
Greek language, 32, 33, 35
Green, A. A. (London), 303
Green, J. R.—"History of the English People," 32
Greenberg, Joseph, 214
Greenstone, Julius H., 184
Gruenberg, Samuel, 425
Gruenstein, Moritz, 190
Gruenstein, Sophie, 190
Guggenheim, Adolph, 208, 214
Gutmann, Martha, 114, 256
Halpern, (Rabbi, of Denver), 343
Hamburg
Harris, George, 212
Harris, Mrs. George, 212
Harris, Mrs. Jacob, 212
Harris, Rose, 215
Hebrew culture & Literature, 12-14
Hebrew Free Loan Society
Hebrew grammar, 36
Hebrew language, 12-14, 404, 405
Hebrew Preparatory School, 40-45, 57, 164
"Hebrew Standard, The"
Hebrew studies and education, 12, 13, 36, 40-45
Heidelberg (Germany) and Heidelberg University, 152-5
Heller, Carl, 208
Hertz, Emanuel, 184
Hertz, Joseph H. (Dr., Chief Rabbi), 184, 222, 223, 238, 421, 446
Herzberg, Eliezer
Hildesheimer, Israel (Berlin), 100, 425
Hildesheimer, Meyer
Hildesheimer Seminary
Hilkowitz, (Dr., of Denver), 343
Hirsch, Meyer (of San Francisco), 346
Hirsch, Paul, 213
Hirsch, Samson Raphael
Hirth, Prof. Doktor, of Breslau, 110-112
Hith-galluth-ha-Rib
   (See also: *Dibre ha-Riboth*
Hobebei Zion, 45
Hoffman, Jacob, 444
Hoffman, John
Homiletics
Horovitz
Hotel Hirschel (Hamburg), 62
Houdini, Harry, 337-9, 417
Huebsch, Adolph, 28, 29
Hungary, Hungarian Jews, 29
Hurlwitz, Nathan (*Dayan*), 259
Hutter, Leo, 208
Hyamson, Moses, 336, 420
hymn-singing, 38-40
Illich, Abraham, 44
Immigrants, 19, 20
Intercession (for Sabbath observance) 230, 231
"Israel's Messenger" (of Shanghai)
Isserres, Moses (Rabbi), 136, 140
Italy and Italian Jews, 141

454 Index

Jackson, Judge (Sharon Springs), 245
Jacob Joseph School
Jacobus (Dr., of Berlin), 425
Janowsky, Oscar J., 446
Jarmulowsky, Sender, 213
Jastrow, Morris, 102, 117
Jersey City, 4-10, 20, 31-40, 149
Jersey City High School, 31-40, 46, 51
Jerusalem
Jesus, Virgin Mary, etc., 39
Jewish Center (West 86th Street), 373
Jewish Consumptive Relief Society (Denver) Sanatorium, 343, 344
Jewish dietary laws, 15, 58, 62, 63, 354 ff
The Jewish Encyclopedia, 14, 342
Jewish Endeavor Society, 225, 226
Jewish farmers
Jewish history
Jewish nation
Jewish National Home, 506
Jewish "Race"
Jewish Parade (1921, in New York) 381, 382
Jewish press, 336
The Jewish Review
Jewish Sabbath, 24, 228
  (See also: Sabbath)
Jewish Sabbath Alliance of America, 24, 231
Jewish Sabbath Association, 228
"Jewish vote"
Jewish Theological Seminary of America (of New York), 176-182, 183-5, 187, 189, 197, 220-4, 225, 253-261, 272, 372, 374
Jewish Theological Seminary of Breslau (Also called: Breslau Seminary and *Juedisch-Theologisches Seminar, Fraenkelscher Stiftung*), 67, 68, 88, 100-9, 114-7, 148, 151, 156, 157, 256
Jewish Welfare Board, 364, 365
Joel, Manuel (Rabbi, of Breslau), 96, 113, 257
Joel, Moritz (*Referendar*), 113
Joffe, A. J., 221
Joint Distribution Committee (organized) 336
Joseph, Jacob
Judah ha-Levi, 42
Juedisch-Deutsch, 15
Kamniky, Leon (Editor, the *Jewish Morning Journal*), 336
Kantrowitz, Hyman, 209, 211, 284
Kaplan, Baruch David, 213
Kaplan, Bernard S., 184
Kaplan, Mordecai M., 184, 372-7
Karaites, *Poets and Poetry of*, 51
Katz, Jacob, 214
Katz, Rose Szobotka
Kauvar, Hirschman Hillel (Charles), 184, 226, 343, 344
Kehillath Yeshurun Congregation (Syracuse, N. Y.), 373
Kevutzoth
Kingsbury (Dep't of Charities, New York, 1915), 354, 355
Klein, Philip, 278, 281, 321, 336, 378
Koenigsburg, Herman, 232
Kohler, Kaufman, 43, 177
Kohn, Jacob, 173-4
Kohn, Rose (Mrs.), 173, 174
Kohut, Alexander, 172, 176, 179, 221, 223
Kohut, George Alexander, 260
Kolinsky, I. J., 343
Kosher, Kashruth (See: Jewish dietary laws)
Kosher kitchen, City Hospital, 354-6
Kothel Maaravi (See: Wailing Wall, Jerusalem)
Kussy, Sarah, 173
Labor
Landauer, Max, 214
Latin language and literature, 32-35

League for Safeguarding the Fixity of the Sabbath, 420
League of Nations
Lebanon Hospital, 218
Leeds (England), 310, 311
Leeser, Isaac, 173
Lehman, Herbert (Governor, New York State), 446
Lemberg (Galicia), 139-144
Levi, Samuel Mordecai 307, 308, 310
Levine Hadassah, 411-5
Levine, Fisher, 213
Levov (or Lwow)
  (See: Lemberg)
Lewisohn, Adolph, 367, 386
Lewy, Israel (Rabbi, Breslau), 68, 103, 107, 116, 257
Liberalism
Liebermann, Gustave, 183, 184, 214, 221
Lilienthal, William
Linsley, George H. (Principal, P.S. 1, J. C.)
Lipzin, M, 370
Lithuania, Lithuanian Jews, 29
Liverpool, 314, 315
Loew, Elazar
London (England), 157, 162, 290-304, 315, 316
London, N. T.
"Looking at America"
Los Angeles, 173, 345, 346
Low, Seth, 272-4
Lublinsky, Moses (also Lublinski, 209, 211, 284
Lucas, Albert, 35, 36
Luria, Zvi Jacob, 228
Maisner, Moses, 178, 179, 188, 221, 321
Manchester (England), 311-5
Mandate (for Palestine), 406
Mandel, Morris, 184
Mandelbaum, Samuel, 445
Manishewitz (Cincinnatti), 351
Margolies, M. Z., 336
Martin, W. R., 32-35
Marvin, Charles F., 418
Materialism—a Satisfactory Explanation of Mind?, 50
Mandel, Morris, 184
Marx, Alexander, 254, 258
Masseches America, 267
Massachusetts Legislature
Materialism
Mayer, Bernhard, 190
McMillan, Duncan J. (Director, Lord's Day Congress, Oakland, Calif., July, 1915), 347, 348
The Melancholy Club, 52
Mellrichstadt, 64, 69
Mendes, H. Pereira, 178, 221, 321, 414
Menkes, Simchah (*Reb*), 140, 141
Menorah Society, 337
Messiah (*Moshiach*), 9
Meyer, Martin A. (Rabbi, San Francisco), 346
Mikra-Ki-Peshuto, 41
Minyan, 285
Missionaries
Mizrachi Organization, 384
Mizrachi "Bank", 407
Mizrachi Conference in Antwerp, 1925, 406, 407
Montefiore, Sir Moses, 158
Montreal
Morais, Sabato, 178, 181, 182, 221, 223
Murphy, Deas, 53
Myers, Isidore (Rev., of Los Angeles), 345, 346
Myers, Lewis, 208, 213
Neckar River (Germany), 153
Nethanneh Tokef, 41
Netherlands, 376
Neuhausen, Simon, A., 260

Neuman, Moritz, 378, 379
New Canaan, Conn., 53
Norotoa, Conn., 53
Newman, H.
Newark
New York
New York Times
New York Public Library
Niantic, Conn., 234 ff
Nies, James Buchanan, 53 ff, 117-20
Nieto, Abraham H., 346
Nieto, Jacob (Rabbi, of San Francisco), 346
"Nineteen Letters of Ben Uziel"
(*Neunzehn Briefe uber Judentum*)
See also: Ben Uziel
Nordheim (vor der Rhon), 3, 16-18, 70, 71, 158
Religious life of, 83, 86, 87
Oakland, Calif., 347
Ohab Zedek Congregation, 278, 284, 289, 378, 379
(See also: First Nungarian Congregation)
Oheb Sholom Congregation
(See: Congregation *Oheb Sholom*)
Ohole Shem Society (Tents of Shem), 266
Onderwyzer, Abraham Cohen (Chief Rabbi, Amsterdam, Holland), 376
Orthodoxy
Orthodox Judaism, 44, 45
Oshrinsky, Joseph, 213
Oswiecim, 129
Pacific, Angelo, 425
Palestine, 43, 45
Passover Relief Association, 212
Peck, Edwards S. (Vice-Principal, Jersey City High School), 32
Pedagogical methods, 41
Phelps, William Lyon, 35
Phi Beta Kappa, 51, 52
Philosophic Terms
Philosophy, 51
Pittsburgh Conference (1885), 177
Piza, David, 228
Polack, Isaac
Pollack, Abraham, 444
Poland, 11, 29, 139, 140
Polish language, 12
Politics
Polstein, Joseph, 213
Pool, David de Sola
Posquieres, Abraham ben David of—
(See also: *Abraham* . . .)
James Pott and Company
Praetorius (Professor, Breslau) 107
Prager, William, 208
Propaganda
Proselytes
Proselytizing
Psalms
Public School No. 1, 6-10, 31
Pullan family (Toronto), 394
Rappaport, Solomon, 173, 174
Raunheim, Julia, 24
Reform Judaism, 42, 44, 165, 167, 100, 177
Revel, Bernard, 350, 368, 369, 386
Reznik, Isser, 228
Ritter, Osias, 143
Roeder, Simon M.
Republican Party
Rogers, Gustavus, 384
Rogow, David, 276
Roosevelt, Franklin Delano (President, United States), 445
Rosalsky, Otto (Judge), 336
Rosenberg, Adam, 44, 45, 59
Rosenberg, Amelia, 188, 246
Rosenberg, William, 215, 384
Rosenblatt, Joseph, 282, 283
Rosengarten, Isaac, 375

Rosenthal, Herman, 266
Rosenzweig, Gerson, 267
Rosin, David (Professor, Breslau) 68, 103, 105, 257
Roth, Mathilde, 114
Roth, Xavier, 218, 354
Rothschild, Baron Edmond de, 401
Rothschild, Lord Lionel Evelyn de, 299
Rothschild, Evelyn de, 302
Rothschild, Lionel, 310, 311
Russia and Russian Jews, 19, 29
Rothstein, Abraham, 208
Sabbatarians, Christian, 452-8
Sabbath, 30, 68, 70-2, 74, 225, 227-233, 347-9
(See also: *Jewish Sabbath*)
Sabbath Legislation, 231, 232, 347 ff, 320 ff
Sachs, Michael, 106
Samaritans
Samuel, Mrs. Herbert, 303
Samuelson, Jacob, 276
San Francisco, 346, 347
Sanitarium (Denver), 343, 344
Sar, Samuel, 369
Sassoon (family, of London and Bombay), 296
Sassoon, Lady Solomon, 296, 297
Schechter, Solomon, 114, 253, 259, 261
Schiff, Jacob H., 222, 253, 336, 337
Schnabel, Louis, 40, 41
Schneeberger, Henry W., 178, 179
Schneider and Herter, architects
Schoen, Mrs. Marcus, 212
Schulman, Samuel, 386
Schwartz, Isaac, 172
Schwartz, Israel, 172, 173
Schwartz, Joseph, 172, 173
Schweinfurt (Germany) 81, 82
Seminars, 40
Semitics, 44
Sephardim (Spanish Jews) 29, 357 ff
Seventh-Day Adventists
Shealoth (technical questions) 356 ff
Shanghai
Sharon Springs, N. Y., 243 ff, 254, 380
Sharon Spring Synagogue, 248-252
Short, Prof, *Short comments on the Latin Language and Literature*, 47
Siegel, Abraham, 213
Singer, Isadore, 267
Sisterhood of Congregation *Zichron Ephraim* 212
Smith, Nathan (of Toronto), 392
Solomon, Elias S., 184, 226
Solomon, J. P. (Editor, "The Hebrew Standard"), 340
Solomons, A. S., 180
Soloweitzik, 240-242
Somberg, Y. Etta, 212
Sonnenschein, S. H. (St. Louis), 177
South Africa, 184
Spanish and Portuguese Congregation *Shearith Israel*
Speaker, Henry, 184
Spiritualists, 416
Spivak, (Dr., of Denver), 343
Staatszeitung, 40
Stein, Adolph, 77, 78
Stein, Mathilde, 15-20
Stein, Samuel, 2
Stein, Shemayh (Rabbi, of Nordheim) 16, 72-3
Stein, Solomon (Rabbi, of Schweinfurt), 69, 77-79, 80, 81
Stern, Simon, 214
Strauss, Herr and Frau Badt, 426
Student spirit, songs, customs, 48, 49
Sturman, Barnett, 208
S. S. "Suevia",", 58
Sulzberger, Ferdinand, 190

Index

Sulzberger, Rosa, 190
Sunday Legislation
Swaythling, (Lord, of London), 299
Synagogue, 3
  Jersey City, 27-30
Syracuse (N. Y.), 184
Talmai, (Dr.)
Talmud, 6, 12, 41, 42
Talmud Torah
  Jersey City, 27, 28
Tammany Hall, 273 ff
Tel Aviv
Temple Beth El, 40
Temple Emanu-El, 40, 164-7
Testimonial Dinner, 387, 388
"The Jew and Philosophy"
"The Real Jew"
Tiberias
Tiktin, Gedaliah, (Rabbi, of Breslau), 96
Tisha b'Ab, 58, 186, 240-2
Tomche Shabbath (Organization), 228
Torah
Trans-Jordania, 45
Toronto (Canada), 392 ff
Tuck, Sir Adolph, 301
Tulsa (Okla.), 351
Ungar, Jonas, 214
Union of Orthodox Jewish Congregations of America, 333
Union Theological Seminary, 272
'Unitarian", 54
Upton's Tactics, 23
Vacations
Valdez
Verband der Sabbat-Freunde
Vessell, Meyer, 213
Vizitelly, Frank H., 269-271
Von Suttner, Baroness, 334
Wailing Wall (Jerusalem), 399

Weil, Adele, 190
Weil, Babbette, 190
Weil, Moretz, 190
Weil, Lazarus, 190
Weil, Belle
Weil, Benjamin J., 219, 244, 444
Weil, Ephraim
Weil, Gustave (Prof. of Heidelberg), 153
Weil, Jonas, 189, 206, 208, 213, 232
Weil, L. Victor, 219
Weil, Samuel, 190
Weil, Sarah, 190, 191, 193, 194
Weil, Theresa (Mrs.), 246, 414
Weisz, David, 214
Westerly, R. I., 239-242
Wheeler, Leonard (Erothanatos), 52
Wiley, William Ogden, 53
Wilinsky, Isaac, 236 ff
Will, August, 16
Wilson, Woodrow (Pres.), 312, 335
Wintner, Leopold, 331, 332
Wise, Aaron, 192
Wise, Stephen, 192
Wise, Isaac M., 167, 177, 327
World Congress of Jewish Sabbath Observers 422 ff
Wuertzberg (Ger.), 68, 123
"Ralkut Maarabi" (Hebrew Magazine), 266
Yeshiva College, 368 ff
Yeshivoth, 399
Yiddish, 12, 28, 301, 302, 405
Yiddish Press
Yishruv, 399 ff
Yorkville, 188
Young Israel, 226
Young People's Societies, 215
Zarahia ben Isaac ha-Levi (Rabbi, of Gerona), 258
Zionism, 44, 383 ff, 386 ff

Printed in the USA
CPSIA information can be obtained
at www.ICGtesting.com
LVHW022332210624
783675LV00001B/17